IDOL dreams

STORY & ART BY

ARINA TANEMURA

3

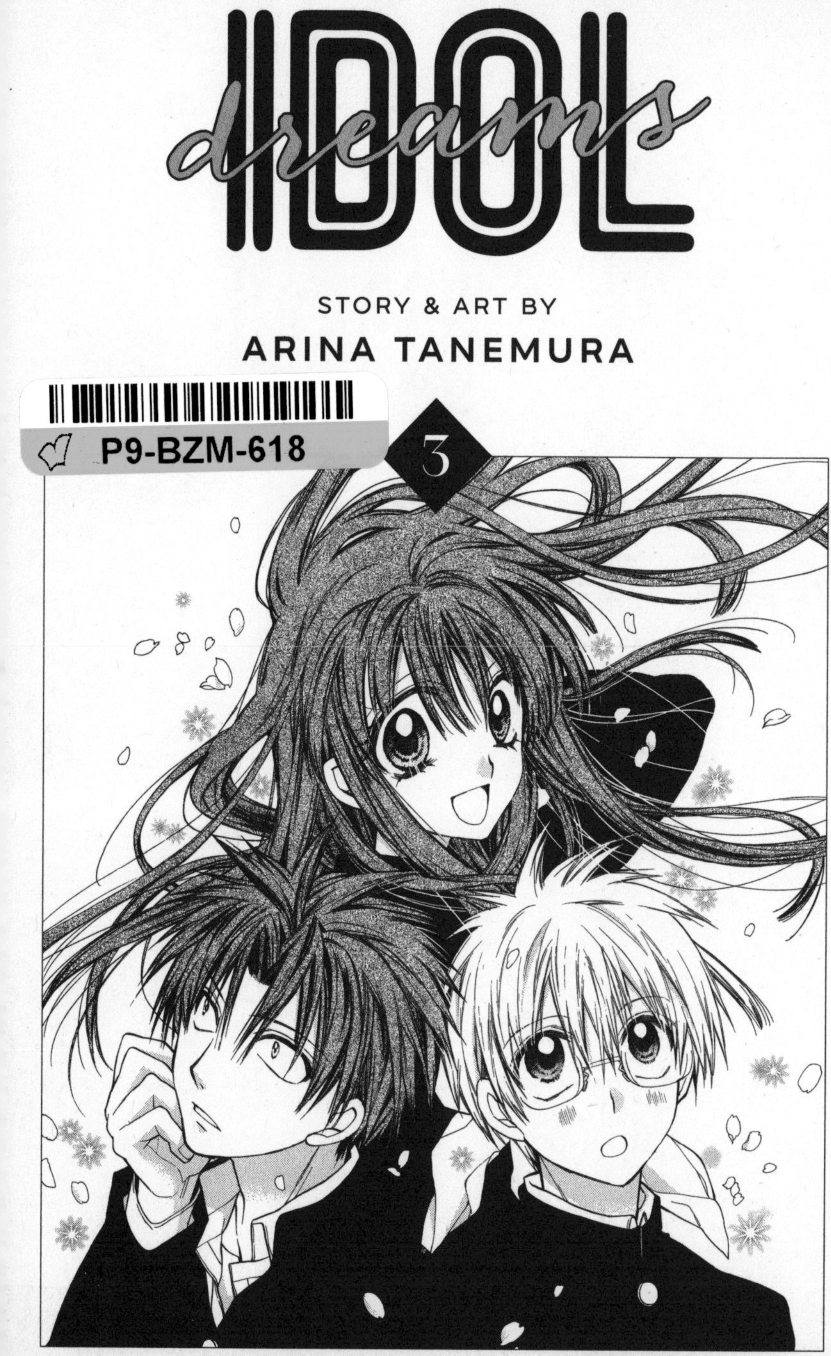

IDOL dreams 3

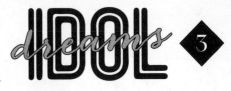

CONTENTS

IDOL dreams

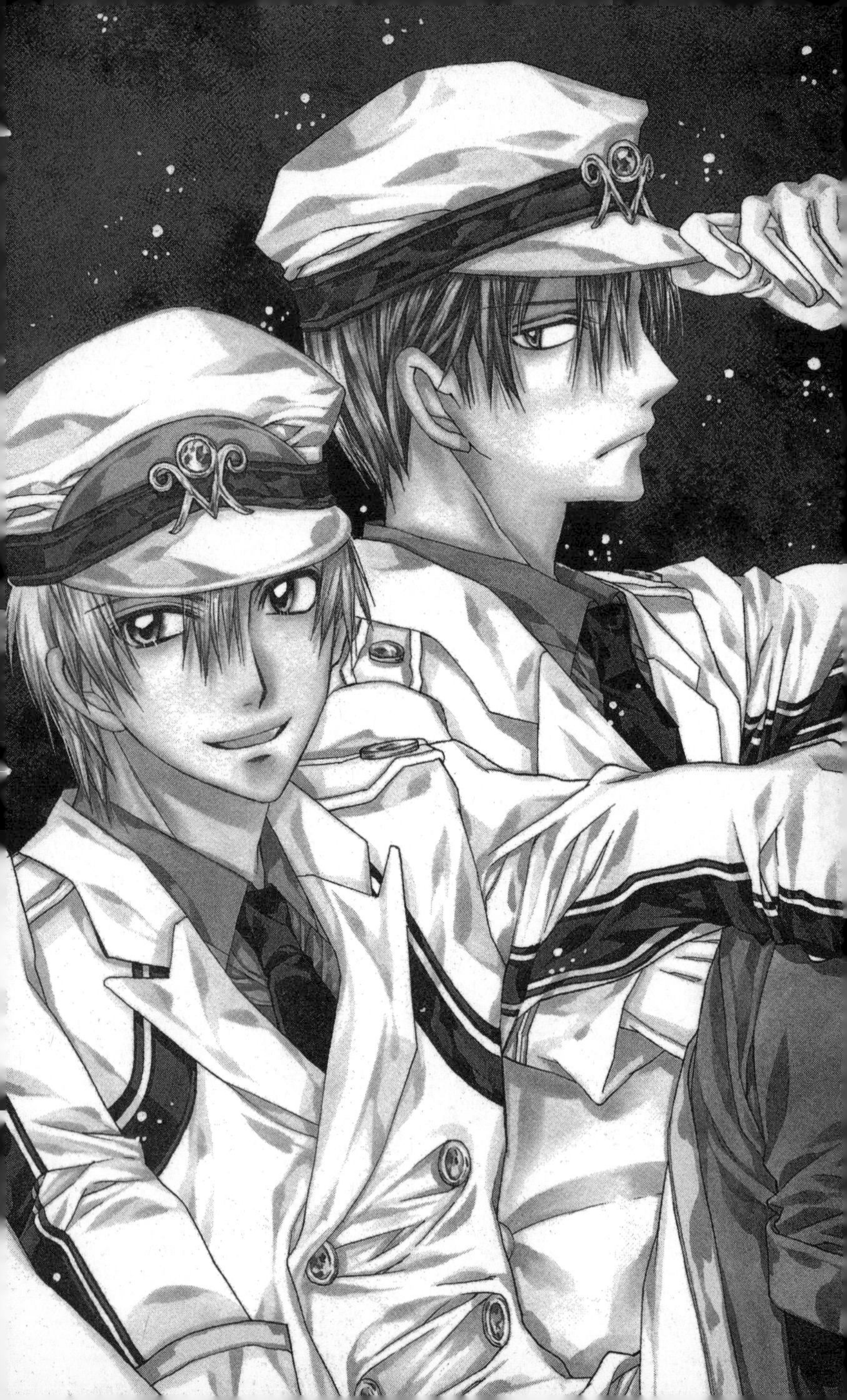

Chapter 11

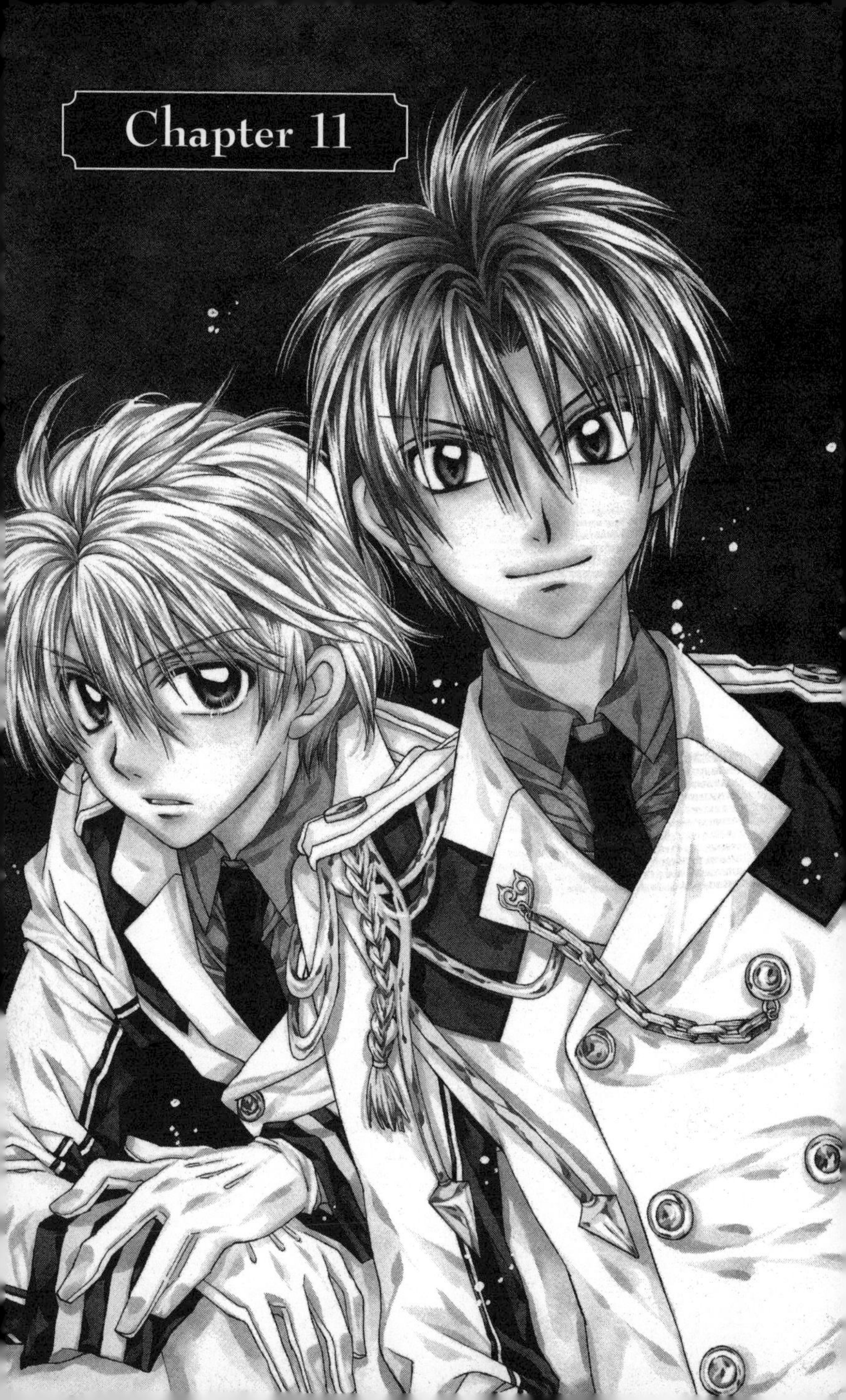

IDOL dreams

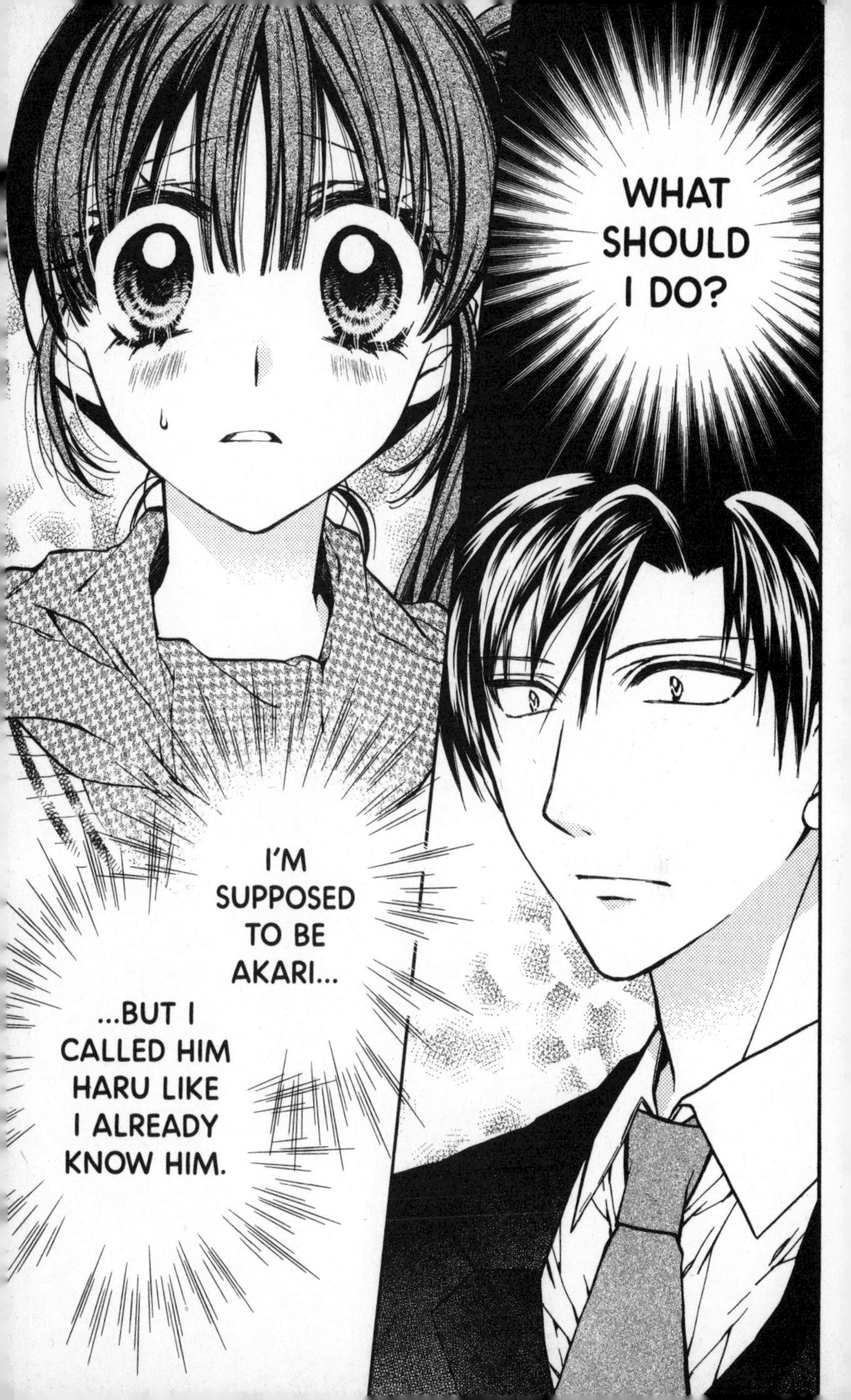
WHAT SHOULD I DO?
I'M SUPPOSED TO BE AKARI...
...BUT I CALLED HIM HARU LIKE I ALREADY KNOW HIM.

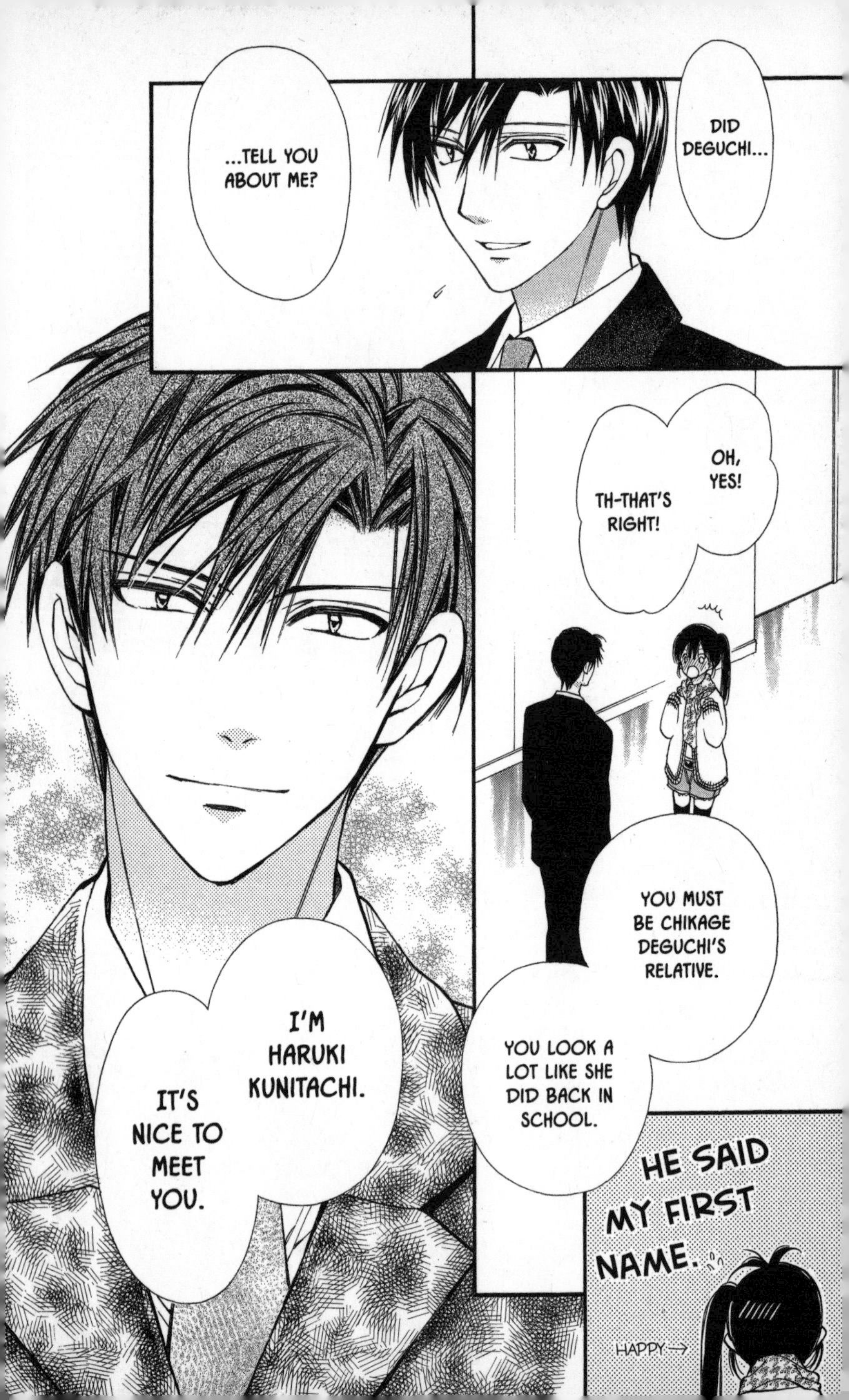
DID DEGUCHI...
...TELL YOU ABOUT ME?
OH, YES!
TH-THAT'S RIGHT!
YOU MUST BE CHIKAGE DEGUCHI'S RELATIVE.
YOU LOOK A LOT LIKE SHE DID BACK IN SCHOOL.
HE SAID MY FIRST NAME.
HAPPY→
I'M HARUKI KUNITACHI.
IT'S NICE TO MEET YOU.

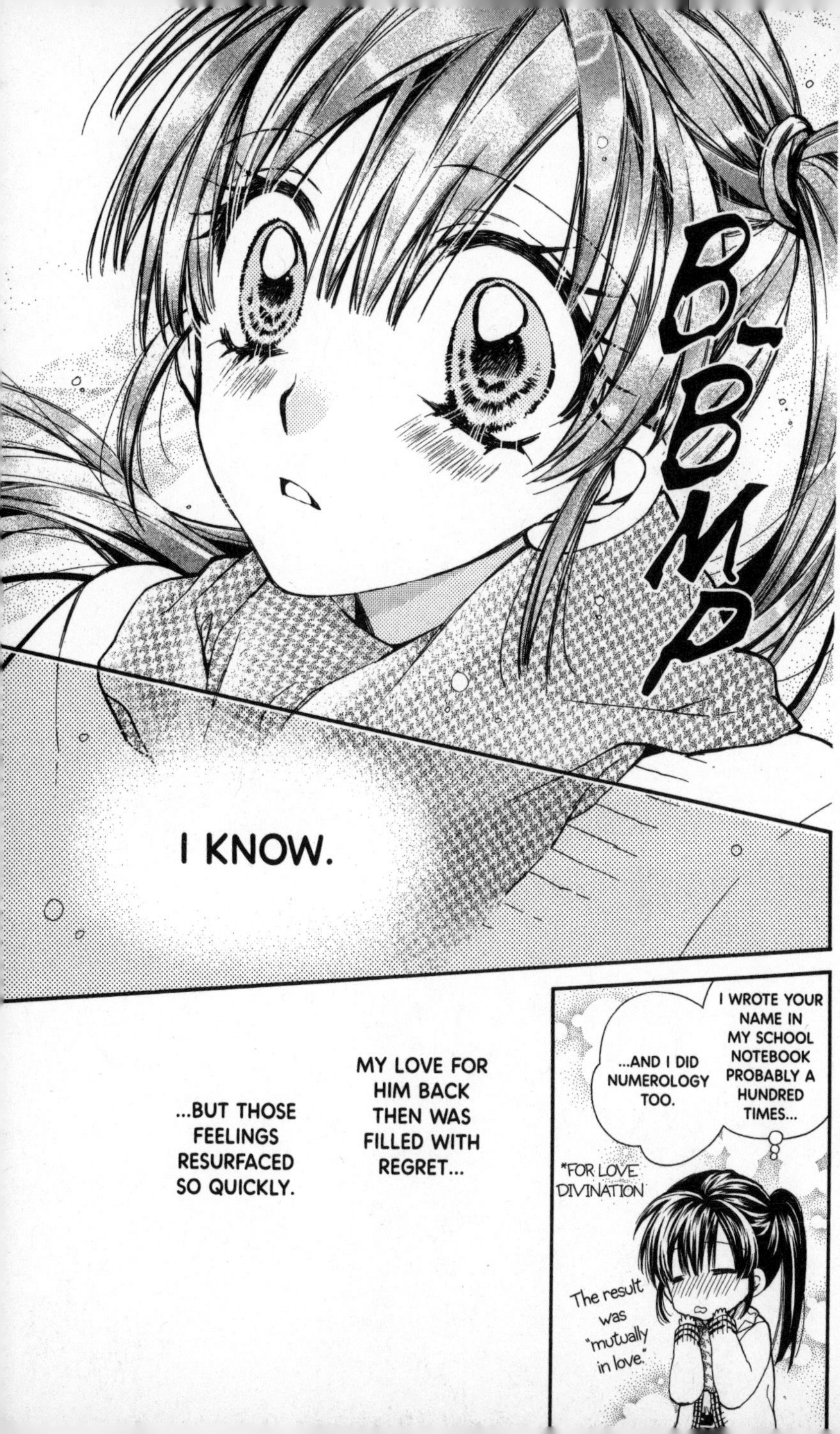
B-BMP
I KNOW.
I WROTE YOUR NAME IN MY SCHOOL NOTEBOOK PROBABLY A HUNDRED TIMES...
...AND I DID NUMEROLOGY TOO.
*FOR LOVE DIVINATION
The result was "mutually in love."
MY LOVE FOR HIM BACK THEN WAS FILLED WITH REGRET...
...BUT THOSE FEELINGS RESURFACED SO QUICKLY.

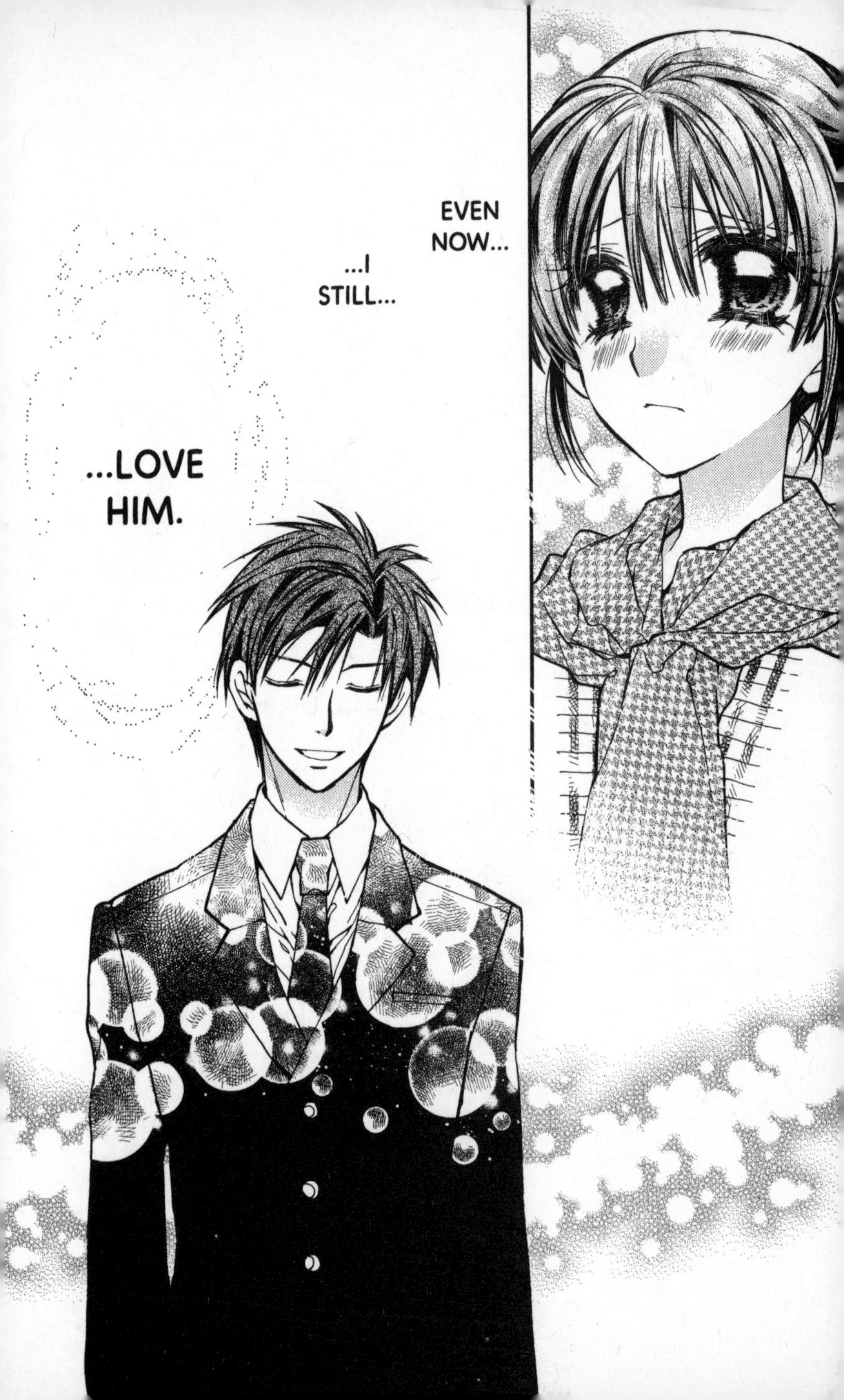
EVEN NOW...
...I STILL...
...LOVE HIM.

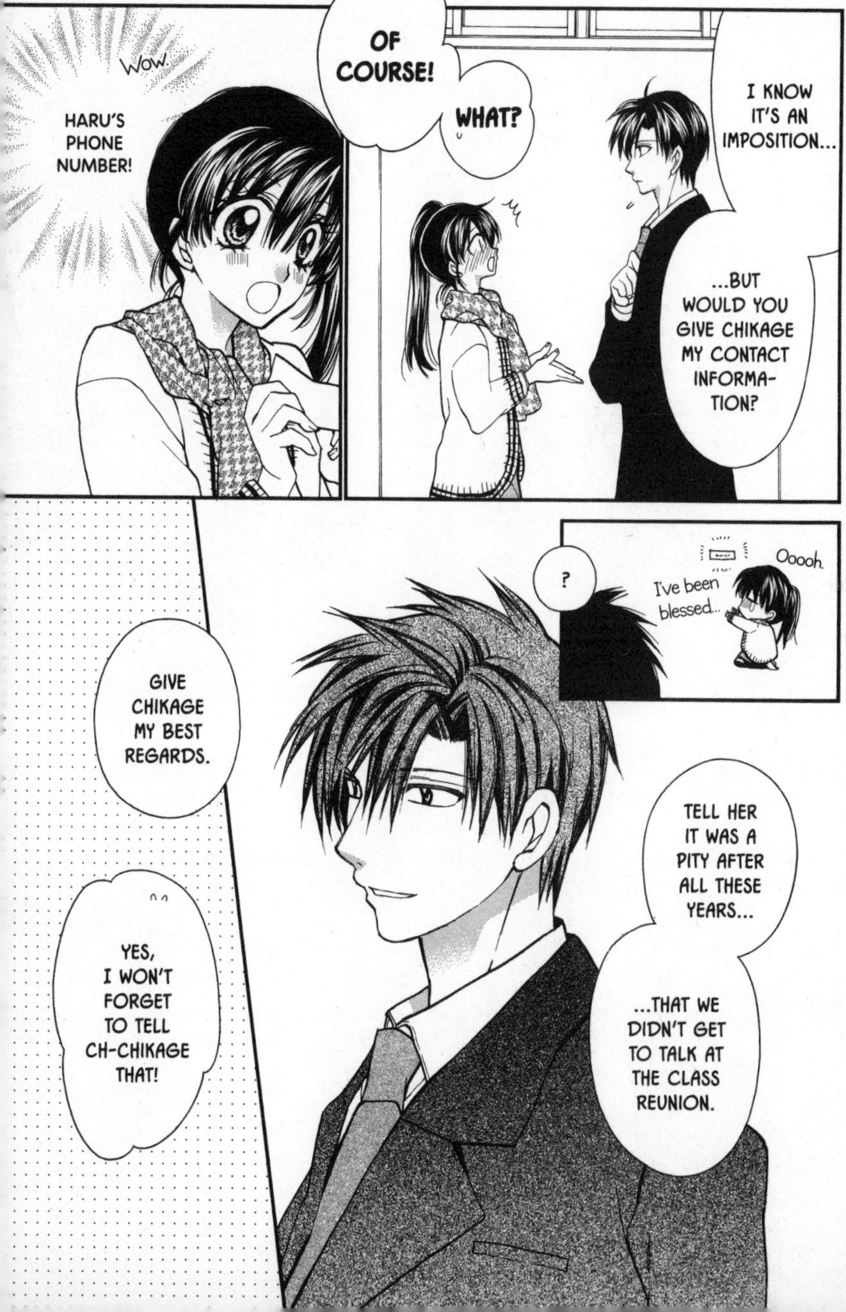
I KNOW IT'S AN IMPOSITION...
...BUT WOULD YOU GIVE CHIKAGE MY CONTACT INFORMATION?
WHAT?
OF COURSE!
WOW.
HARU'S PHONE NUMBER!
Ooooh.
I've been blessed...
?
TELL HER IT WAS A PITY AFTER ALL THESE YEARS...
...THAT WE DIDN'T GET TO TALK AT THE CLASS REUNION.
GIVE CHIKAGE MY BEST REGARDS.
YES, I WON'T FORGET TO TELL CH-CHIKAGE THAT!

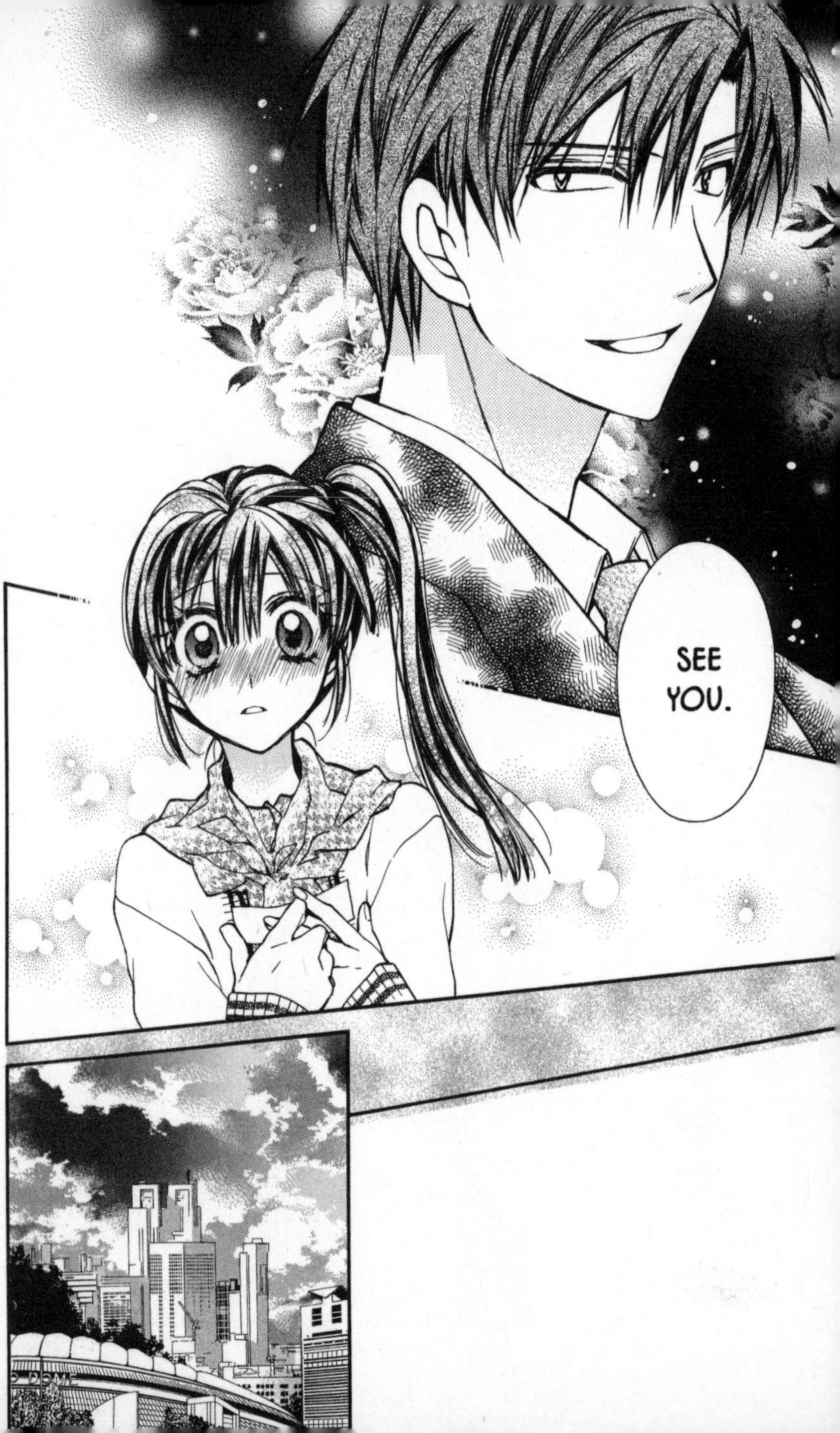
SEE YOU.

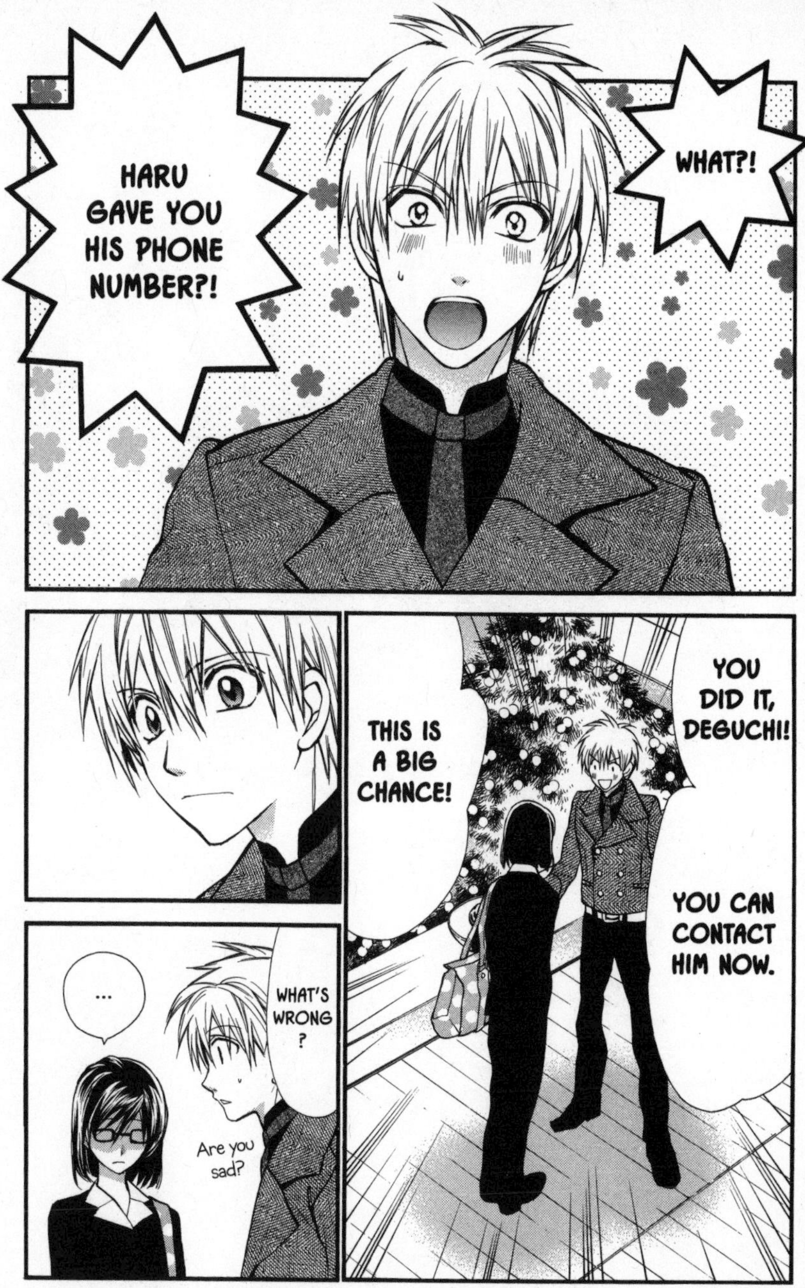
WHAT?!
HARU GAVE YOU HIS PHONE NUMBER?!
YOU DID IT, DEGUCHI!
YOU CAN CONTACT HIM NOW.
THIS IS A BIG CHANCE!
WHAT'S WRONG?
Are you sad?
...

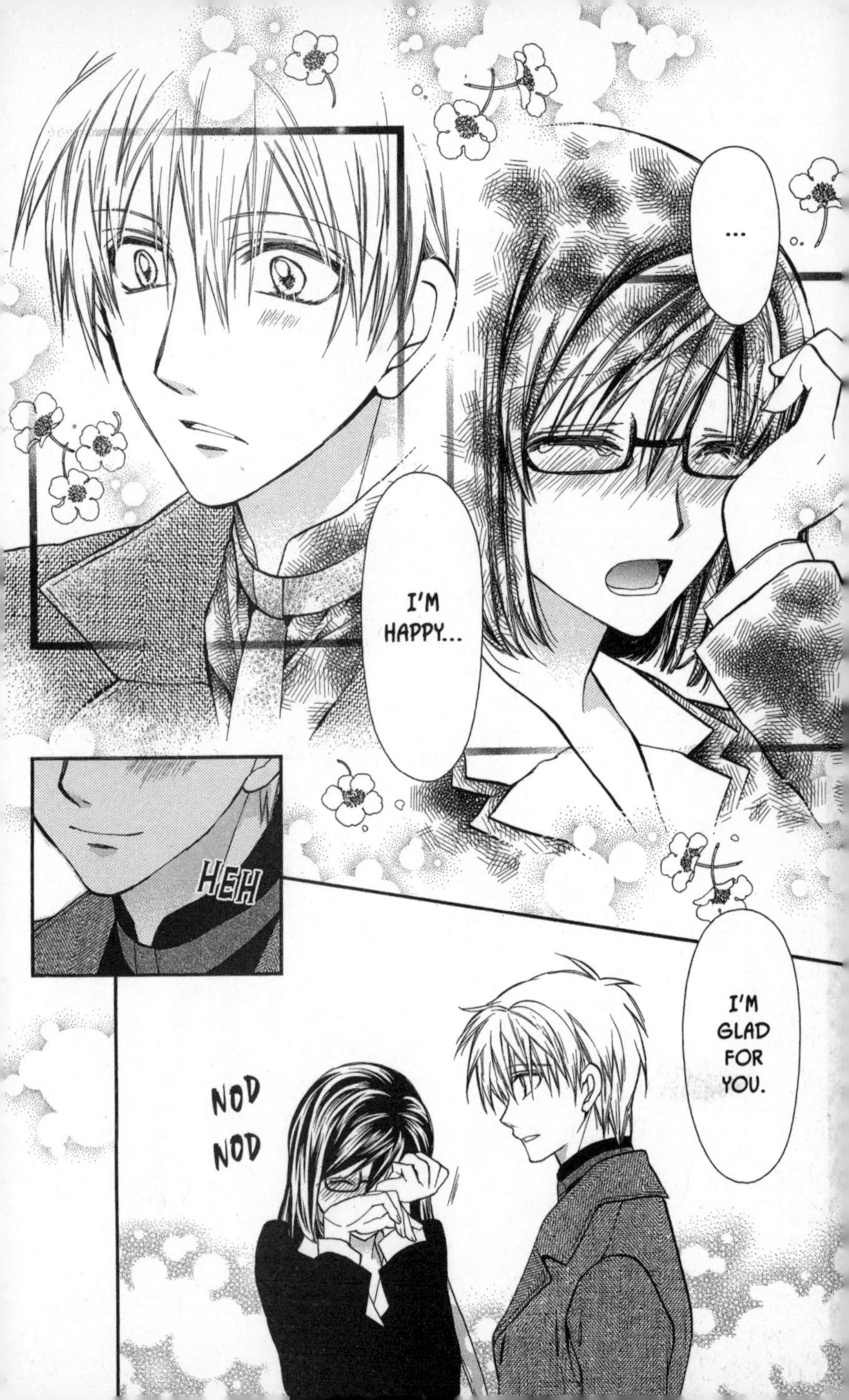
...
I'M HAPPY...
HEH
I'M GLAD FOR YOU.
NOD NOD

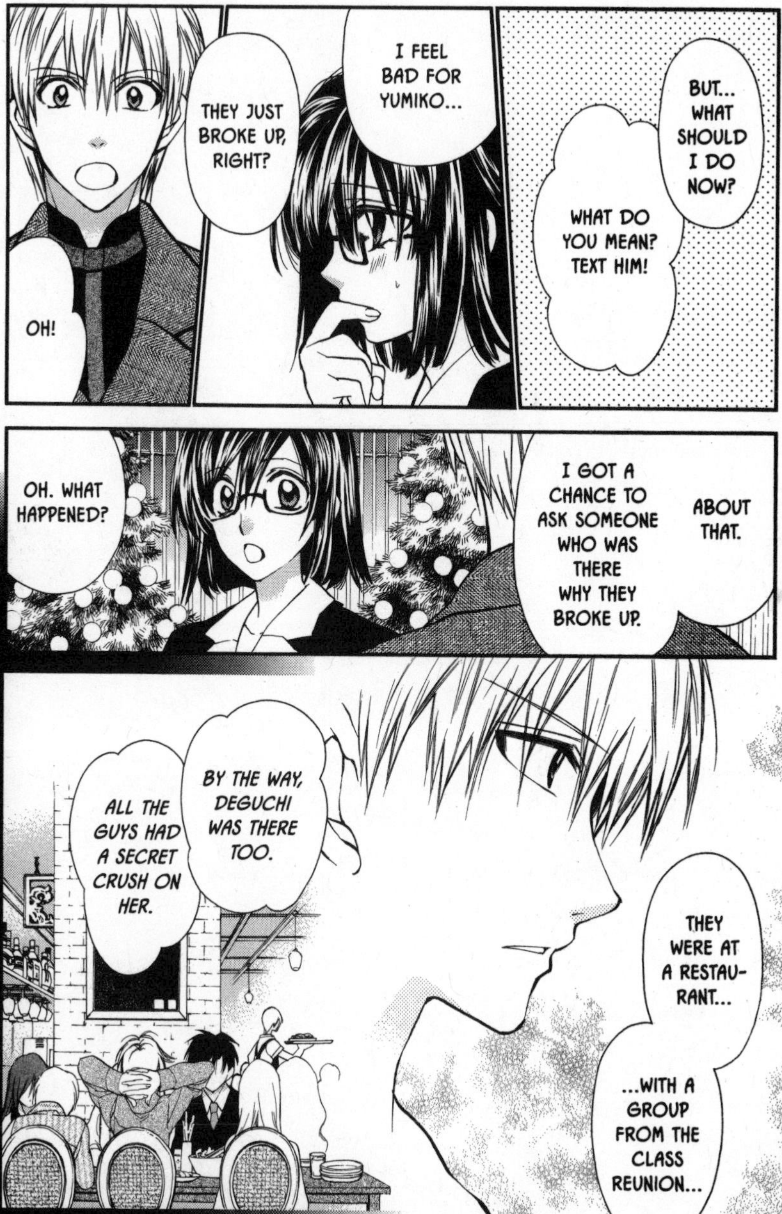
BUT... WHAT SHOULD I DO NOW?
WHAT DO YOU MEAN? TEXT HIM!
I FEEL BAD FOR YUMIKO...
THEY JUST BROKE UP, RIGHT?
OH!
ABOUT THAT.
I GOT A CHANCE TO ASK SOMEONE WHO WAS THERE WHY THEY BROKE UP.
OH. WHAT HAPPENED?
THEY WERE AT A RESTAU-RANT...
...WITH A GROUP FROM THE CLASS REUNION...
BY THE WAY, DEGUCHI WAS THERE TOO.
ALL THE GUYS HAD A SECRET CRUSH ON HER.

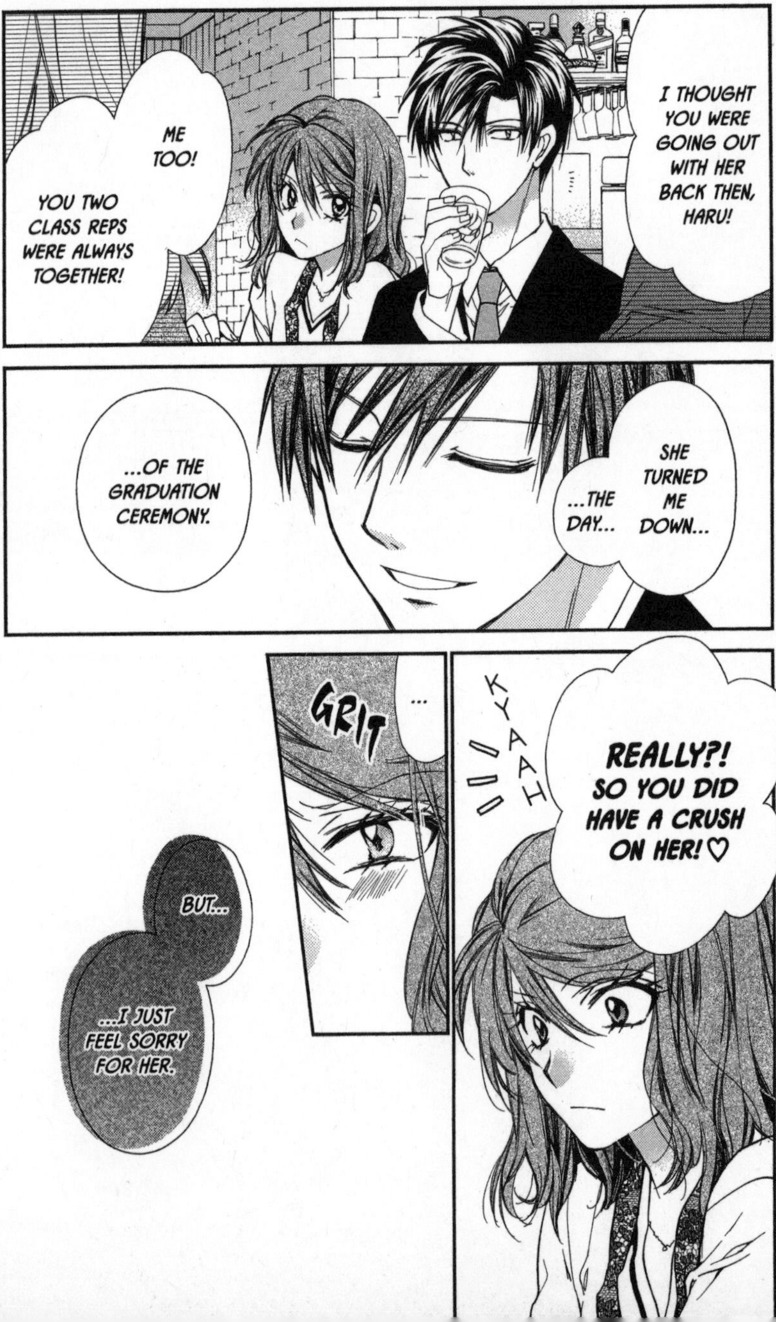
I THOUGHT YOU WERE GOING OUT WITH HER BACK THEN, HARU!
ME TOO!
YOU TWO CLASS REPS WERE ALWAYS TOGETHER!
SHE TURNED ME DOWN...
...THE DAY...
...OF THE GRADUATION CEREMONY.
KYAAH
REALLY?! SO YOU DID HAVE A CRUSH ON HER!♡
...
GRIT
BUT...
...I JUST FEEL SORRY FOR HER.

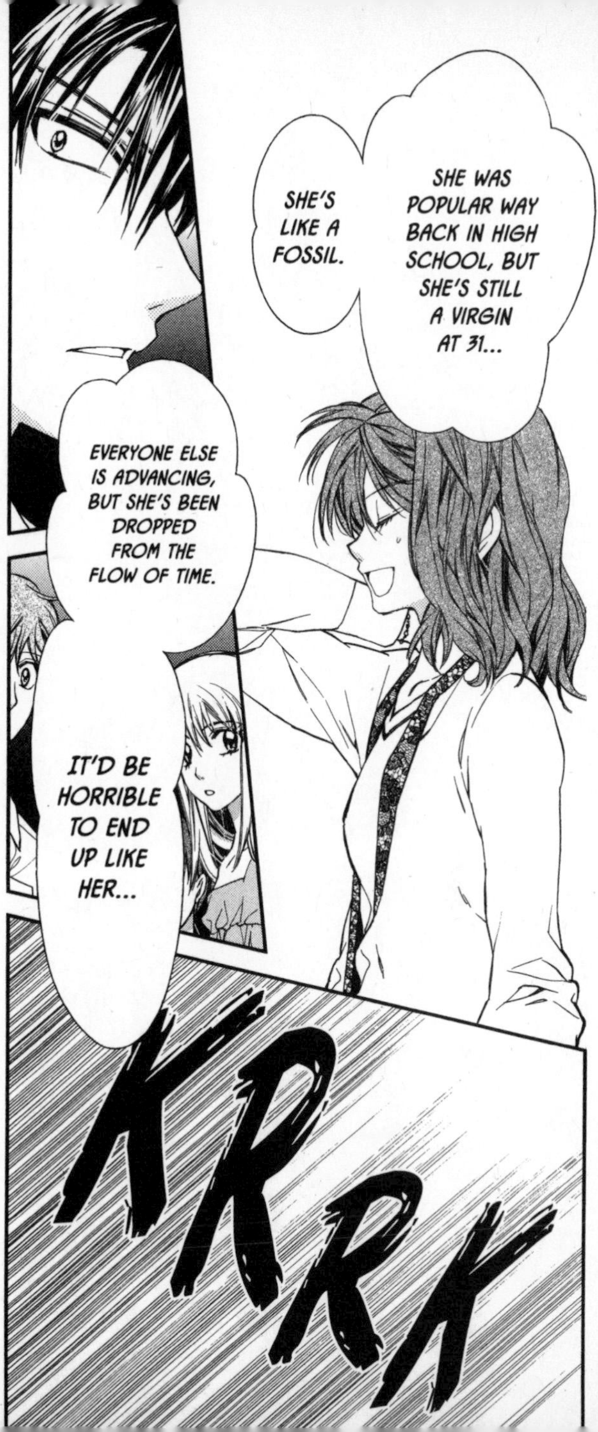
SHE WAS POPULAR WAY BACK IN HIGH SCHOOL, BUT SHE'S STILL A VIRGIN AT 31...
SHE'S LIKE A FOSSIL.
EVERYONE ELSE IS ADVANCING, BUT SHE'S BEEN DROPPED FROM THE FLOW OF TIME.
IT'D BE HORRIBLE TO END UP LIKE HER...
KRRK

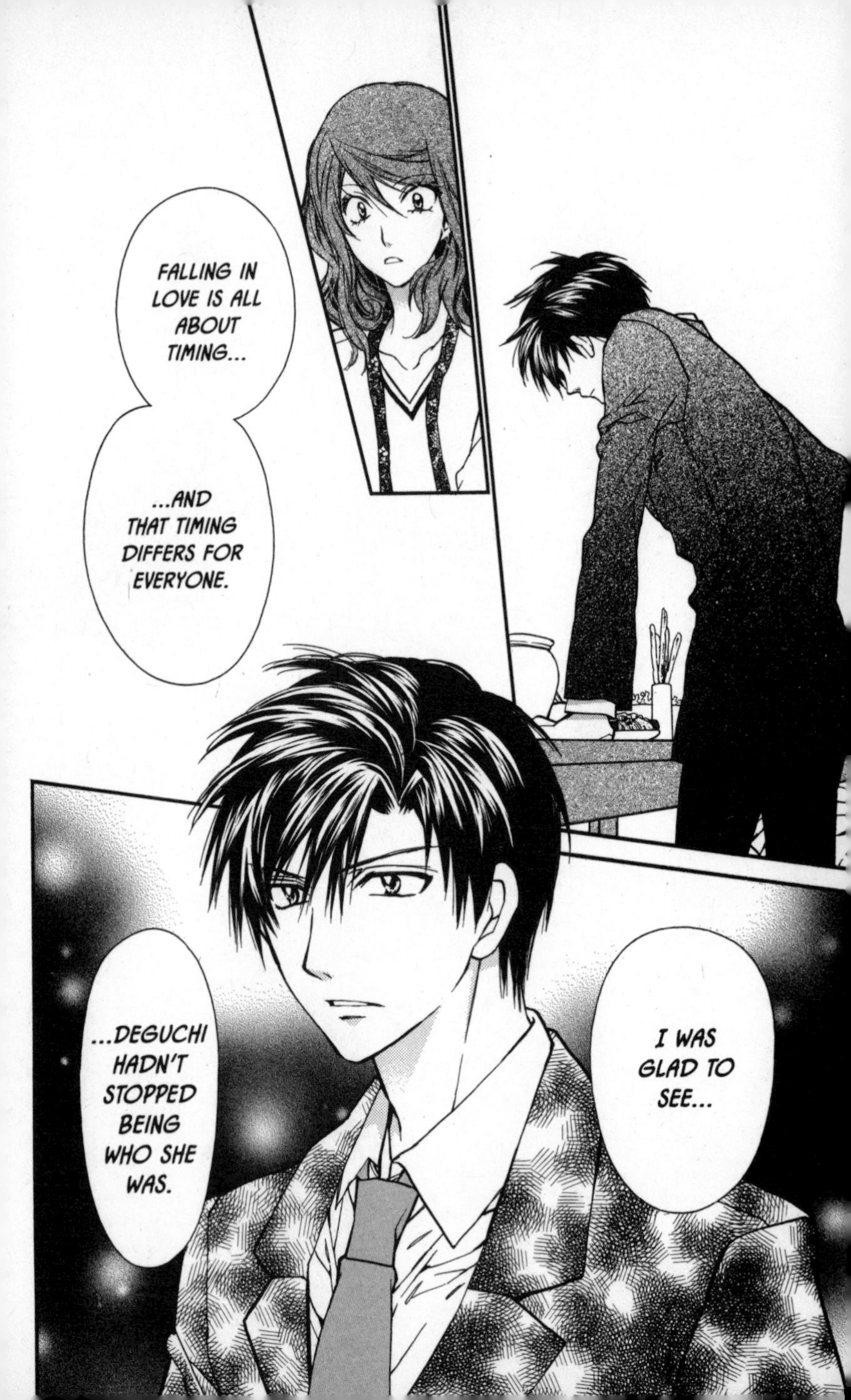
FALLING IN LOVE IS ALL ABOUT TIMING...
...AND THAT TIMING DIFFERS FOR EVERYONE.
I WAS GLAD TO SEE...
...DEGUCHI HADN'T STOPPED BEING WHO SHE WAS.

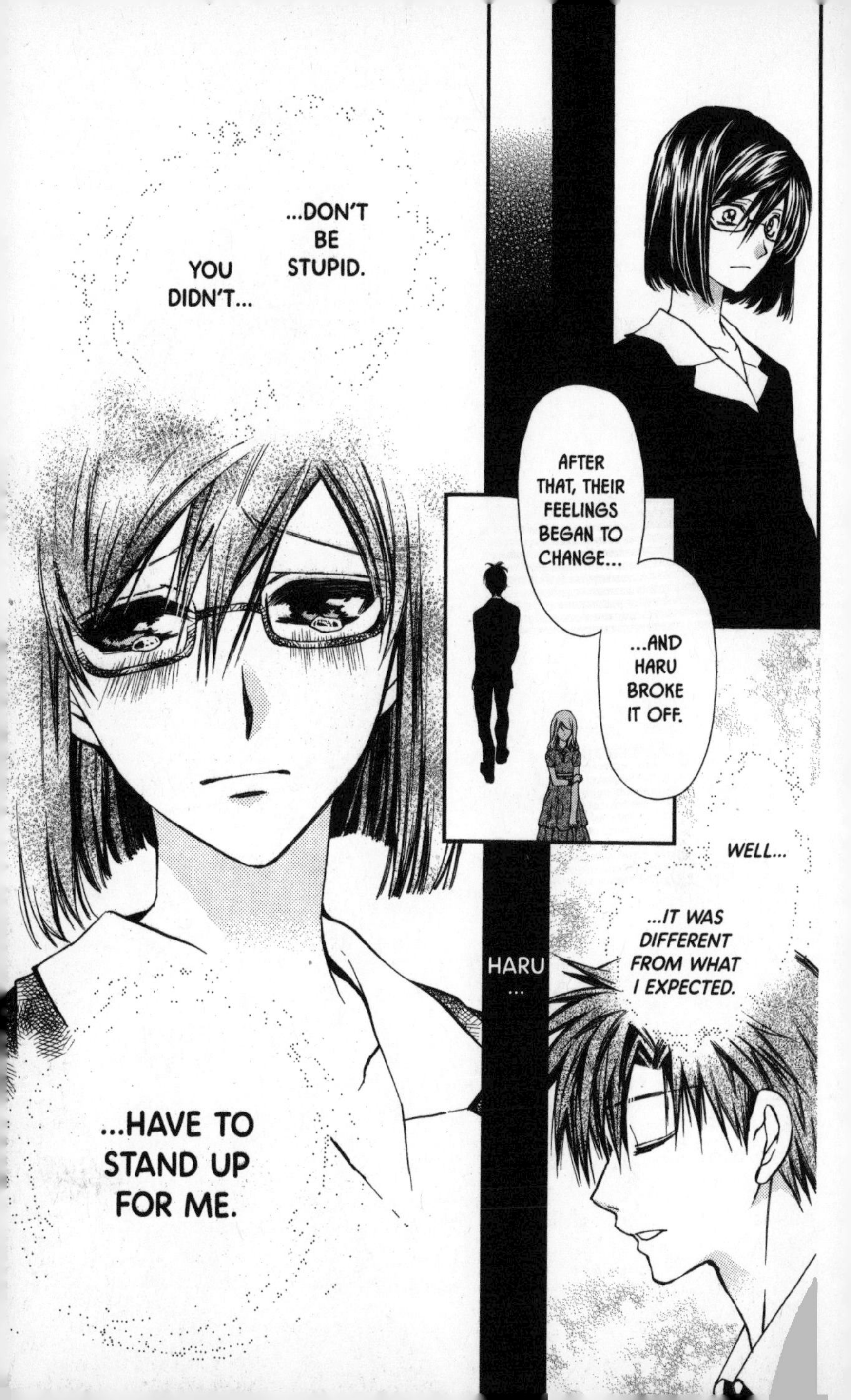
AFTER THAT, THEIR FEELINGS BEGAN TO CHANGE...
...AND HARU BROKE IT OFF.
WELL...
...IT WAS DIFFERENT FROM WHAT I EXPECTED.
HARU...
...DON'T BE STUPID.
YOU DIDN'T...
...HAVE TO STAND UP FOR ME.

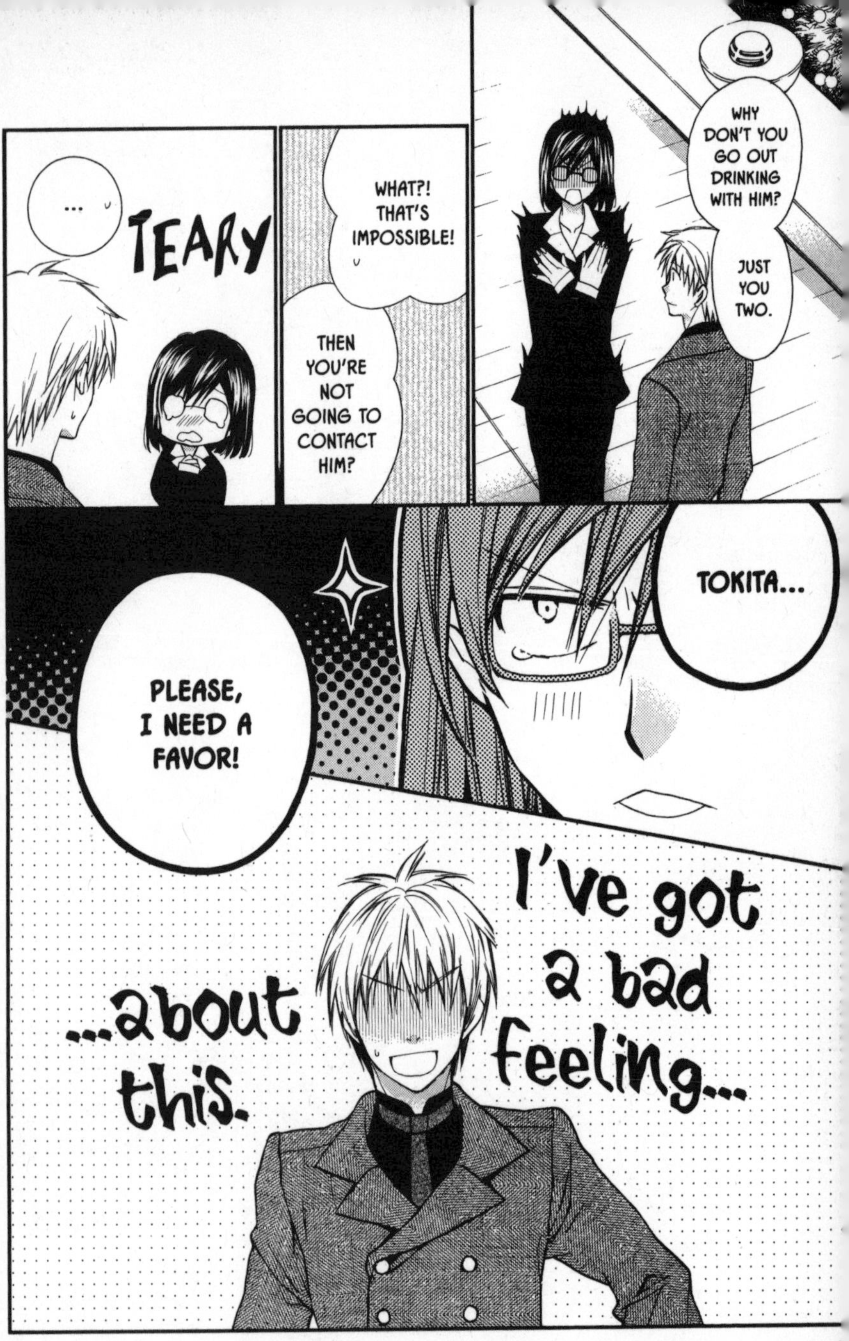
WHY DON'T YOU GO OUT DRINKING WITH HIM?
JUST YOU TWO.
WHAT?! THAT'S IMPOSSIBLE!
THEN YOU'RE NOT GOING TO CONTACT HIM?
...
TEARY
TOKITA...
PLEASE, I NEED A FAVOR!
I've got a bad feeling...
...about this.

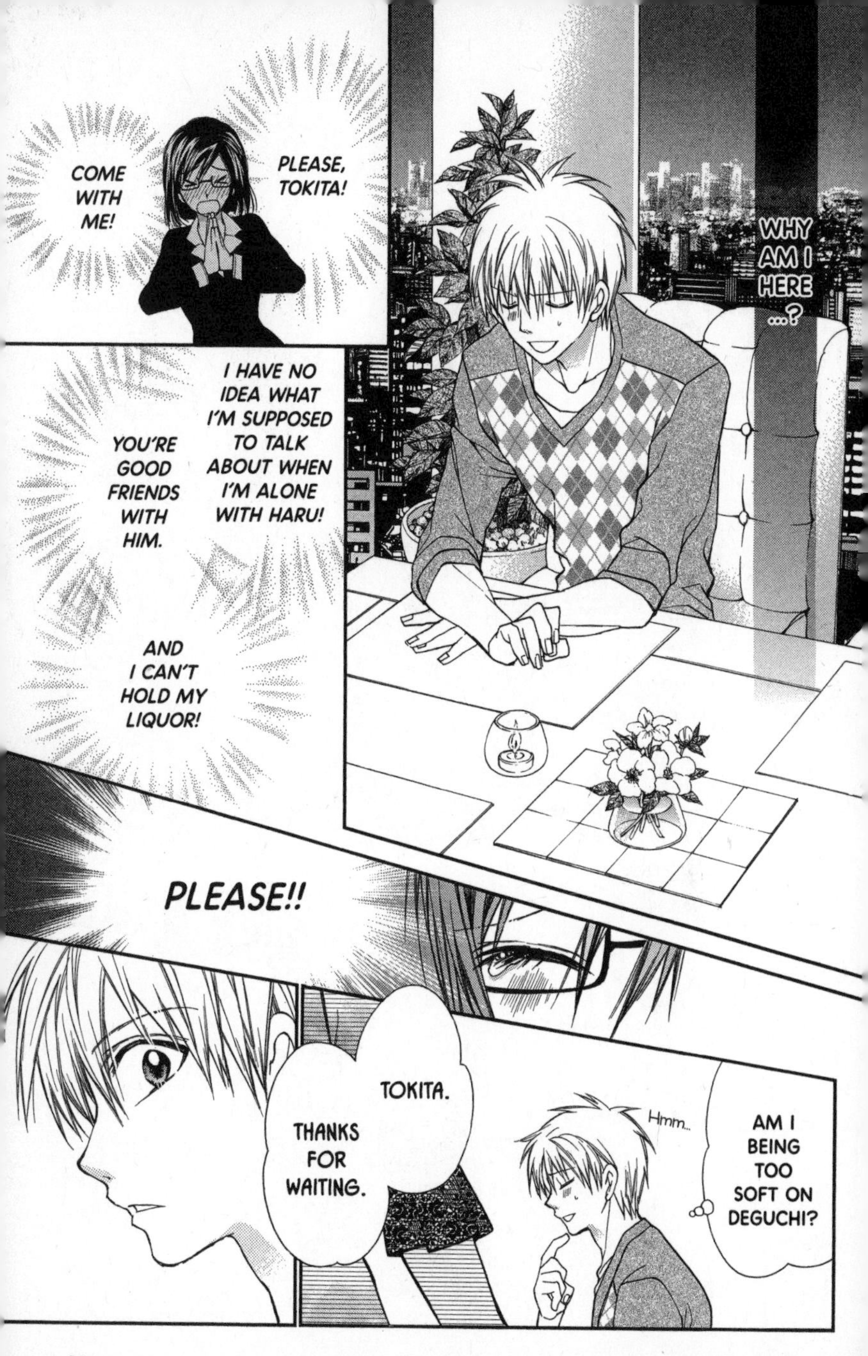
WHY AM I HERE ...?
PLEASE, TOKITA!
COME WITH ME!
I HAVE NO IDEA WHAT I'M SUPPOSED TO TALK ABOUT WHEN I'M ALONE WITH HARU!
YOU'RE GOOD FRIENDS WITH HIM.
AND I CAN'T HOLD MY LIQUOR!
PLEASE!!
Hmm..
AM I BEING TOO SOFT ON DEGUCHI?
TOKITA.
THANKS FOR WAITING.

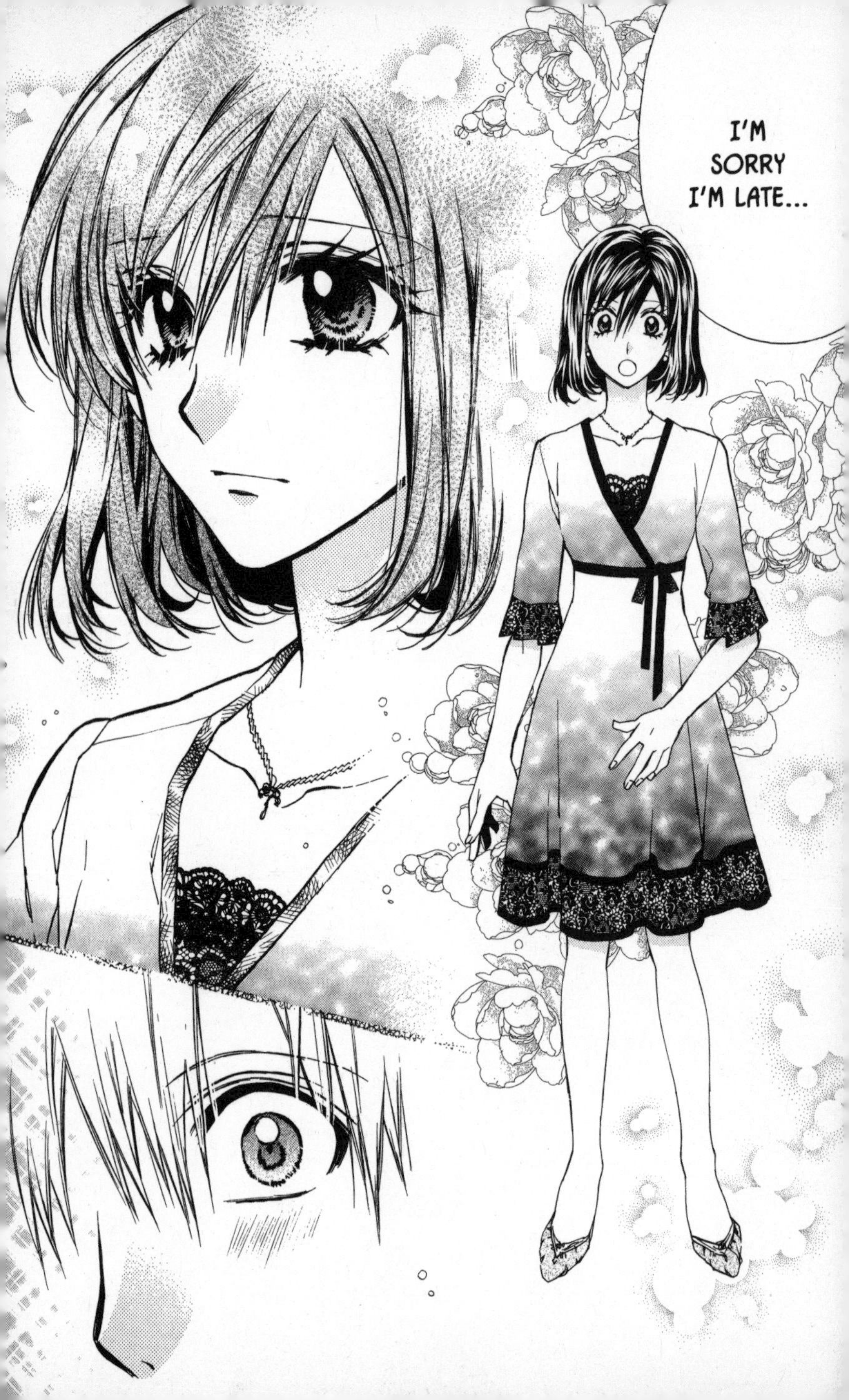
I'M SORRY I'M LATE...

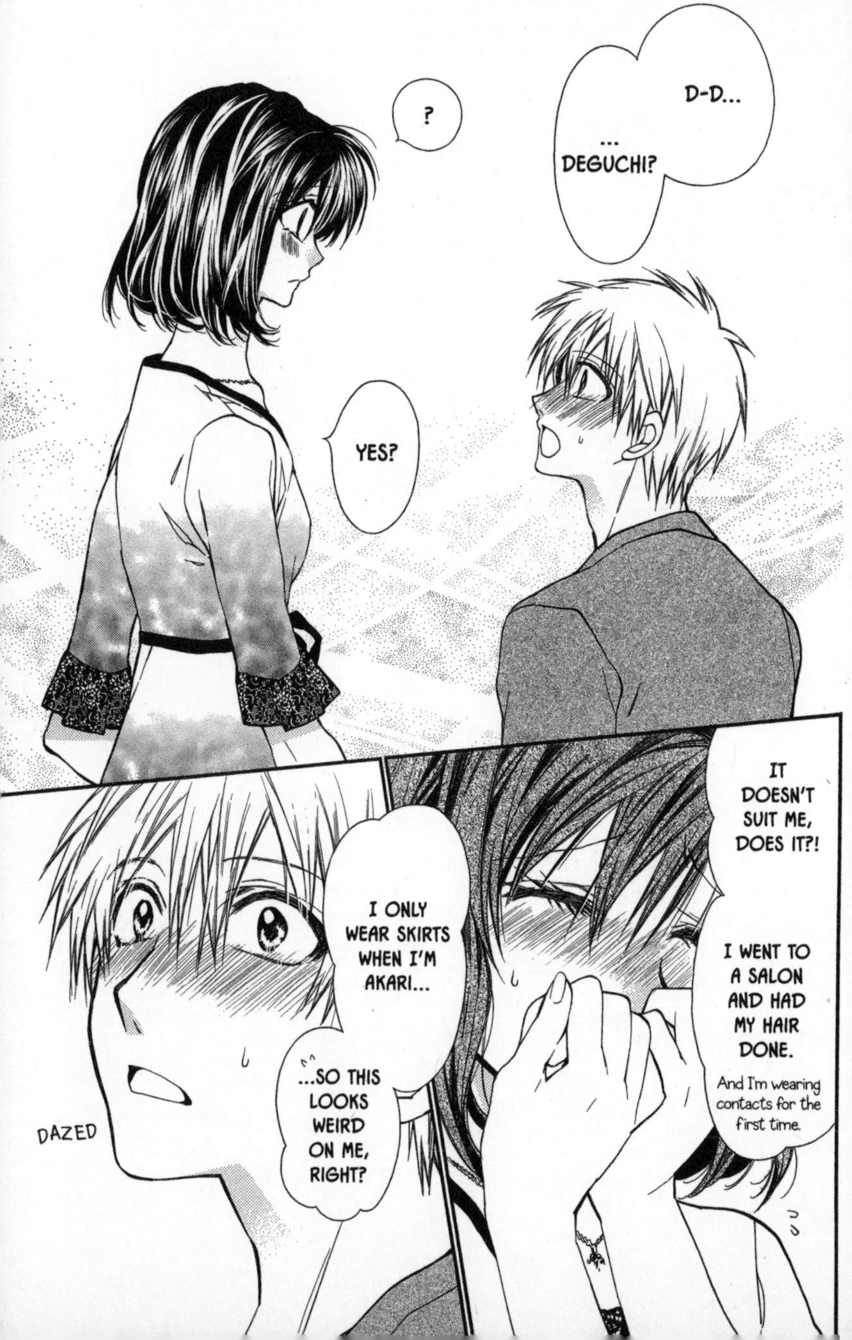
D-D...
...DEGUCHI?
?
YES?
IT DOESN'T SUIT ME, DOES IT?!
I WENT TO A SALON AND HAD MY HAIR DONE.
And I'm wearing contacts for the first time.
I ONLY WEAR SKIRTS WHEN I'M AKARI...
...SO THIS LOOKS WEIRD ON ME, RIGHT?
DAZED

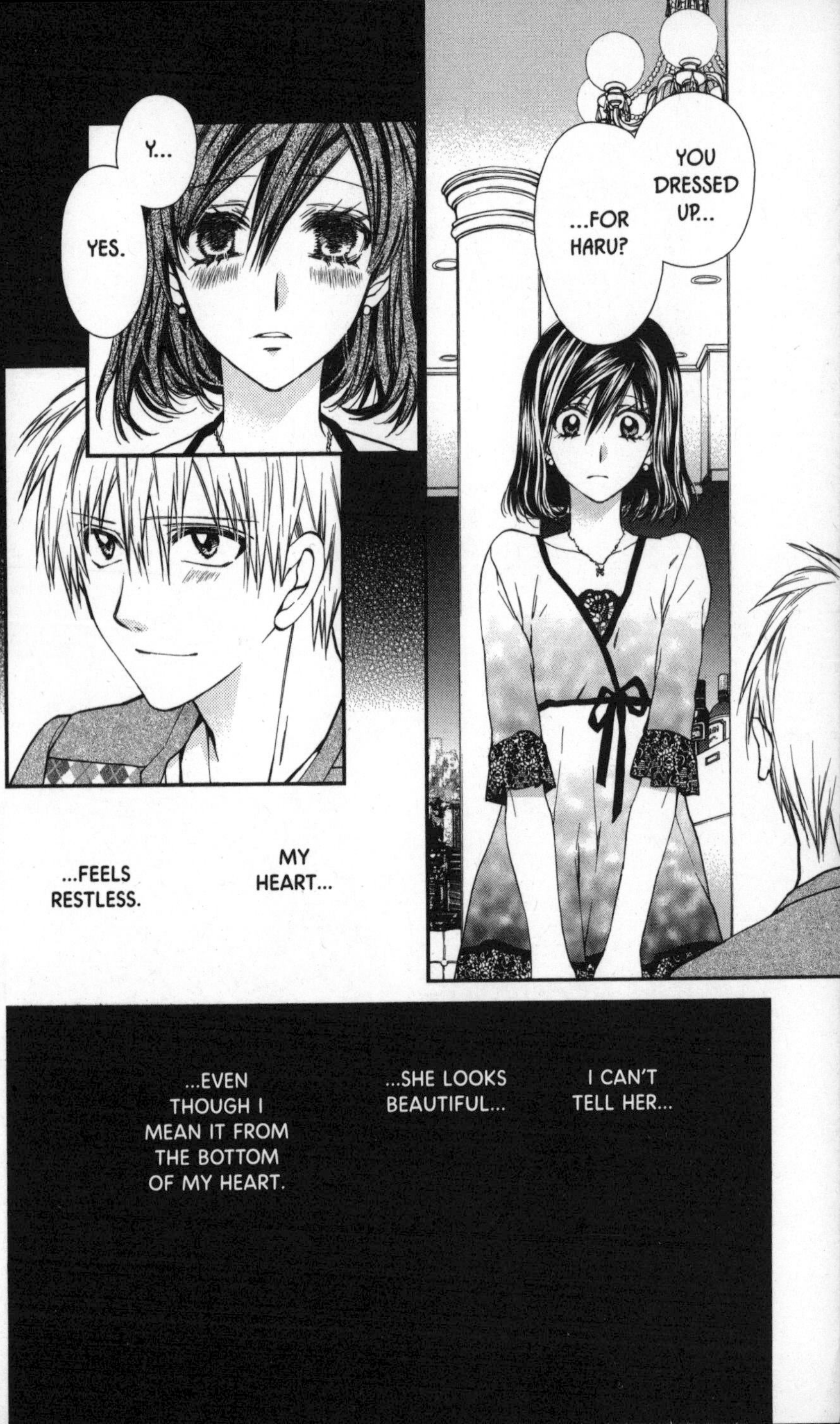
YOU DRESSED UP...
...FOR HARU?
Y...
YES.
MY HEART...
...FEELS RESTLESS.
I CAN'T TELL HER...
...SHE LOOKS BEAUTIFUL...
...EVEN THOUGH I MEAN IT FROM THE BOTTOM OF MY HEART.

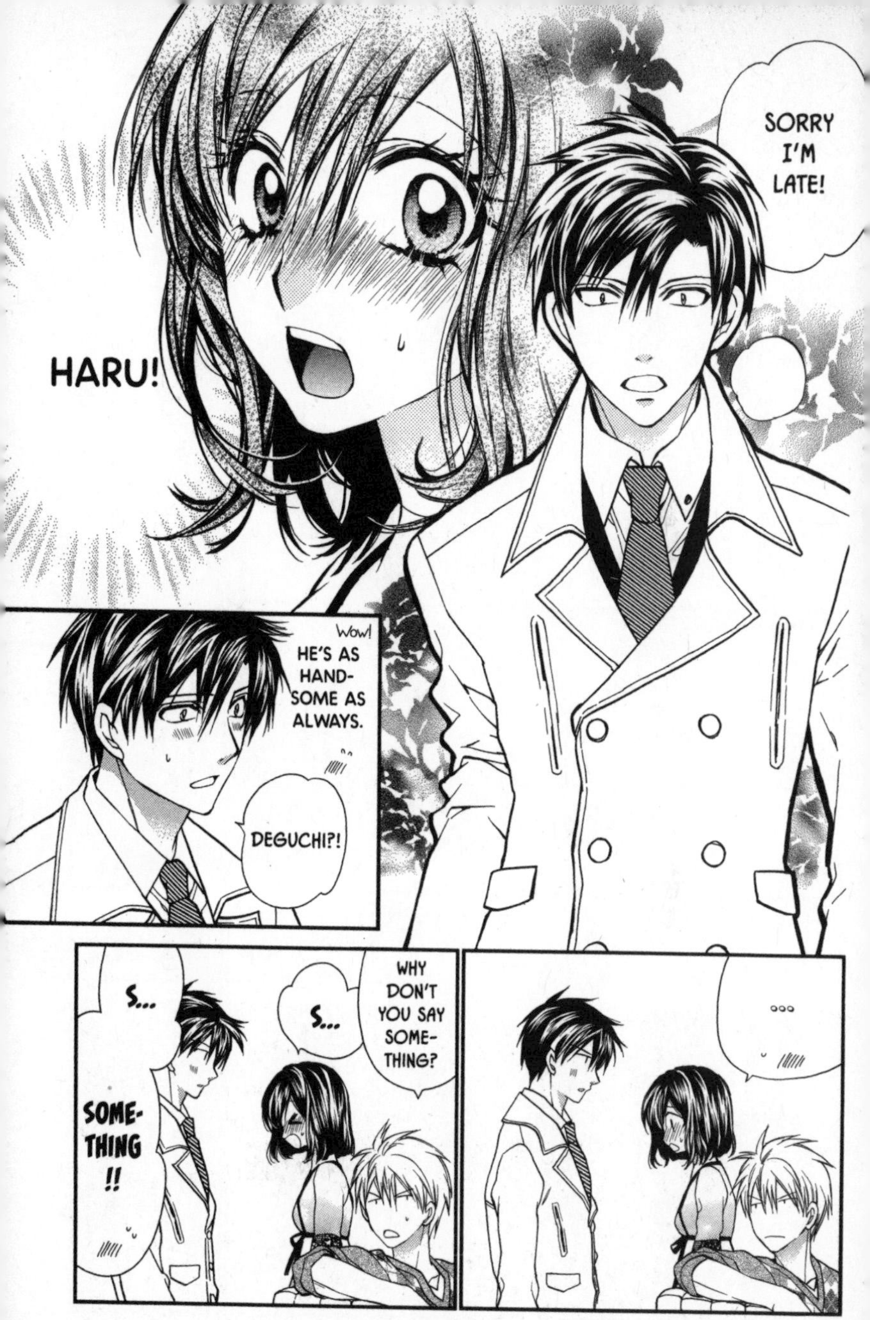
SORRY I'M LATE!
HARU!
Wow! HE'S AS HAND-SOME AS ALWAYS.
DEGUCHI?!
...
WHY DON'T YOU SAY SOME-THING?
S...
S...
SOME-THING !!

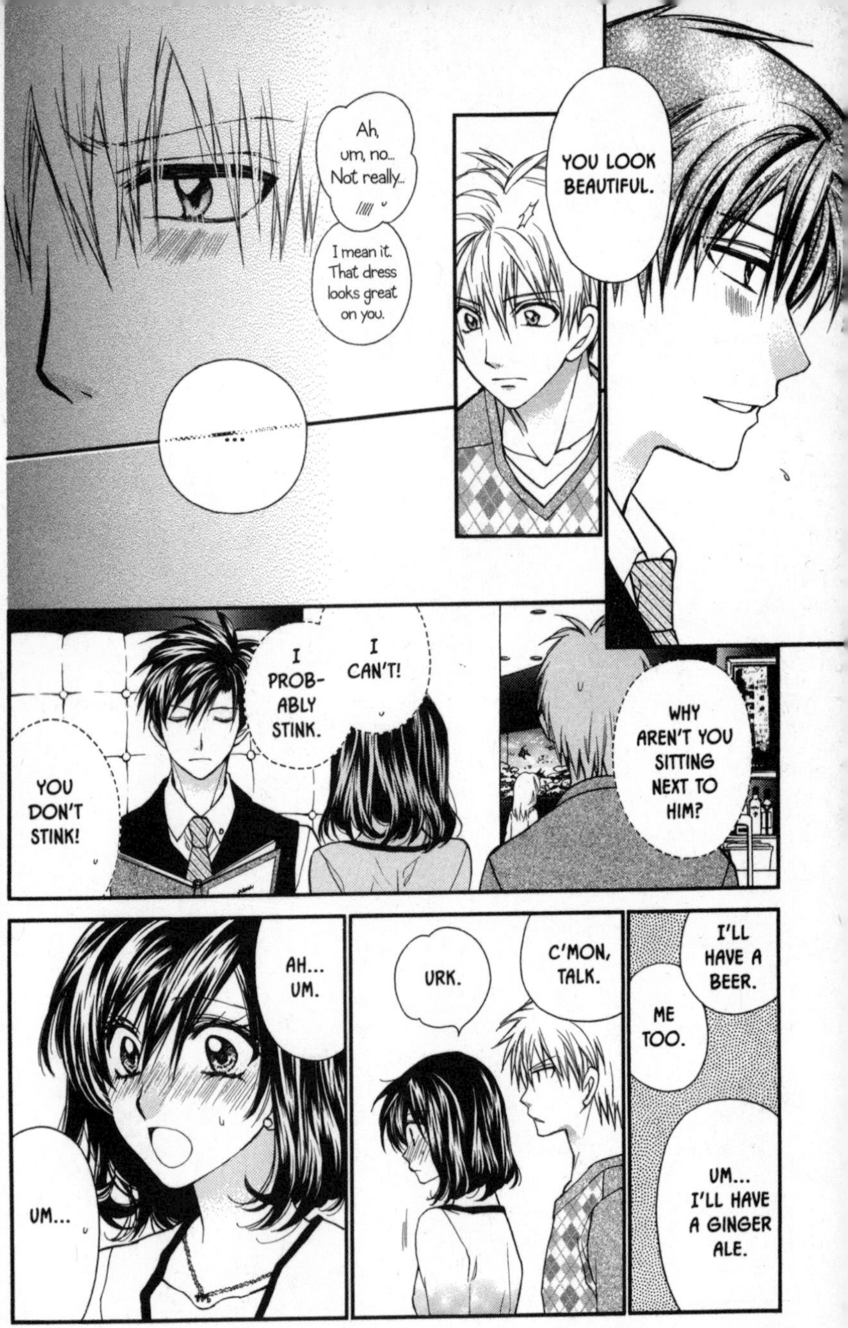
YOU LOOK BEAUTIFUL.
Ah, um, no... Not really...
I mean it. That dress looks great on you.
...
WHY AREN'T YOU SITTING NEXT TO HIM?
I CAN'T!
I PROBABLY STINK.
YOU DON'T STINK!
I'LL HAVE A BEER.
ME TOO.
UM... I'LL HAVE A GINGER ALE.
C'MON, TALK.
URK.
AH... UM.
UM...

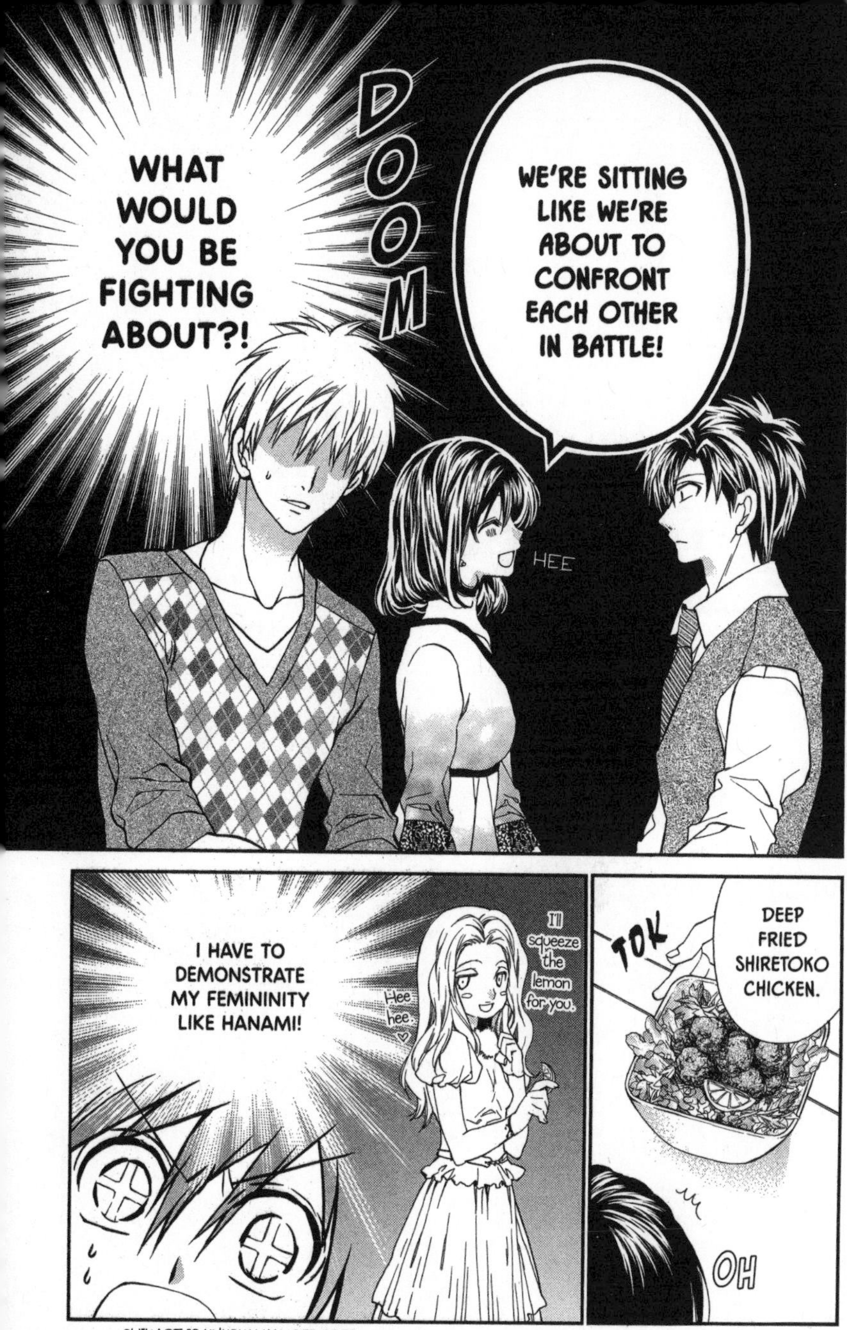
WE'RE SITTING LIKE WE'RE ABOUT TO CONFRONT EACH OTHER IN BATTLE!
DOOM
WHAT WOULD YOU BE FIGHTING ABOUT?!
HEE
TOK
DEEP FRIED SHIRETOKO CHICKEN.
OH
I'll squeeze the lemon for you.
Hee hee.
I HAVE TO DEMONSTRATE MY FEMININITY LIKE HANAMI!

CHIKAGE IS UNUSUALLY MOTIVATED.

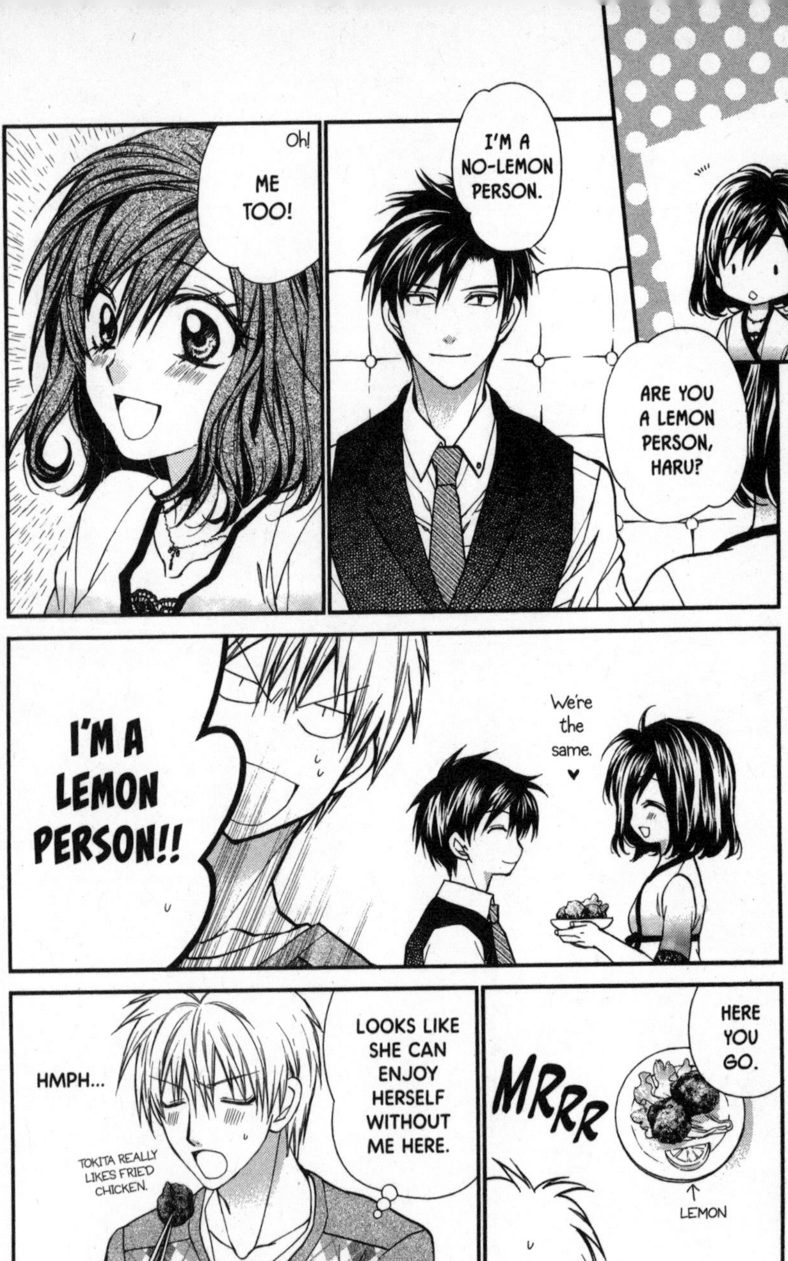
ARE YOU A LEMON PERSON, HARU?
I'M A NO-LEMON PERSON.
Oh!
ME TOO!
We're the same.
I'M A LEMON PERSON!!
HERE YOU GO.
MRRR
LEMON
LOOKS LIKE SHE CAN ENJOY HERSELF WITHOUT ME HERE.
HMPH...
TOKITA REALLY LIKES FRIED CHICKEN.

A SHOW OF "SQUEEZE AS MUCH LEMON JUICE AS YOU WANT" TO BE KIND (OR SO SHE THINKS).

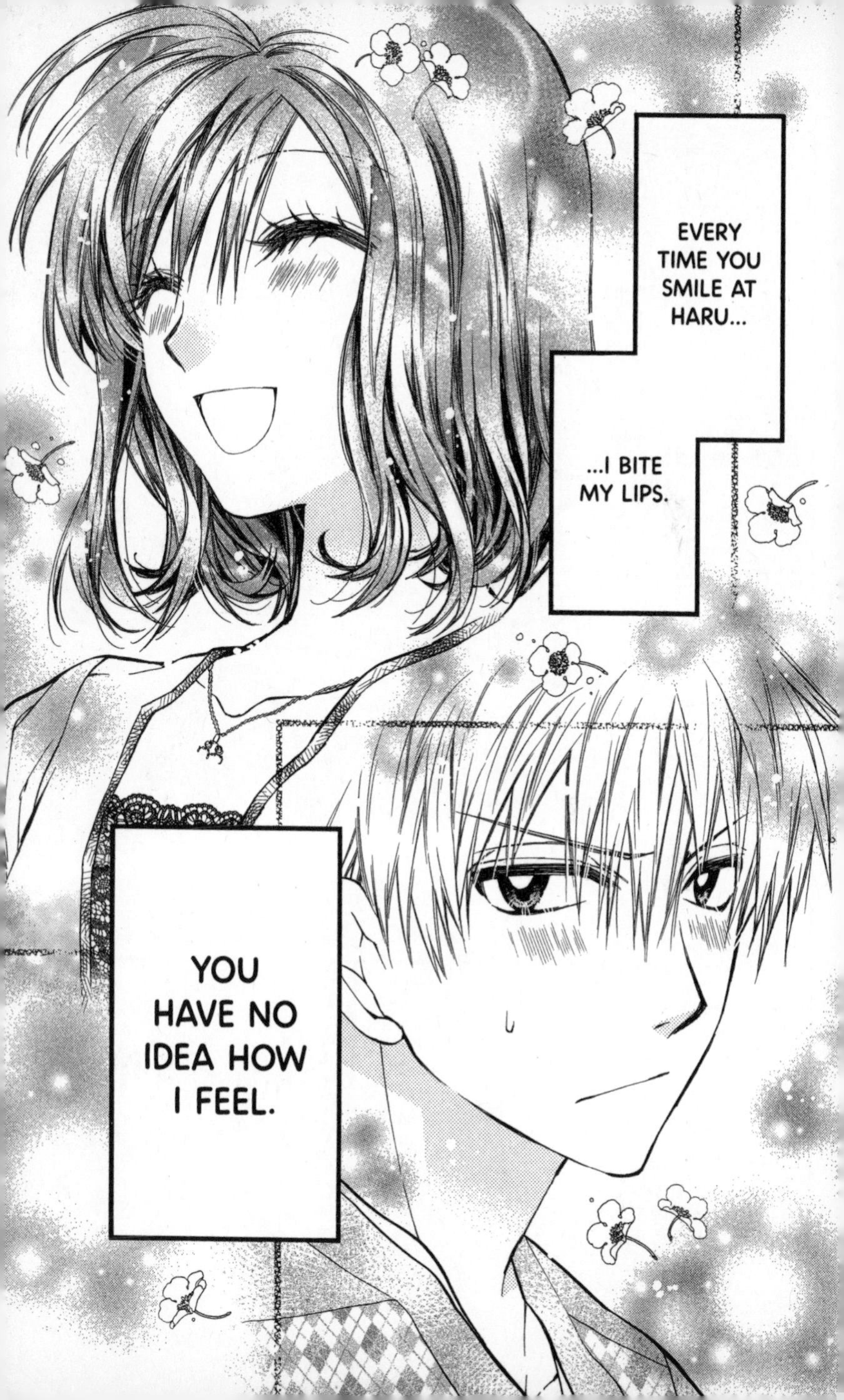
EVERY TIME YOU SMILE AT HARU...
...I BITE MY LIPS.
YOU HAVE NO IDEA HOW I FEEL.

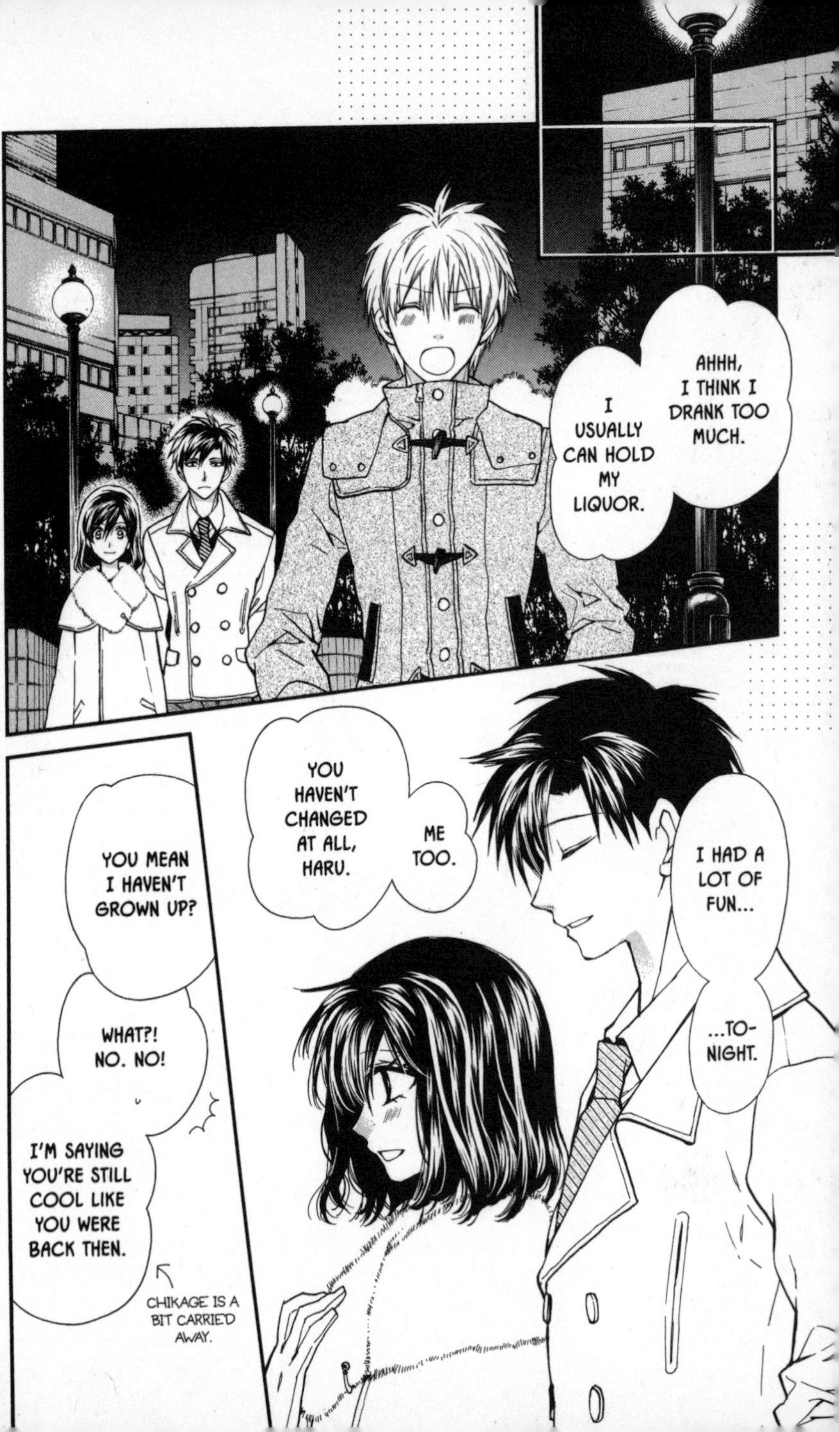
AHHH, I THINK I DRANK TOO MUCH.
I USUALLY CAN HOLD MY LIQUOR.
I HAD A LOT OF FUN...
...TO-NIGHT.
ME TOO.
YOU HAVEN'T CHANGED AT ALL, HARU.
YOU MEAN I HAVEN'T GROWN UP?
WHAT?! NO. NO!
I'M SAYING YOU'RE STILL COOL LIKE YOU WERE BACK THEN.
CHIKAGE IS A BIT CARRIED AWAY.

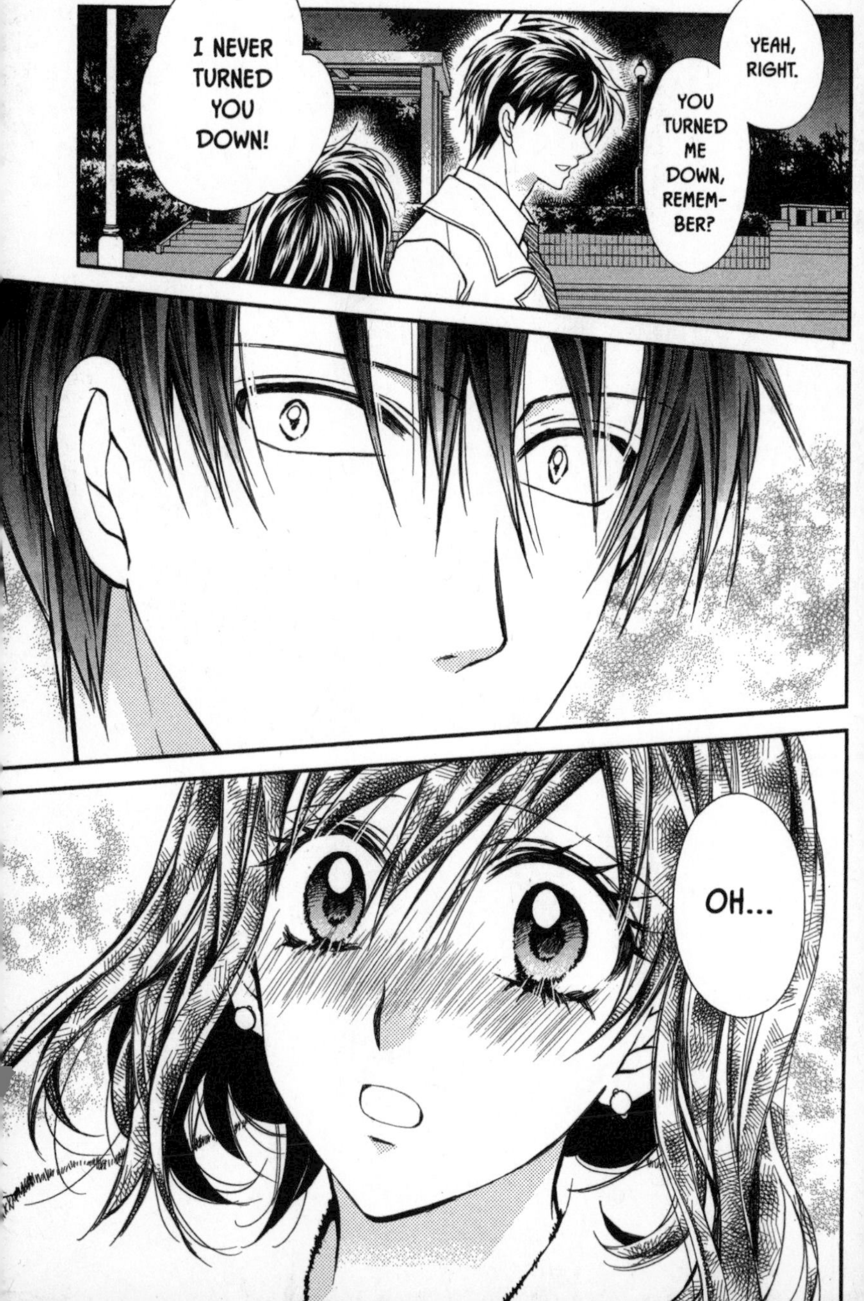
YEAH, RIGHT.
YOU TURNED ME DOWN, REMEMBER?
I NEVER TURNED YOU DOWN!
OH...

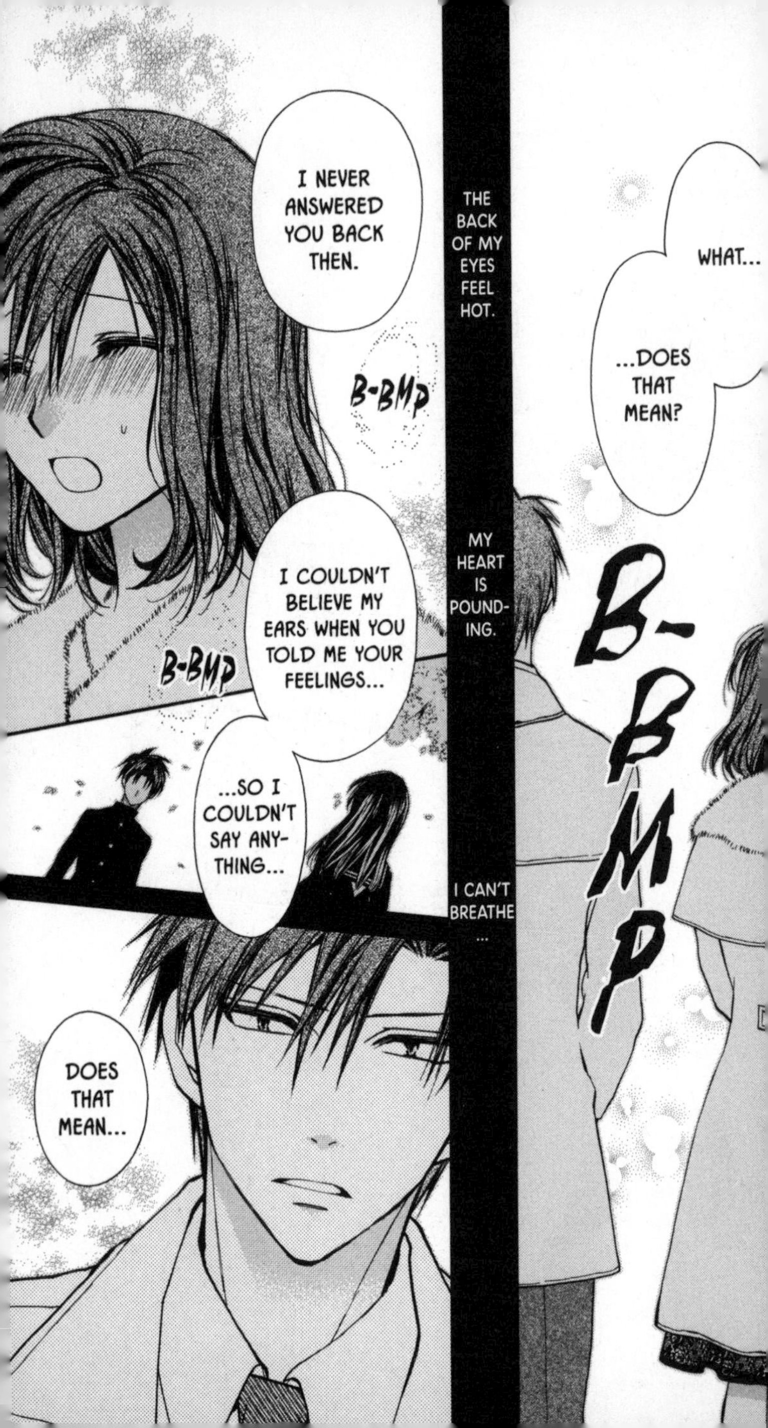
WHAT...
...DOES THAT MEAN?
B-BMP
THE BACK OF MY EYES FEEL HOT.
MY HEART IS POUNDING.
I CAN'T BREATHE...
I NEVER ANSWERED YOU BACK THEN.
B-BMP
I COULDN'T BELIEVE MY EARS WHEN YOU TOLD ME YOUR FEELINGS...
B-BMP
...SO I COULDN'T SAY ANYTHING...
DOES THAT MEAN...

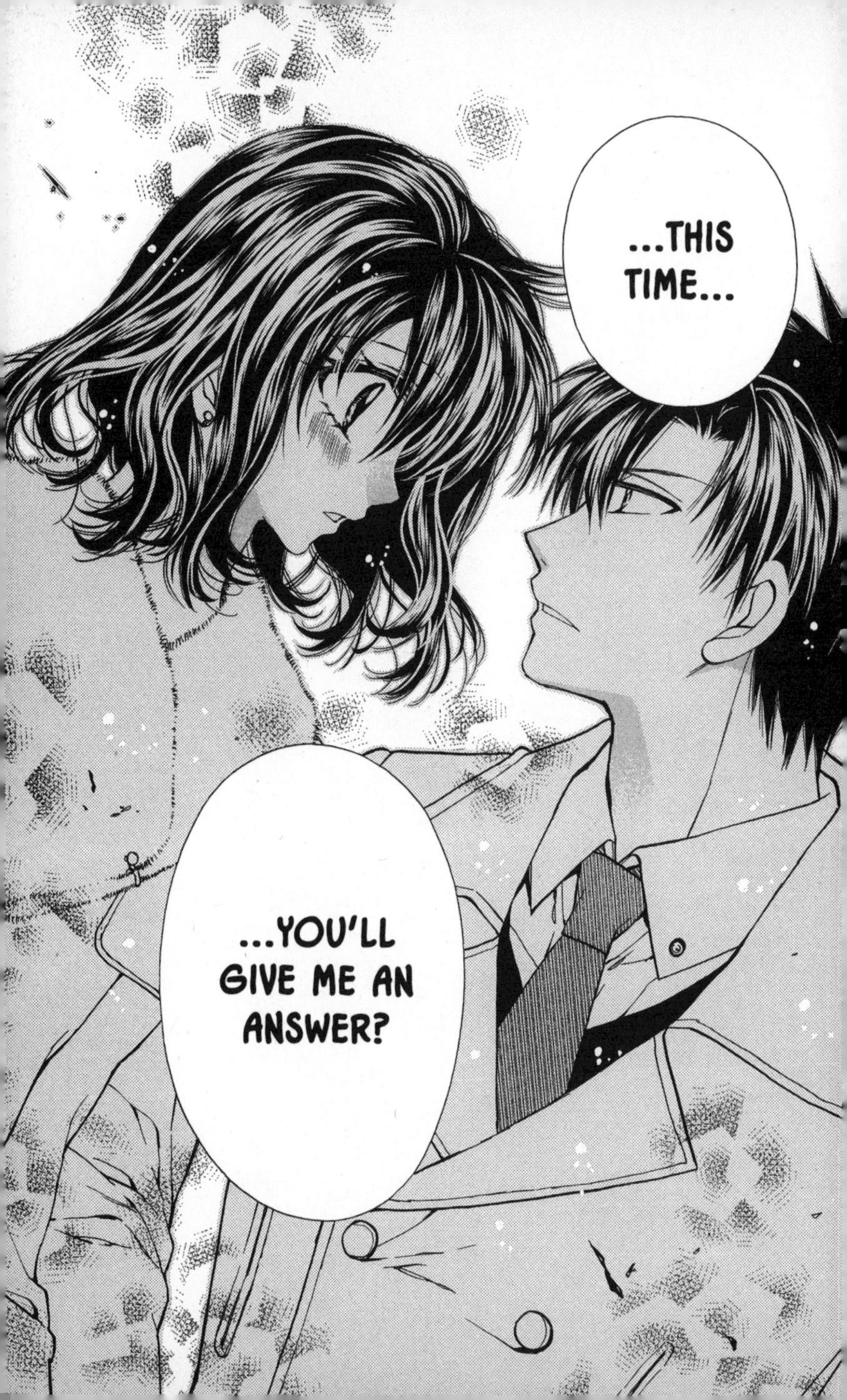
...THIS TIME...
...YOU'LL GIVE ME AN ANSWER?

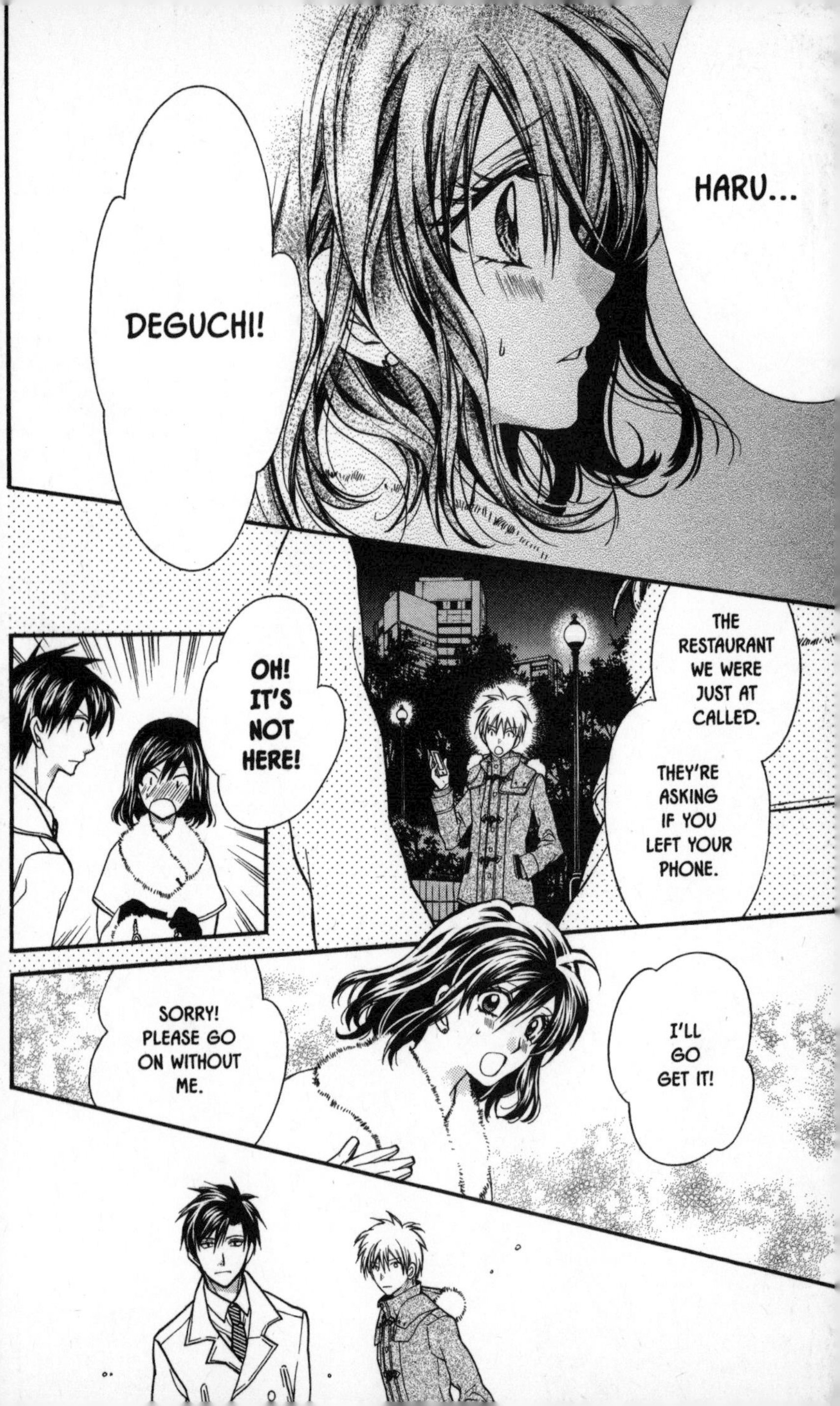
HARU...
DEGUCHI!
THE RESTAURANT WE WERE JUST AT CALLED.
THEY'RE ASKING IF YOU LEFT YOUR PHONE.
OH! IT'S NOT HERE!
I'LL GO GET IT!
SORRY! PLEASE GO ON WITHOUT ME.

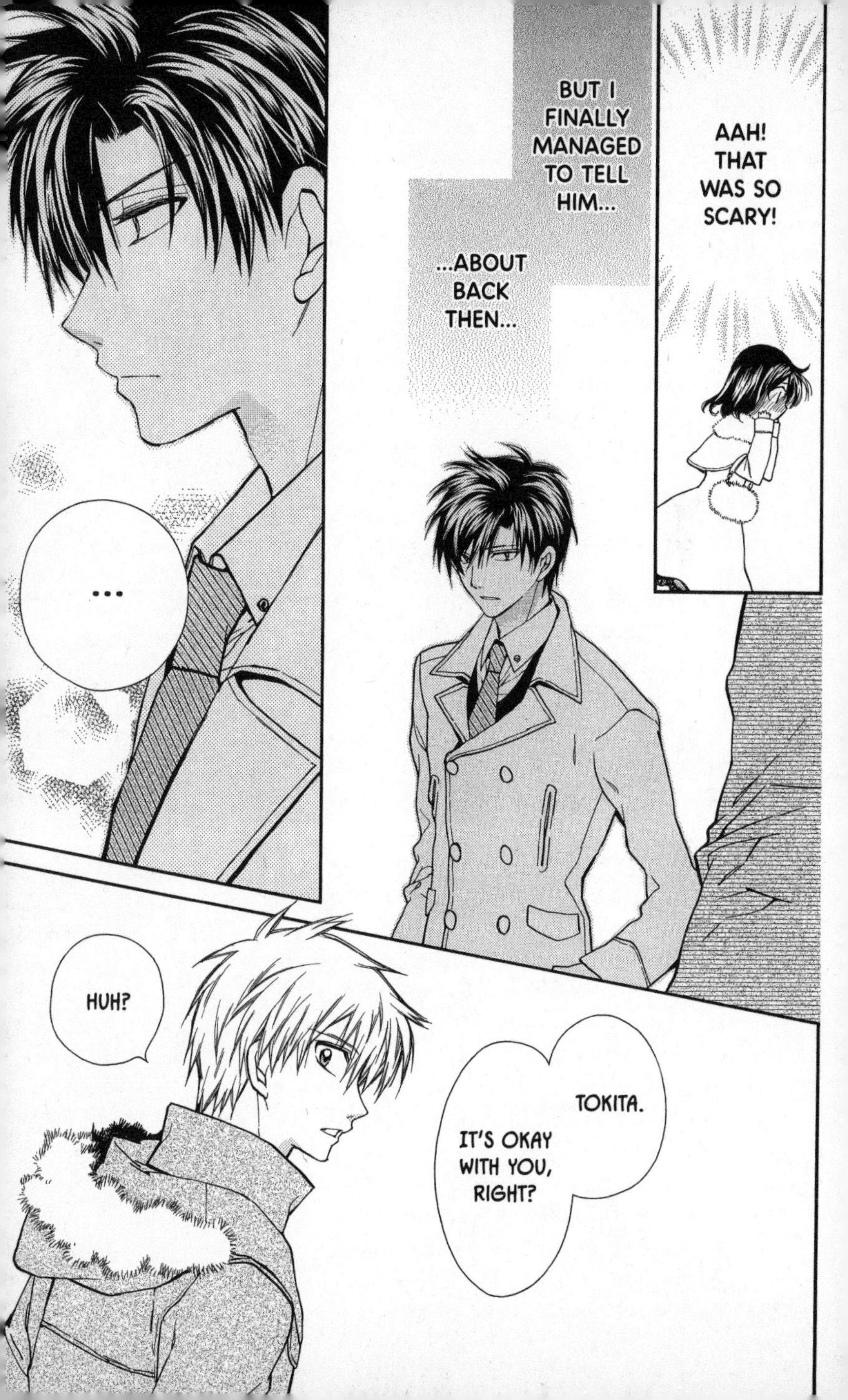
AAH! THAT WAS SO SCARY!
BUT I FINALLY MANAGED TO TELL HIM...
...ABOUT BACK THEN...
...
TOKITA.
IT'S OKAY WITH YOU, RIGHT?
HUH?

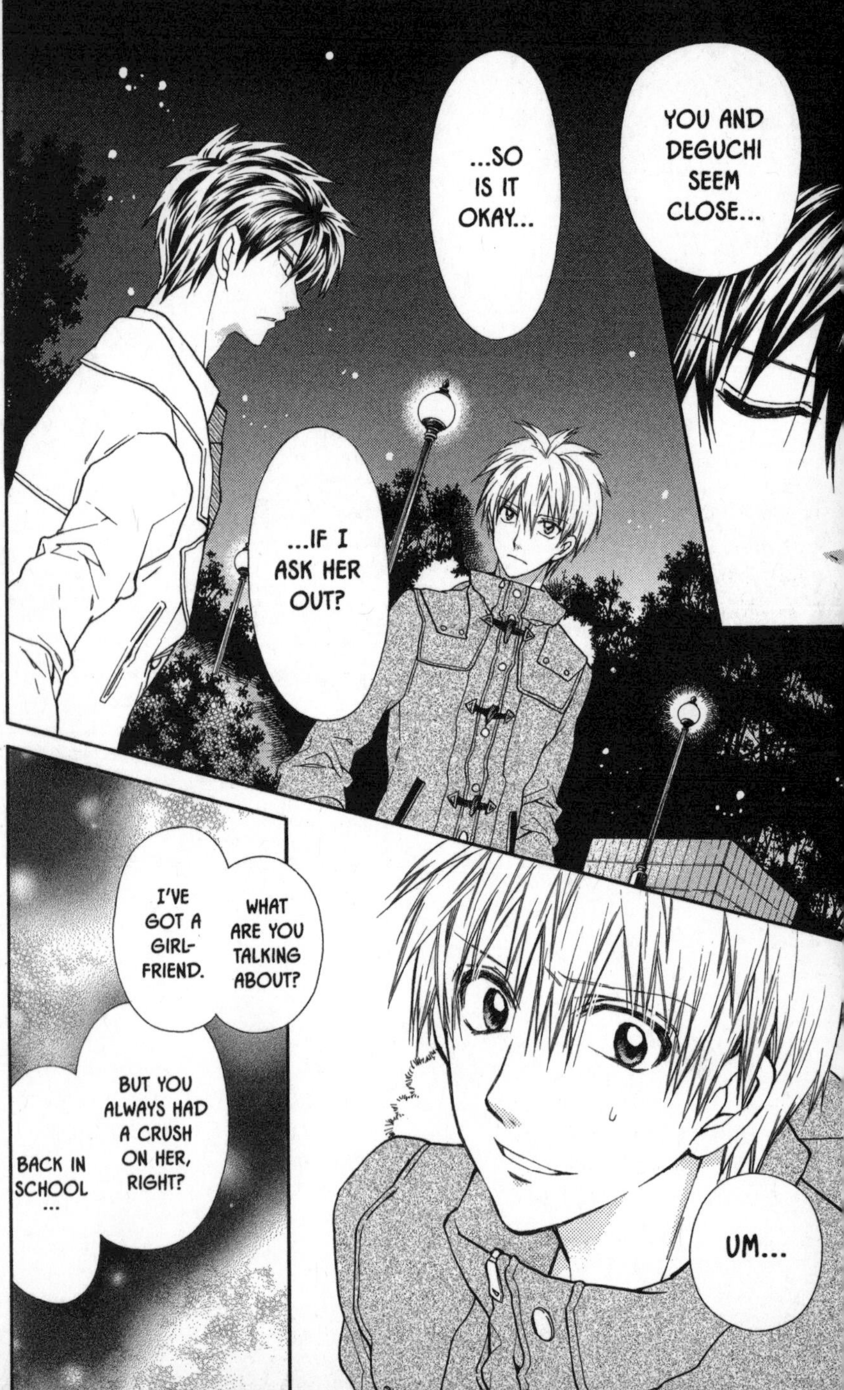
YOU AND DEGUCHI SEEM CLOSE...
...SO IS IT OKAY...
...IF I ASK HER OUT?
UM...
WHAT ARE YOU TALKING ABOUT?
I'VE GOT A GIRL-FRIEND.
BUT YOU ALWAYS HAD A CRUSH ON HER, RIGHT?
BACK IN SCHOOL...

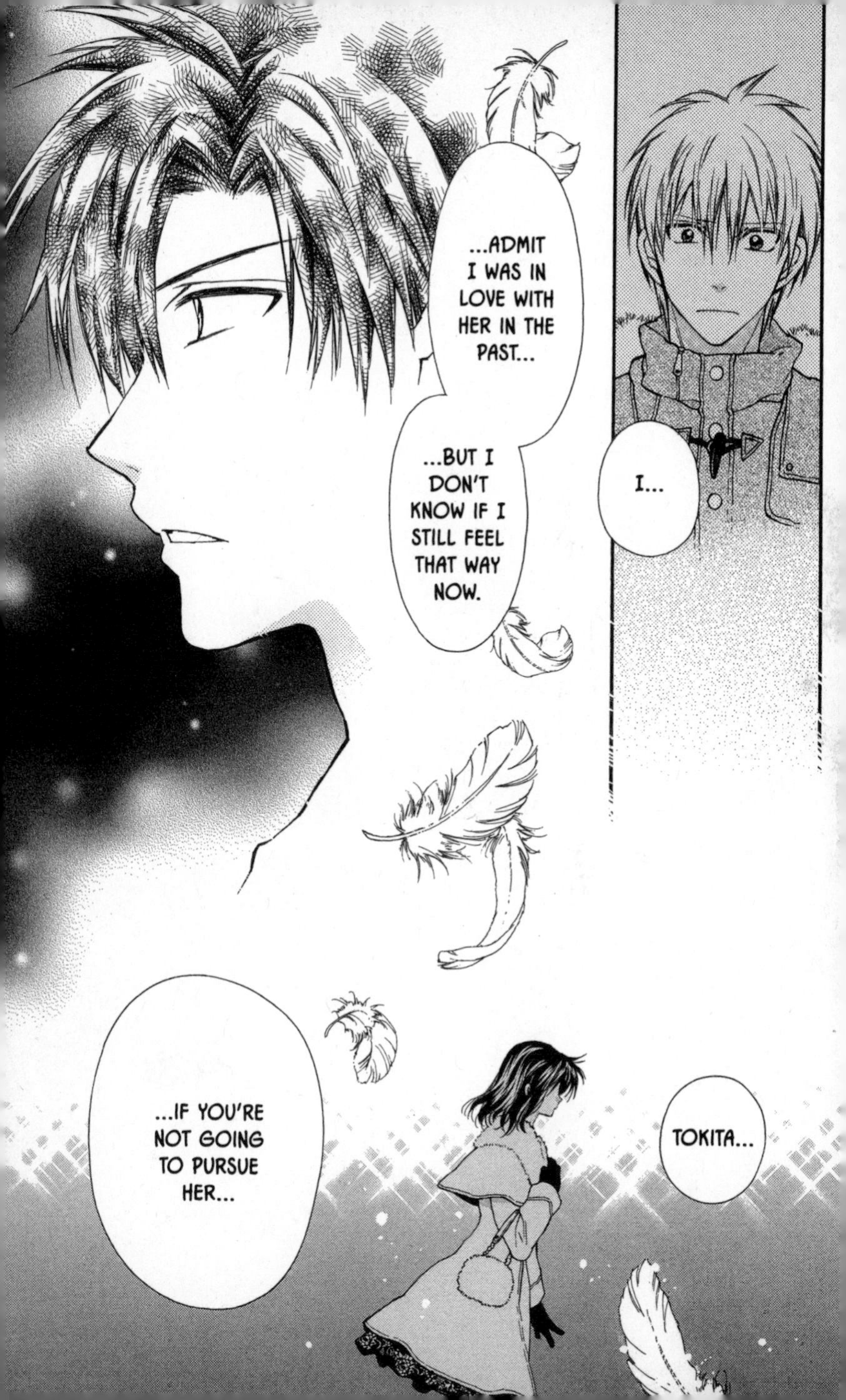
I...
...ADMIT I WAS IN LOVE WITH HER IN THE PAST...
...BUT I DON'T KNOW IF I STILL FEEL THAT WAY NOW.
TOKITA...
...IF YOU'RE NOT GOING TO PURSUE HER...

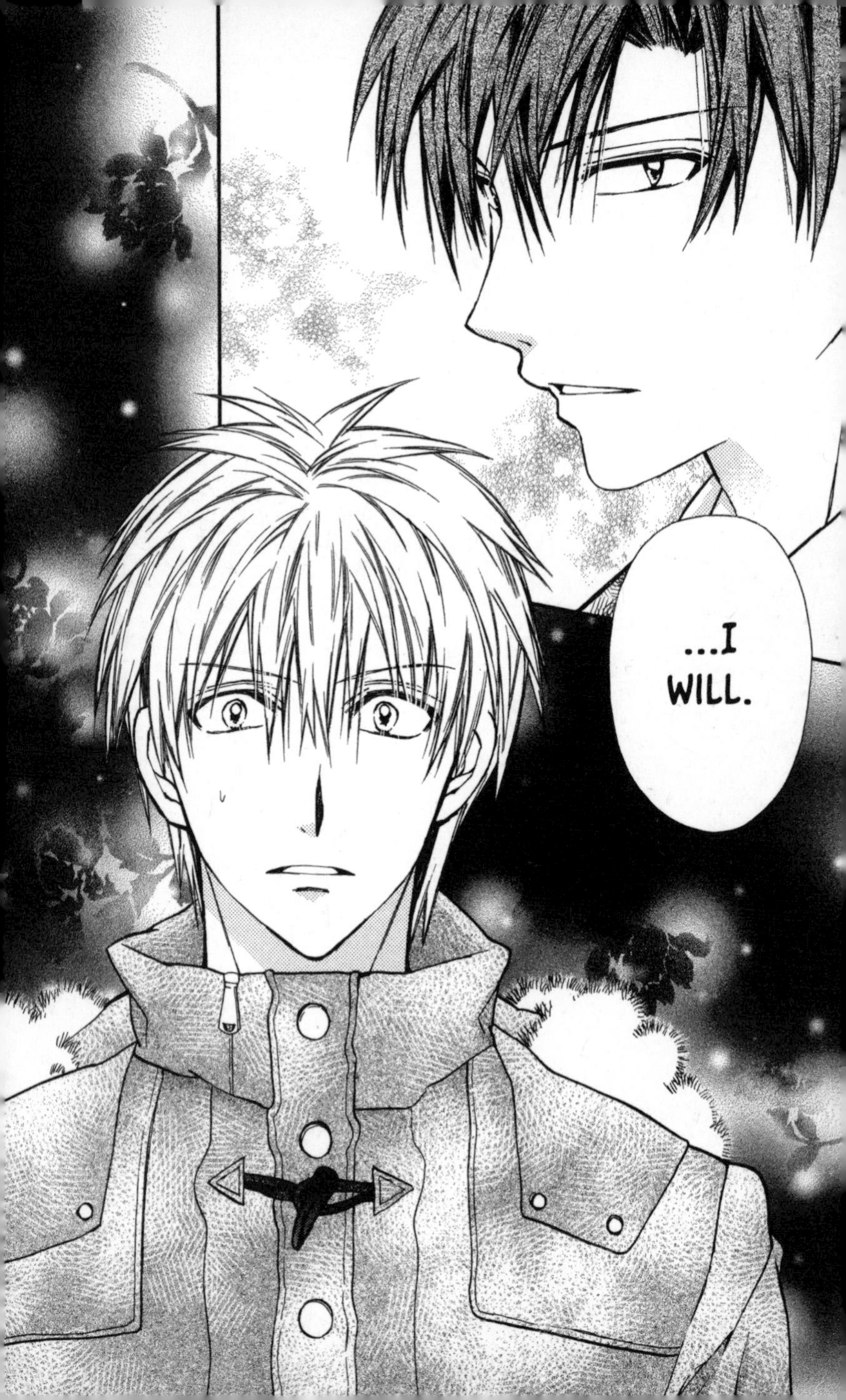
...I WILL.

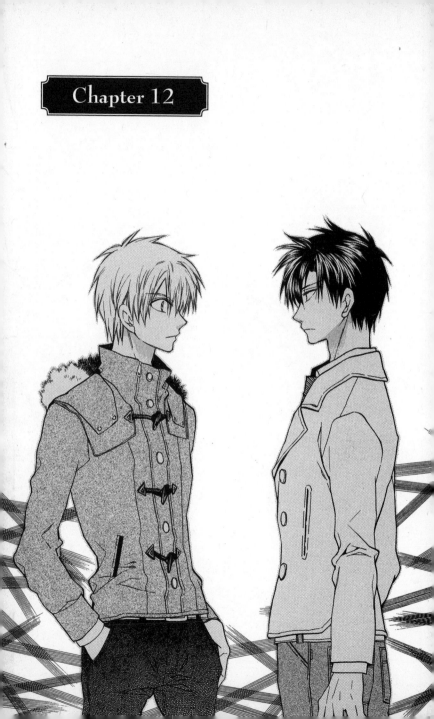

Chapter 12

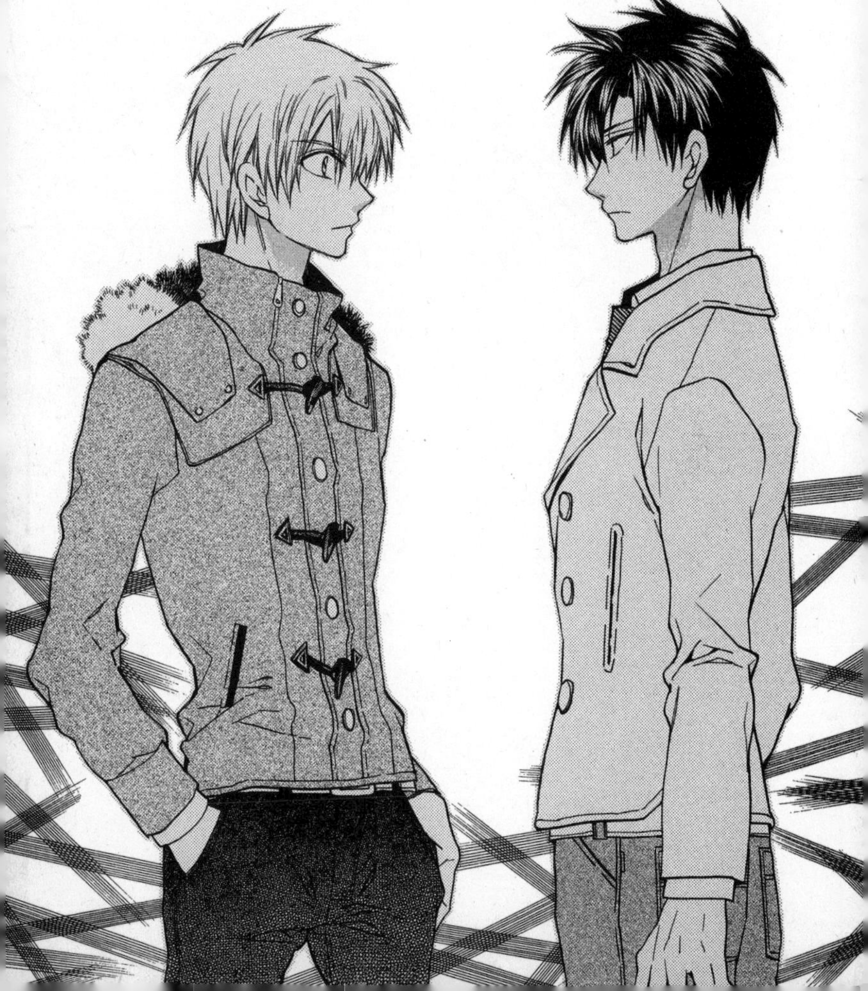

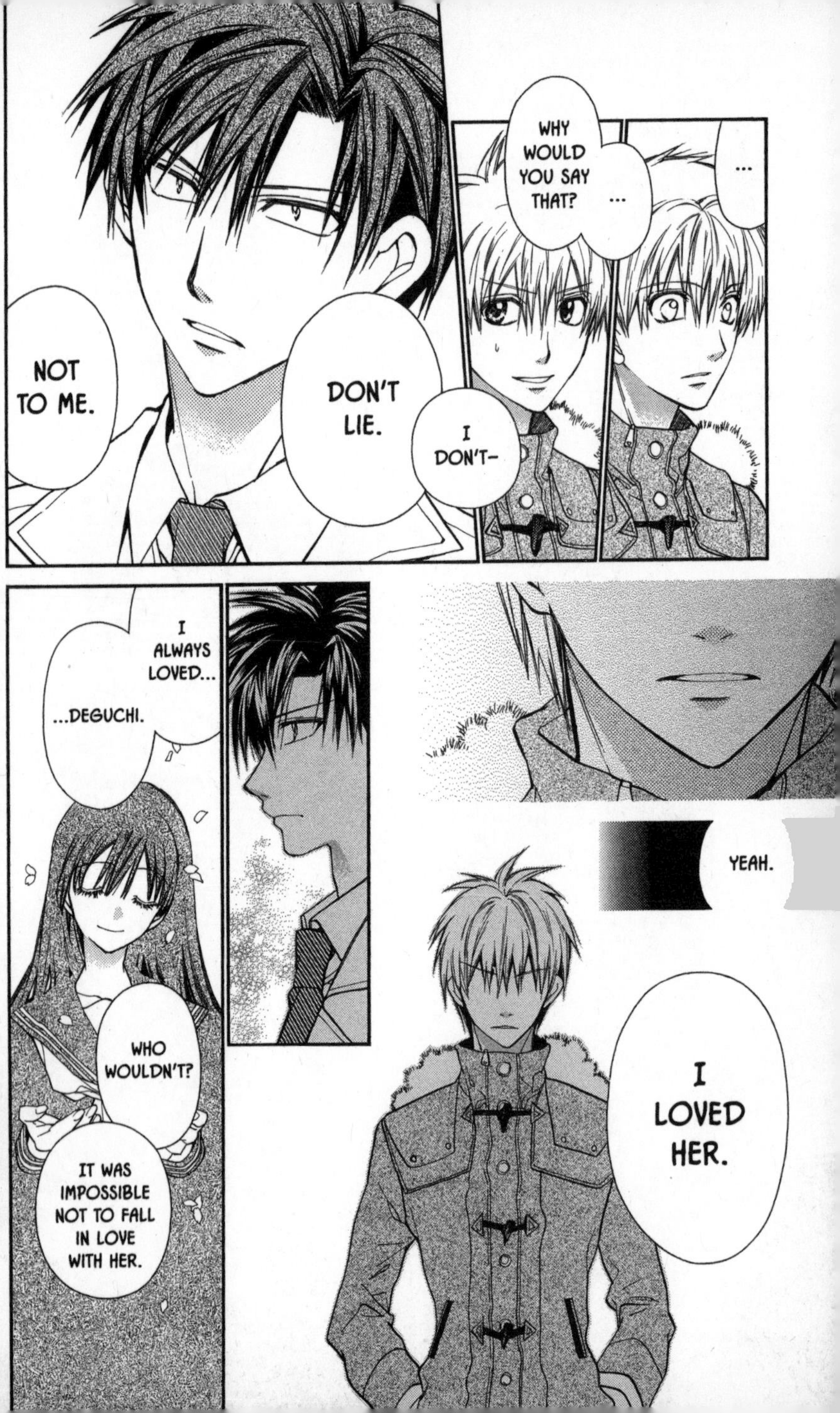
...
WHY WOULD YOU SAY THAT?
...
I DON'T-
DON'T LIE.
NOT TO ME.
YEAH.
I LOVED HER.
I ALWAYS LOVED...
...DEGUCHI.
WHO WOULDN'T?
IT WAS IMPOSSIBLE NOT TO FALL IN LOVE WITH HER.

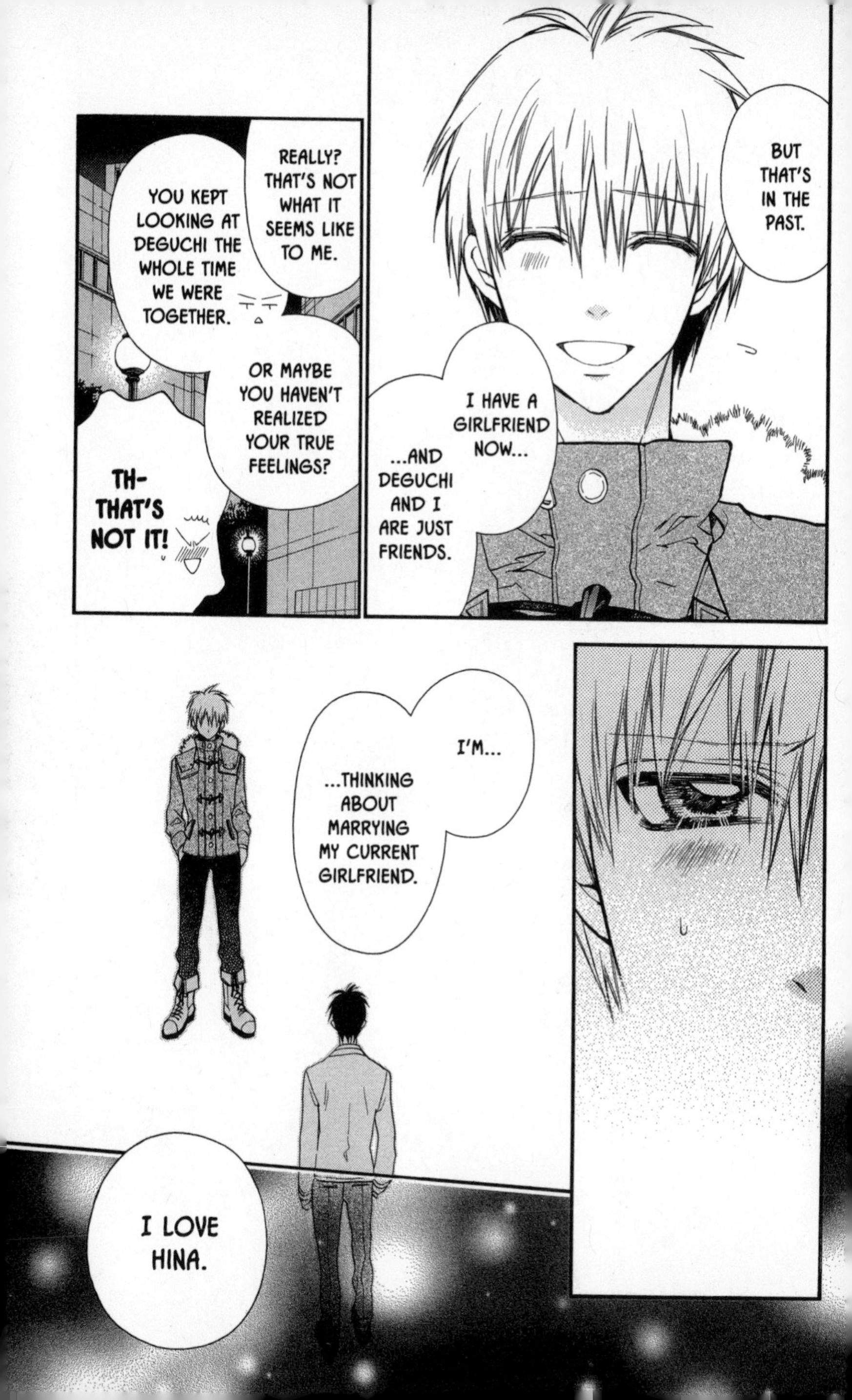
BUT THAT'S IN THE PAST.
I HAVE A GIRLFRIEND NOW...
...AND DEGUCHI AND I ARE JUST FRIENDS.
REALLY? THAT'S NOT WHAT IT SEEMS LIKE TO ME.
YOU KEPT LOOKING AT DEGUCHI THE WHOLE TIME WE WERE TOGETHER.
OR MAYBE YOU HAVEN'T REALIZED YOUR TRUE FEELINGS?
TH- THAT'S NOT IT!
I'M...
...THINKING ABOUT MARRYING MY CURRENT GIRLFRIEND.
I LOVE HINA.

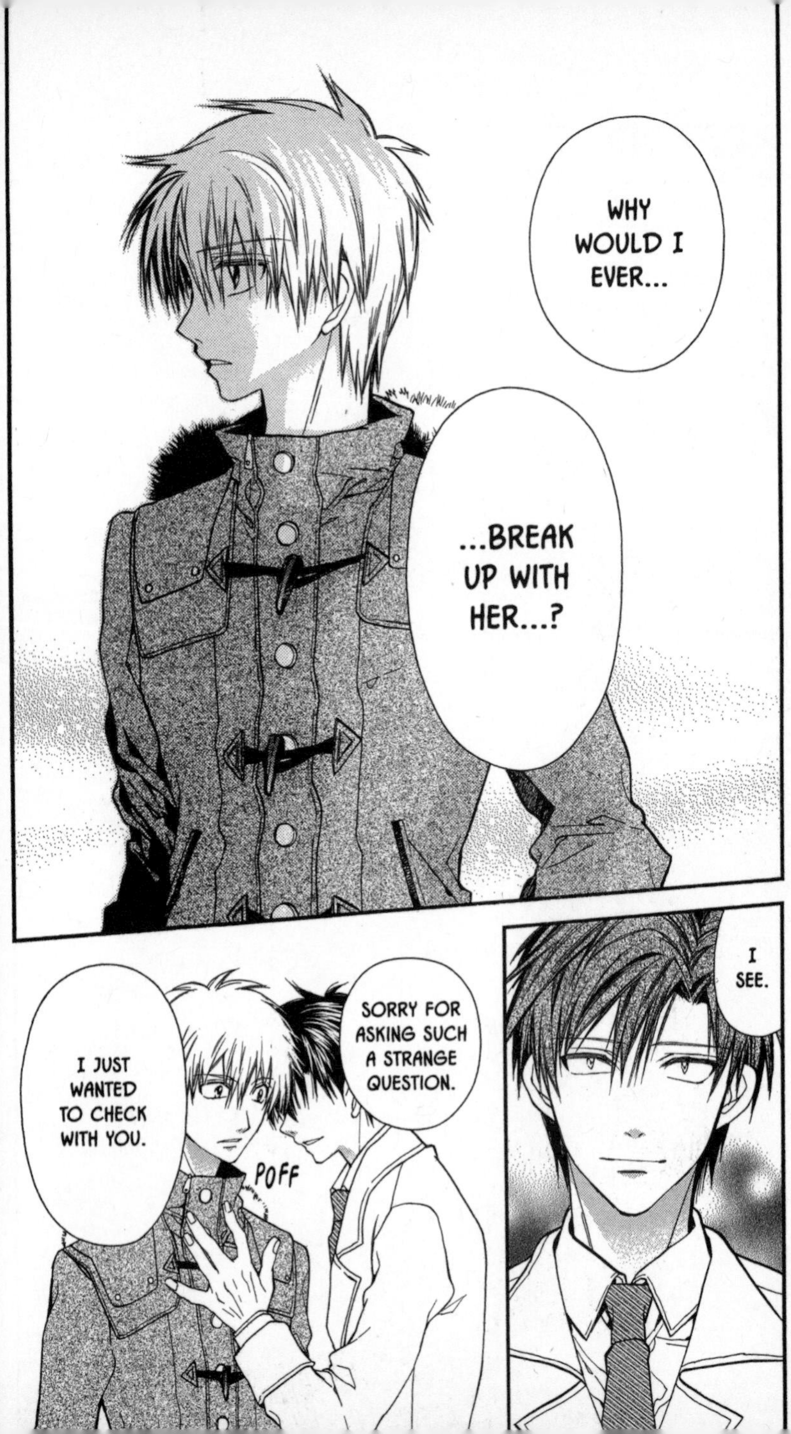
WHY WOULD I EVER...
...BREAK UP WITH HER...?
I SEE.
SORRY FOR ASKING SUCH A STRANGE QUESTION.
POFF
I JUST WANTED TO CHECK WITH YOU.

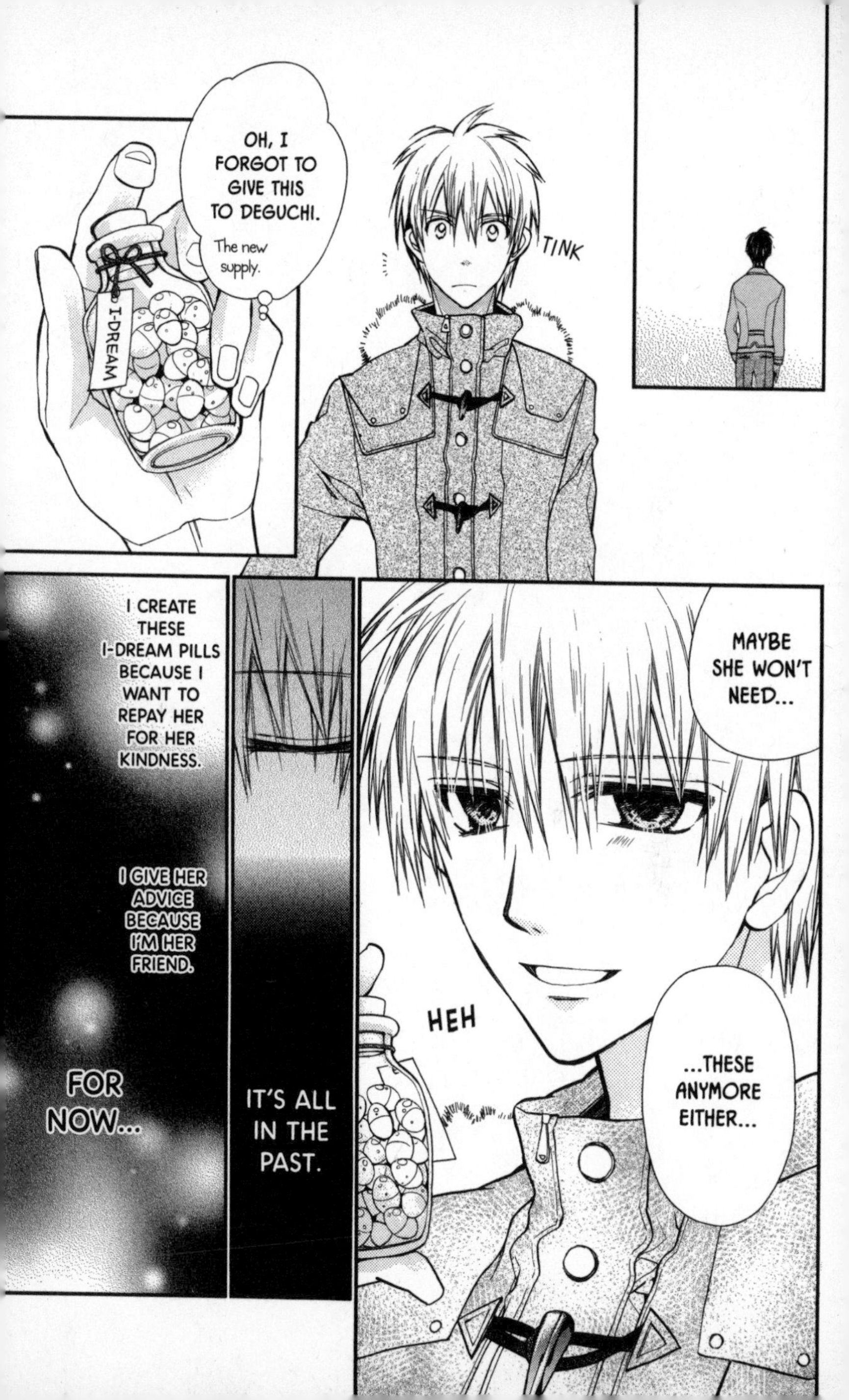
TINK
OH, I FORGOT TO GIVE THIS TO DEGUCHI.
The new supply.
I-DREAM
MAYBE SHE WON'T NEED...
HEH
...THESE ANYMORE EITHER...
IT'S ALL IN THE PAST.
I CREATE THESE I-DREAM PILLS BECAUSE I WANT TO REPAY HER FOR HER KINDNESS.
I GIVE HER ADVICE BECAUSE I'M HER FRIEND.
FOR NOW...

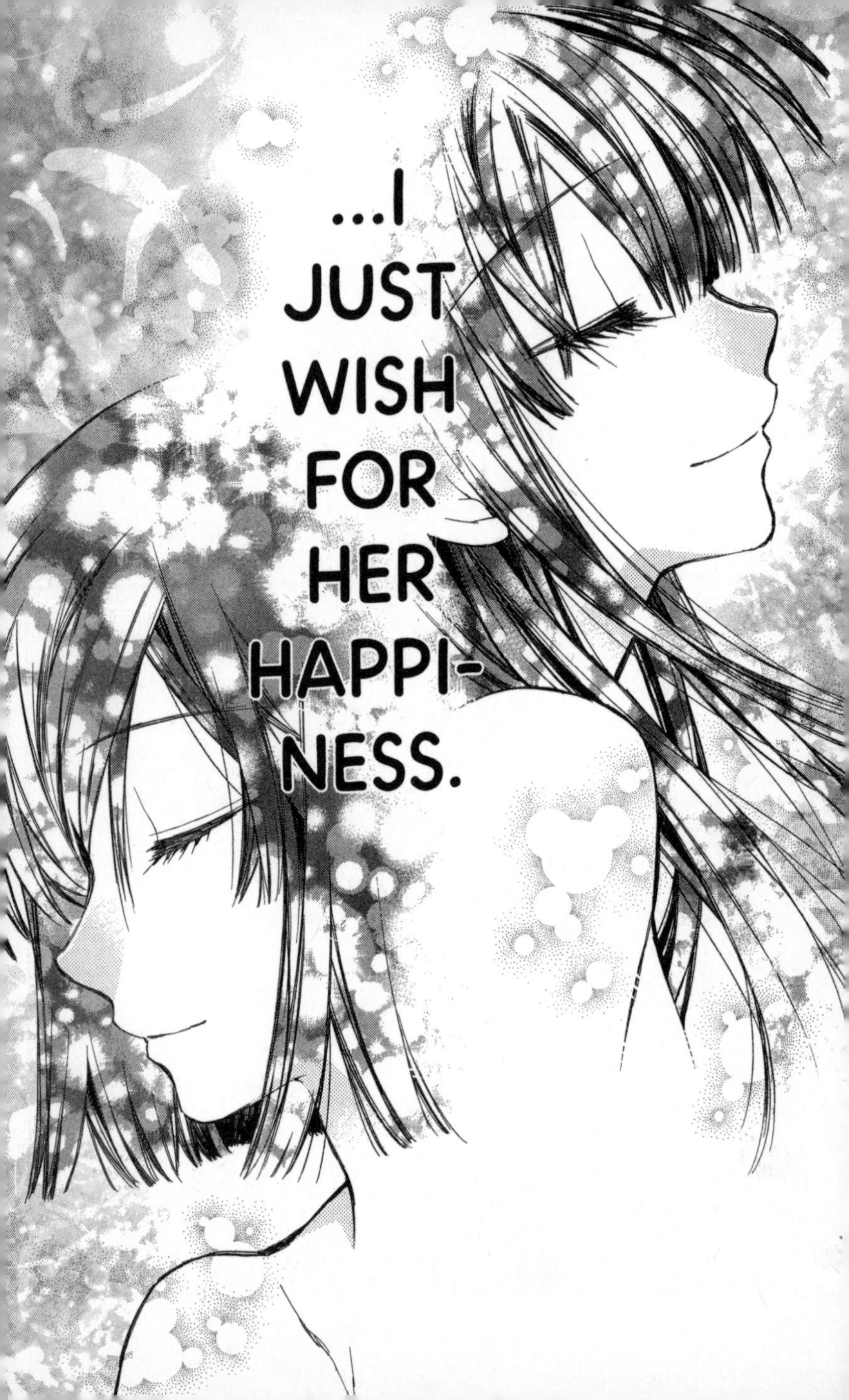
...I JUST WISH FOR HER HAPPI- NESS.

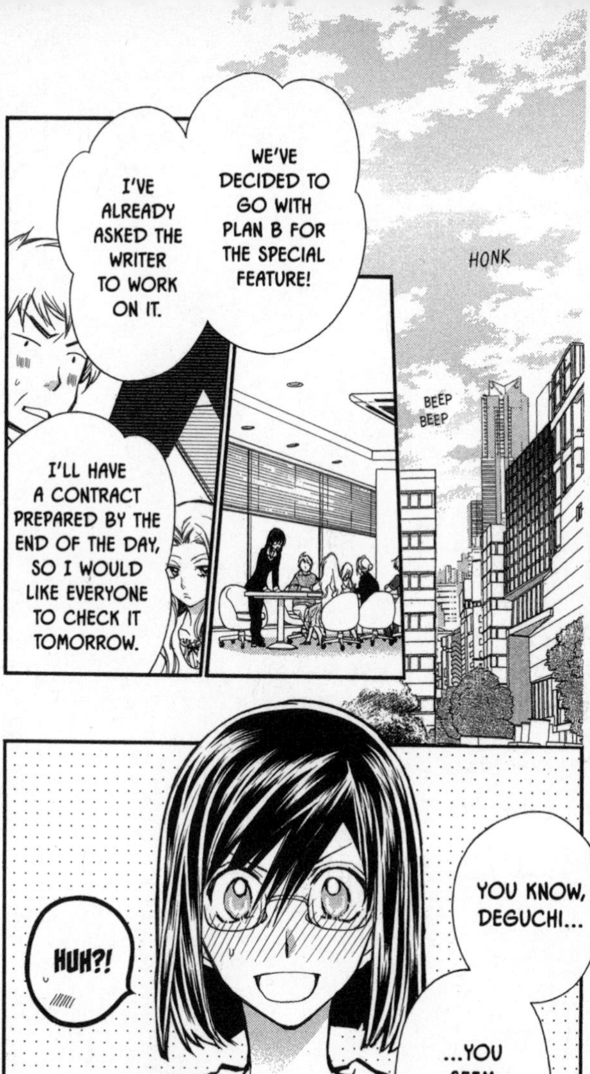
HONK
BEEP BEEP
WE'VE DECIDED TO GO WITH PLAN B FOR THE SPECIAL FEATURE!
I'VE ALREADY ASKED THE WRITER TO WORK ON IT.
I'LL HAVE A CONTRACT PREPARED BY THE END OF THE DAY, SO I WOULD LIKE EVERYONE TO CHECK IT TOMORROW.
YOU KNOW, DEGUCHI...
...YOU SEEM DIFFERENT SOMEHOW.
HUH?!

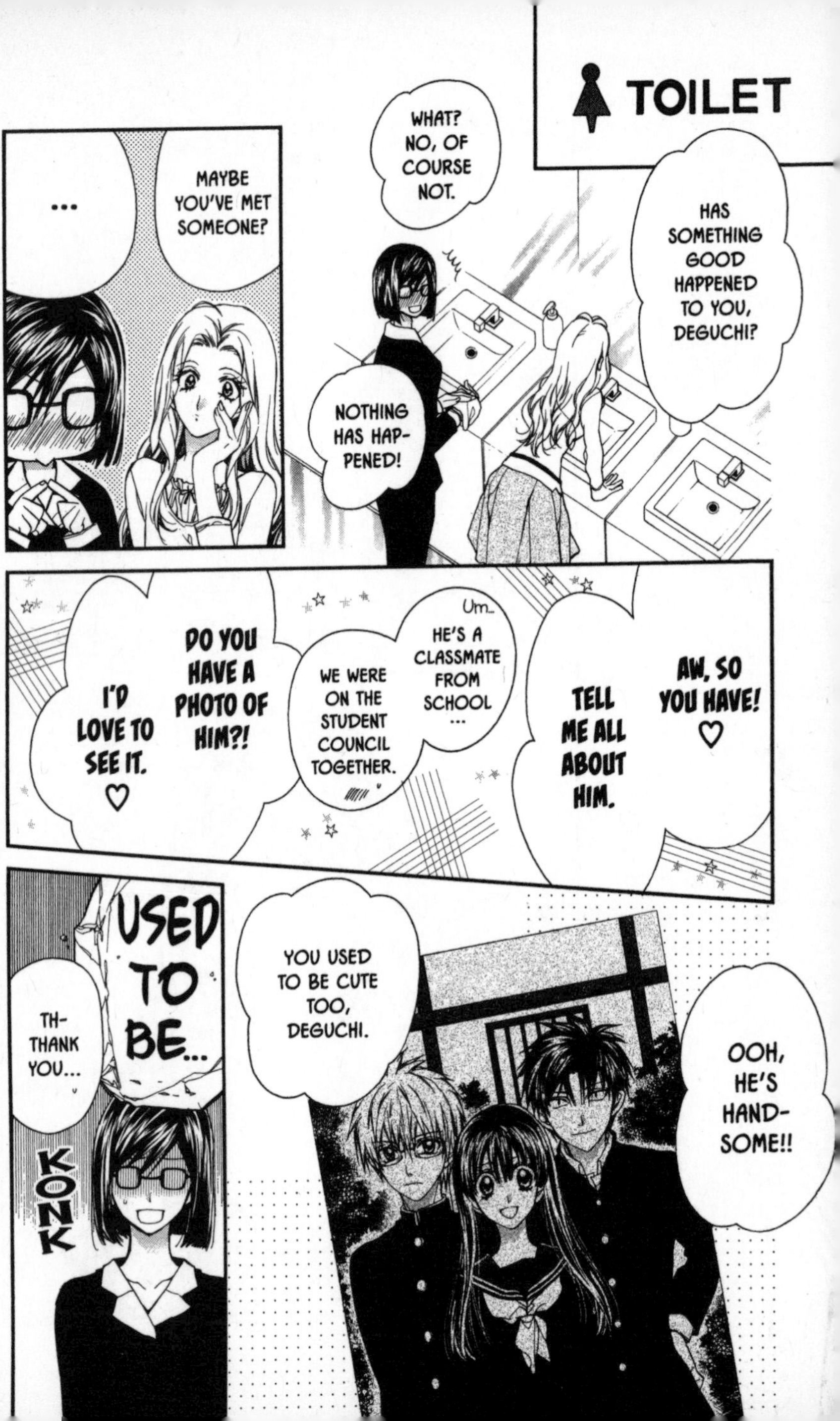
TOILET
HAS SOMETHING GOOD HAPPENED TO YOU, DEGUCHI?
WHAT? NO, OF COURSE NOT.
NOTHING HAS HAP-PENED!
MAYBE YOU'VE MET SOMEONE?
...
AW, SO YOU HAVE! ♡
TELL ME ALL ABOUT HIM.
Um...
HE'S A CLASSMATE FROM SCHOOL...
WE WERE ON THE STUDENT COUNCIL TOGETHER.
DO YOU HAVE A PHOTO OF HIM?!
I'D LOVE TO SEE IT. ♡
OOH, HE'S HAND-SOME!!
YOU USED TO BE CUTE TOO, DEGUCHI.
USED TO BE...
TH-THANK YOU...
KONK

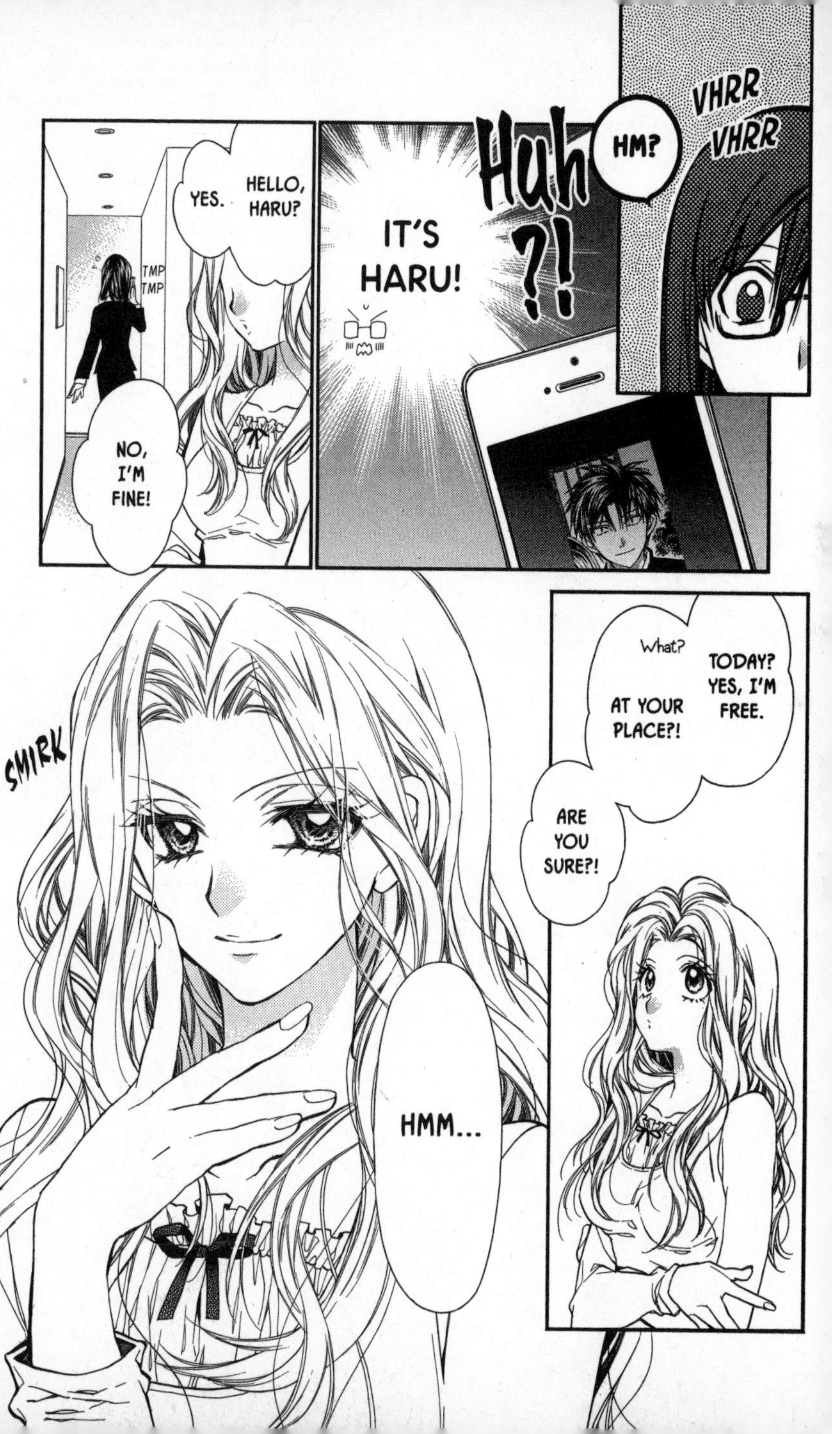
VHRR
VHRR
HM?
Huh ?!
IT'S HARU!
HELLO, HARU?
YES.
TMP TMP
NO, I'M FINE!
TODAY? YES, I'M FREE.
What?
AT YOUR PLACE?!
ARE YOU SURE?!
SMIRK
HMM...

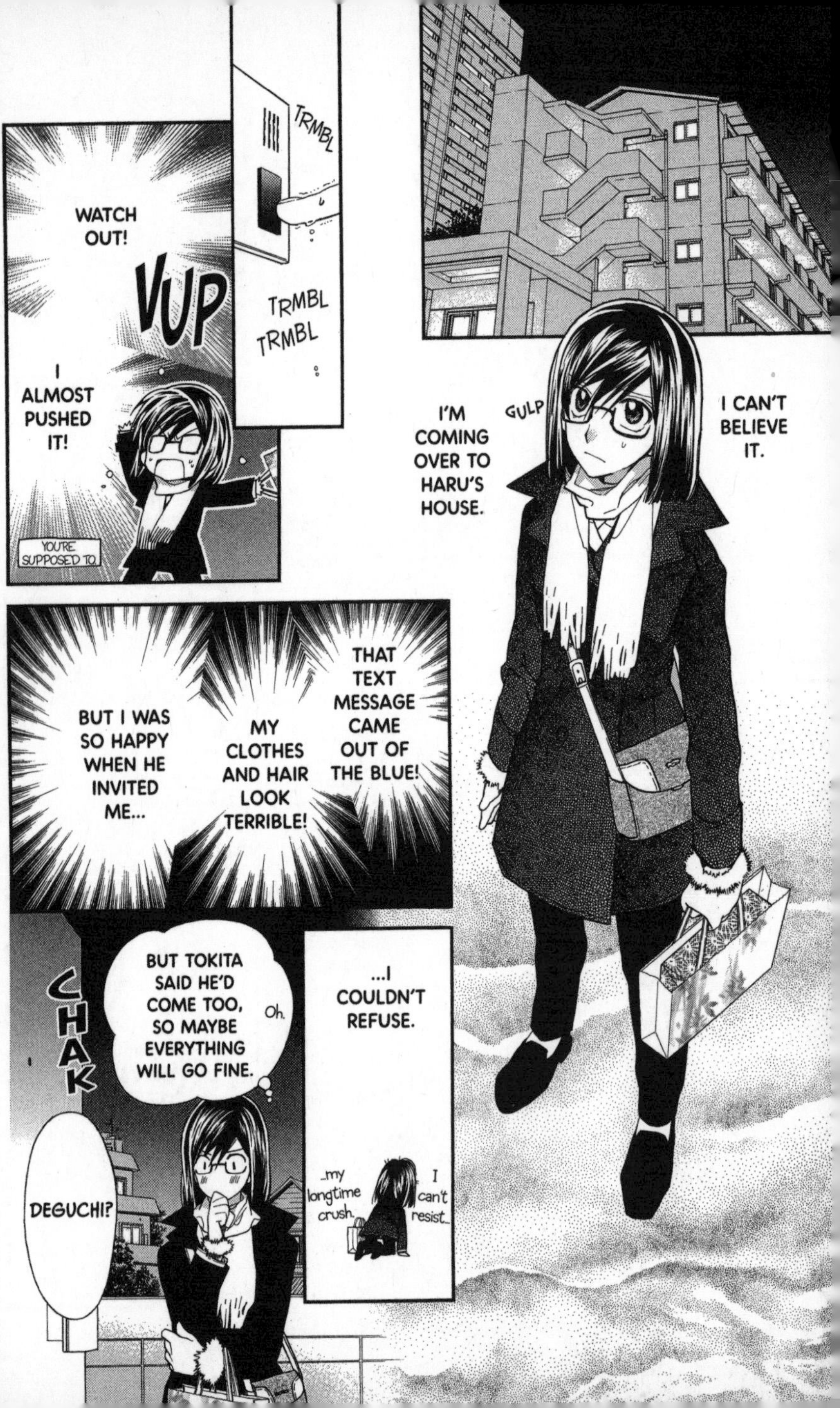
I CAN'T BELIEVE IT.
GULP
I'M COMING OVER TO HARU'S HOUSE.
TRMBL
TRMBL TRMBL
WATCH OUT!
VUP
I ALMOST PUSHED IT!
YOU'RE SUPPOSED TO.
THAT TEXT MESSAGE CAME OUT OF THE BLUE!
MY CLOTHES AND HAIR LOOK TERRIBLE!
BUT I WAS SO HAPPY WHEN HE INVITED ME...
...I COULDN'T REFUSE.
I can't resist...
...my longtime crush.
Oh.
BUT TOKITA SAID HE'D COME TOO, SO MAYBE EVERYTHING WILL GO FINE.
CHAK
DEGUCHI?

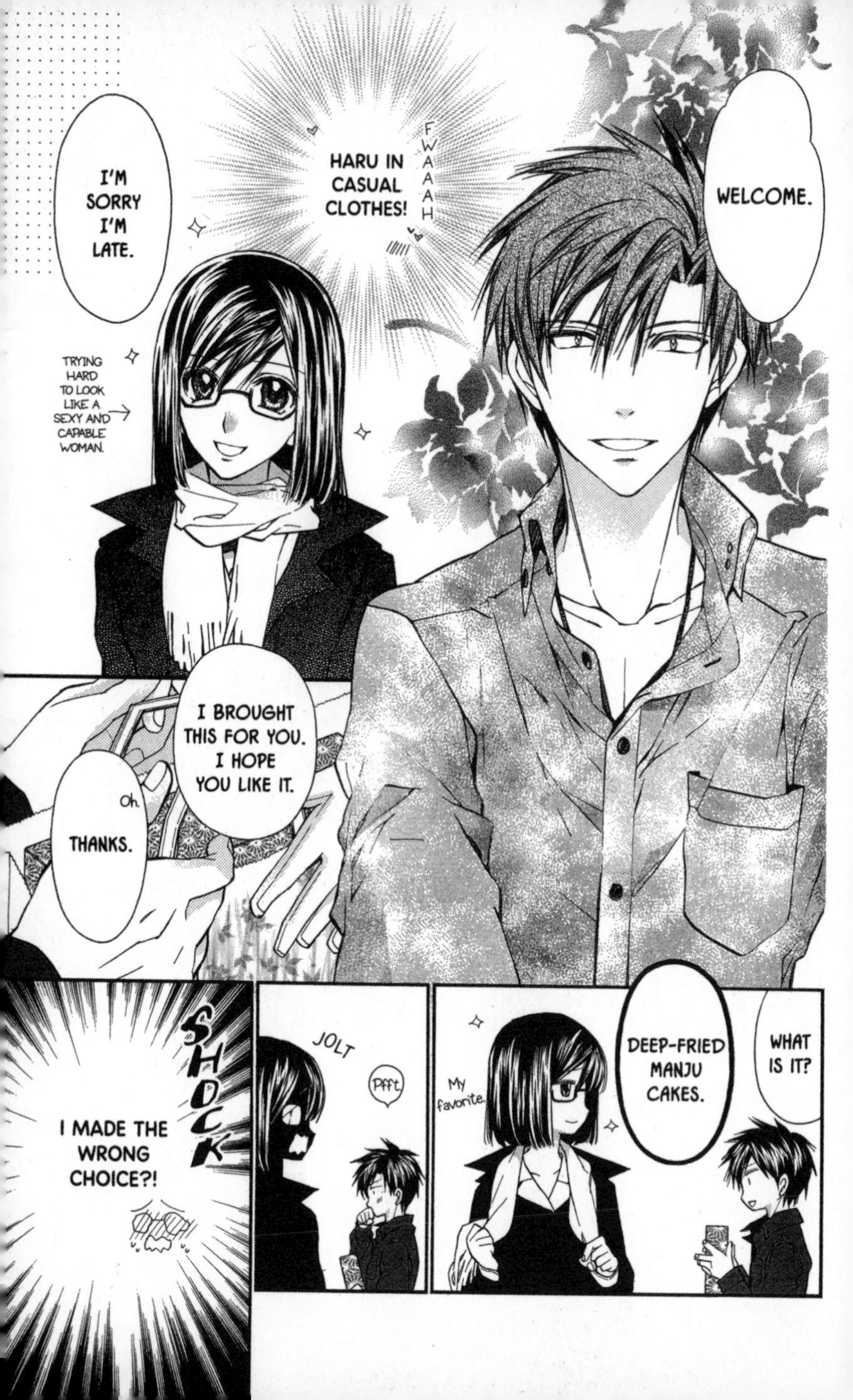
WELCOME.
FWAAAH
HARU IN CASUAL CLOTHES!
I'M SORRY I'M LATE.
TRYING HARD TO LOOK LIKE A SEXY AND CAPABLE WOMAN.
I BROUGHT THIS FOR YOU. I HOPE YOU LIKE IT.
Oh.
THANKS.
WHAT IS IT?
DEEP-FRIED MANJU CAKES.
My favorite.
JOLT
Pfft.
SHOCK
I MADE THE WRONG CHOICE?!

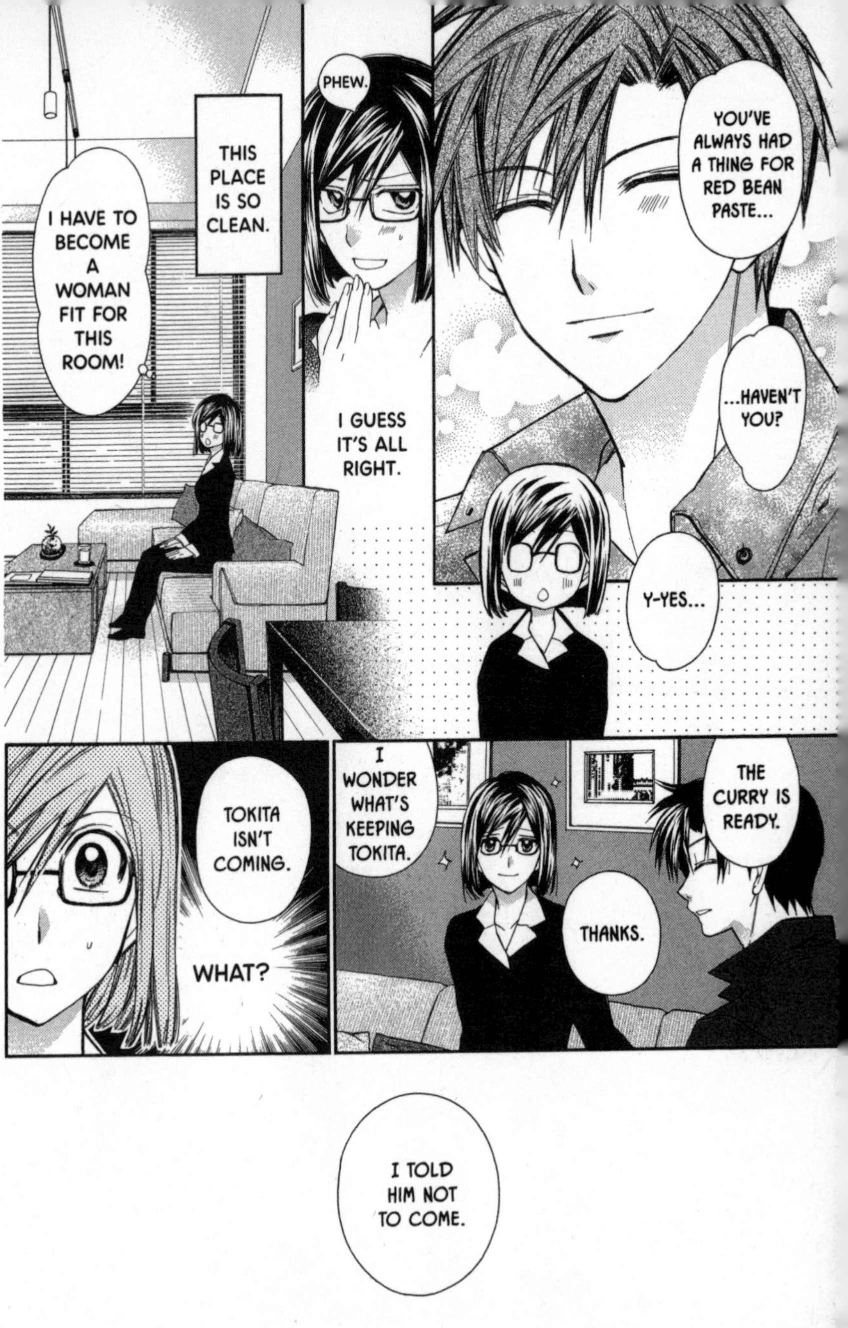
YOU'VE ALWAYS HAD A THING FOR RED BEAN PASTE...
...HAVEN'T YOU?
Y-YES...
PHEW.
I GUESS IT'S ALL RIGHT.
THIS PLACE IS SO CLEAN.
I HAVE TO BECOME A WOMAN FIT FOR THIS ROOM!
THE CURRY IS READY.
THANKS.
I WONDER WHAT'S KEEPING TOKITA.
TOKITA ISN'T COMING.
WHAT?
I TOLD HIM NOT TO COME.

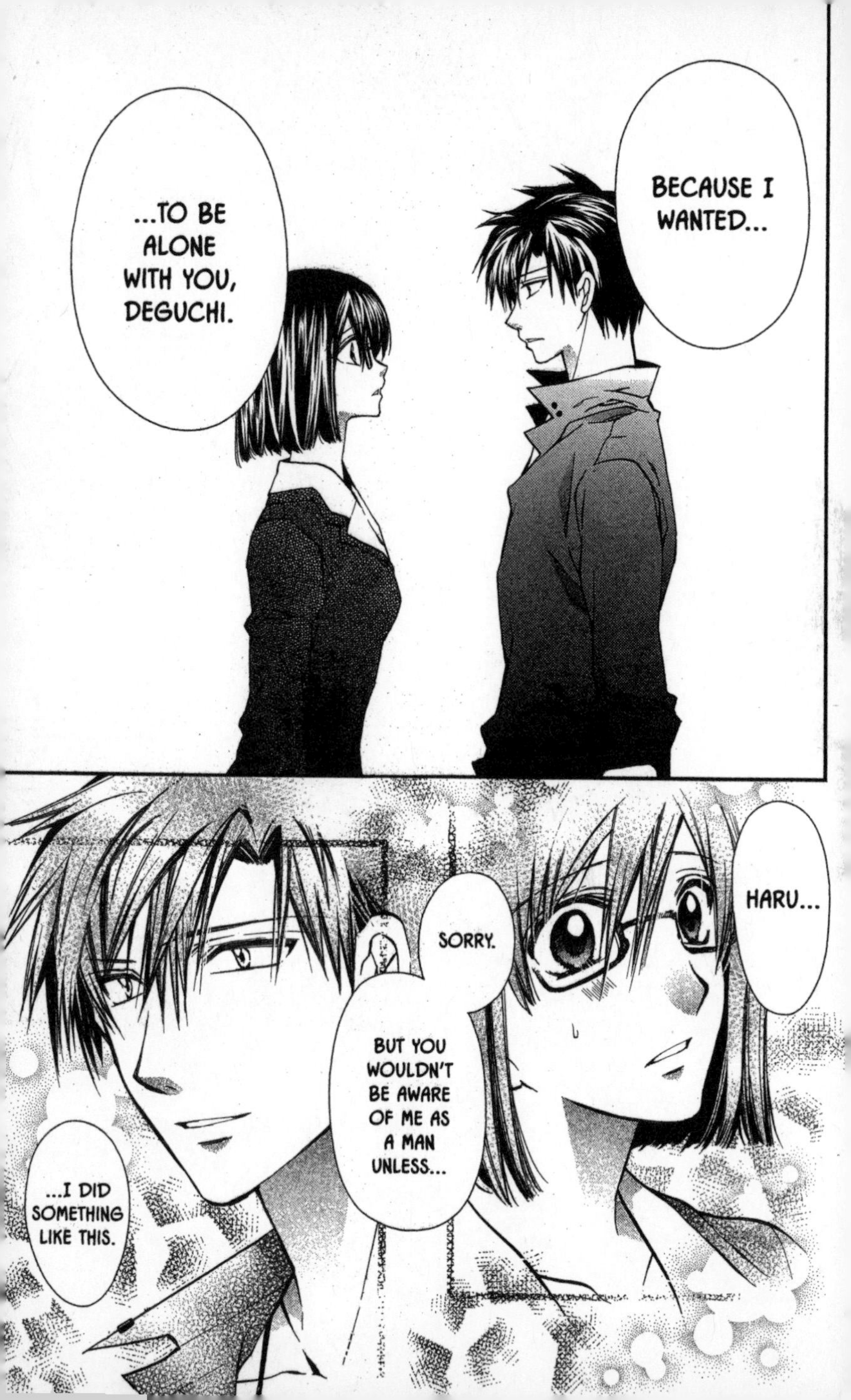
BECAUSE I WANTED...
...TO BE ALONE WITH YOU, DEGUCHI.
HARU...
SORRY.
BUT YOU WOULDN'T BE AWARE OF ME AS A MAN UNLESS...
...I DID SOMETHING LIKE THIS.

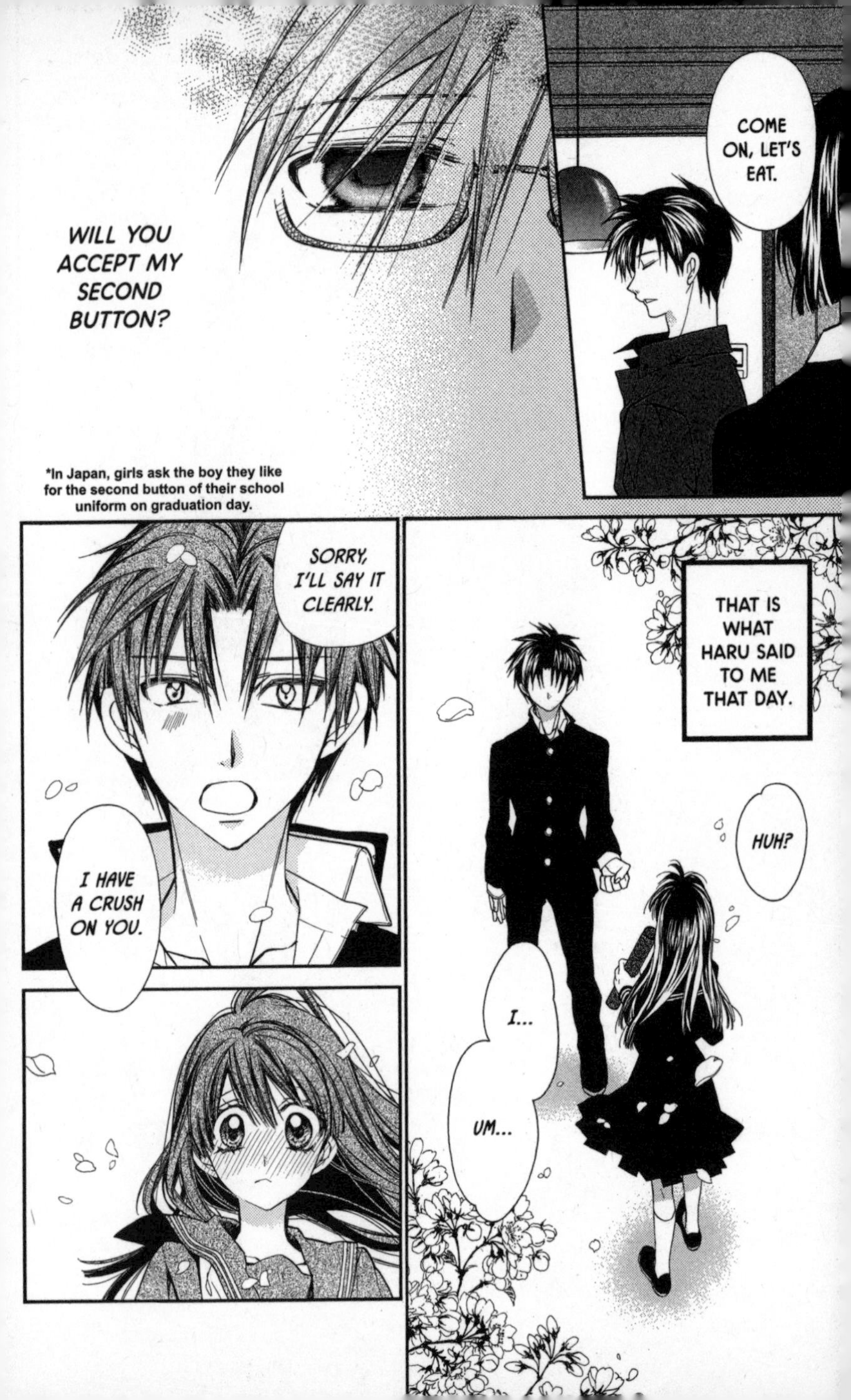
COME ON, LET'S EAT.
WILL YOU ACCEPT MY SECOND BUTTON?
THAT IS WHAT HARU SAID TO ME THAT DAY.
HUH?
I...
UM...
SORRY, I'LL SAY IT CLEARLY.
I HAVE A CRUSH ON YOU.
*In Japan, girls ask the boy they like for the second button of their school uniform on graduation day.

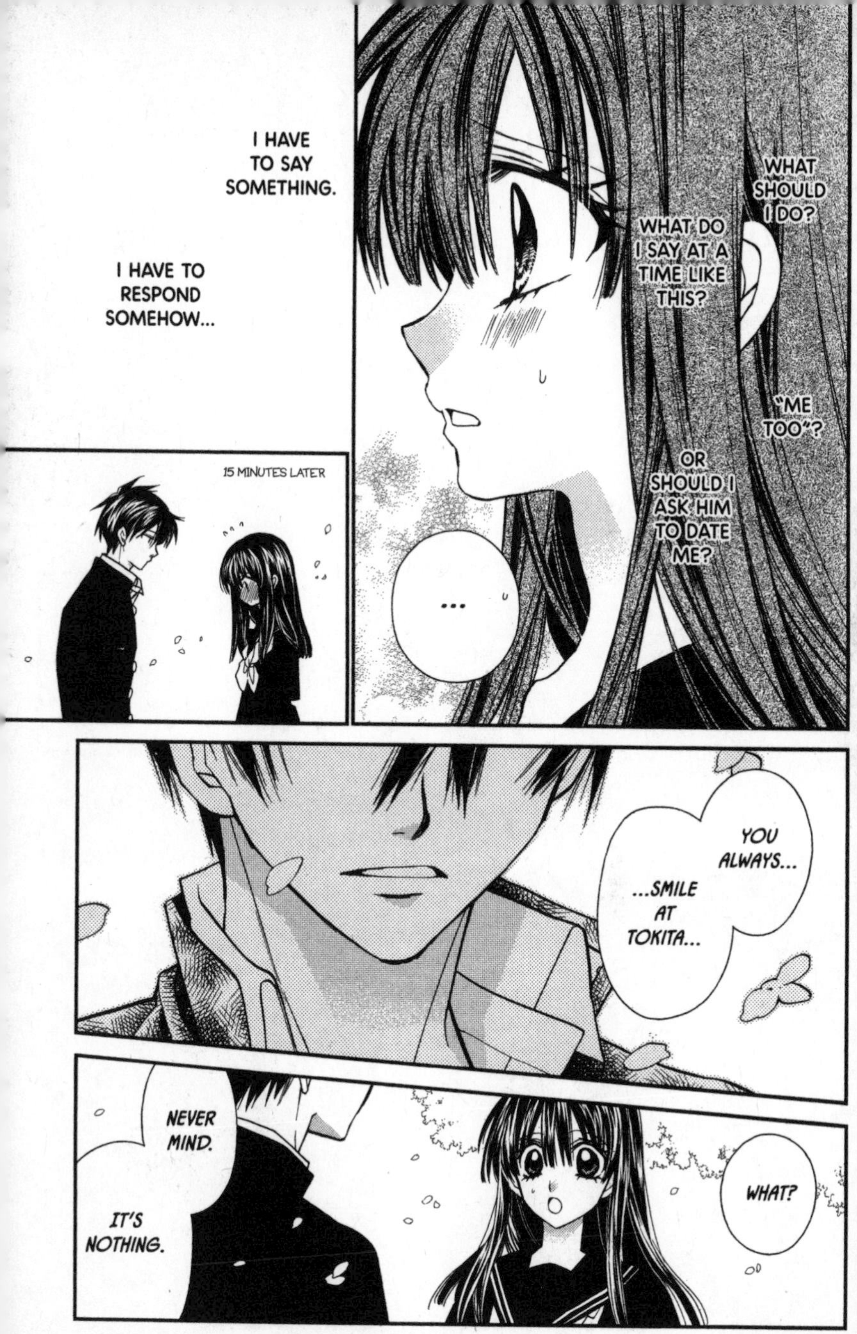
WHAT SHOULD I DO?
WHAT DO I SAY AT A TIME LIKE THIS?
"ME TOO"?
OR SHOULD I ASK HIM TO DATE ME?
...
I HAVE TO SAY SOMETHING.
I HAVE TO RESPOND SOMEHOW...
15 MINUTES LATER
YOU ALWAYS...
...SMILE AT TOKITA...
WHAT?
NEVER MIND.
IT'S NOTHING.

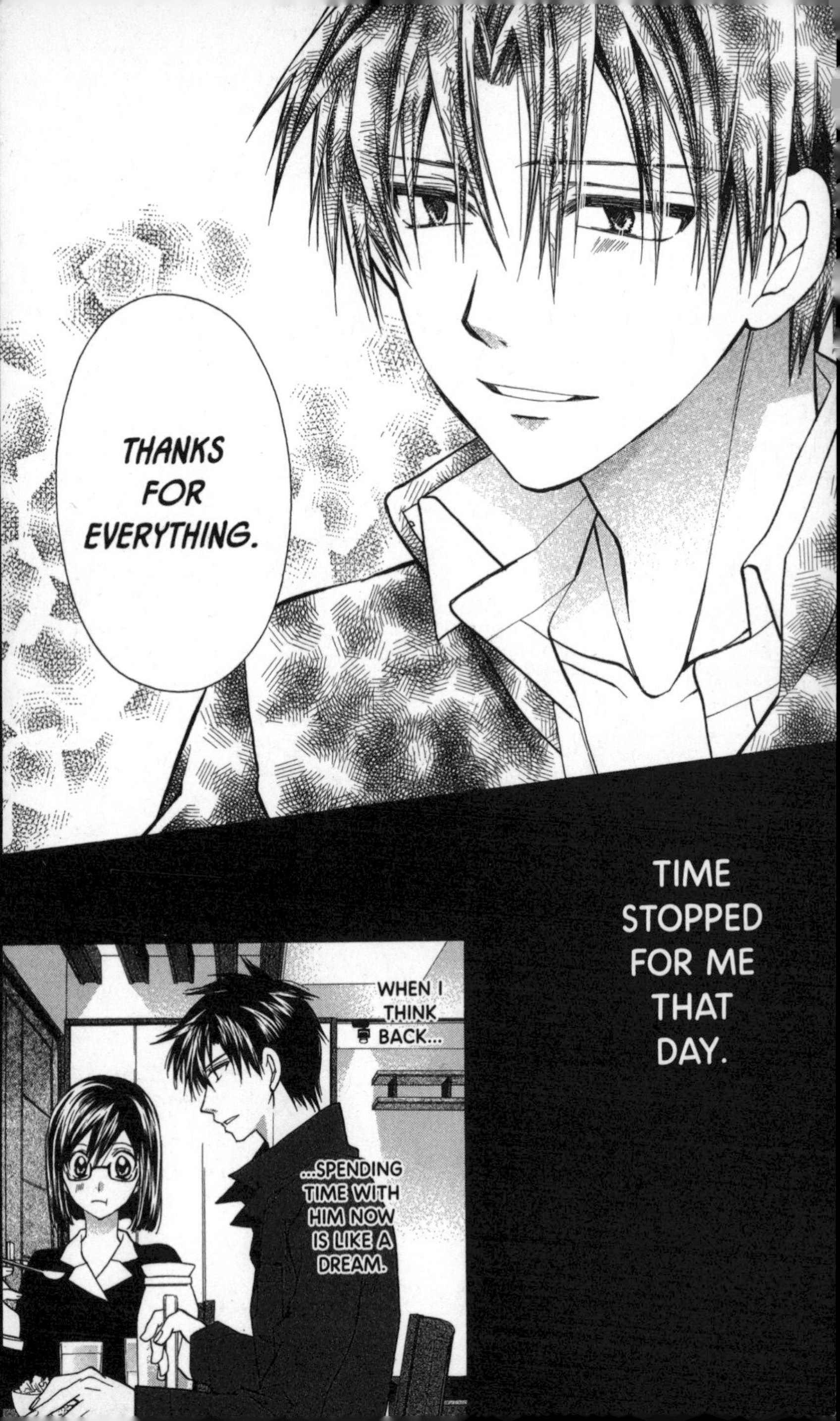
THANKS FOR EVERYTHING.
TIME STOPPED FOR ME THAT DAY.
WHEN I THINK BACK...
...SPENDING TIME WITH HIM NOW IS LIKE A DREAM.

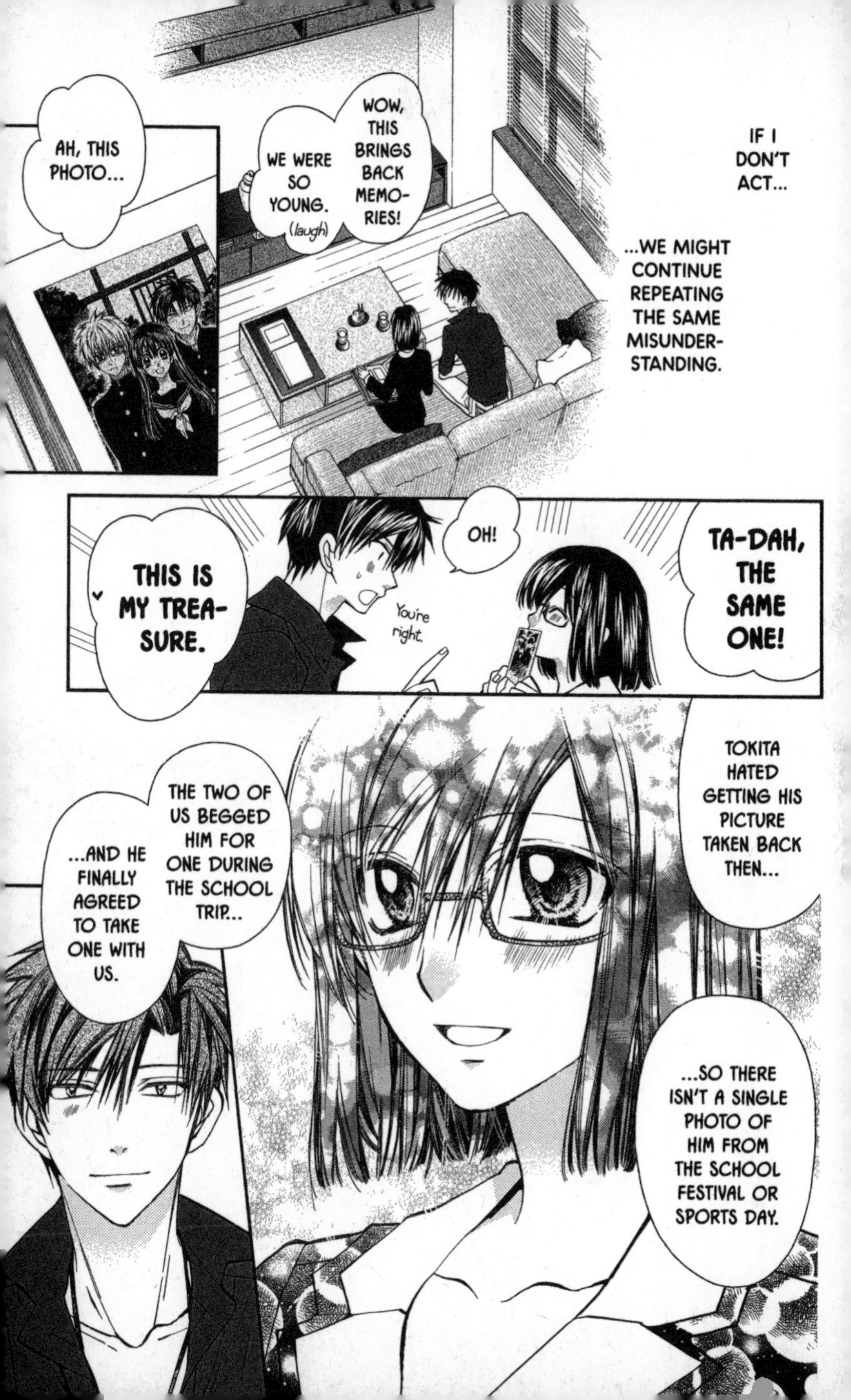
IF I DON'T ACT...
...WE MIGHT CONTINUE REPEATING THE SAME MISUNDERSTANDING.
WOW, THIS BRINGS BACK MEMORIES!
WE WERE SO YOUNG.
(laugh)
AH, THIS PHOTO...
TA-DAH, THE SAME ONE!
OH!
You're right.
THIS IS MY TREASURE.
TOKITA HATED GETTING HIS PICTURE TAKEN BACK THEN...
...SO THERE ISN'T A SINGLE PHOTO OF HIM FROM THE SCHOOL FESTIVAL OR SPORTS DAY.
THE TWO OF US BEGGED HIM FOR ONE DURING THE SCHOOL TRIP...
...AND HE FINALLY AGREED TO TAKE ONE WITH US.

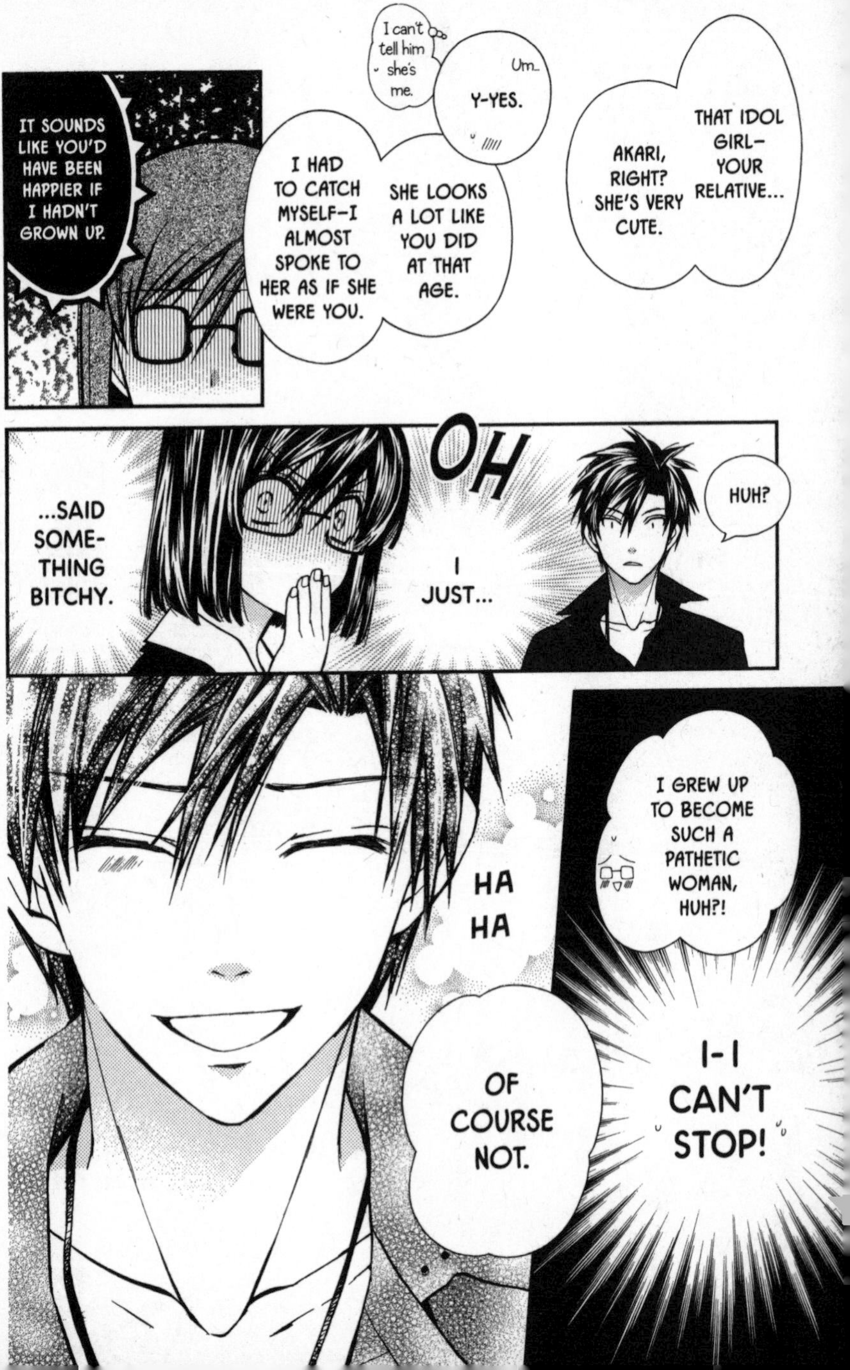
THAT IDOL GIRL— YOUR RELATIVE...
AKARI, RIGHT? SHE'S VERY CUTE.
Um...
Y-YES.
I can't tell him she's me.
SHE LOOKS A LOT LIKE YOU DID AT THAT AGE.
I HAD TO CATCH MYSELF—I ALMOST SPOKE TO HER AS IF SHE WERE YOU.
IT SOUNDS LIKE YOU'D HAVE BEEN HAPPIER IF I HADN'T GROWN UP.
HUH?
OH
I JUST...
...SAID SOME-THING BITCHY.
I GREW UP TO BECOME SUCH A PATHETIC WOMAN, HUH?!
I-I CAN'T STOP!
HA HA
OF COURSE NOT.

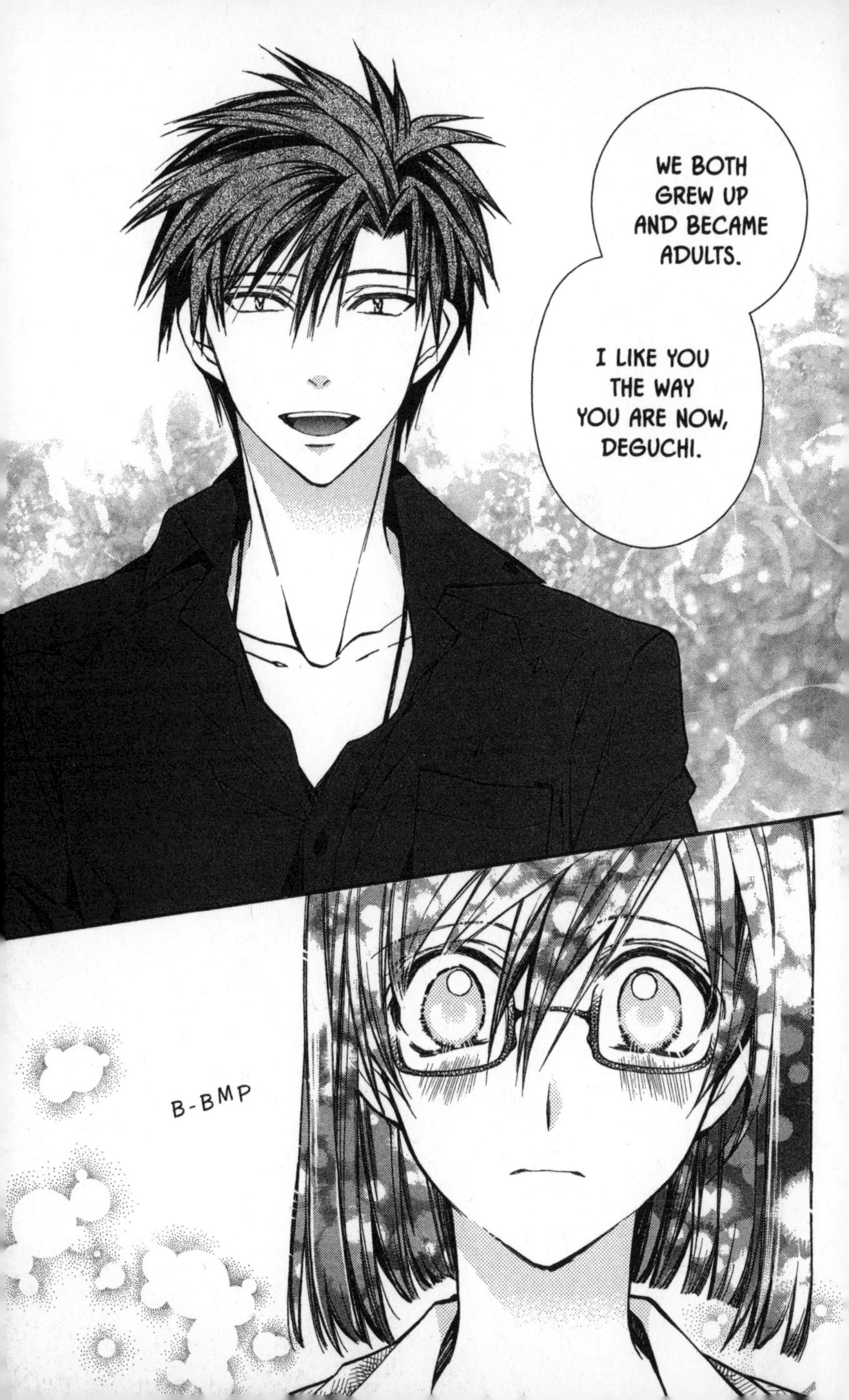
WE BOTH GROW UP AND BECAME ADULTS.
I LIKE YOU THE WAY YOU ARE NOW, DEGUCHI.
B-BMP

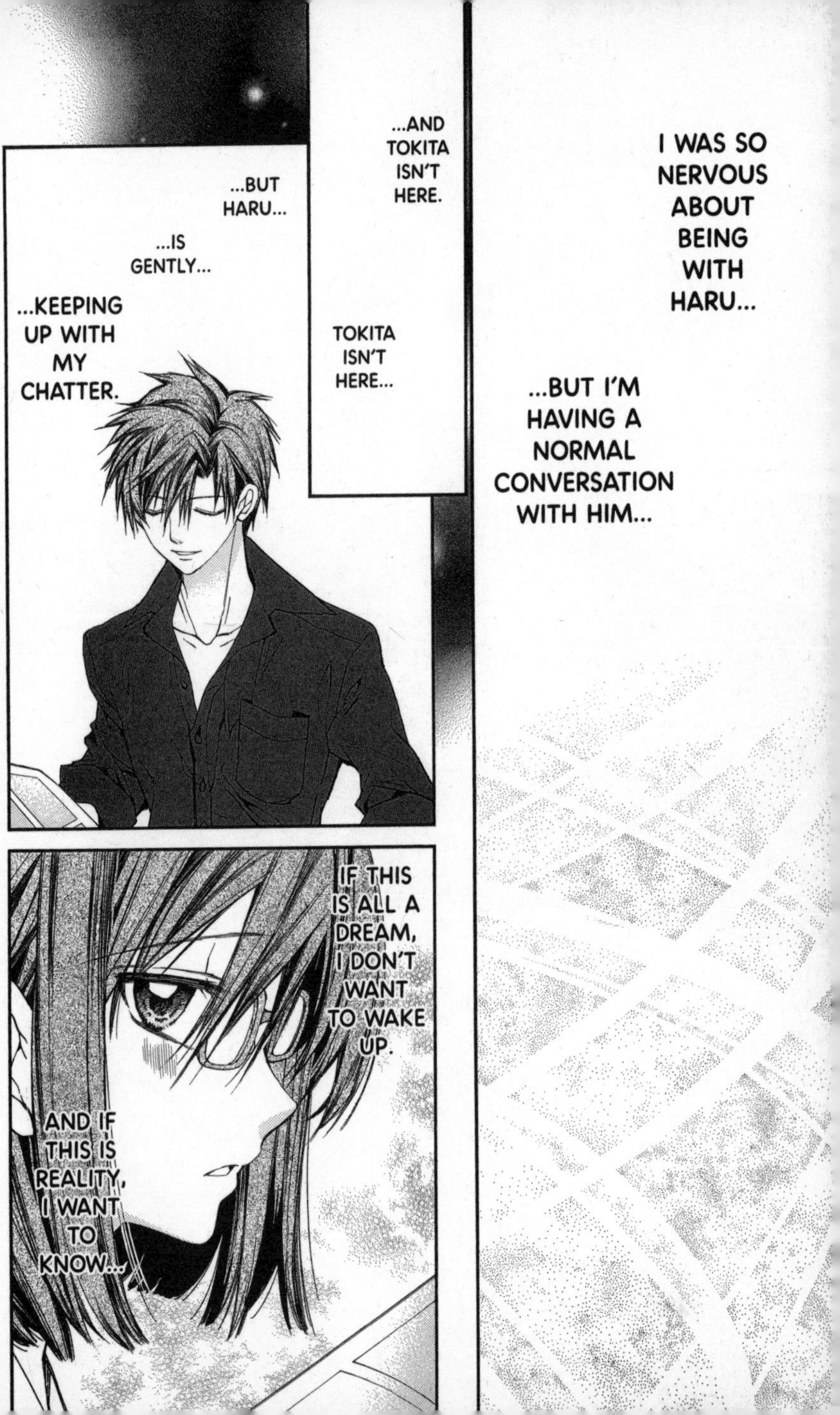
I WAS SO NERVOUS ABOUT BEING WITH HARU...
...BUT I'M HAVING A NORMAL CONVERSATION WITH HIM...
...AND TOKITA ISN'T HERE.
TOKITA ISN'T HERE...
...BUT HARU...
...IS GENTLY...
...KEEPING UP WITH MY CHATTER.
IF THIS IS ALL A DREAM, I DON'T WANT TO WAKE UP.
AND IF THIS IS REALITY, I WANT TO KNOW...

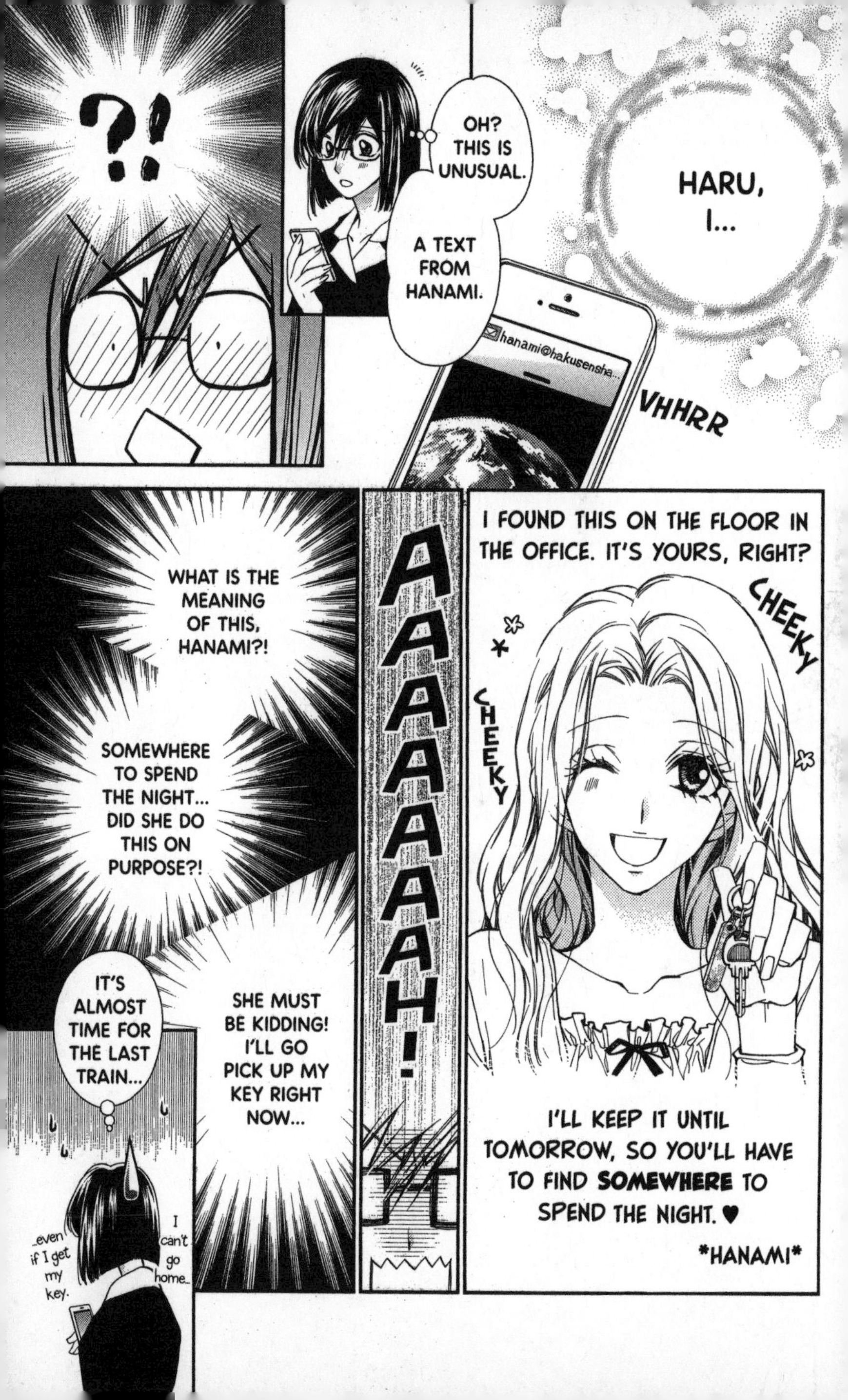
HARU, I...
VHHRR
hanami@hakusensha...
OH? THIS IS UNUSUAL.
A TEXT FROM HANAMI.
?!
I FOUND THIS ON THE FLOOR IN THE OFFICE. IT'S YOURS, RIGHT?
CHEEKY
CHEEKY
I'LL KEEP IT UNTIL TOMORROW, SO YOU'LL HAVE TO FIND **SOMEWHERE** TO SPEND THE NIGHT. ♥
HANAMI
AAAAAAAH!
WHAT IS THE MEANING OF THIS, HANAMI?!
SOMEWHERE TO SPEND THE NIGHT... DID SHE DO THIS ON PURPOSE?!
SHE MUST BE KIDDING! I'LL GO PICK UP MY KEY RIGHT NOW...
IT'S ALMOST TIME FOR THE LAST TRAIN...
I can't go home...
...even if I get my key.

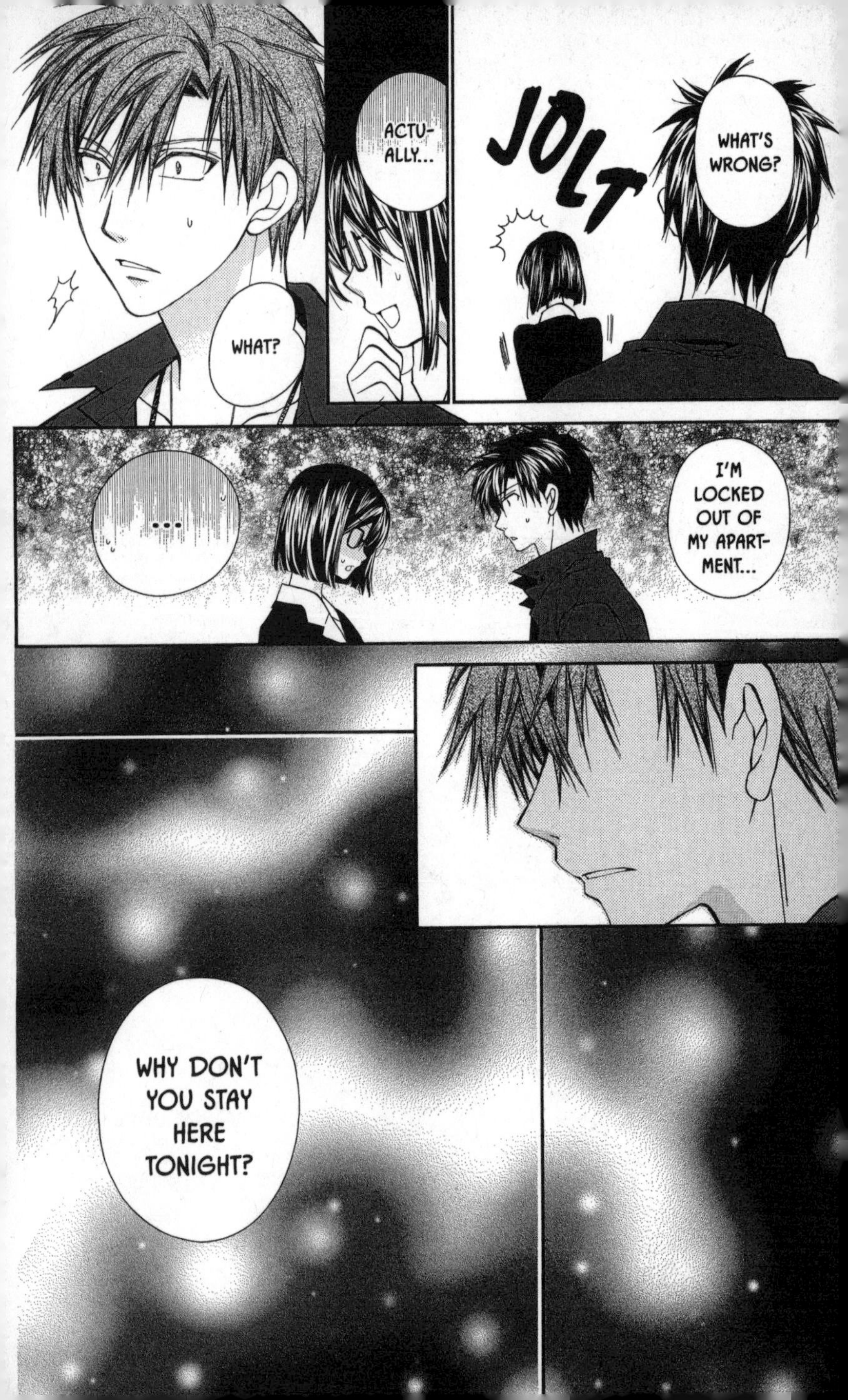
WHAT'S WRONG?
JOLT
ACTU-ALLY...
WHAT?
I'M LOCKED OUT OF MY APARTMENT...
...
WHY DON'T YOU STAY HERE TONIGHT?

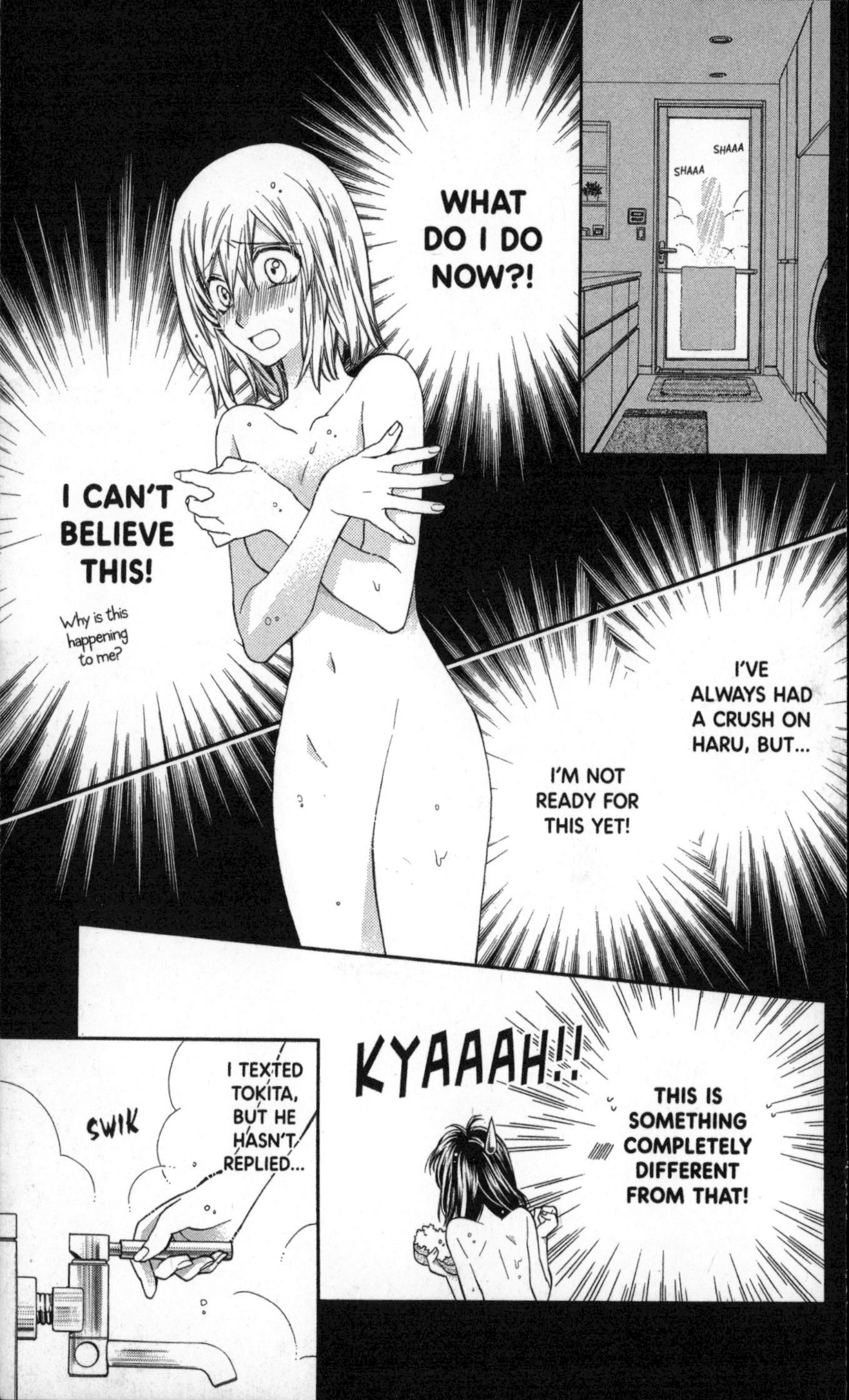
SHAAA
SHAAA
WHAT DO I DO NOW?!
I CAN'T BELIEVE THIS!
Why is this happening to me?
I'VE ALWAYS HAD A CRUSH ON HARU, BUT...
I'M NOT READY FOR THIS YET!
KYAAAH!!
THIS IS SOMETHING COMPLETELY DIFFERENT FROM THAT!
I TEXTED TOKITA, BUT HE HASN'T REPLIED...
SWIK

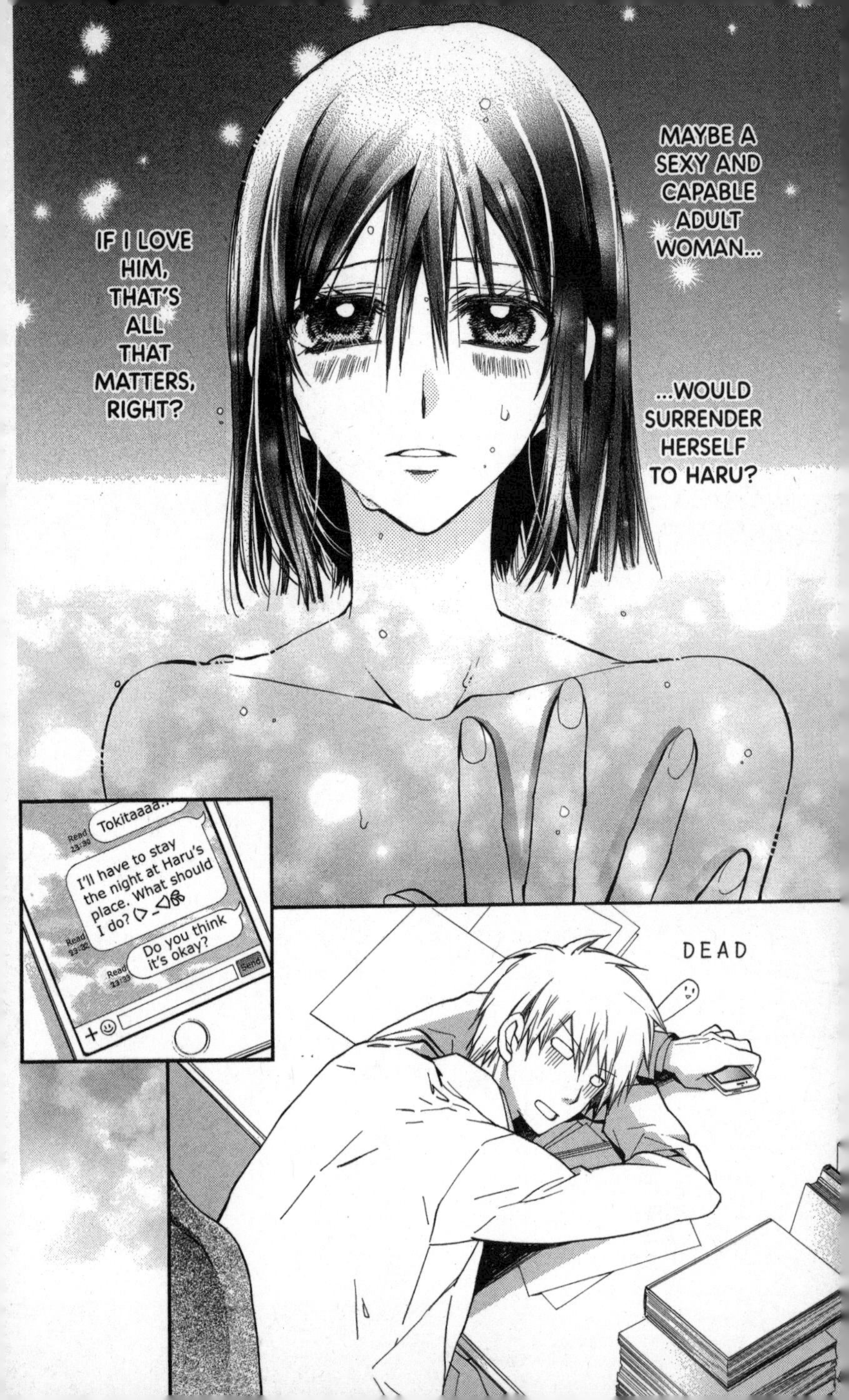
MAYBE A SEXY AND CAPABLE ADULT WOMAN...
...WOULD SURRENDER HERSELF TO HARU?
IF I LOVE HIM, THAT'S ALL THAT MATTERS, RIGHT?
Tokitaaaa...
I'll have to stay the night at Haru's place. What should I do?
Do you think it's okay?
Send
DEAD

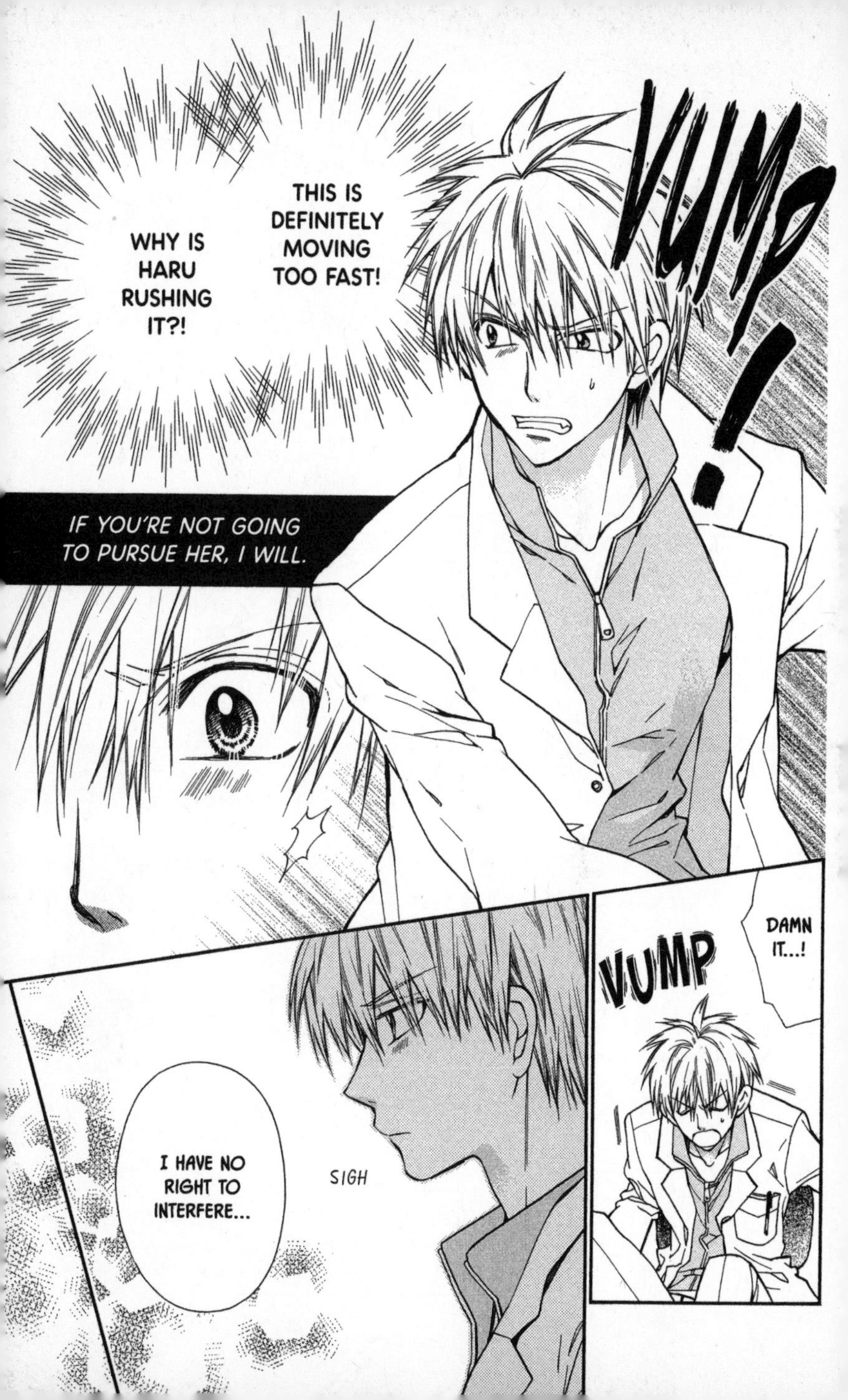
VUMP!
THIS IS DEFINITELY MOVING TOO FAST!
WHY IS HARU RUSHING IT?!
IF YOU'RE NOT GOING TO PURSUE HER, I WILL.
DAMN IT...!
VUMP
SIGH
I HAVE NO RIGHT TO INTERFERE...

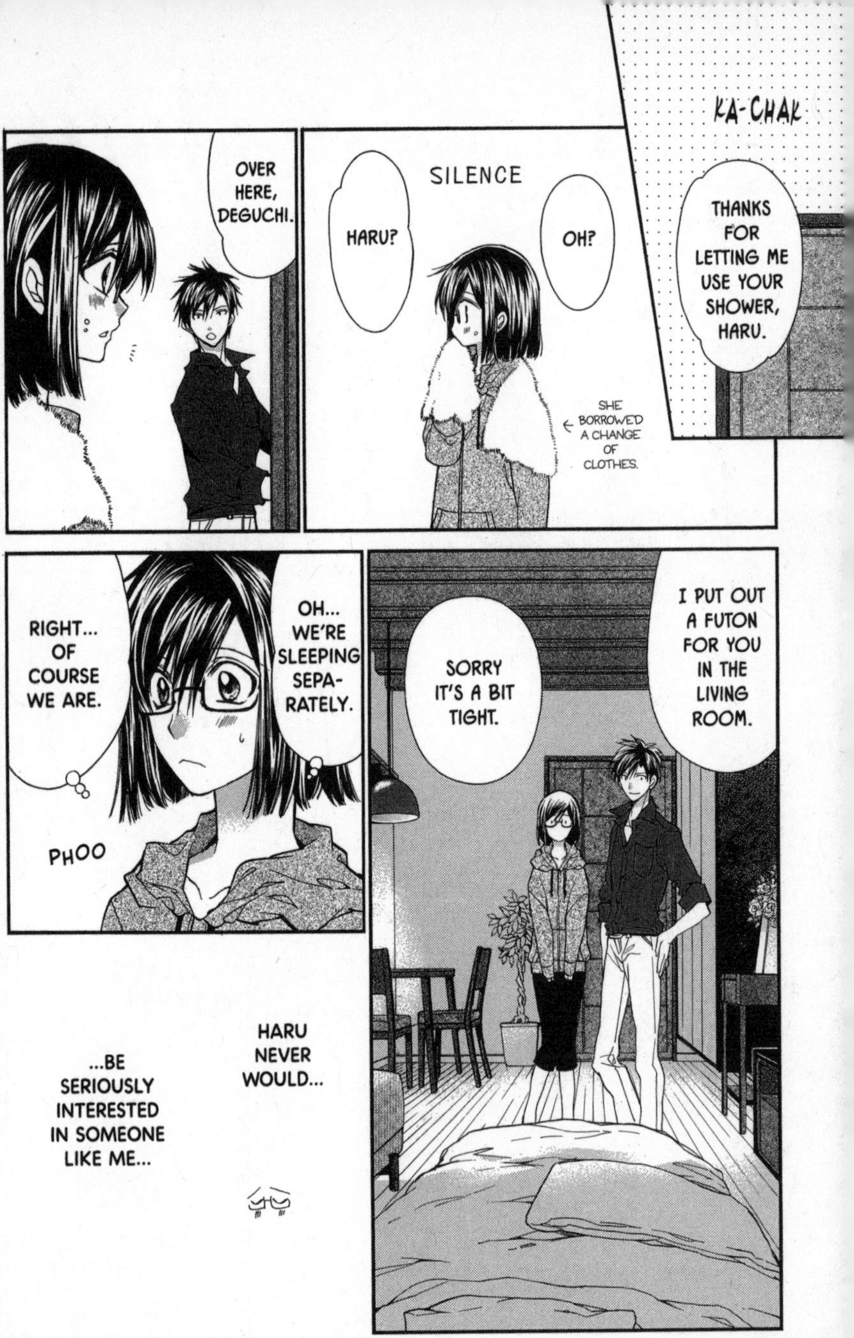
KA-CHAK
THANKS FOR LETTING ME USE YOUR SHOWER, HARU.
OH?
SILENCE
HARU?
SHE BORROWED A CHANGE OF CLOTHES.
OVER HERE, DEGUCHI.
I PUT OUT A FUTON FOR YOU IN THE LIVING ROOM.
SORRY IT'S A BIT TIGHT.
OH... WE'RE SLEEPING SEPA-RATELY.
RIGHT... OF COURSE WE ARE.
PHOO
HARU NEVER WOULD...
...BE SERIOUSLY INTERESTED IN SOMEONE LIKE ME...

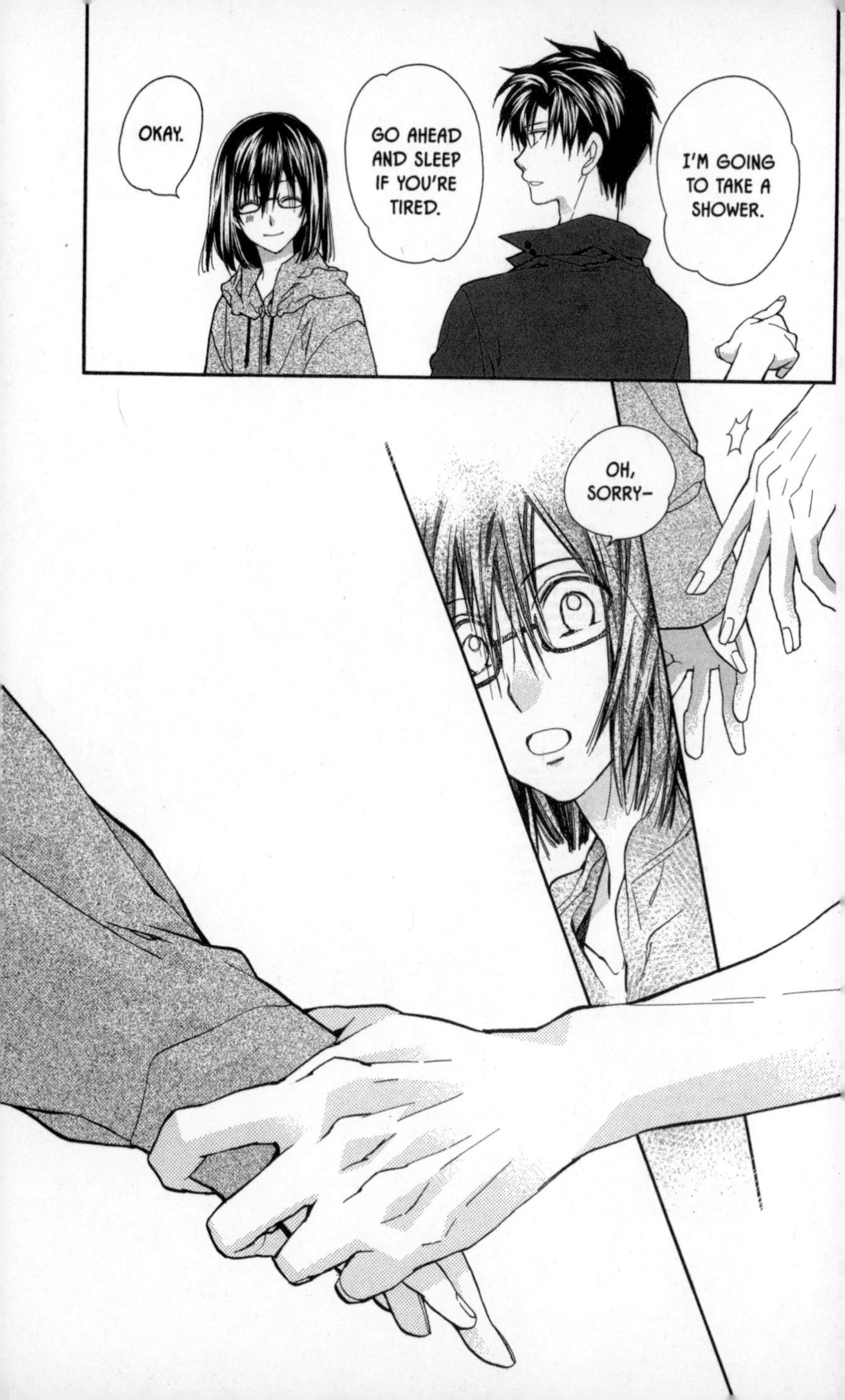
I'M GOING TO TAKE A SHOWER.
GO AHEAD AND SLEEP IF YOU'RE TIRED.
OKAY.
OH, SORRY–

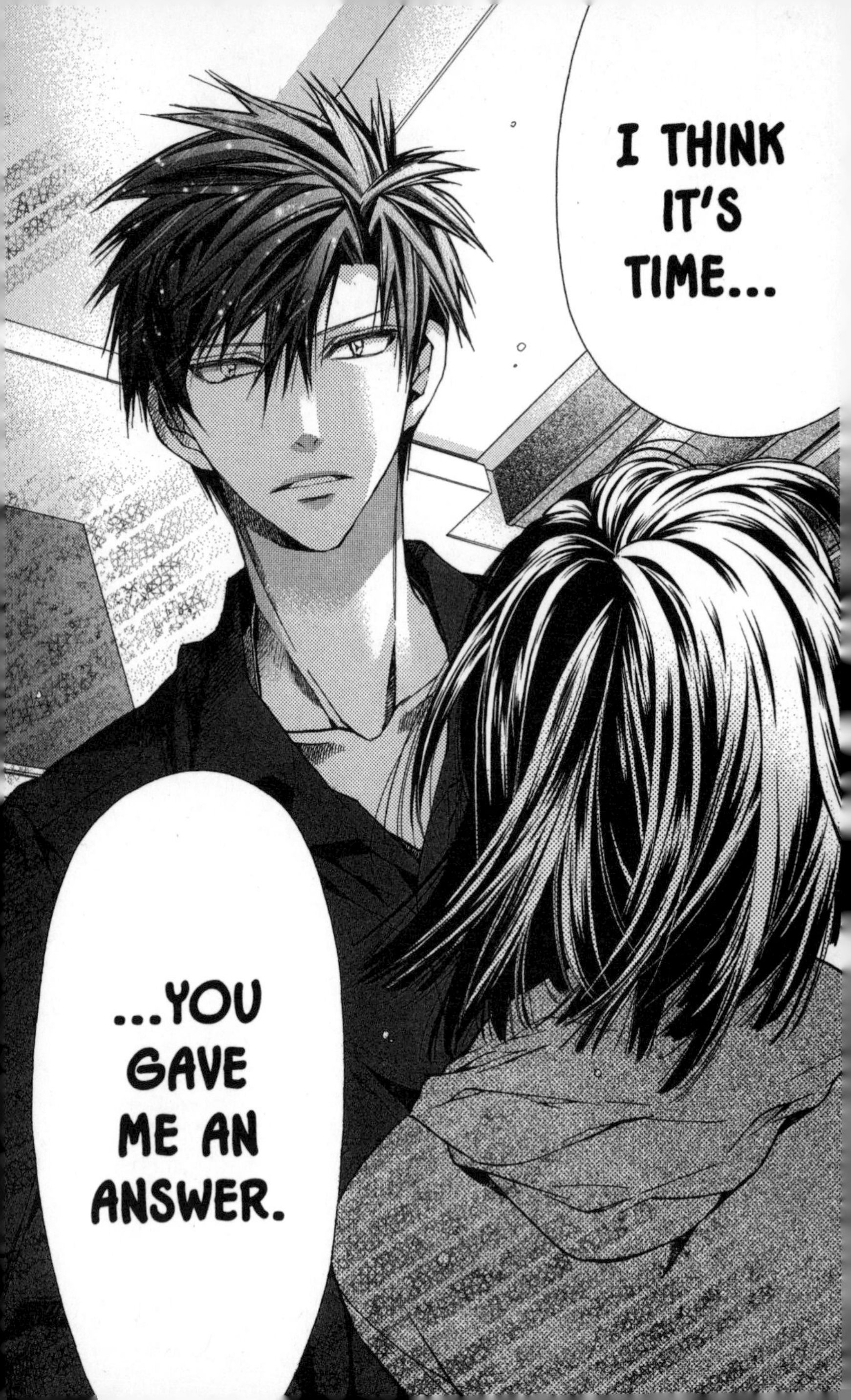
I THINK IT'S TIME...
...YOU GAVE ME AN ANSWER.

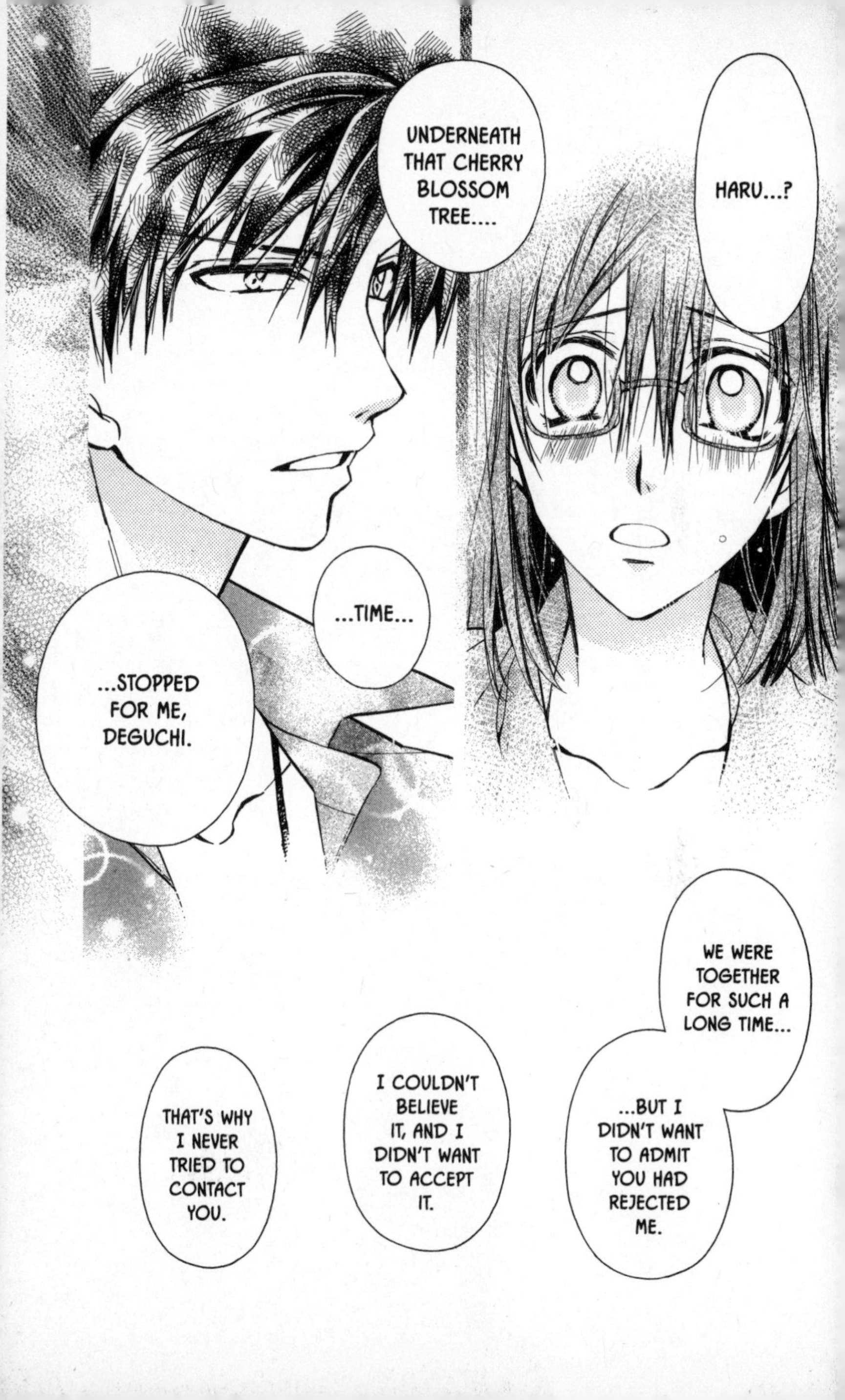
HARU...?
UNDERNEATH THAT CHERRY BLOSSOM TREE....
...TIME...
...STOPPED FOR ME, DEGUCHI.
WE WERE TOGETHER FOR SUCH A LONG TIME...
...BUT I DIDN'T WANT TO ADMIT YOU HAD REJECTED ME.
I COULDN'T BELIEVE IT, AND I DIDN'T WANT TO ACCEPT IT.
THAT'S WHY I NEVER TRIED TO CONTACT YOU.

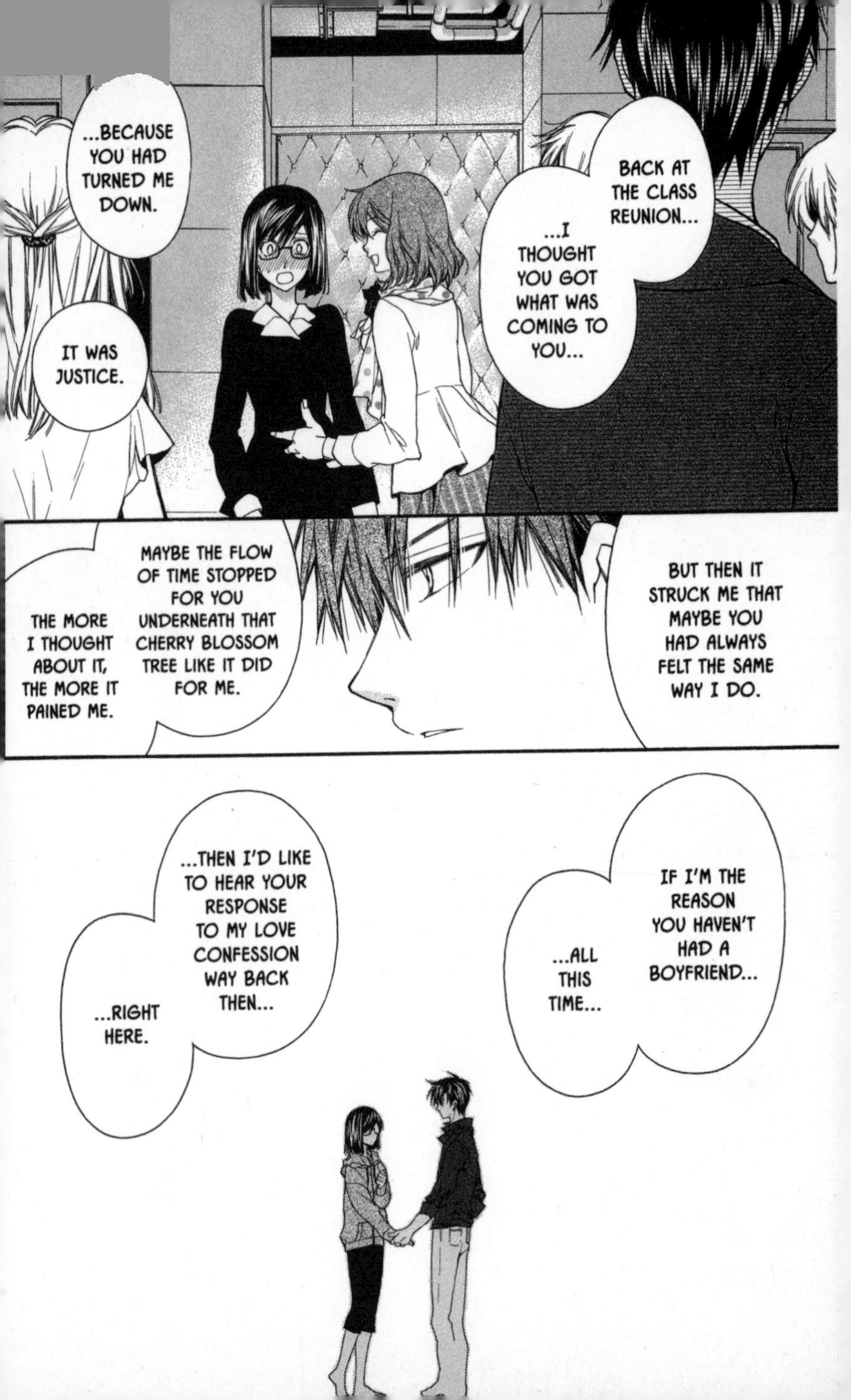
BACK AT THE CLASS REUNION...
...I THOUGHT YOU GOT WHAT WAS COMING TO YOU...
...BECAUSE YOU HAD TURNED ME DOWN.
IT WAS JUSTICE.
BUT THEN IT STRUCK ME THAT MAYBE YOU HAD ALWAYS FELT THE SAME WAY I DO.
MAYBE THE FLOW OF TIME STOPPED FOR YOU UNDERNEATH THAT CHERRY BLOSSOM TREE LIKE IT DID FOR ME.
THE MORE I THOUGHT ABOUT IT, THE MORE IT PAINED ME.
IF I'M THE REASON YOU HAVEN'T HAD A BOYFRIEND...
...ALL THIS TIME...
...THEN I'D LIKE TO HEAR YOUR RESPONSE TO MY LOVE CONFESSION WAY BACK THEN...
...RIGHT HERE.

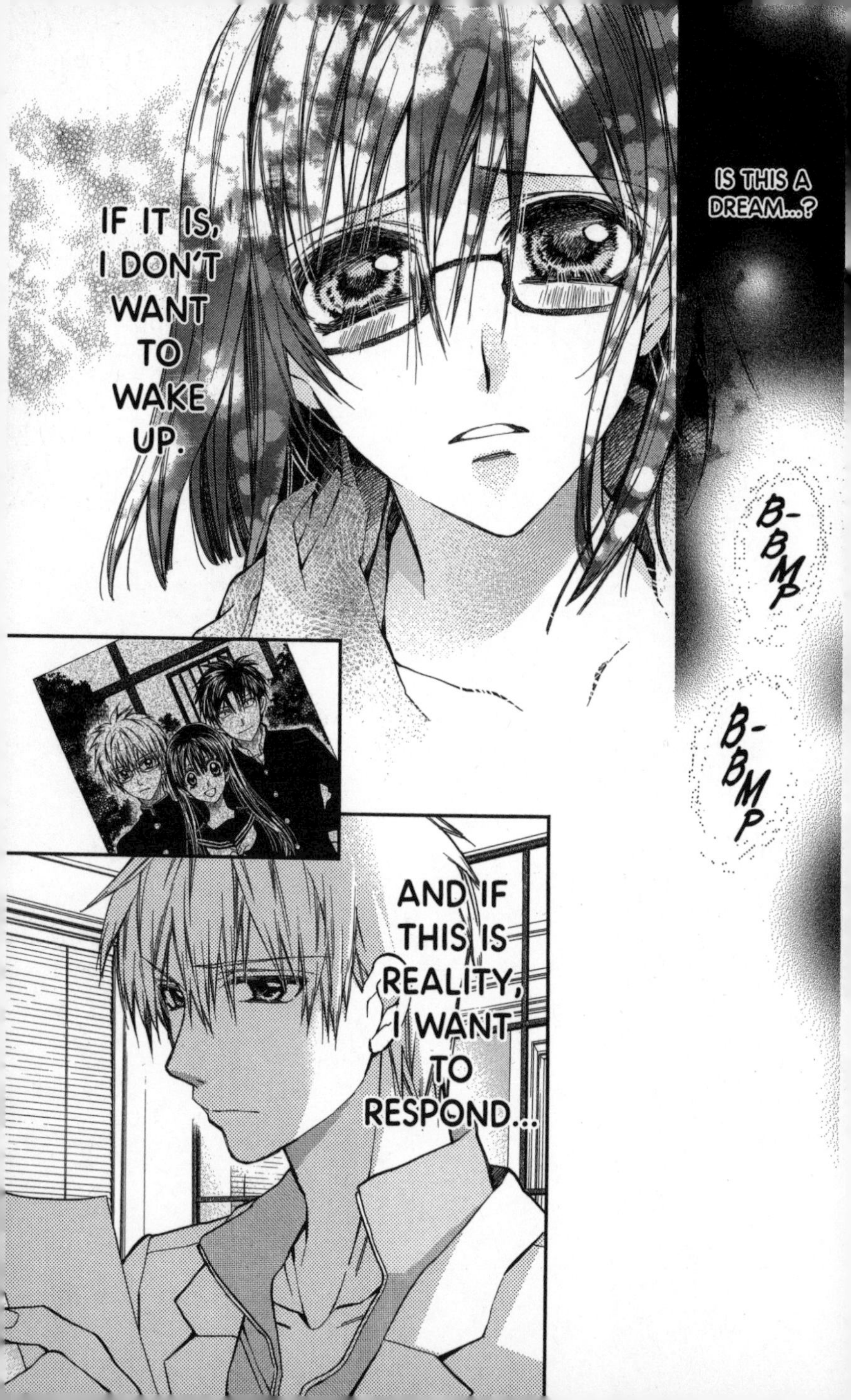
IS THIS A DREAM...?
B-BMP
B-BMP
IF IT IS, I DON'T WANT TO WAKE UP.
AND IF THIS IS REALITY, I WANT TO RESPOND...

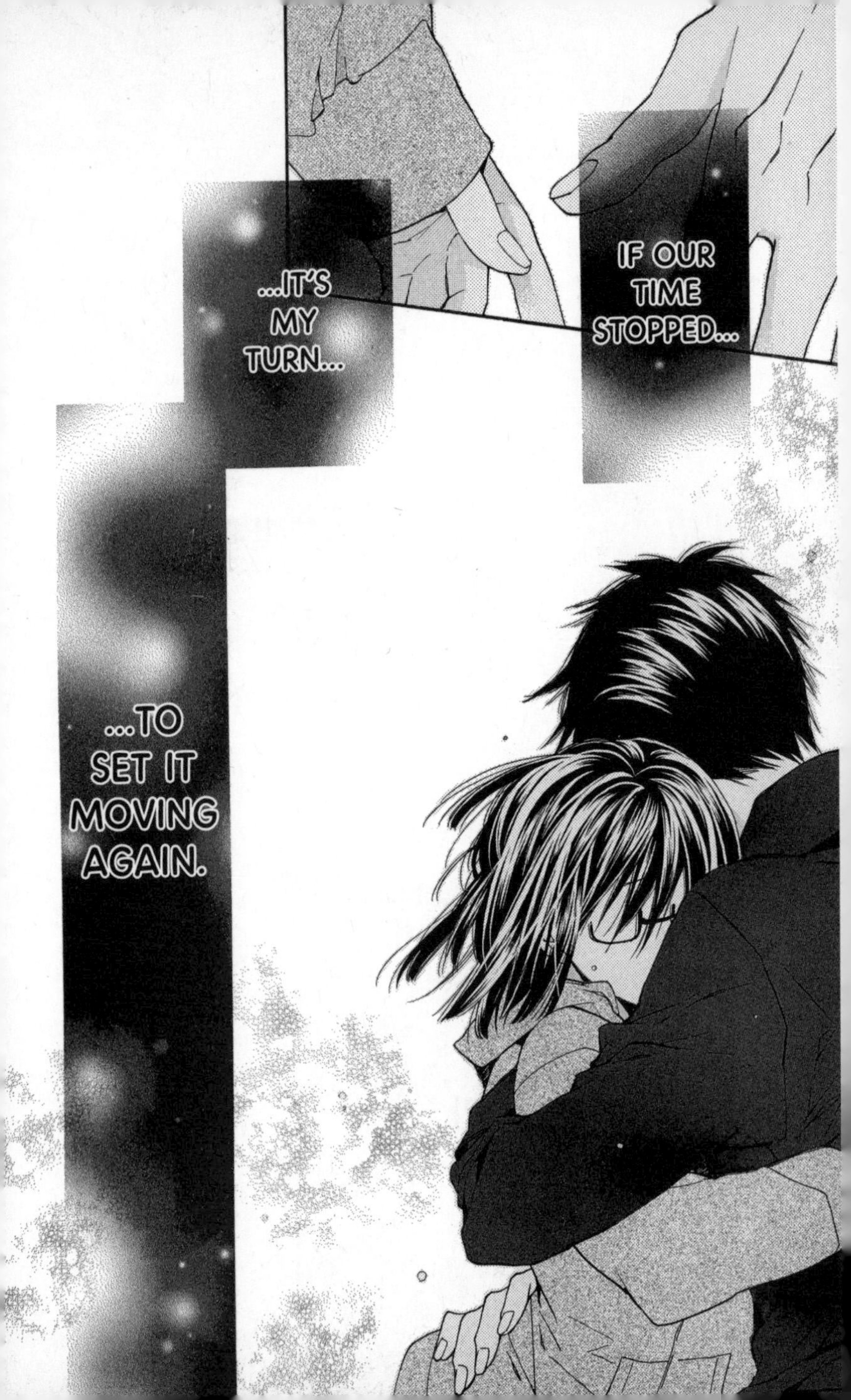
IF OUR TIME STOPPED...
...IT'S MY TURN...
...TO SET IT MOVING AGAIN.

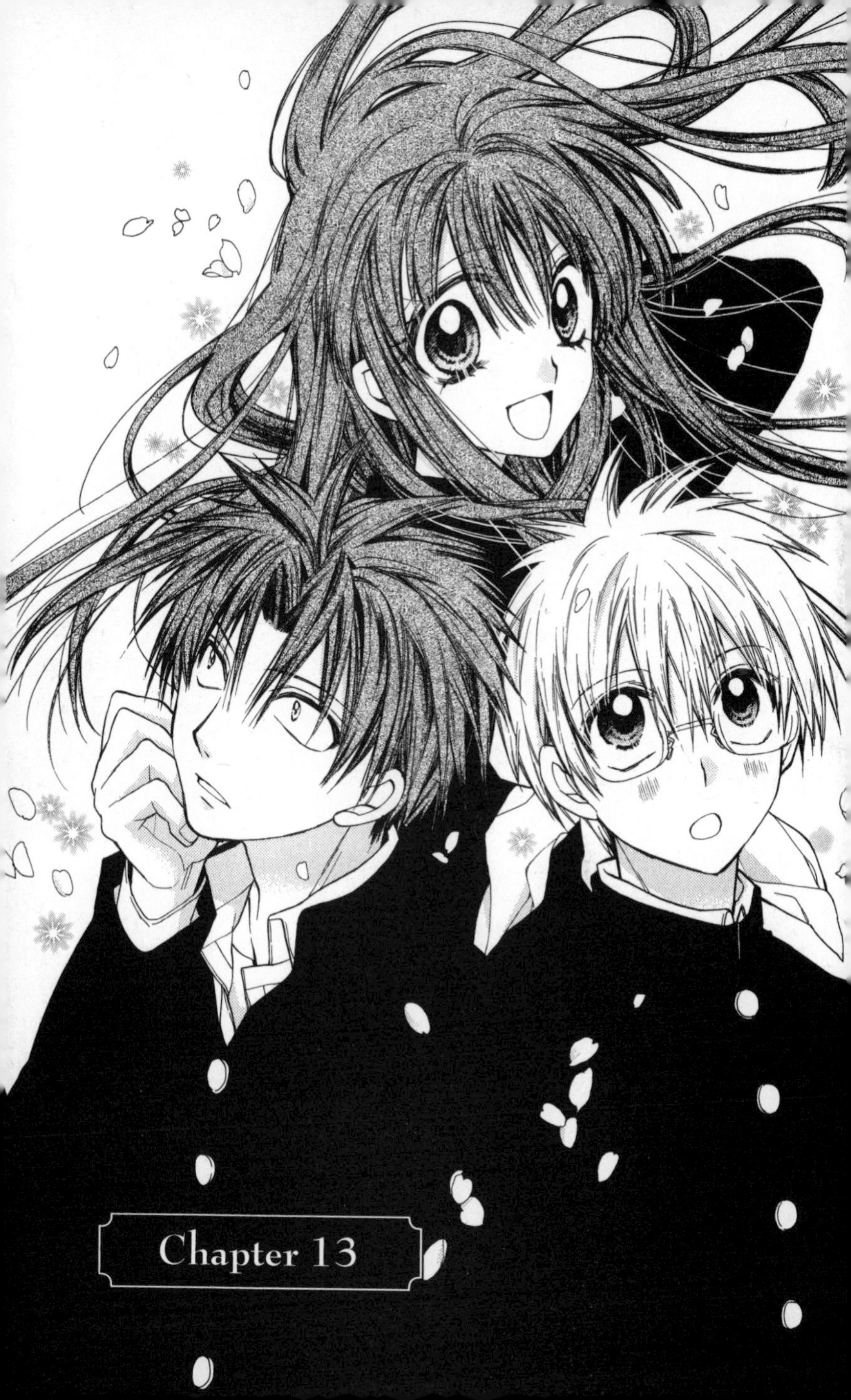
Chapter 13

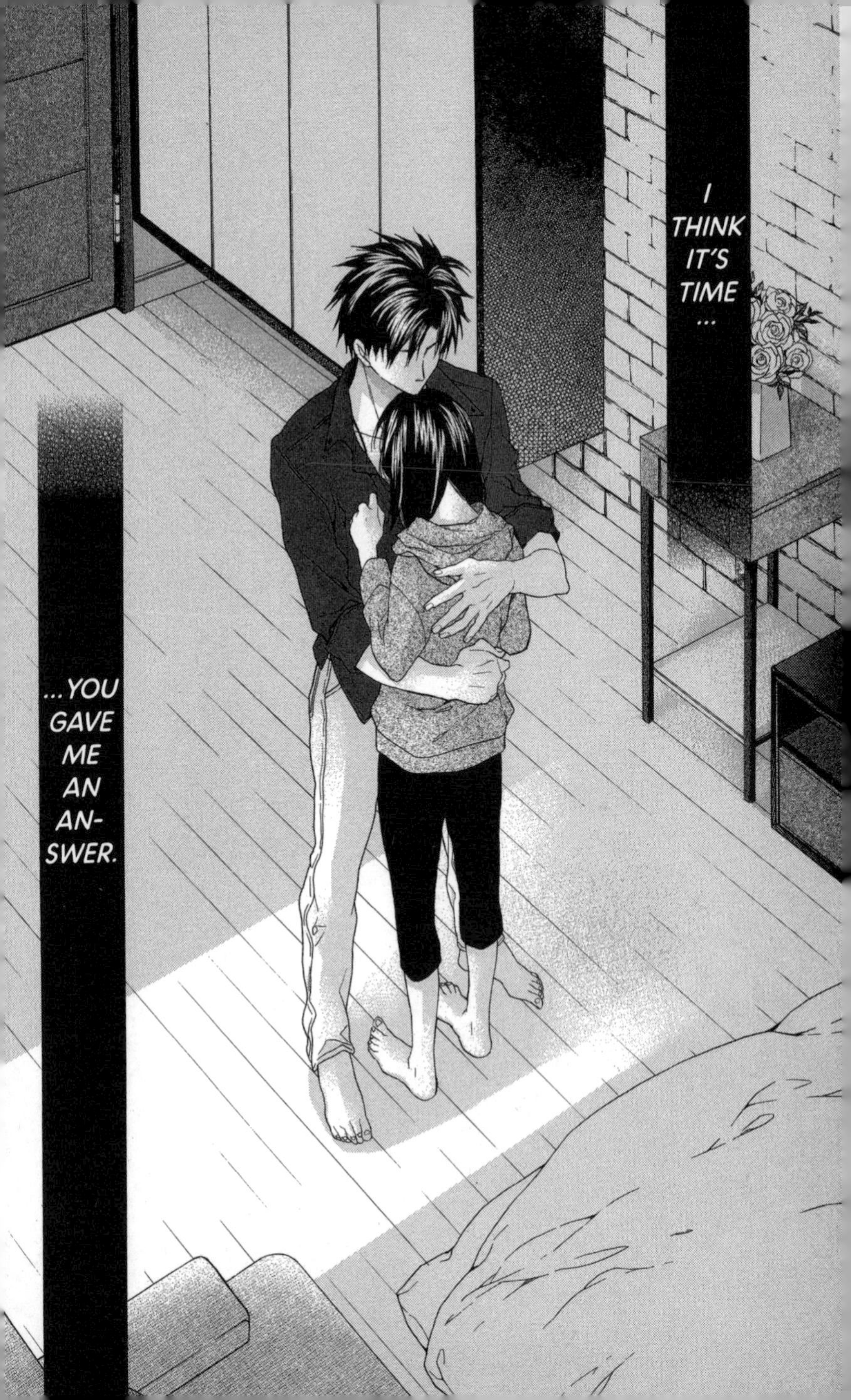
I THINK IT'S TIME...
...YOU GAVE ME AN AN-SWER.

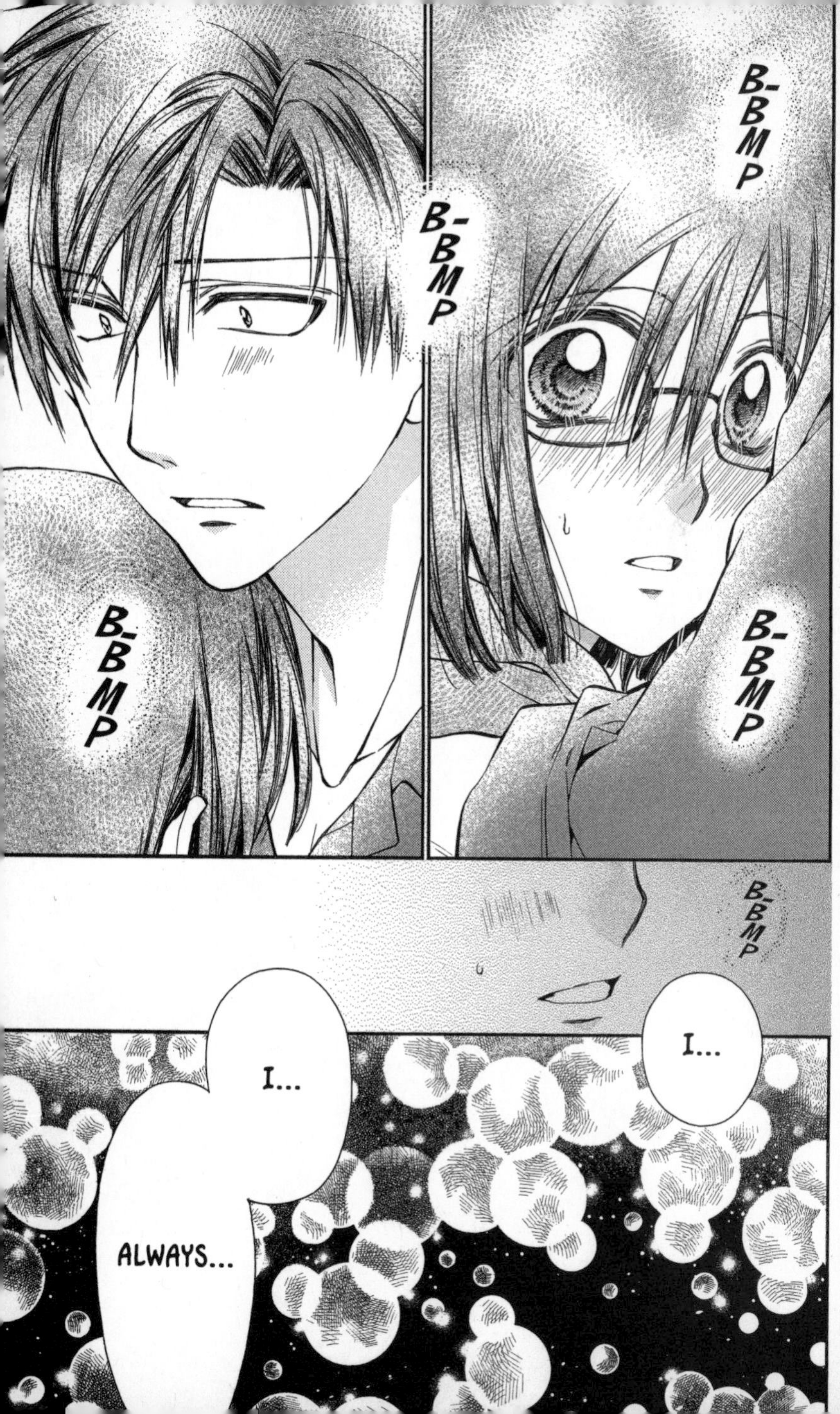
B-BMP
B-BMP
B-BMP
B-BMP
B-BMP
I...
I...
ALWAYS...

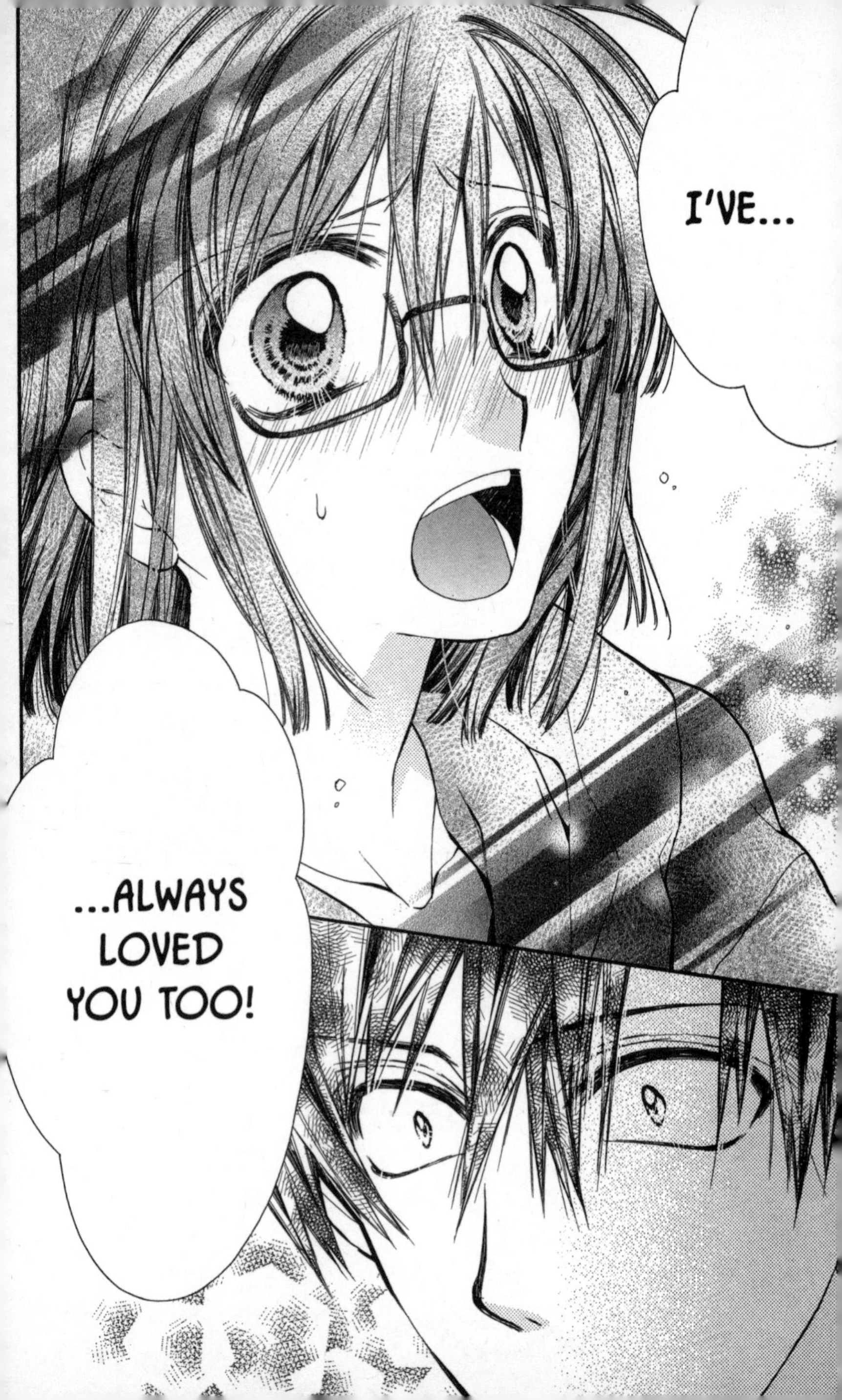
I'VE...
...ALWAYS LOVED YOU TOO!

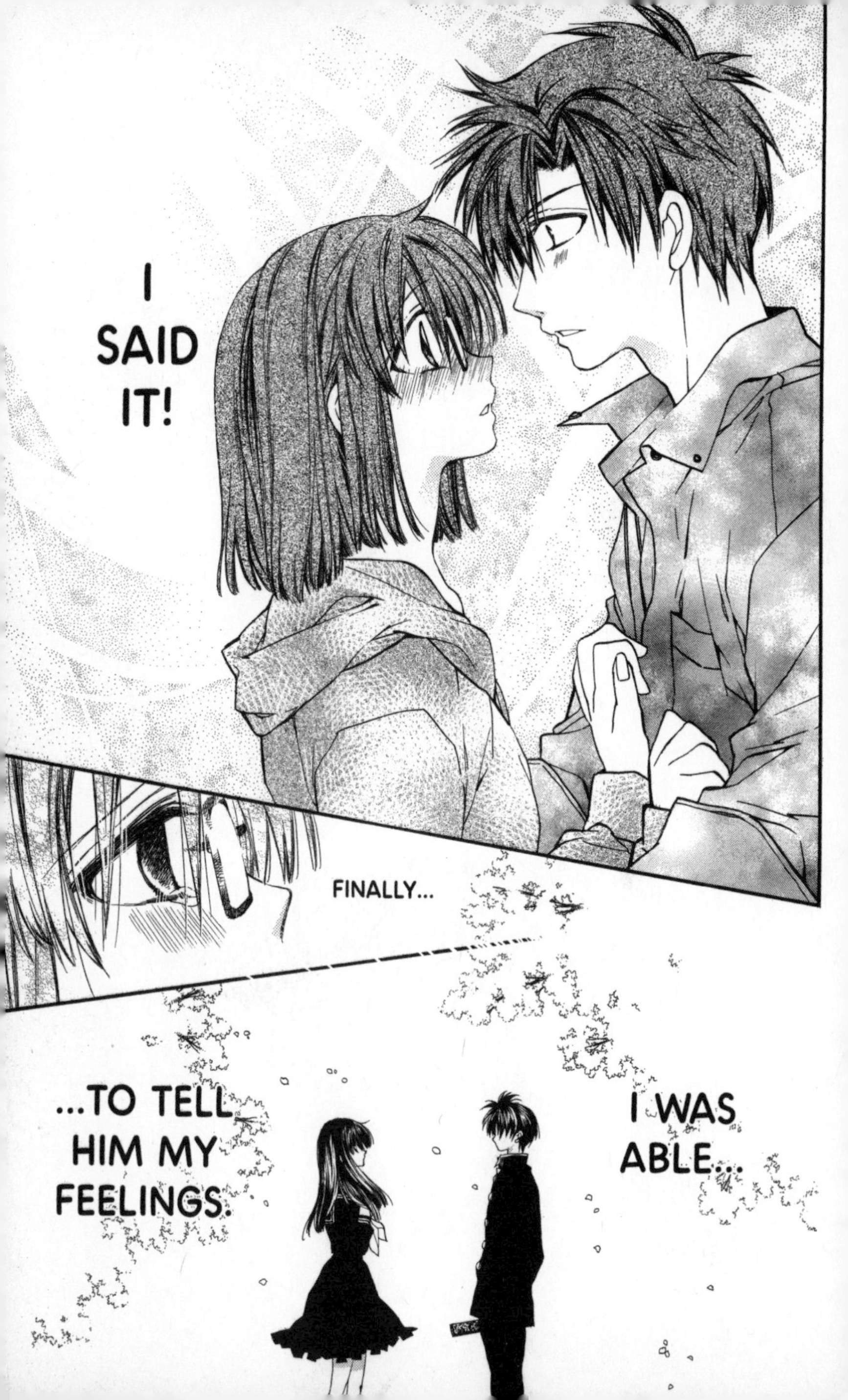
I SAID IT!
FINALLY...
I WAS ABLE...
...TO TELL HIM MY FEELINGS.

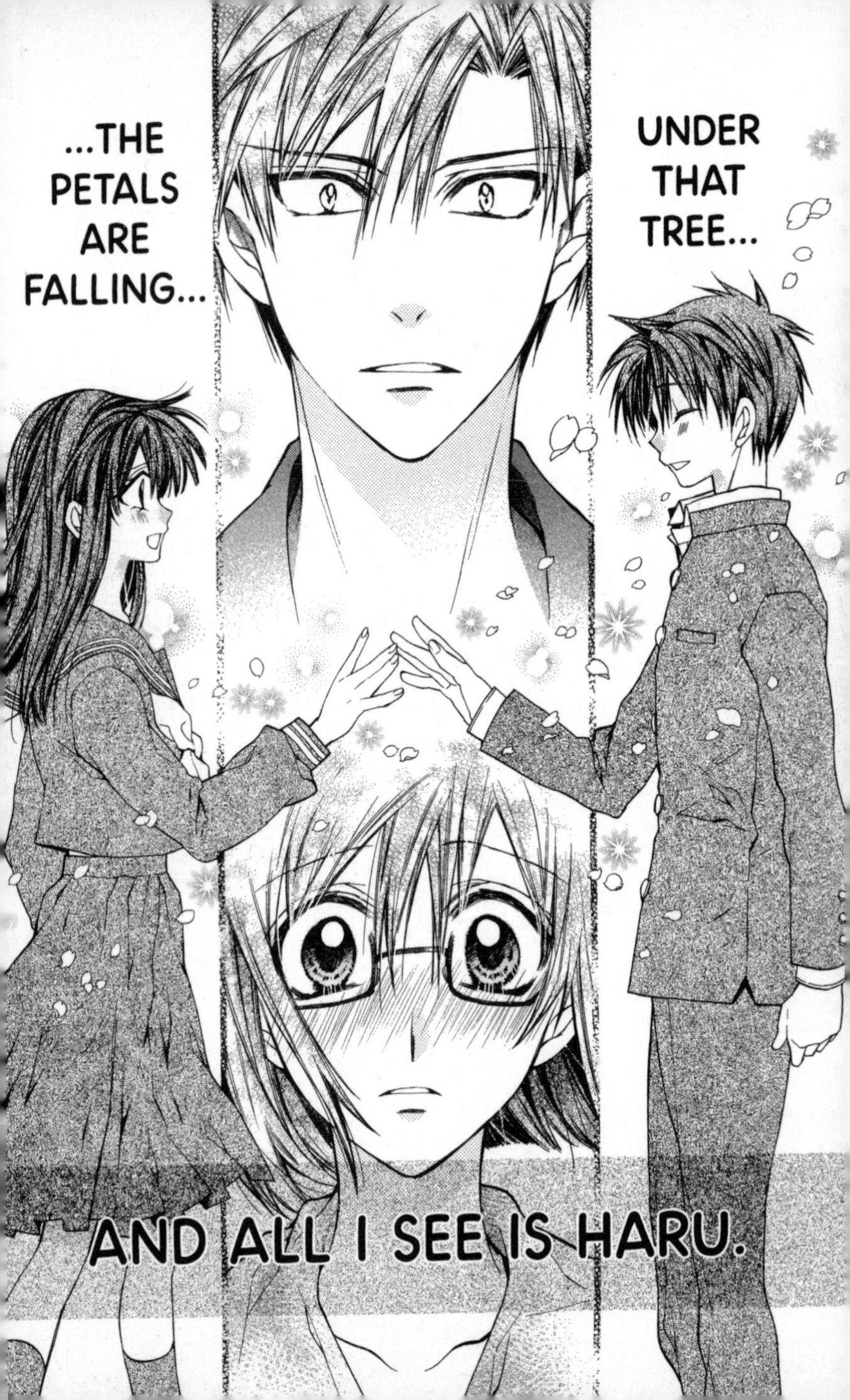
UNDER THAT TREE...
...THE PETALS ARE FALLING...
AND ALL I SEE IS HARU.

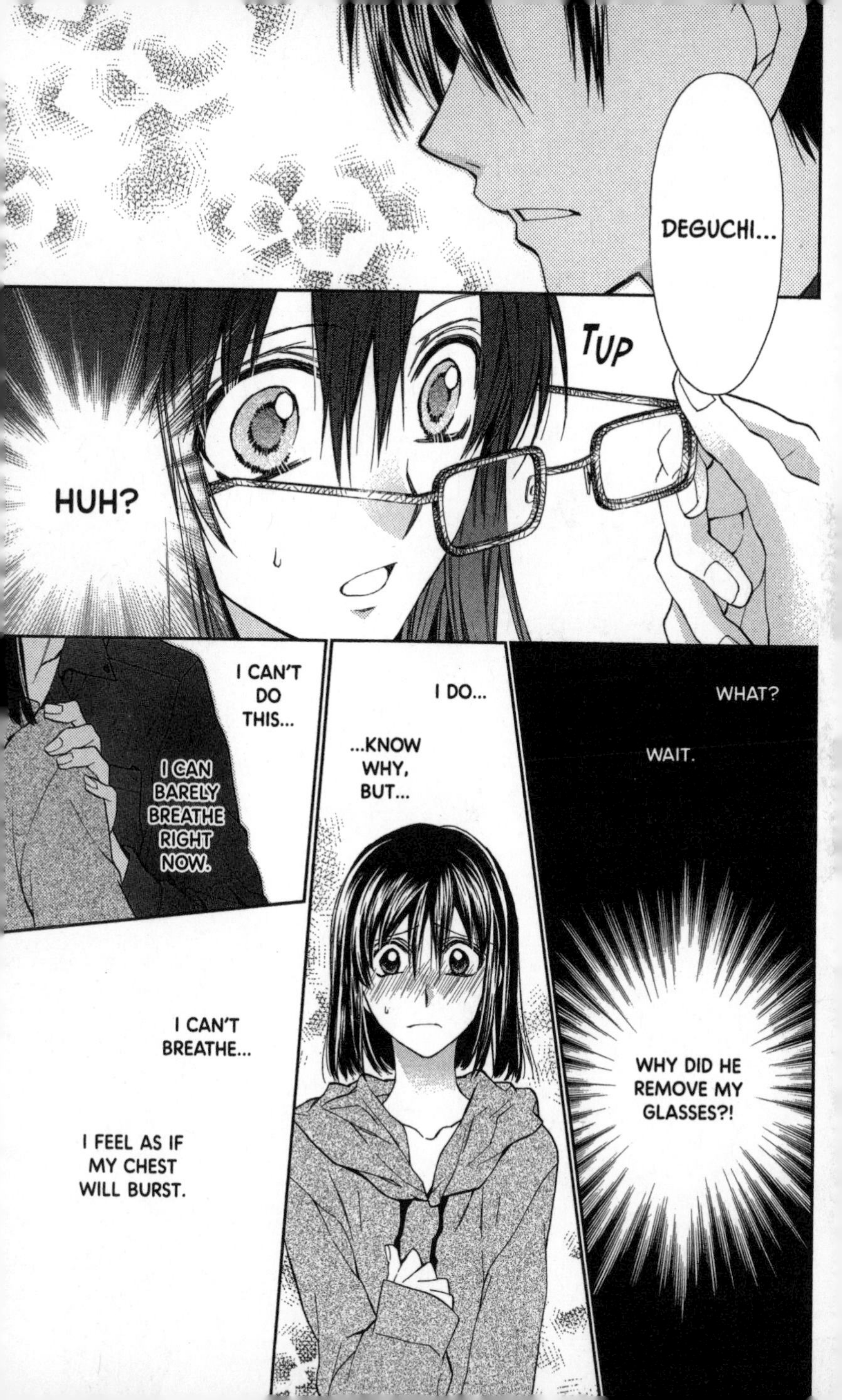
DEGUCHI...
TUP
HUH?
WHAT?
WAIT.
WHY DID HE REMOVE MY GLASSES?!
I DO...
...KNOW WHY, BUT...
I CAN'T DO THIS...
I CAN BARELY BREATHE RIGHT NOW.
I CAN'T BREATHE...
I FEEL AS IF MY CHEST WILL BURST.

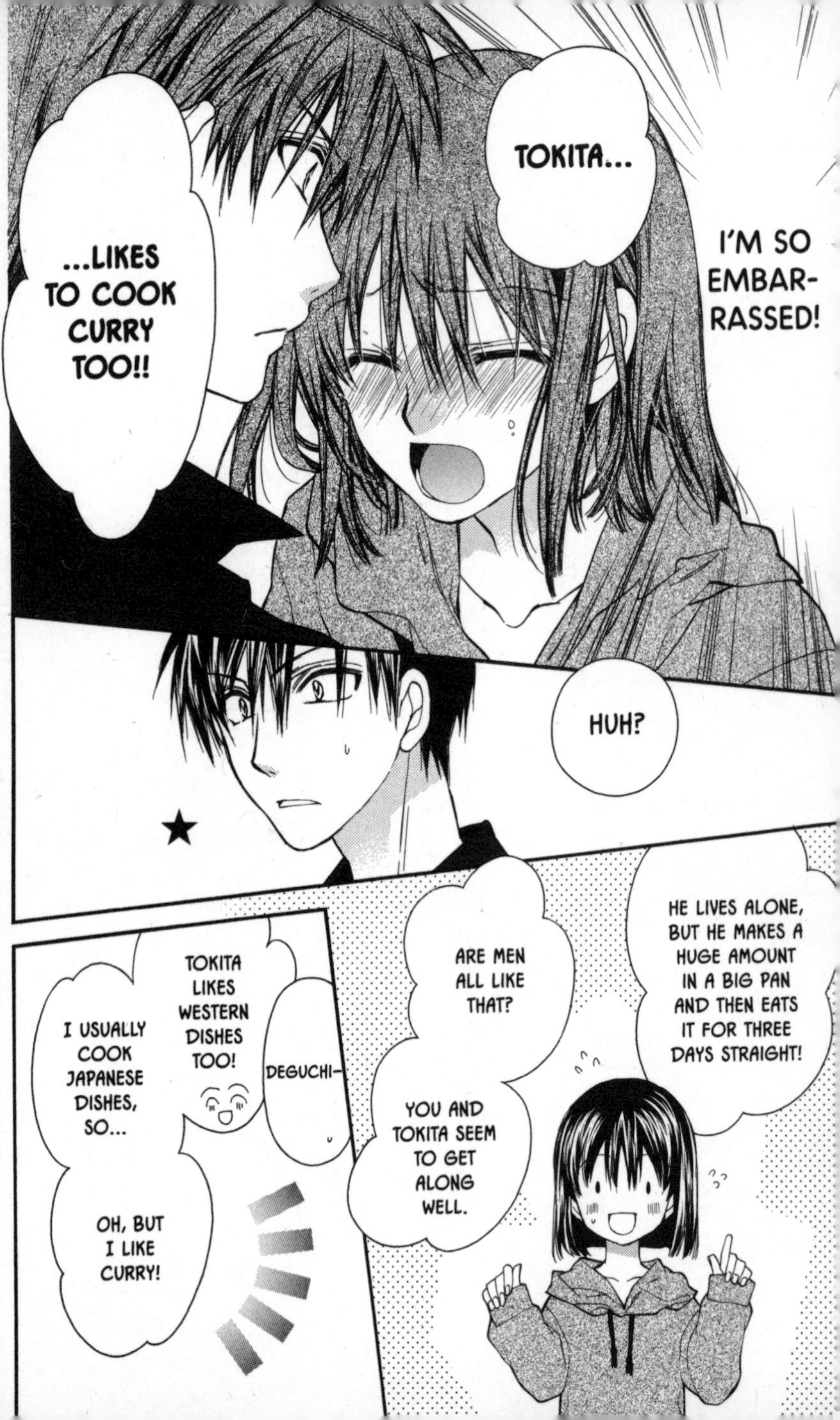
TOKITA...
I'M SO EMBARRASSED!
...LIKES TO COOK CURRY TOO!!
HUH?
HE LIVES ALONE, BUT HE MAKES A HUGE AMOUNT IN A BIG PAN AND THEN EATS IT FOR THREE DAYS STRAIGHT!
ARE MEN ALL LIKE THAT?
YOU AND TOKITA SEEM TO GET ALONG WELL.
TOKITA LIKES WESTERN DISHES TOO!
DEGUCHI-
I USUALLY COOK JAPANESE DISHES, SO...
OH, BUT I LIKE CURRY!

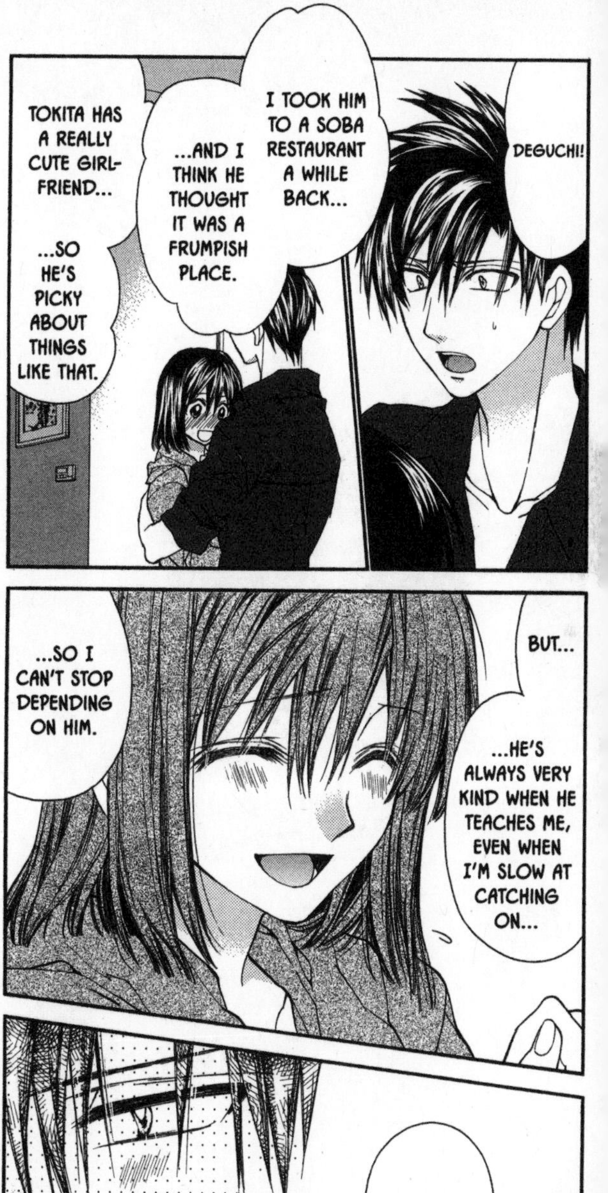
DEGUCHI!
I TOOK HIM TO A SOBA RESTAURANT A WHILE BACK...
...AND I THINK HE THOUGHT IT WAS A FRUMPISH PLACE.
TOKITA HAS A REALLY CUTE GIRL-FRIEND...
...SO HE'S PICKY ABOUT THINGS LIKE THAT.
BUT...
...HE'S ALWAYS VERY KIND WHEN HE TEACHES ME, EVEN WHEN I'M SLOW AT CATCHING ON...
...SO I CAN'T STOP DEPENDING ON HIM.
...

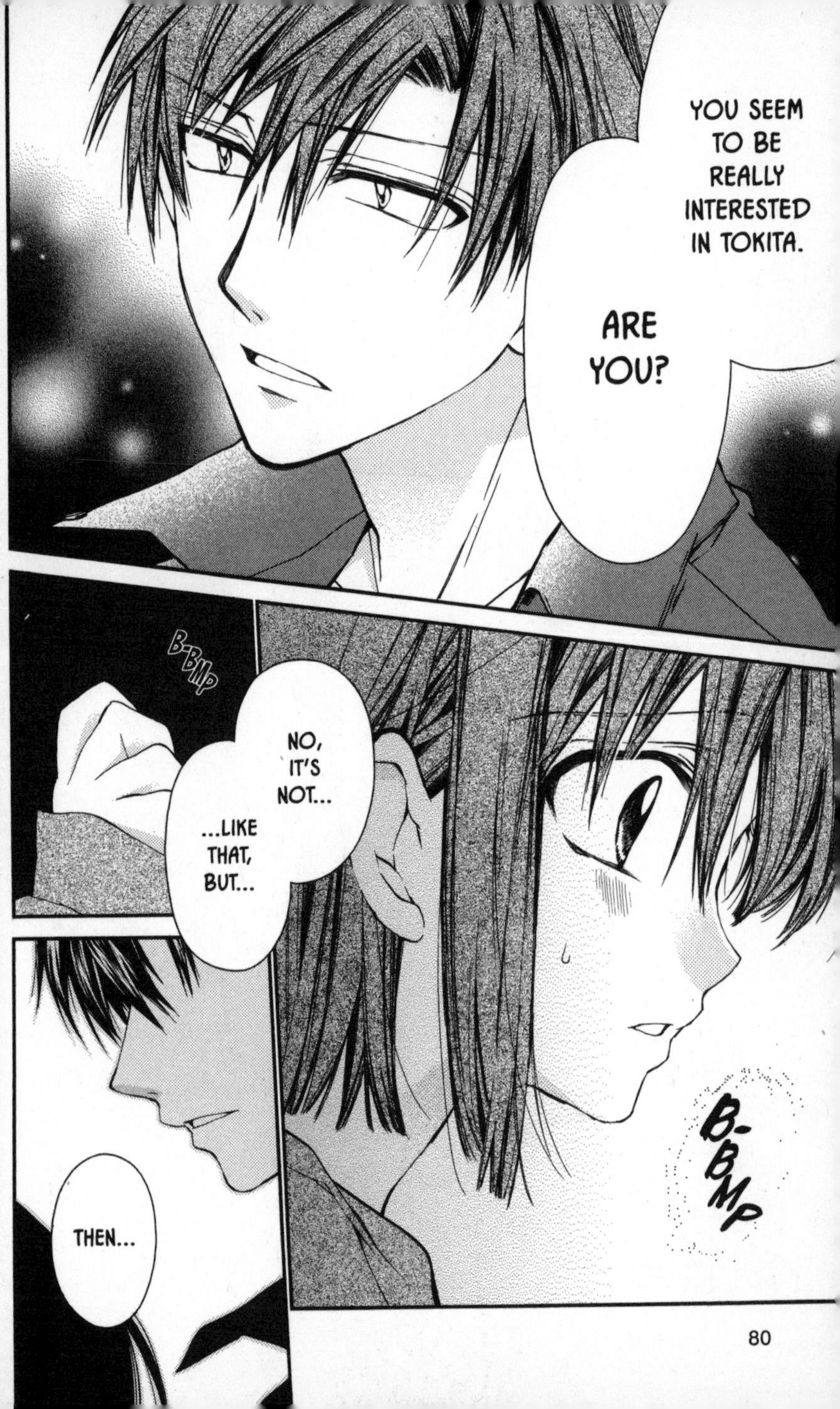
YOU SEEM TO BE REALLY INTERESTED IN TOKITA.
ARE YOU?
NO, IT'S NOT...
...LIKE THAT, BUT...
B-BMP
B-BMP
THEN...

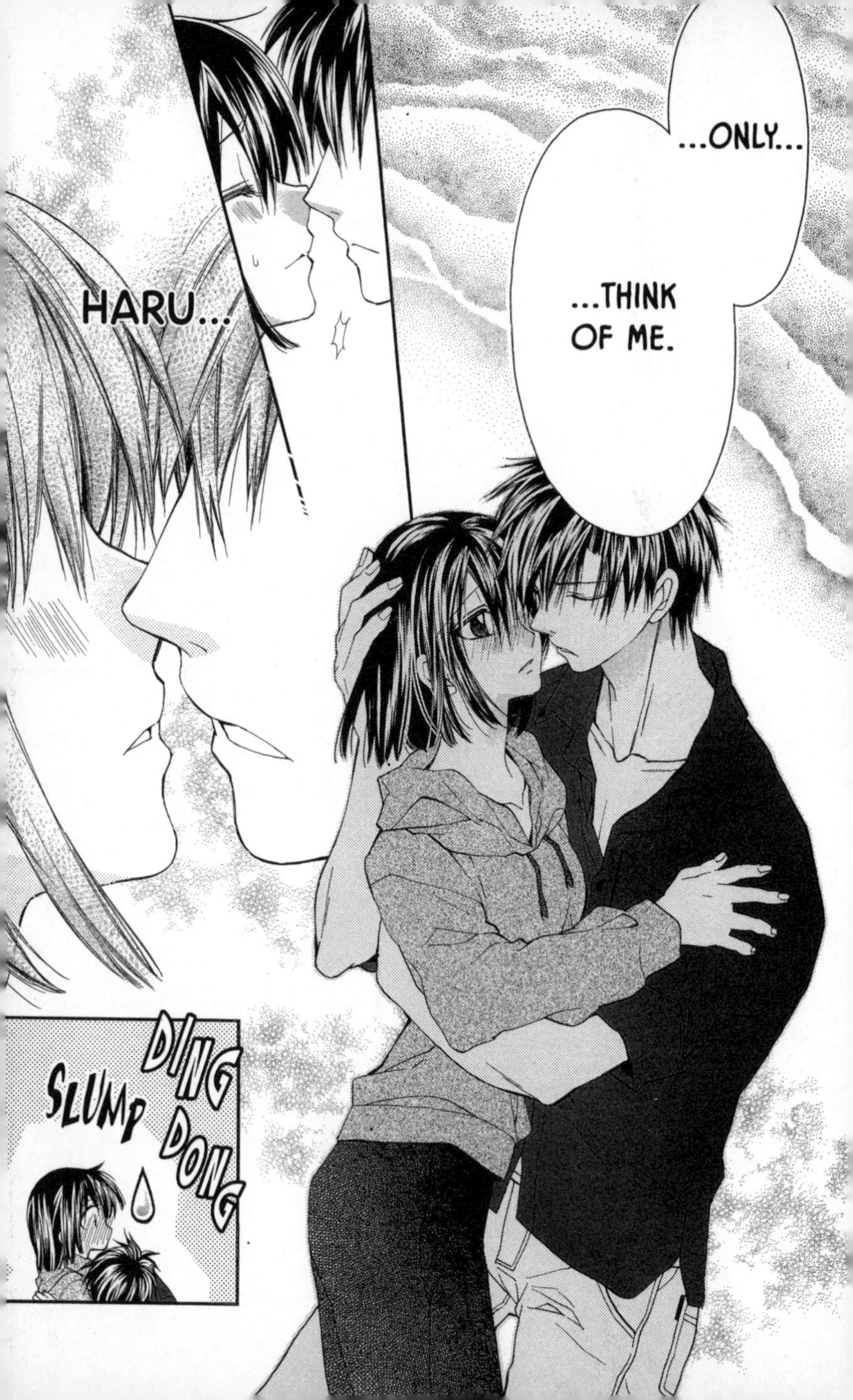
...ONLY...
...THINK OF ME.
HARU...
DING DONG
SLUMP

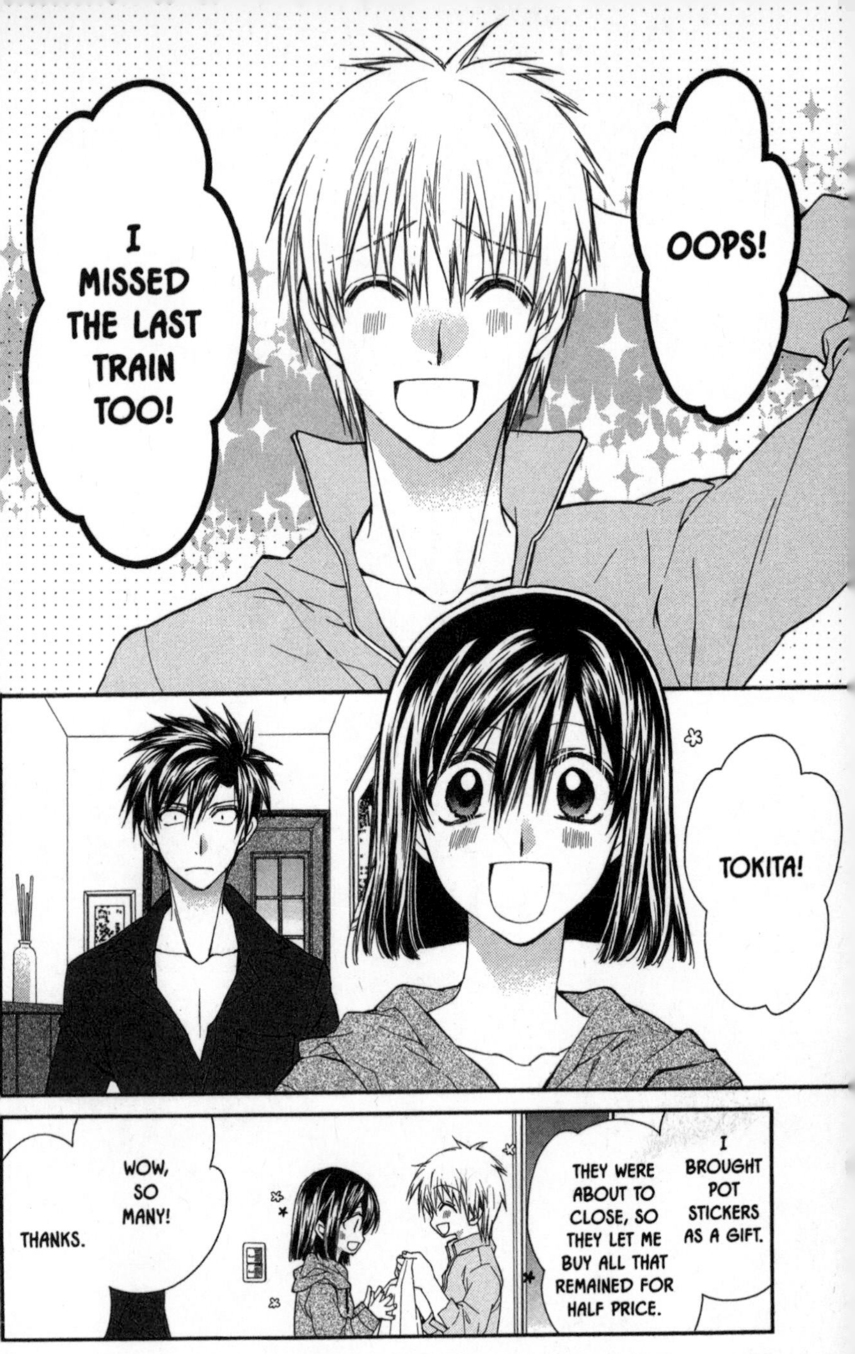
OOPS!
I MISSED THE LAST TRAIN TOO!
TOKITA!
I BROUGHT POT STICKERS AS A GIFT.
THEY WERE ABOUT TO CLOSE, SO THEY LET ME BUY ALL THAT REMAINED FOR HALF PRICE.
WOW, SO MANY!
THANKS.

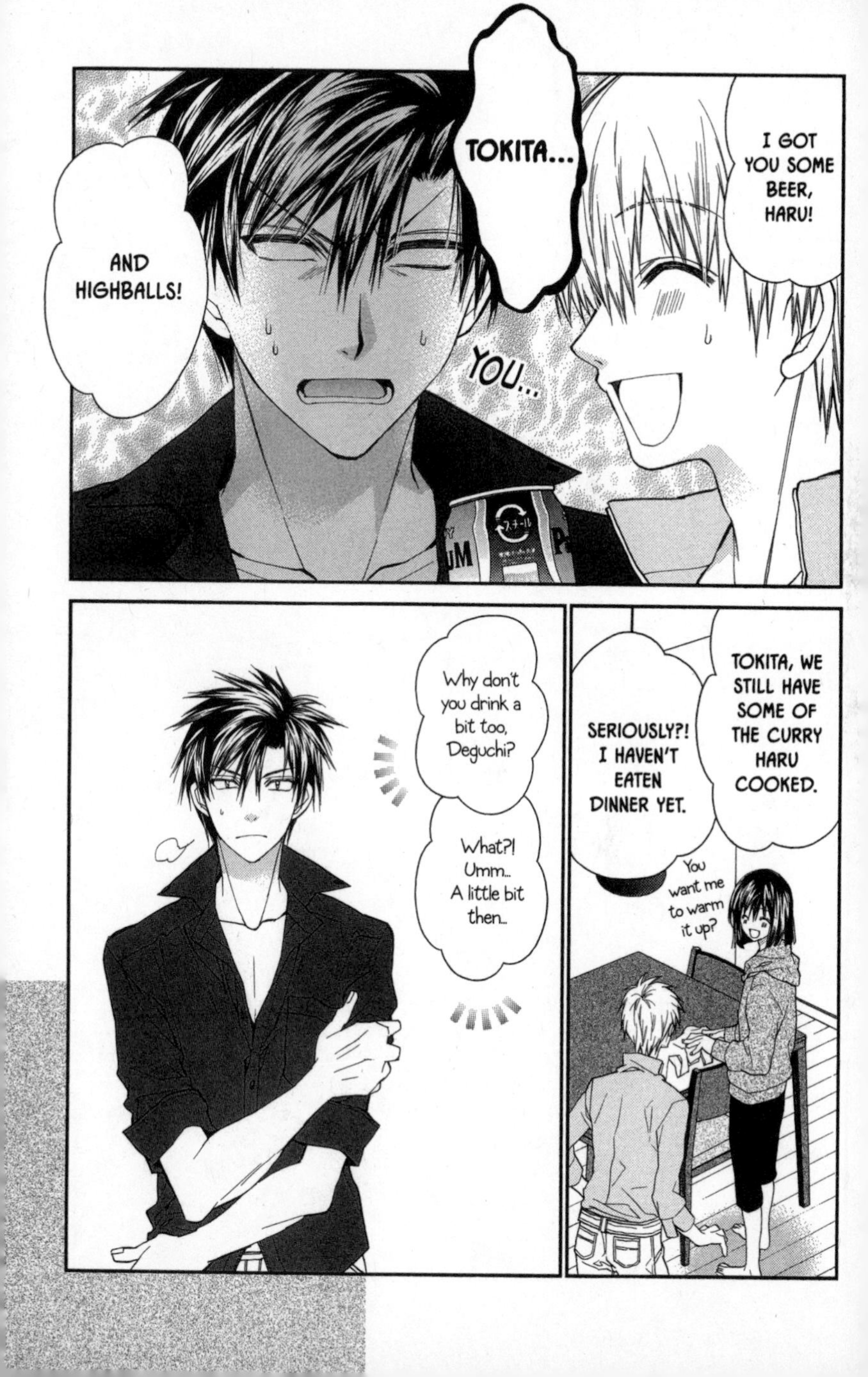
I GOT YOU SOME BEER, HARU!
TOKITA...
YOU...
AND HIGHBALLS!
TOKITA, WE STILL HAVE SOME OF THE CURRY HARU COOKED.
SERIOUSLY?! I HAVEN'T EATEN DINNER YET.
You want me to warm it up?
Why don't you drink a bit too, Deguchi?
What?! Umm... A little bit then...

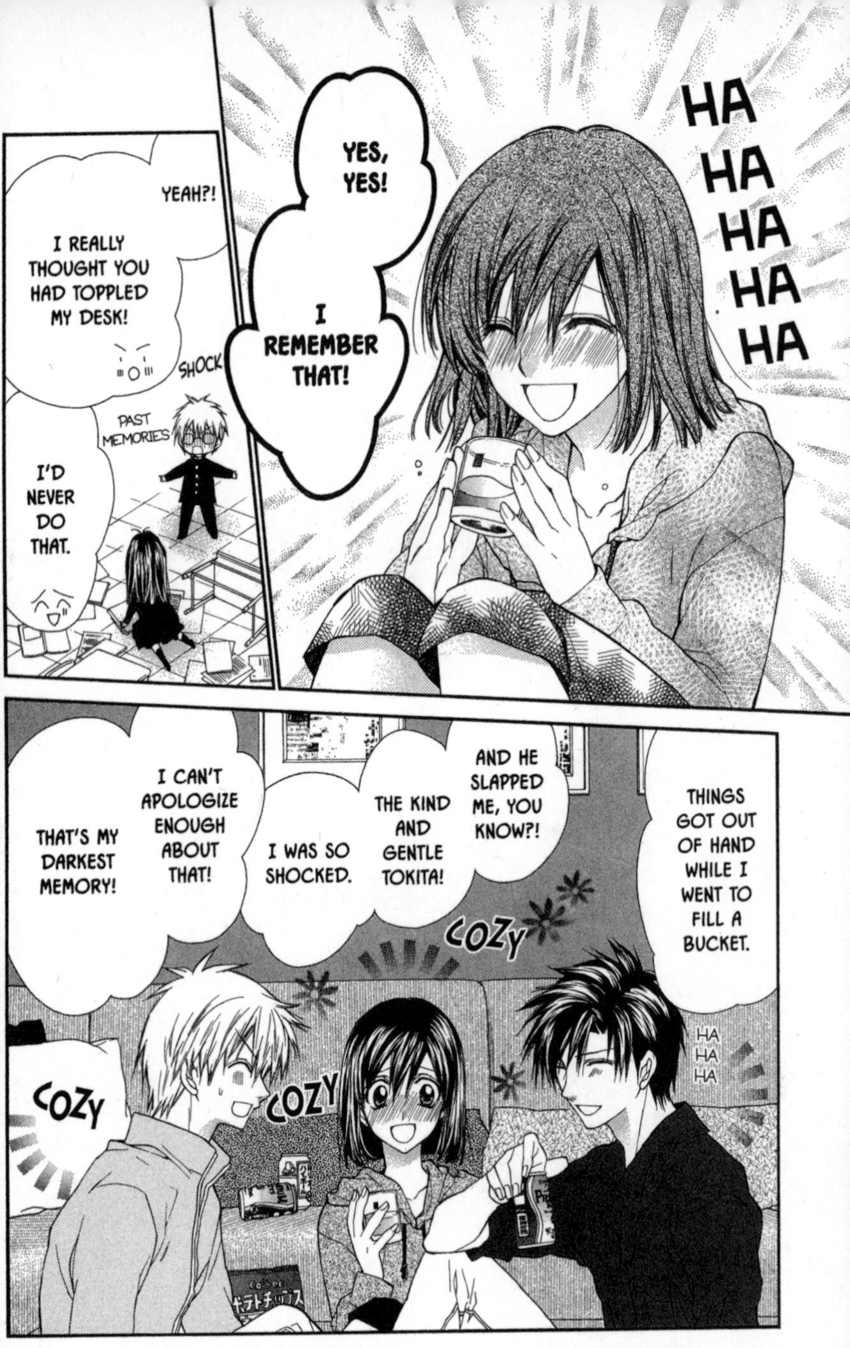
HA HA HA HA HA
YES, YES!
I REMEMBER THAT!
YEAH?!
I REALLY THOUGHT YOU HAD TOPPLED MY DESK!
SHOCK
PAST MEMORIES
I'D NEVER DO THAT.
THINGS GOT OUT OF HAND WHILE I WENT TO FILL A BUCKET.
AND HE SLAPPED ME, YOU KNOW?!
THE KIND AND GENTLE TOKITA!
I WAS SO SHOCKED.
I CAN'T APOLOGIZE ENOUGH ABOUT THAT!
THAT'S MY DARKEST MEMORY!
COZY
HA HA HA
COZY
COZY

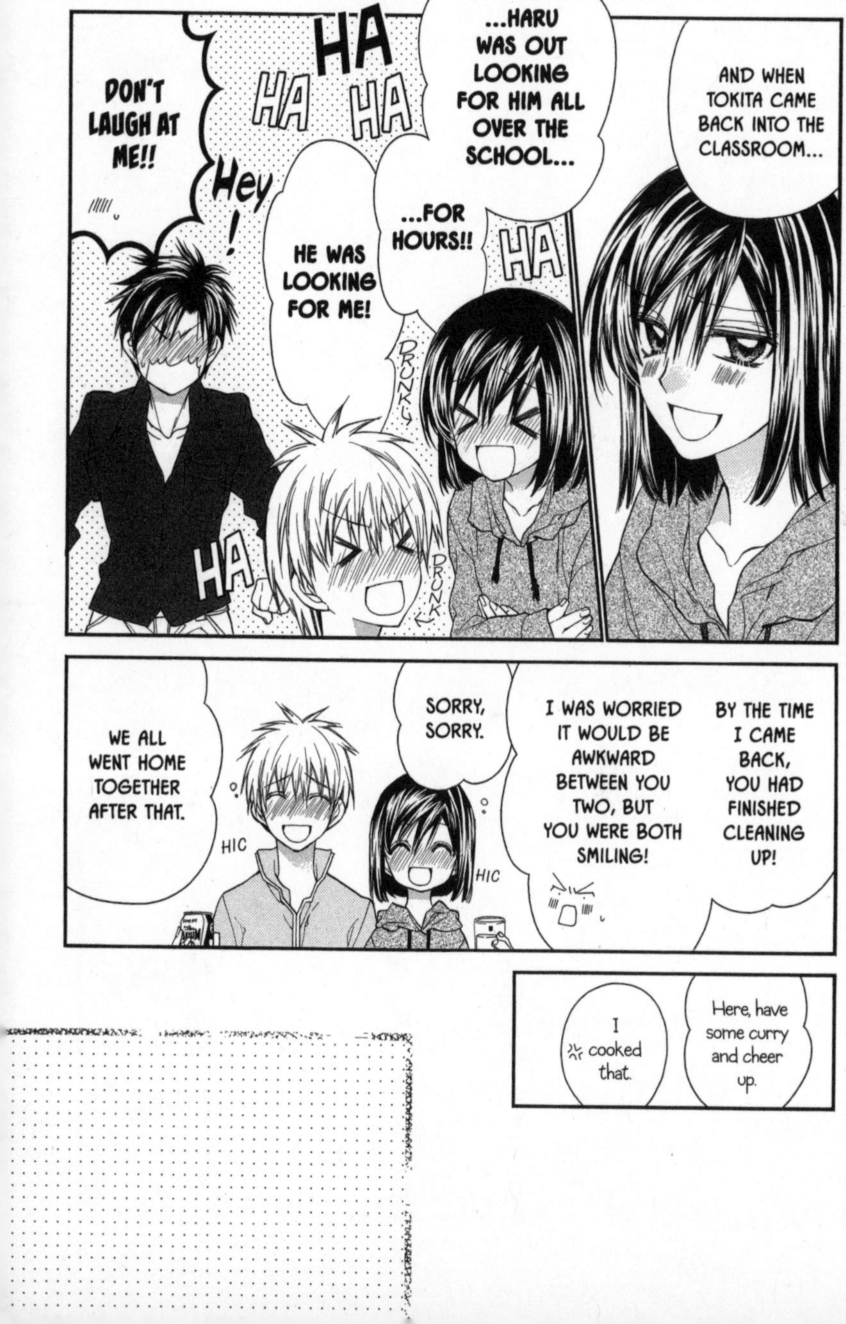
AND WHEN TOKITA CAME BACK INTO THE CLASSROOM...
...HARU WAS OUT LOOKING FOR HIM ALL OVER THE SCHOOL...
HA
HA HA
HA
...FOR HOURS!!
HE WAS LOOKING FOR ME!
DRUNK
Hey!
DON'T LAUGH AT ME!!
HA
DRUNK
BY THE TIME I CAME BACK, YOU HAD FINISHED CLEANING UP!
I WAS WORRIED IT WOULD BE AWKWARD BETWEEN YOU TWO, BUT YOU WERE BOTH SMILING!
SORRY, SORRY.
HIC
HIC
WE ALL WENT HOME TOGETHER AFTER THAT.
Here, have some curry and cheer up.
I cooked that.

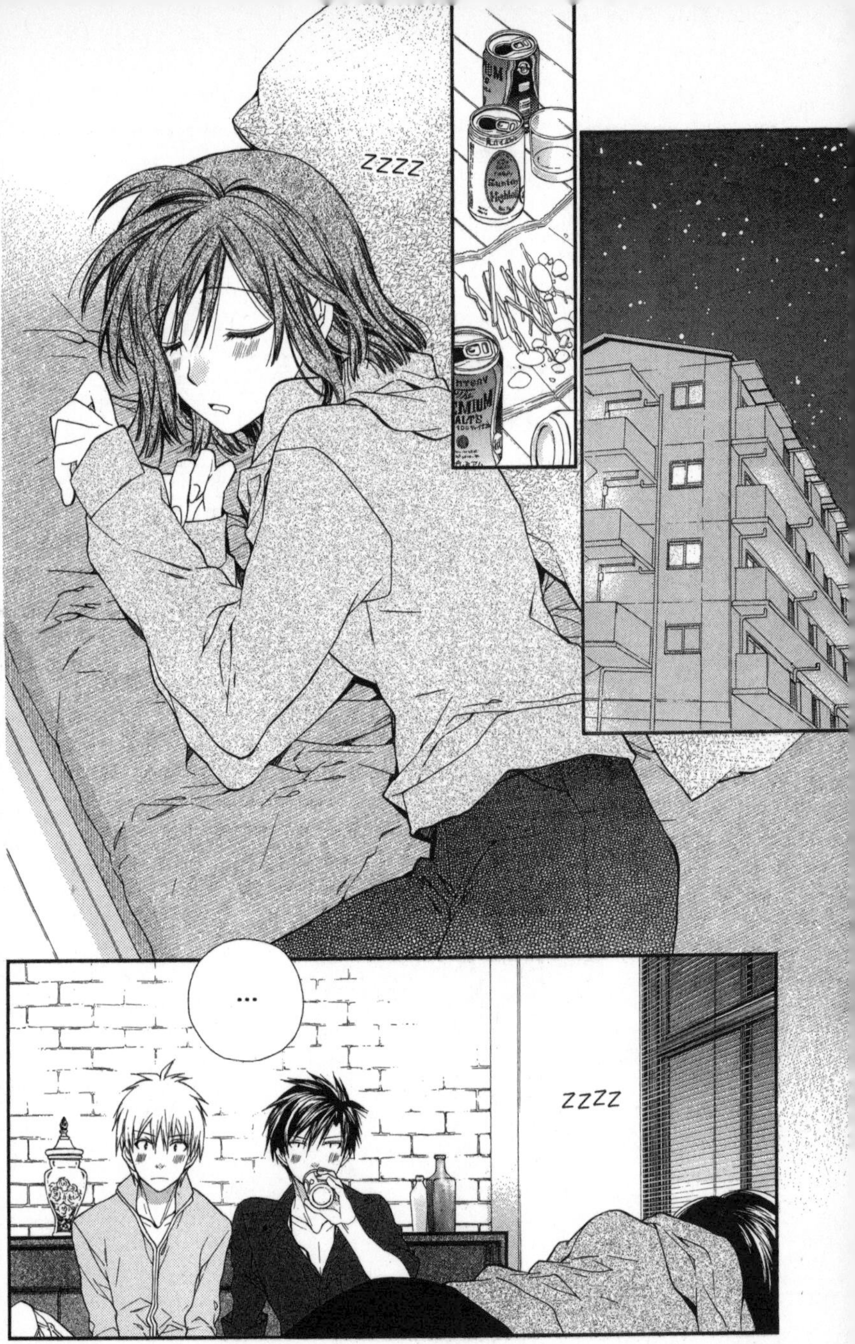
ZZZZ
ZZZZ
...

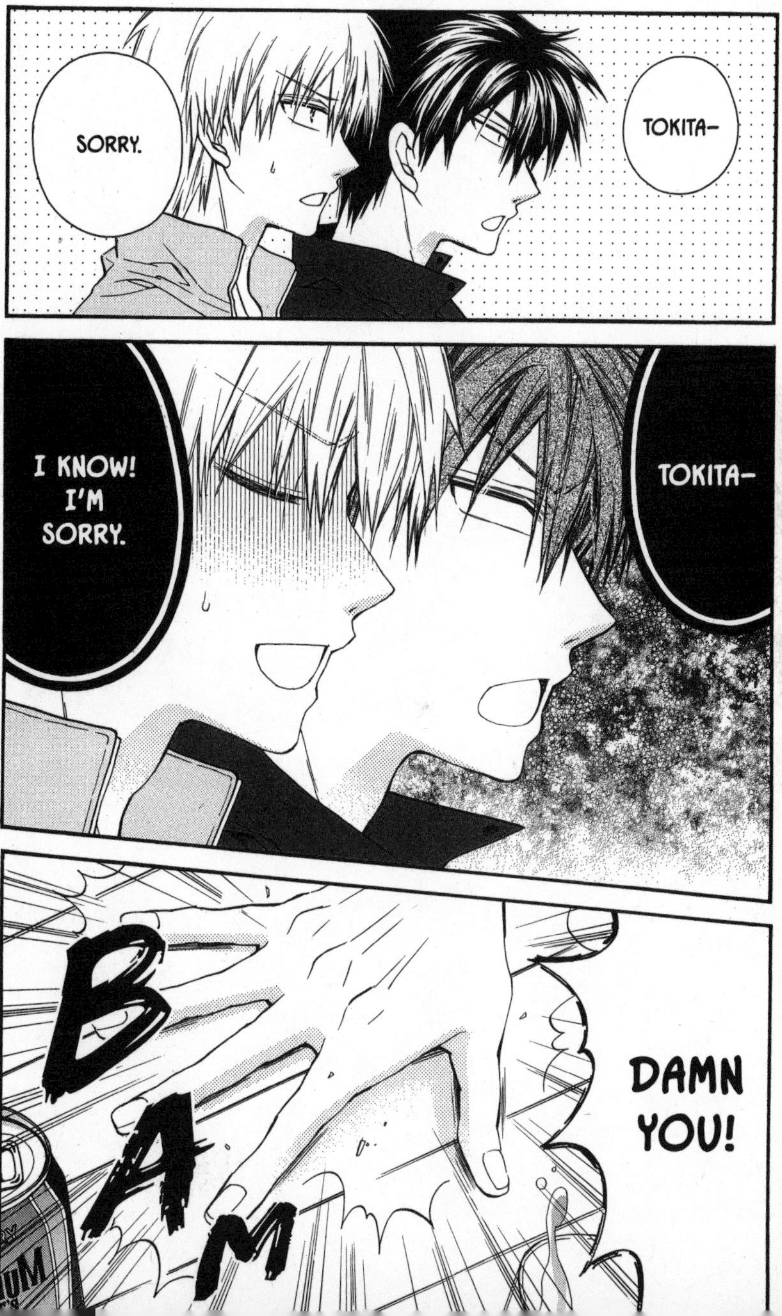
TOKITA-
SORRY.
TOKITA-
I KNOW! I'M SORRY.
DAMN YOU!
BAM

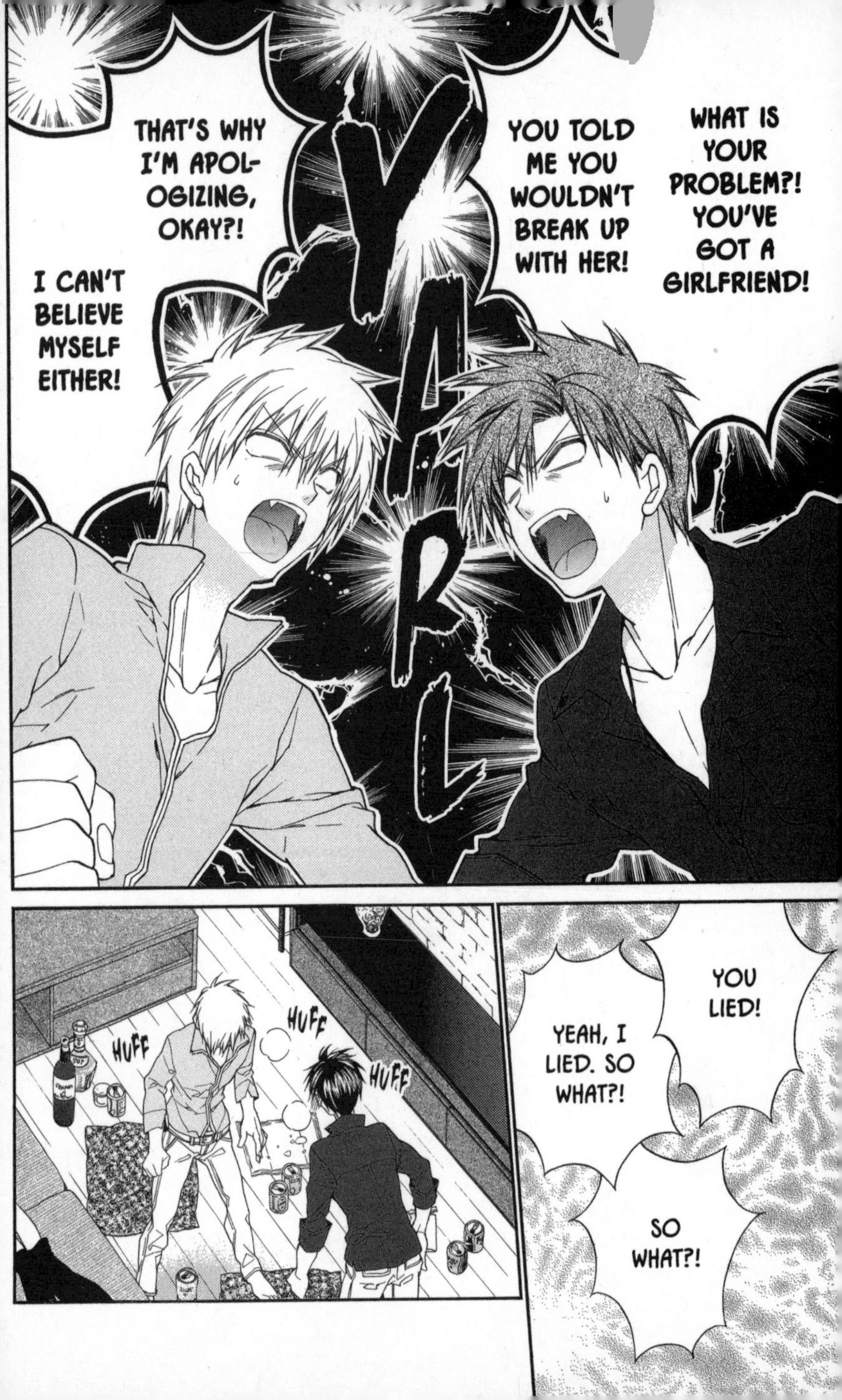
WHAT IS YOUR PROBLEM?! YOU'VE GOT A GIRLFRIEND!
YOU TOLD ME YOU WOULDN'T BREAK UP WITH HER!
THAT'S WHY I'M APOL-OGIZING, OKAY?!
I CAN'T BELIEVE MYSELF EITHER!
YOU LIED!
YEAH, I LIED. SO WHAT?!
SO WHAT?!
HUFF
HUFF
HUFF

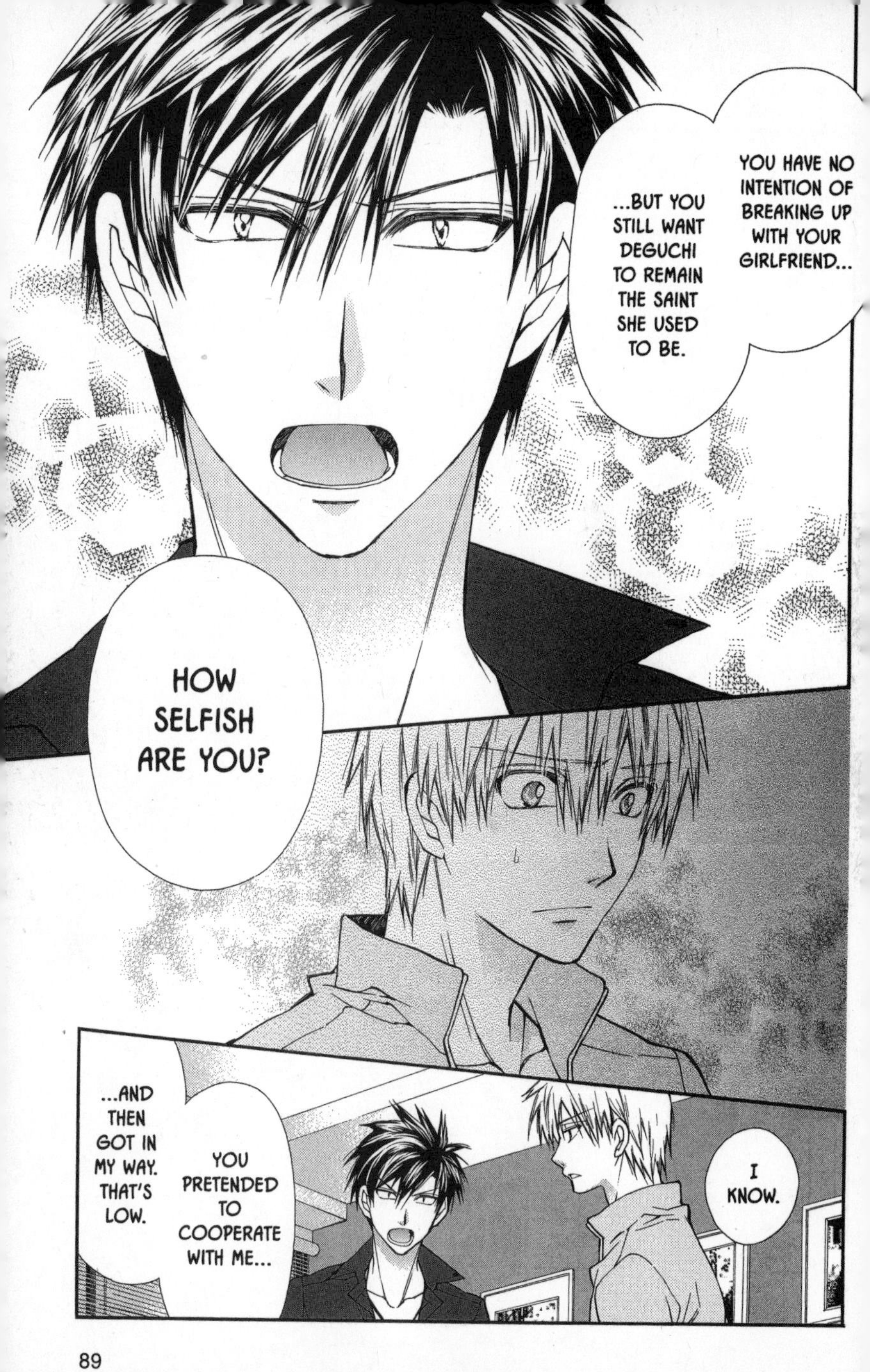
YOU HAVE NO INTENTION OF BREAKING UP WITH YOUR GIRLFRIEND...
...BUT YOU STILL WANT DEGUCHI TO REMAIN THE SAINT SHE USED TO BE.
HOW SELFISH ARE YOU?
I KNOW.
YOU PRETENDED TO COOPERATE WITH ME...
...AND THEN GOT IN MY WAY. THAT'S LOW.

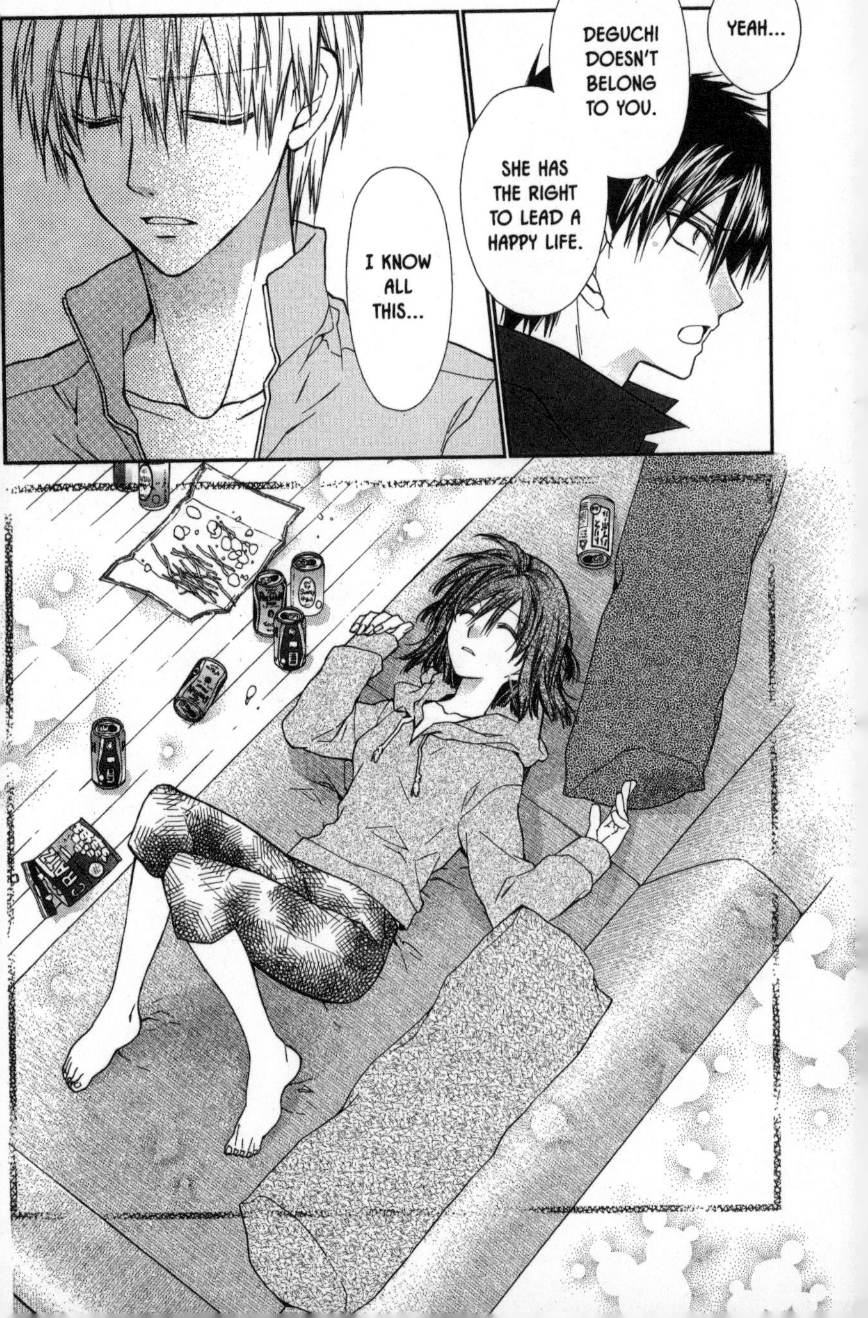
YEAH...
DEGUCHI DOESN'T BELONG TO YOU.
SHE HAS THE RIGHT TO LEAD A HAPPY LIFE.
I KNOW ALL THIS...

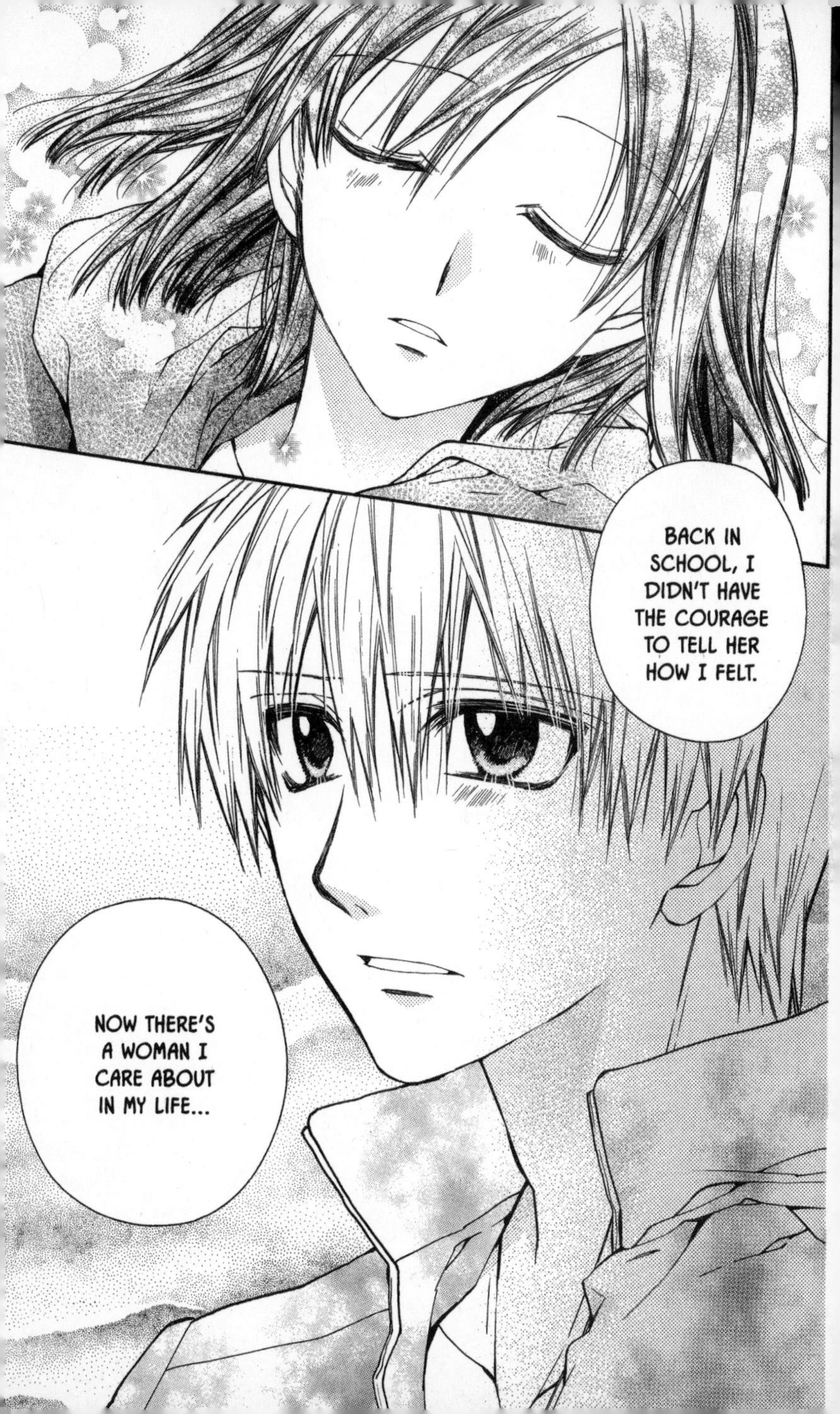
BACK IN SCHOOL, I DIDN'T HAVE THE COURAGE TO TELL HER HOW I FELT.
NOW THERE'S A WOMAN I CARE ABOUT IN MY LIFE...

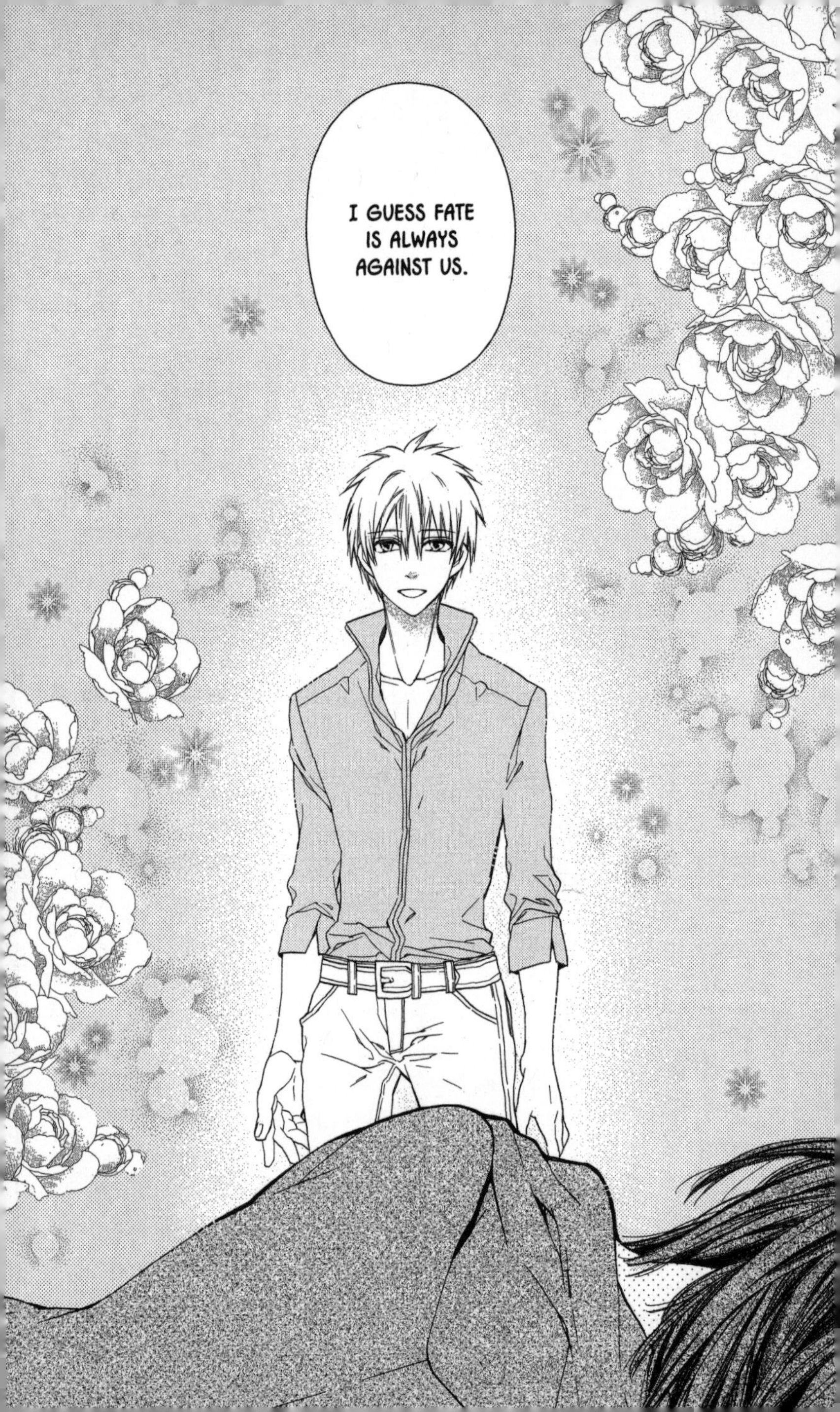
I GUESS FATE IS ALWAYS AGAINST US.

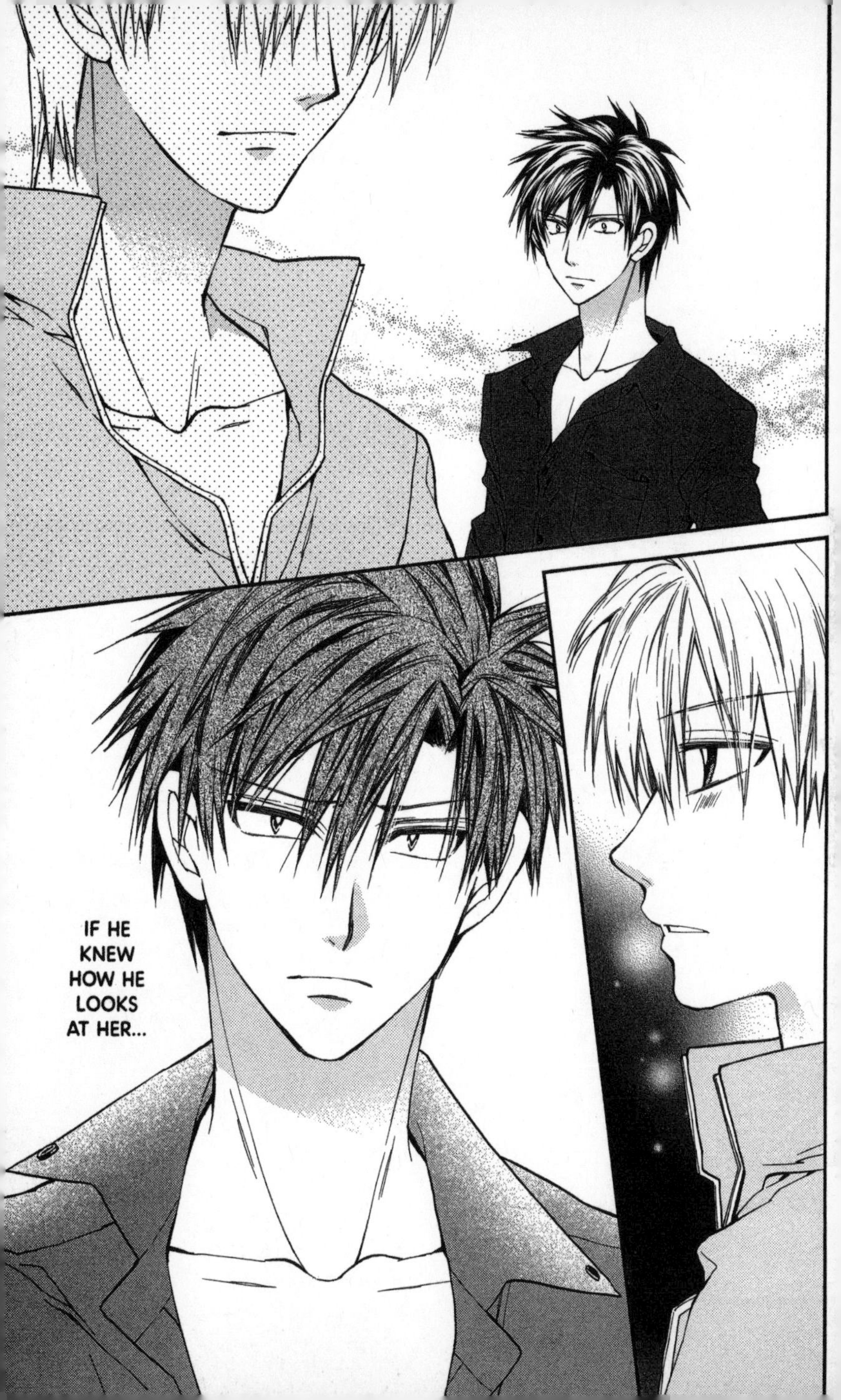
IF HE KNEW HOW HE LOOKS AT HER...

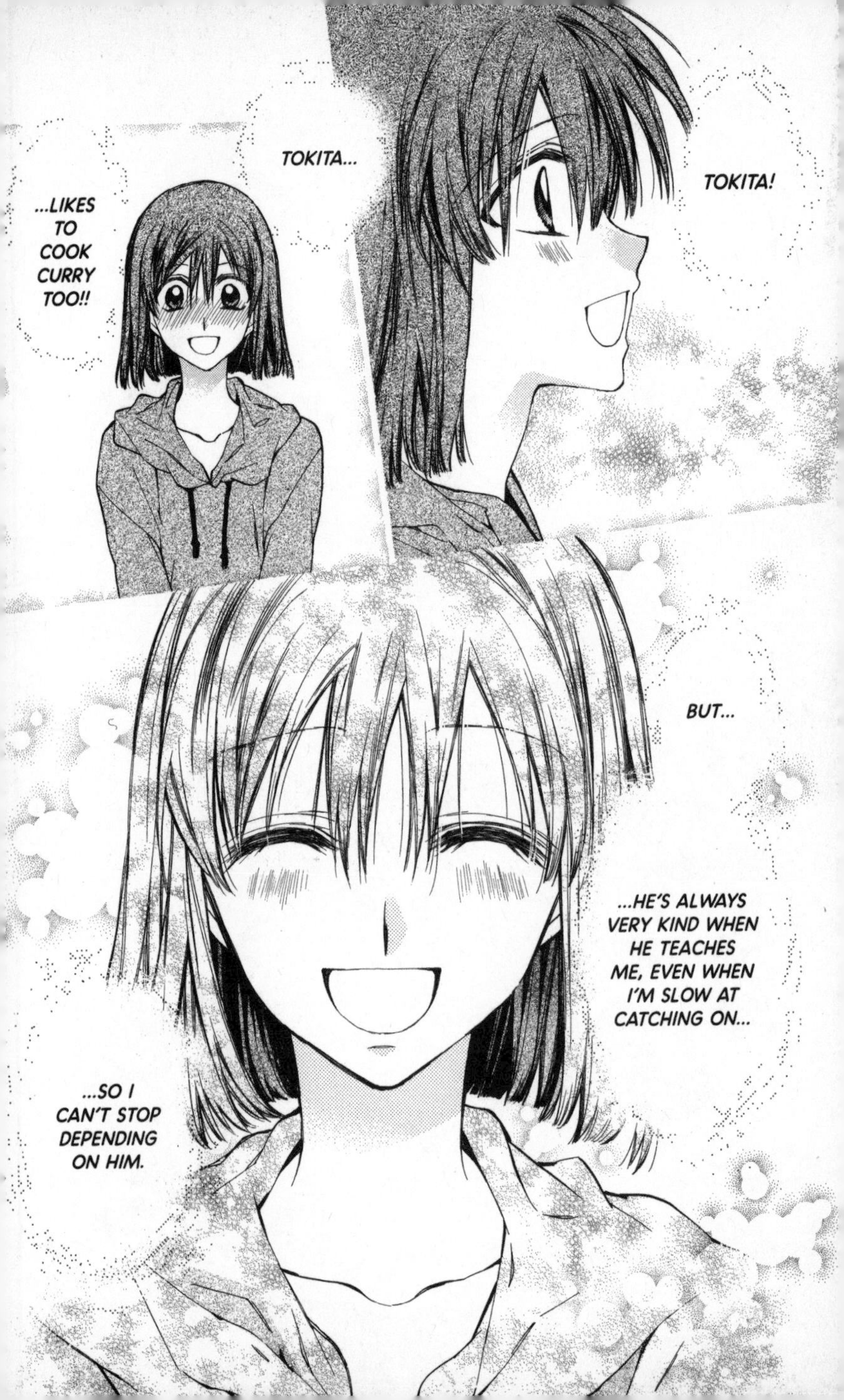
TOKITA!
TOKITA...
...LIKES TO COOK CURRY TOO!!
BUT...
...HE'S ALWAYS VERY KIND WHEN HE TEACHES ME, EVEN WHEN I'M SLOW AT CATCHING ON...
...SO I CAN'T STOP DEPENDING ON HIM.

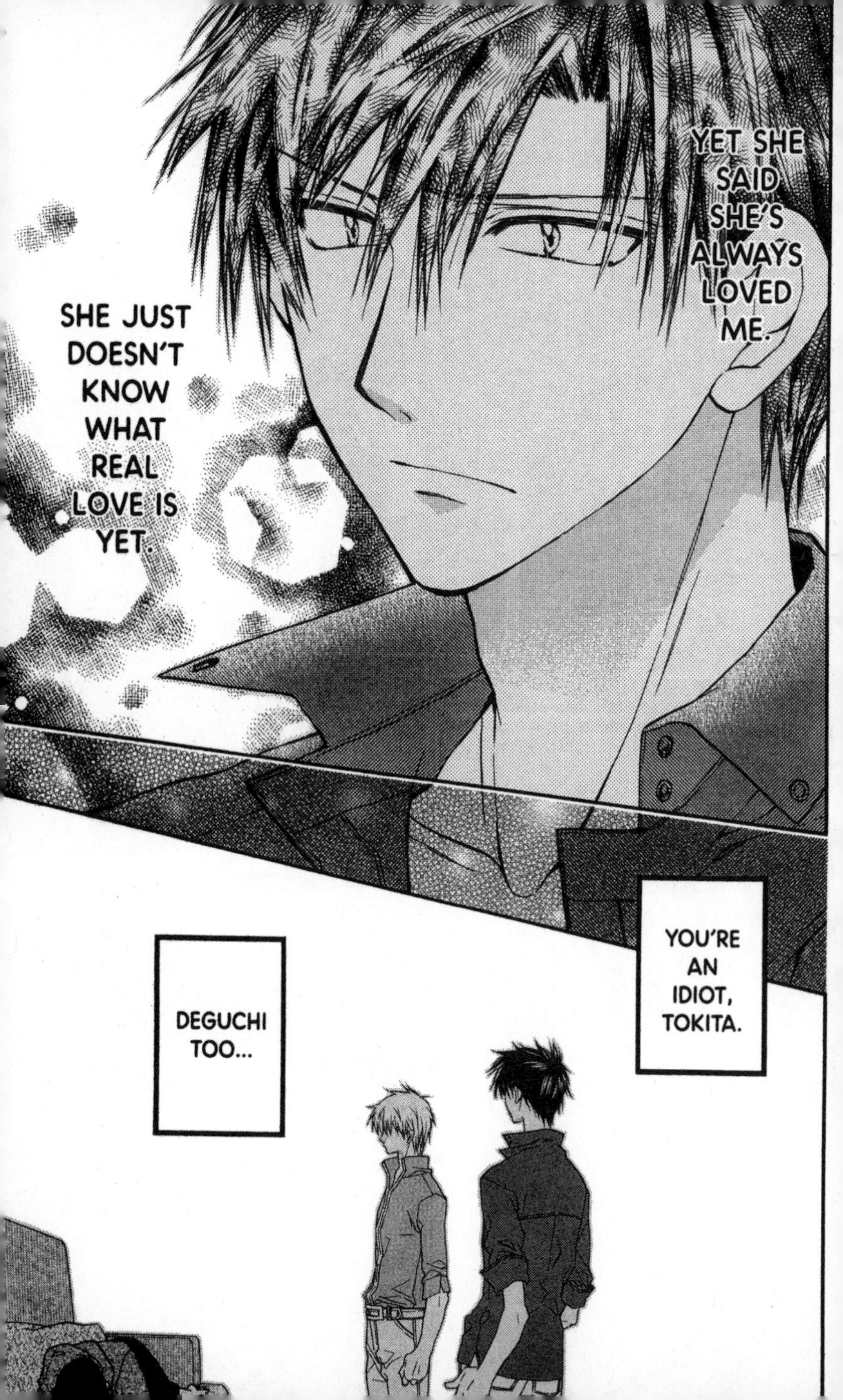
YET SHE SAID SHE'S ALWAYS LOVED ME.
SHE JUST DOESN'T KNOW WHAT REAL LOVE IS YET.
YOU'RE AN IDIOT, TOKITA.
DEGUCHI TOO...

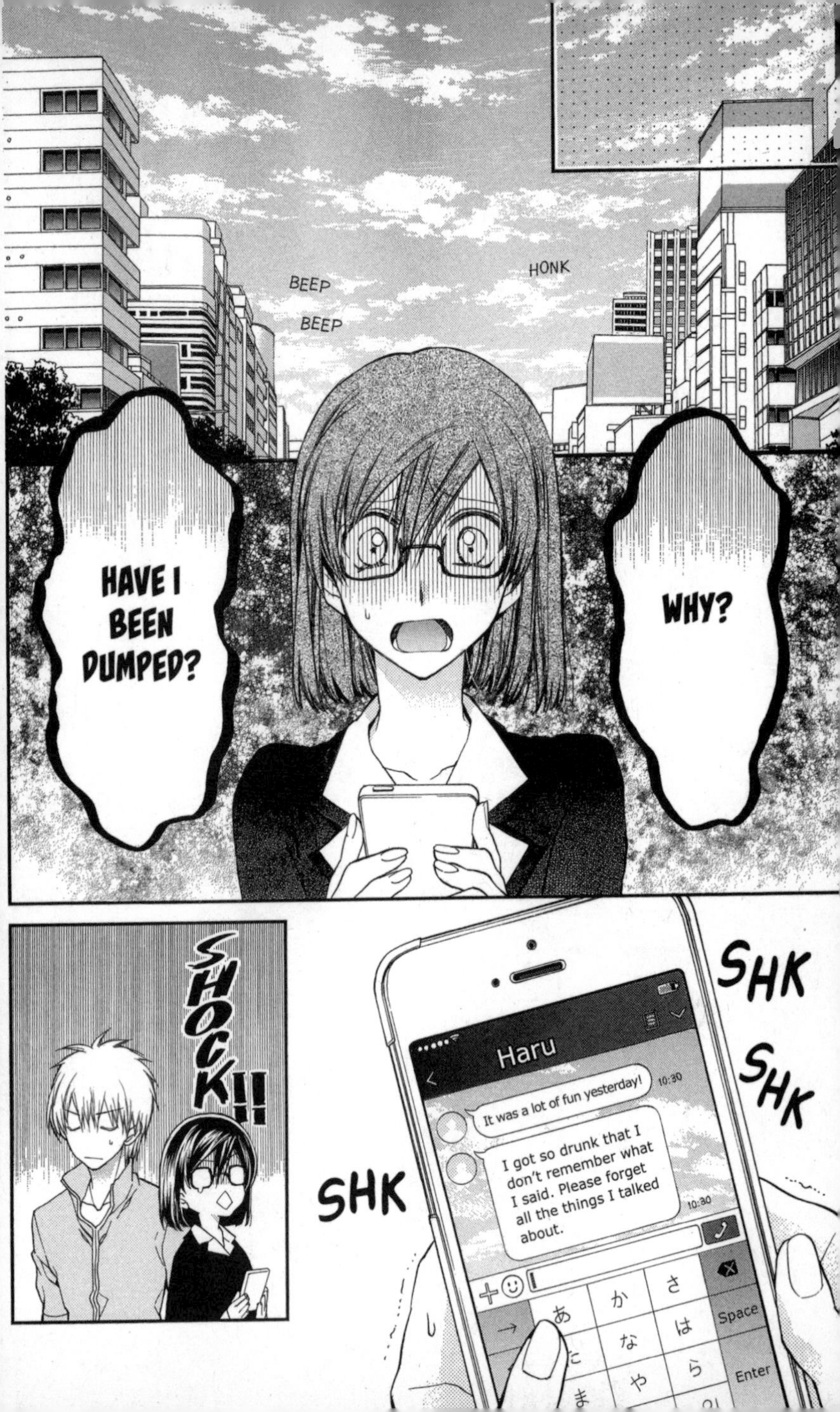
HONK
BEEP
BEEP
WHY?
HAVE I BEEN DUMPED?
SHK
SHK
Haru
It was a lot of fun yesterday!
10:30
I got so drunk that I don't remember what I said. Please forget all the things I talked about.
10:30
あ か さ た な は ま や ら
Space
Enter
SHK
SHOCK!!

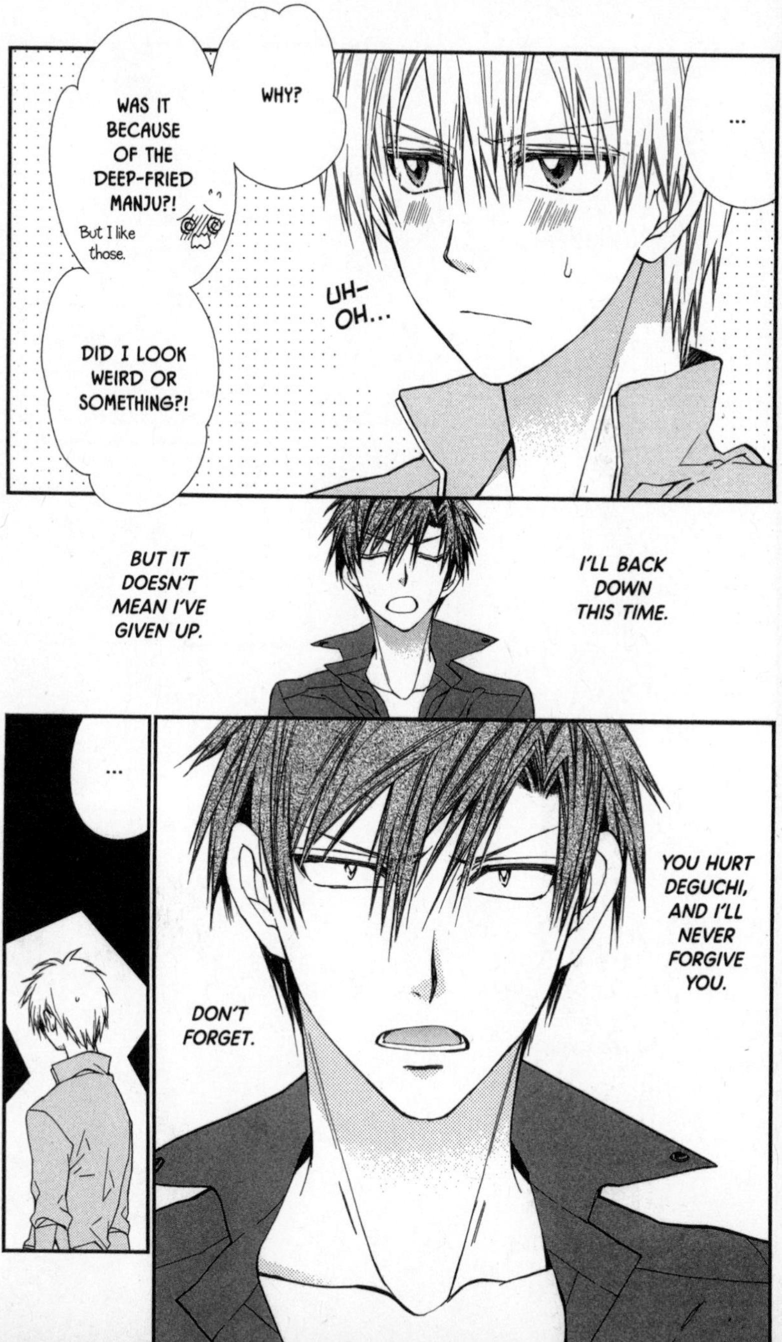
...
WHY?
WAS IT BECAUSE OF THE DEEP-FRIED MANJU?!
But I like those.
UH-OH...
DID I LOOK WEIRD OR SOMETHING?!
I'LL BACK DOWN THIS TIME.
BUT IT DOESN'T MEAN I'VE GIVEN UP.
YOU HURT DEGUCHI, AND I'LL NEVER FORGIVE YOU.
DON'T FORGET.
...

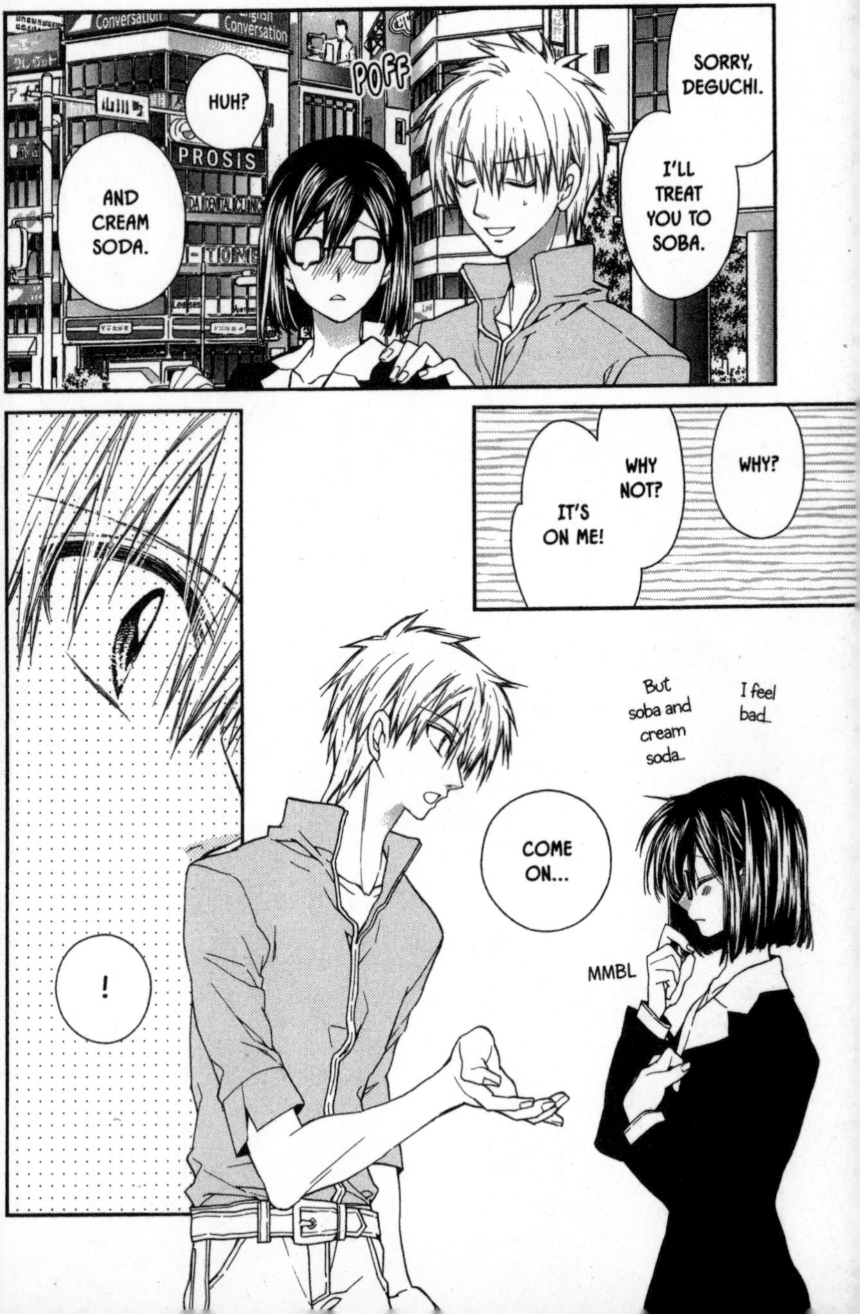
SORRY, DEGUCHI.
I'LL TREAT YOU TO SOBA.
POFF
HUH?
AND CREAM SODA.
English Conversation
Conversation
PROSIS
WHY?
WHY NOT? IT'S ON ME!
I feel bad...
But soba and cream soda...
COME ON...
MMBL
!

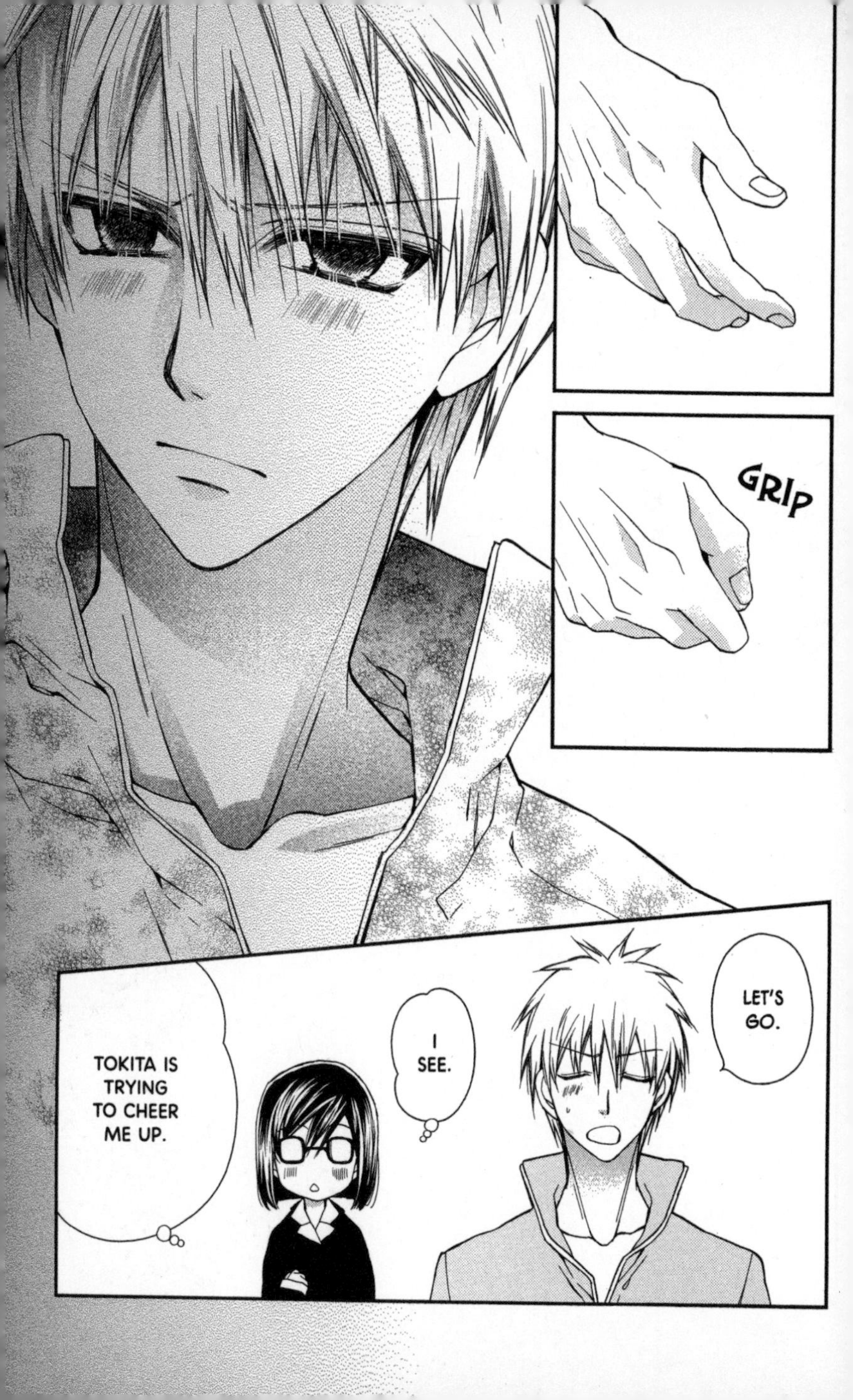
GRIP
LET'S GO.
I SEE.
TOKITA IS TRYING TO CHEER ME UP.

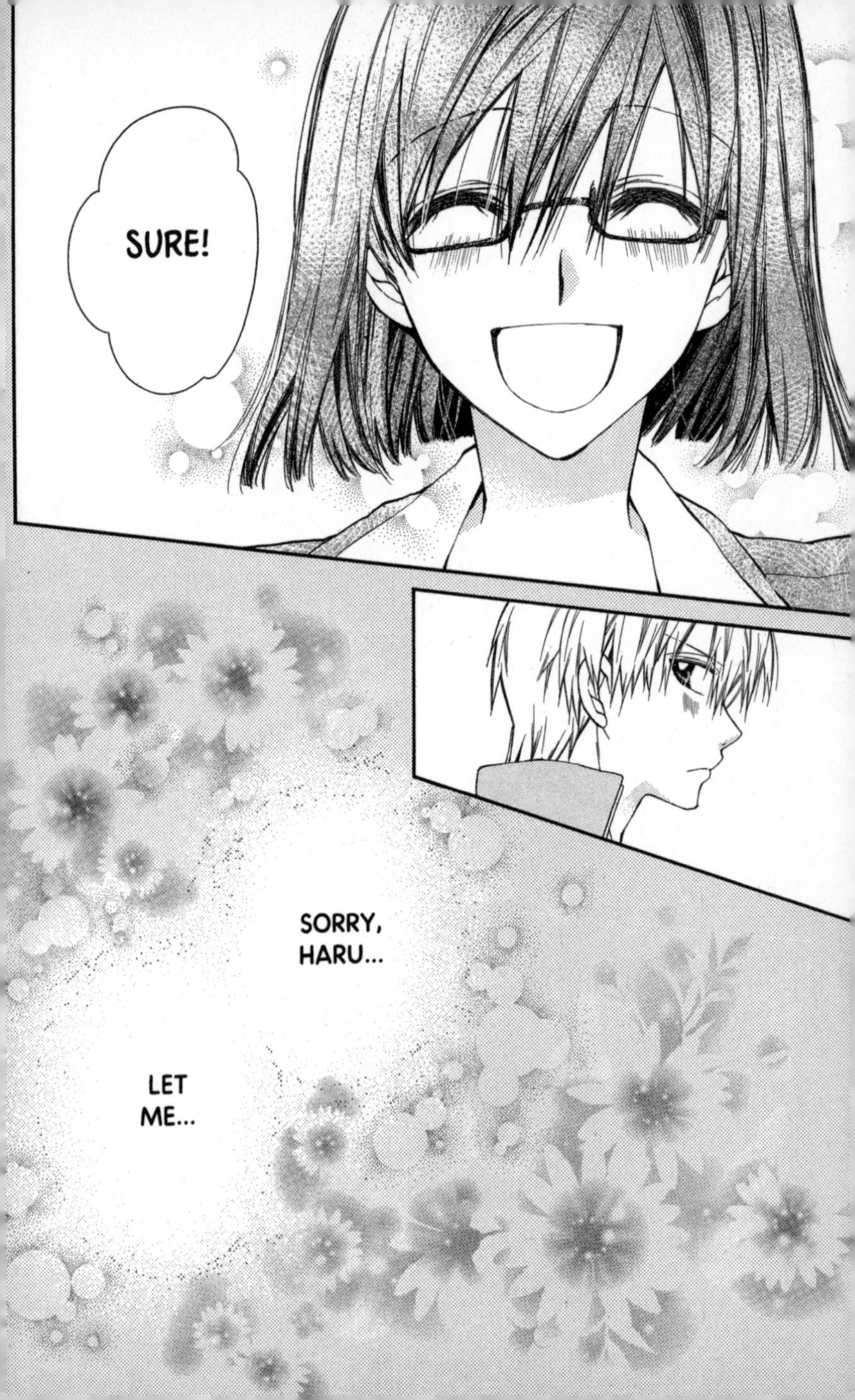
SURE!
SORRY, HARU...
LET ME...

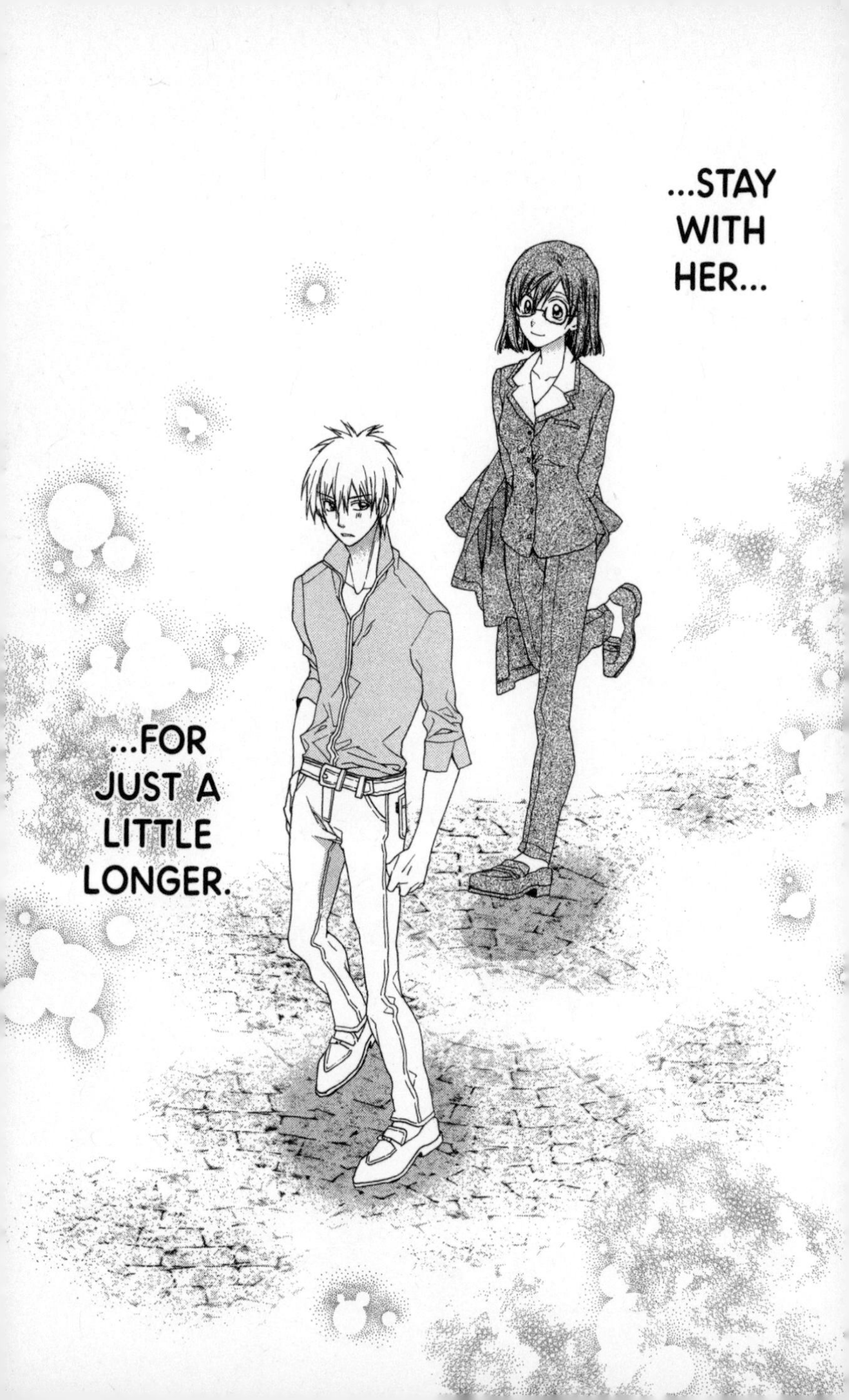
...STAY WITH HER...
...FOR JUST A LITTLE LONGER.

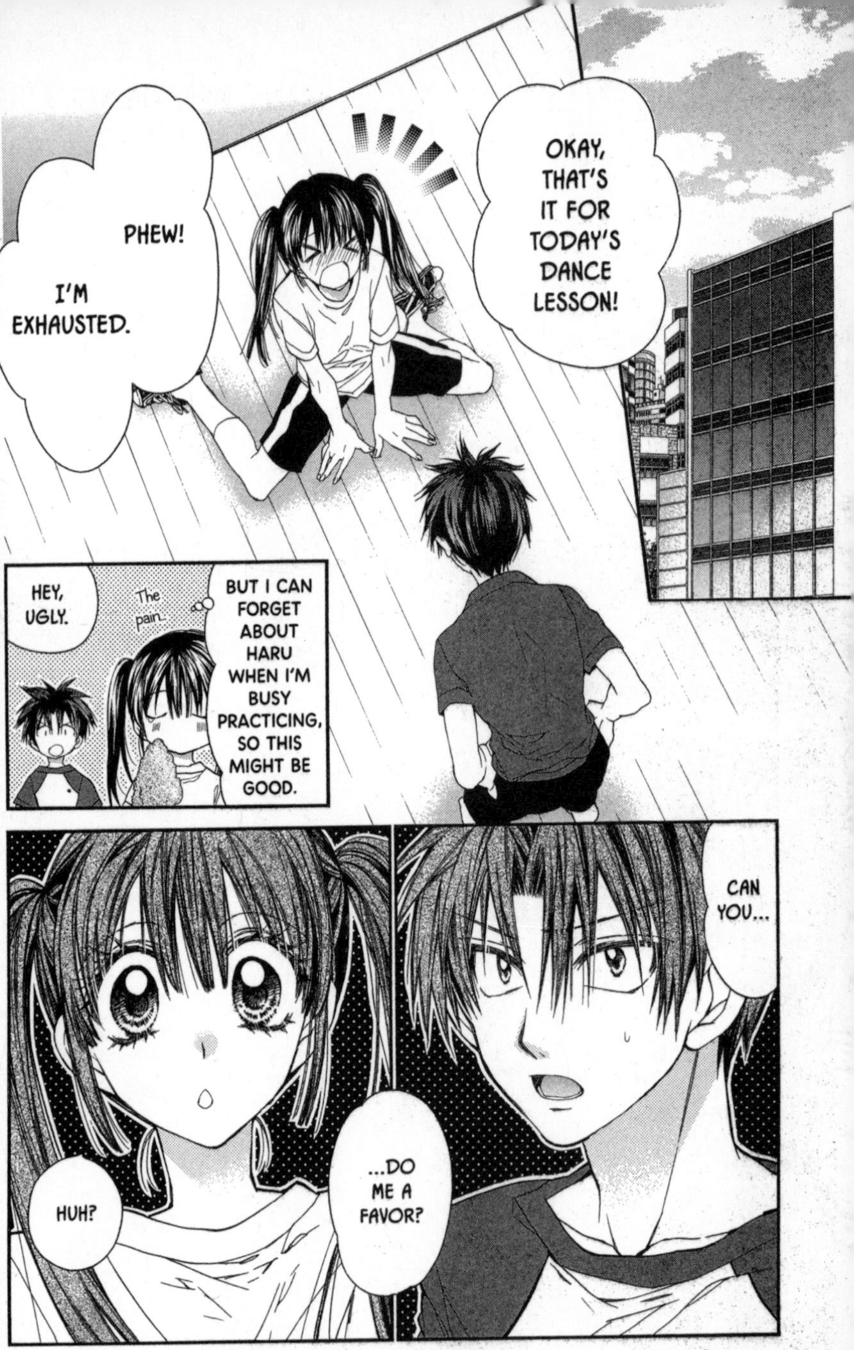
OKAY, THAT'S IT FOR TODAY'S DANCE LESSON!
PHEW!
I'M EXHAUSTED.
BUT I CAN FORGET ABOUT HARU WHEN I'M BUSY PRACTICING, SO THIS MIGHT BE GOOD.
The pain..
HEY, UGLY.
CAN YOU...
...DO ME A FAVOR?
HUH?

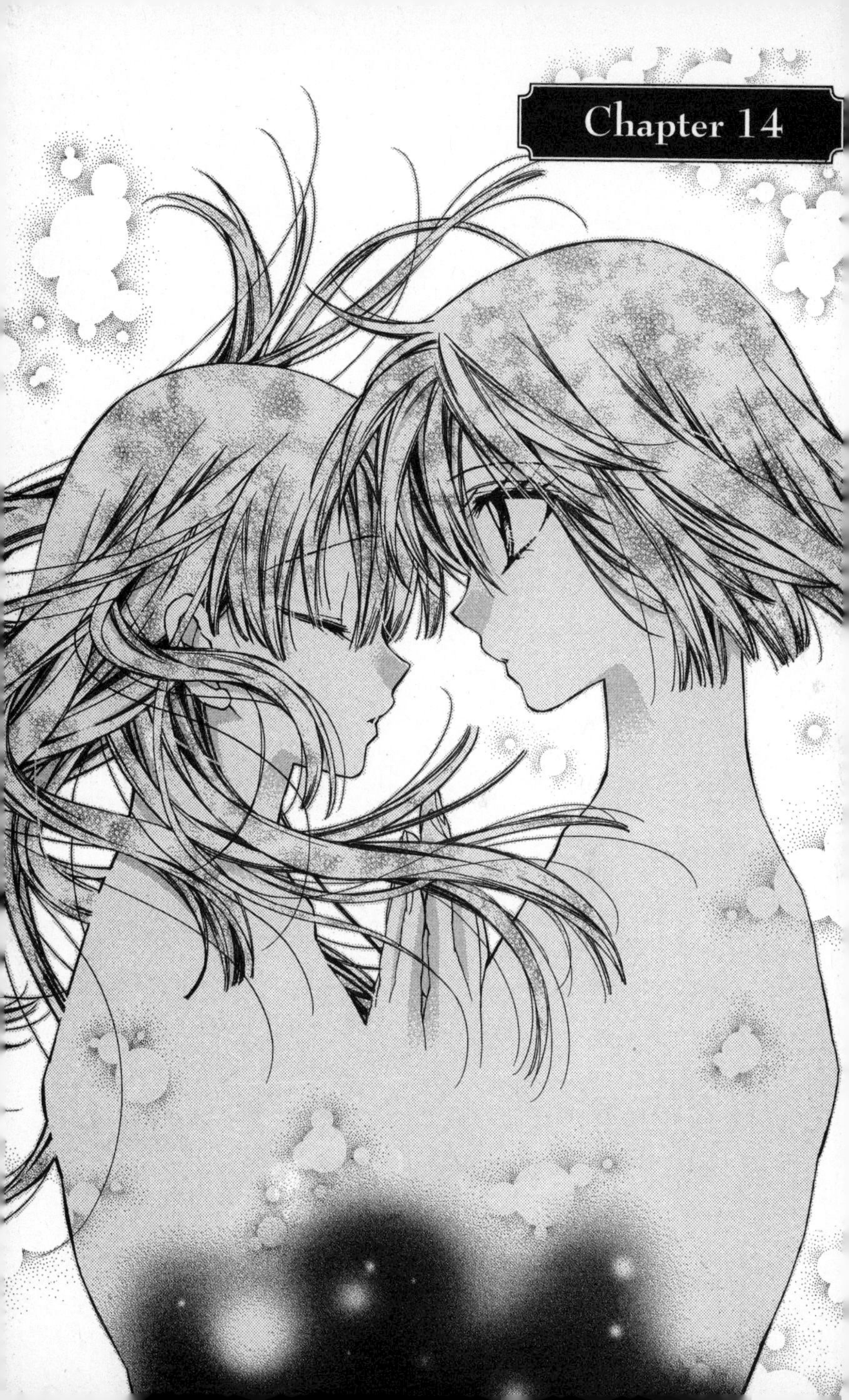
Chapter 14

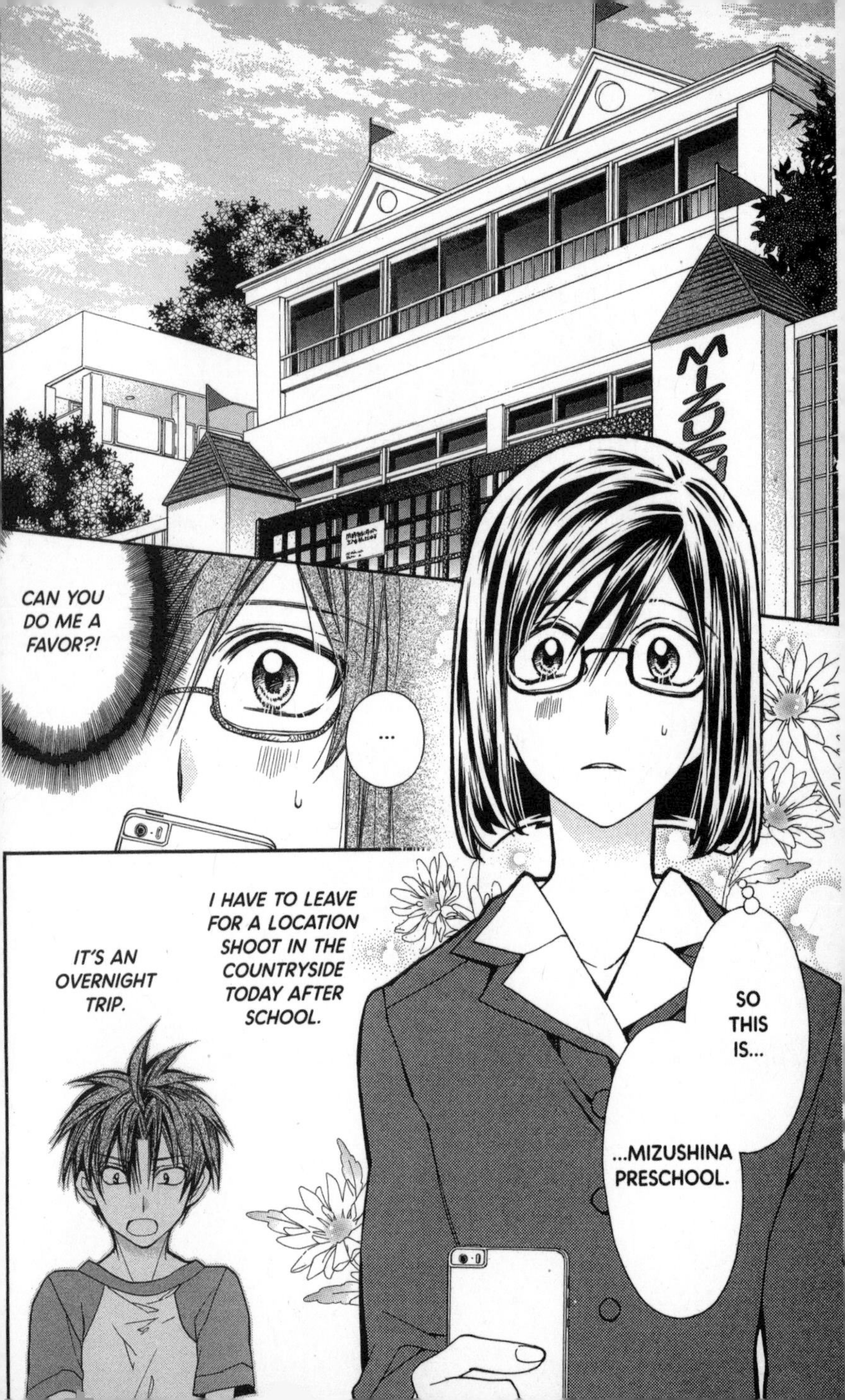
SO THIS IS...
...MIZUSHINA PRESCHOOL.
CAN YOU DO ME A FAVOR?!
...
I HAVE TO LEAVE FOR A LOCATION SHOOT IN THE COUNTRYSIDE TODAY AFTER SCHOOL.
IT'S AN OVERNIGHT TRIP.

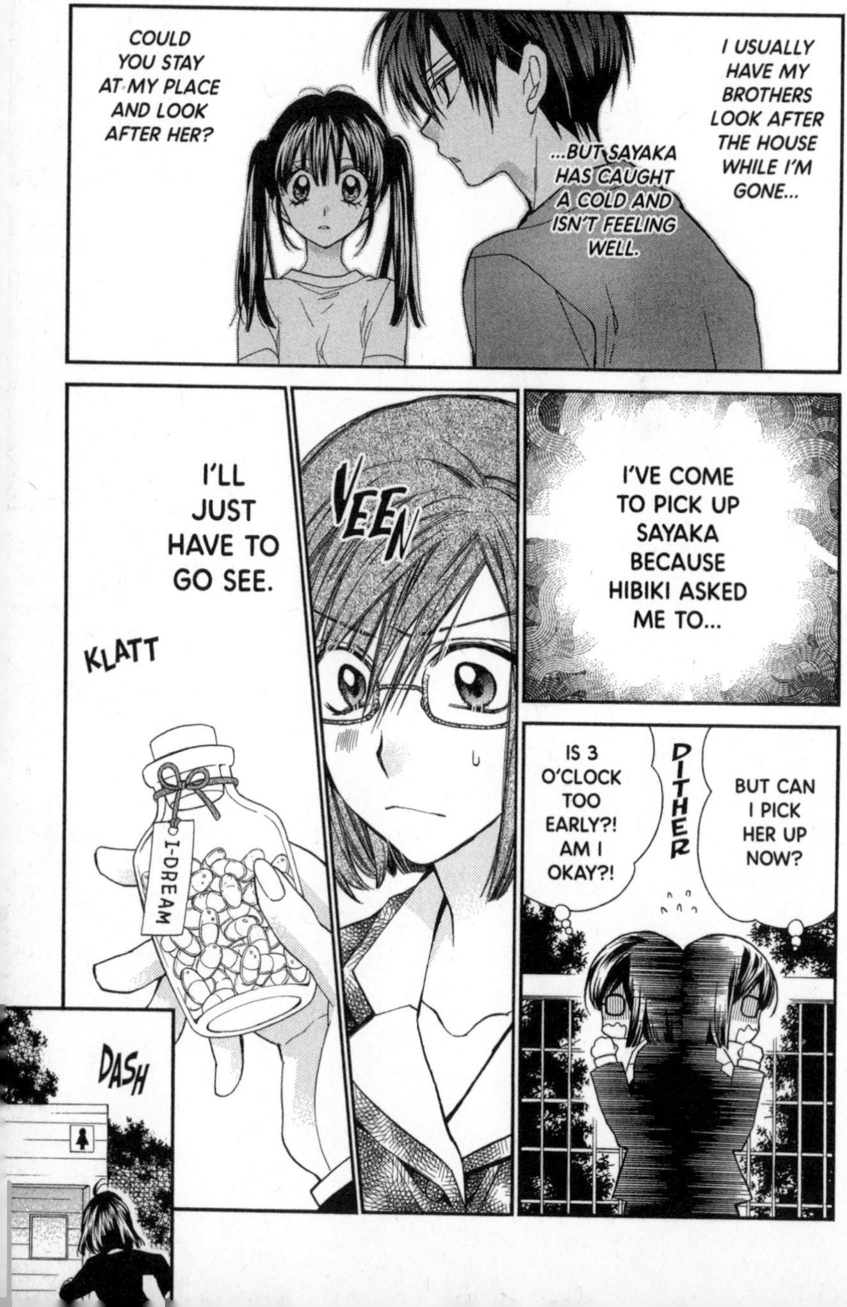
I USUALLY HAVE MY BROTHERS LOOK AFTER THE HOUSE WHILE I'M GONE...
...BUT SAYAKA HAS CAUGHT A COLD AND ISN'T FEELING WELL.
COULD YOU STAY AT MY PLACE AND LOOK AFTER HER?
I'VE COME TO PICK UP SAYAKA BECAUSE HIBIKI ASKED ME TO...
BUT CAN I PICK HER UP NOW?
DITHER
IS 3 O'CLOCK TOO EARLY?! AM I OKAY?!
VEEN
I'LL JUST HAVE TO GO SEE.
KLATT
I-DREAM
DASH

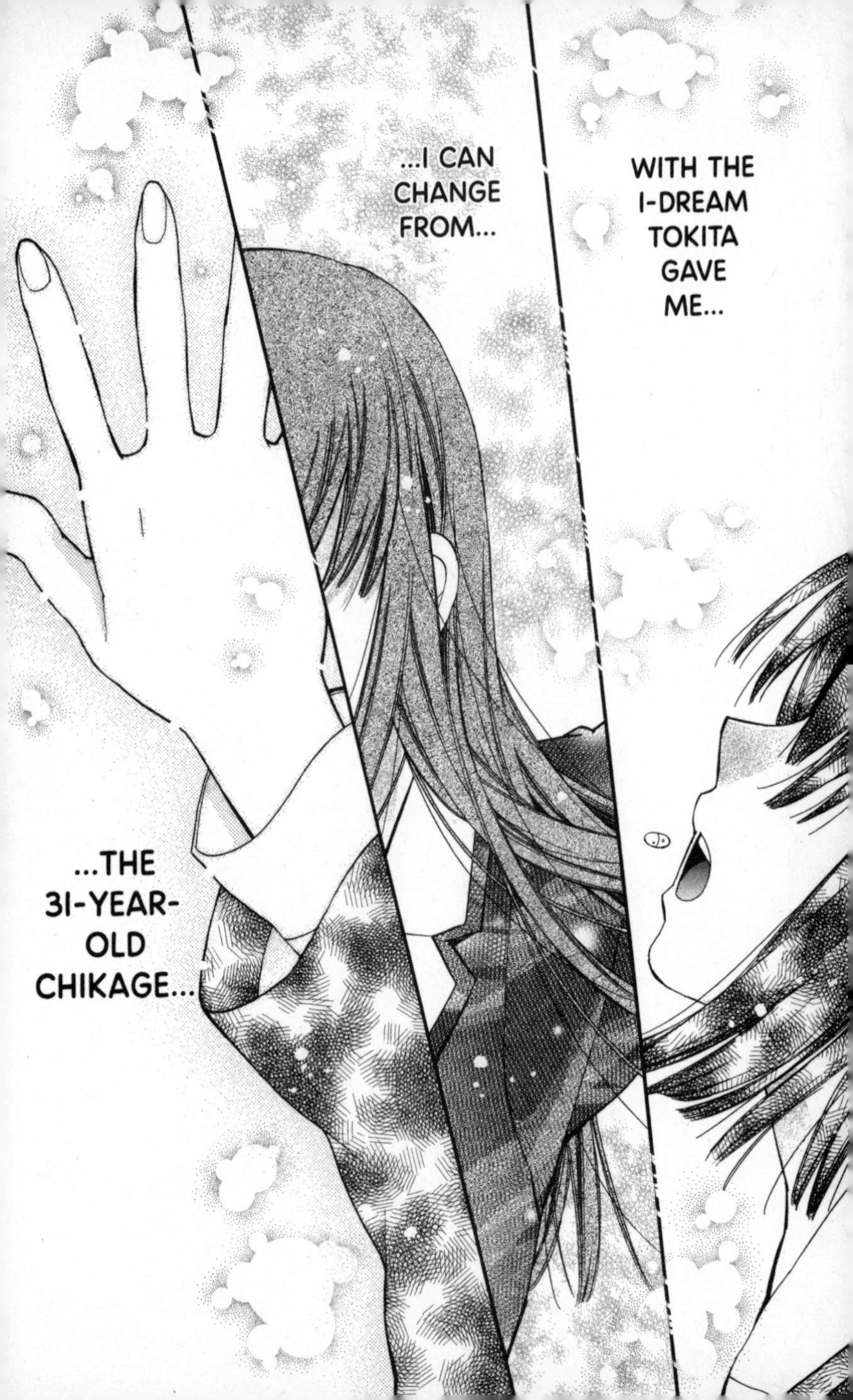
WITH THE I-DREAM TOKITA GAVE ME...
...I CAN CHANGE FROM...
...THE 31-YEAR-OLD CHIKAGE...

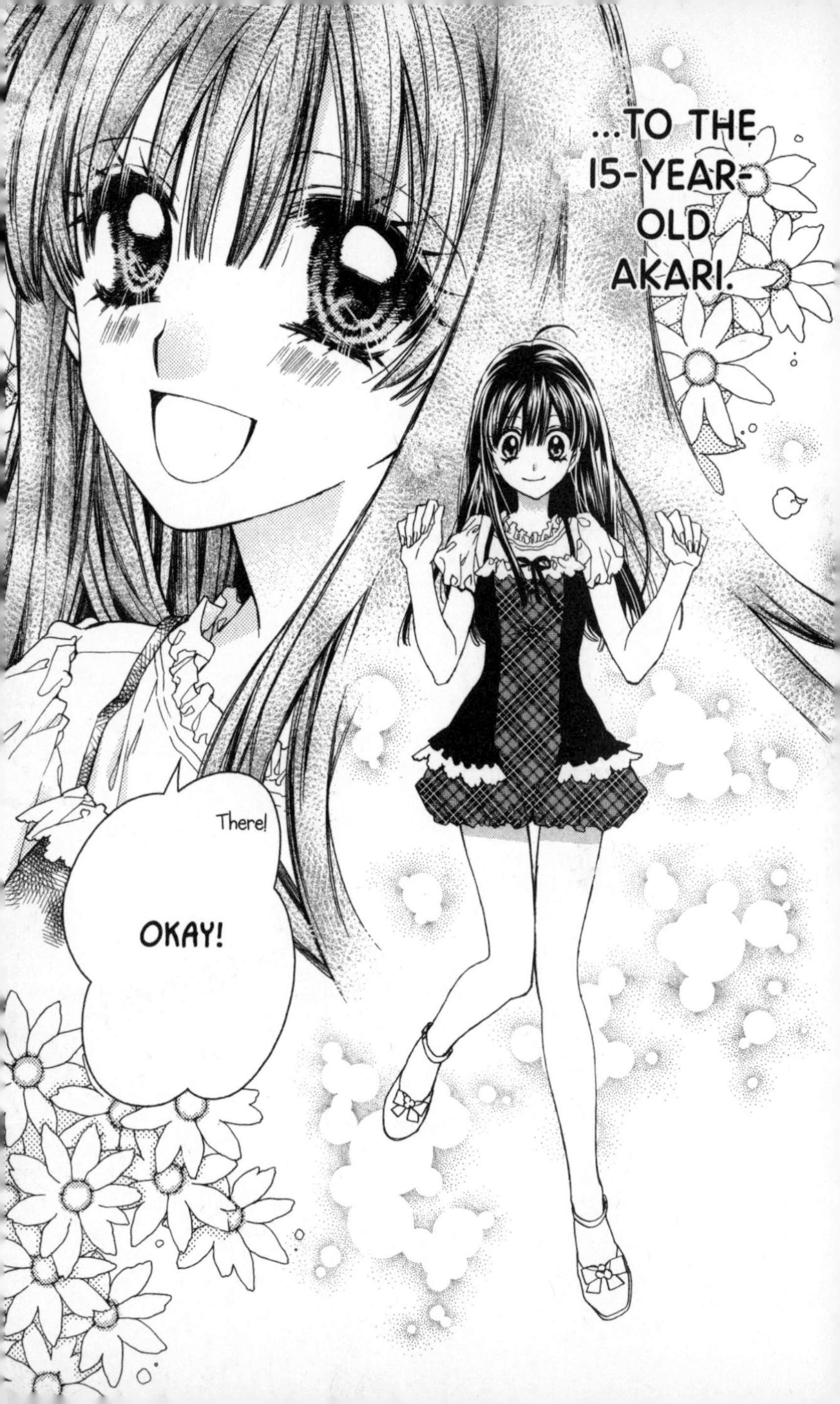
...TO THE 15-YEAR-OLD AKARI.
There!
OKAY!

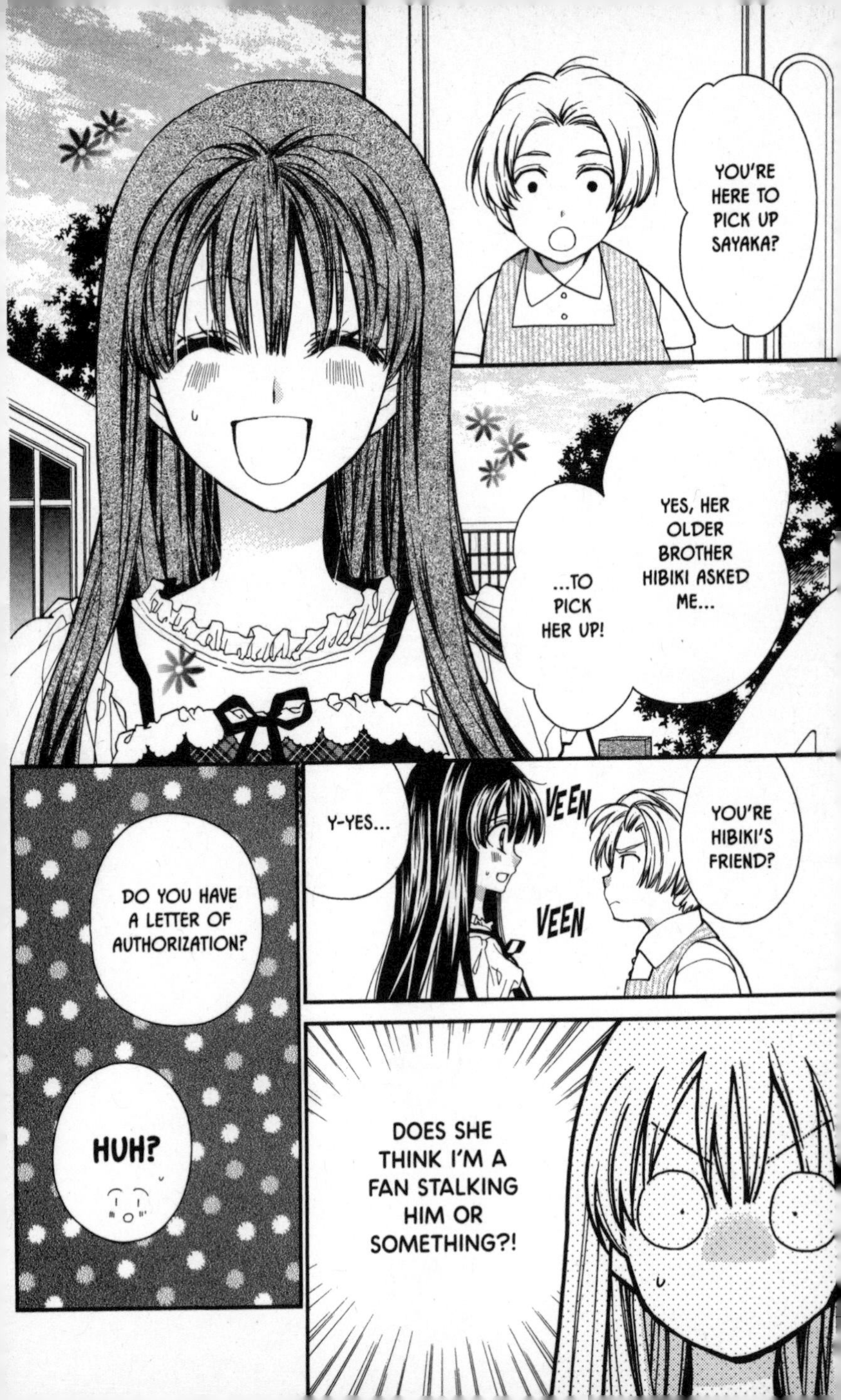
YOU'RE HERE TO PICK UP SAYAKA?
YES, HER OLDER BROTHER HIBIKI ASKED ME...
...TO PICK HER UP!
YOU'RE HIBIKI'S FRIEND?
VEEN
Y-YES...
VEEN
DOES SHE THINK I'M A FAN STALKING HIM OR SOMETHING?!
DO YOU HAVE A LETTER OF AUTHORIZATION?
HUH?

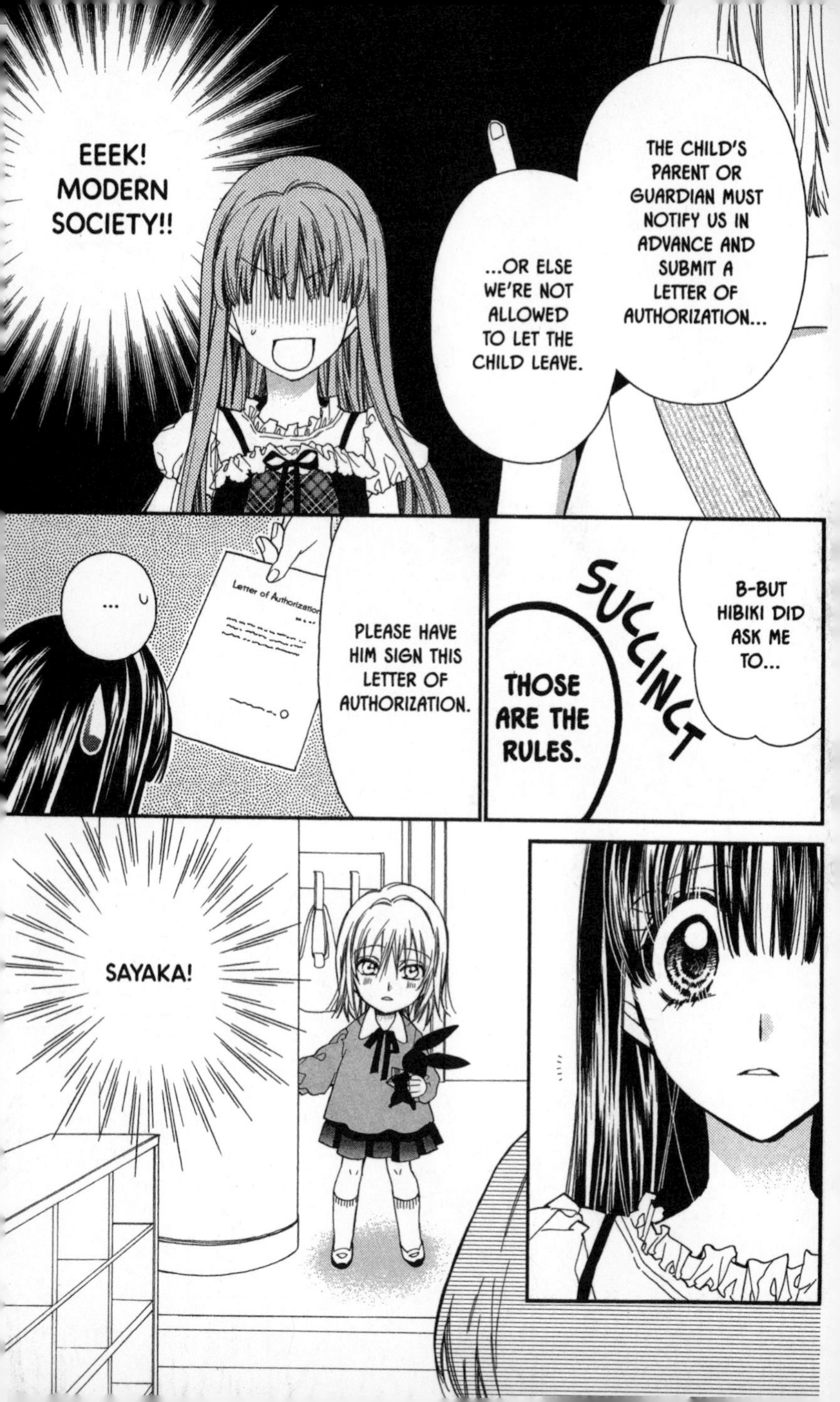
THE CHILD'S PARENT OR GUARDIAN MUST NOTIFY US IN ADVANCE AND SUBMIT A LETTER OF AUTHORIZATION...
...OR ELSE WE'RE NOT ALLOWED TO LET THE CHILD LEAVE.
EEEK! MODERN SOCIETY!!
B-BUT HIBIKI DID ASK ME TO...
SUCCINCT
THOSE ARE THE RULES.
PLEASE HAVE HIM SIGN THIS LETTER OF AUTHORIZATION.
Letter of Authorization
...
SAYAKA!

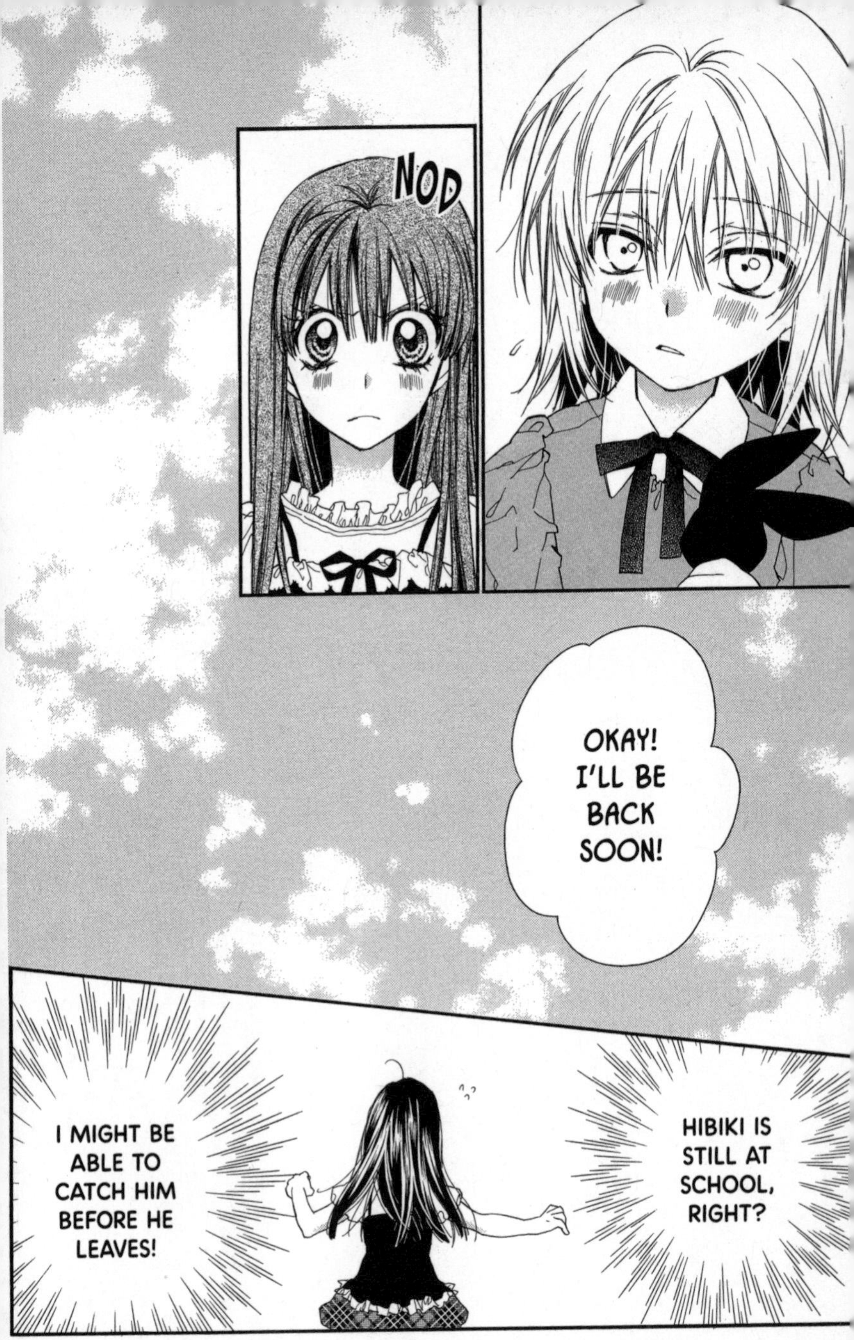
NOD
OKAY! I'LL BE BACK SOON!
HIBIKI IS STILL AT SCHOOL, RIGHT?
I MIGHT BE ABLE TO CATCH HIM BEFORE HE LEAVES!

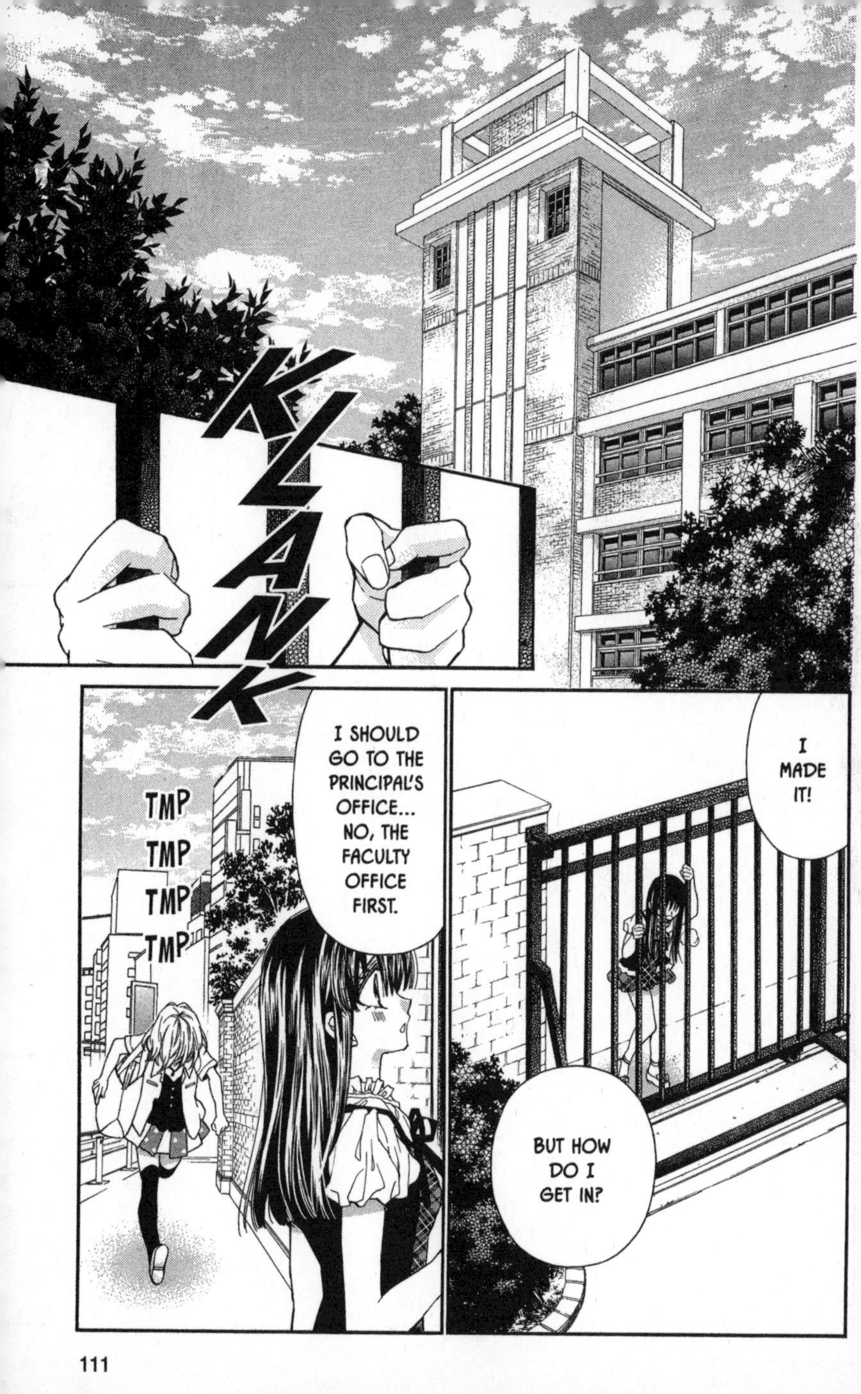
KLANK
I MADE IT!
BUT HOW DO I GET IN?
TMP TMP TMP TMP
I SHOULD GO TO THE PRINCIPAL'S OFFICE... NO, THE FACULTY OFFICE FIRST.

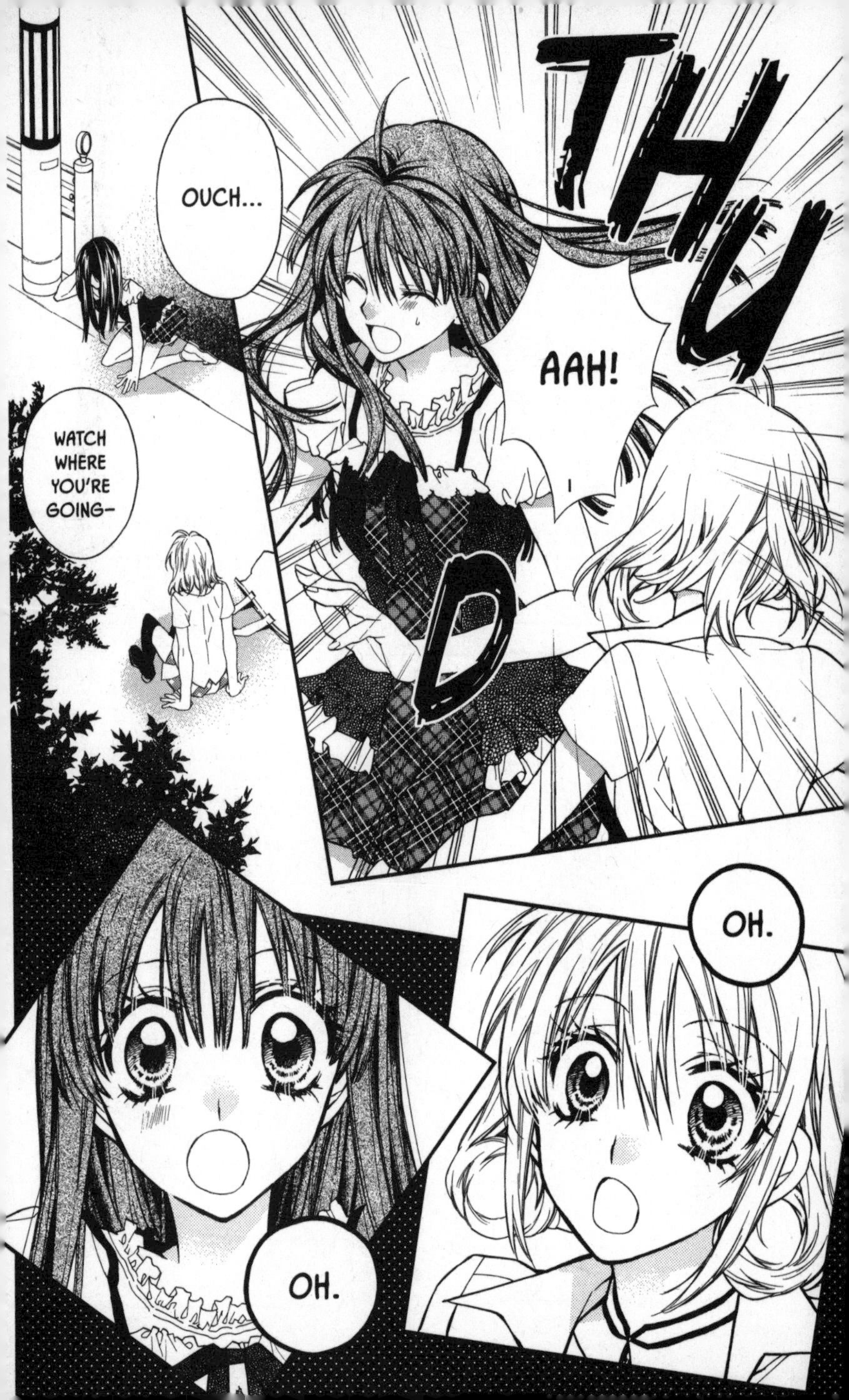
THUD
AAH!
OUCH...
WATCH WHERE YOU'RE GOING–
OH.
OH.

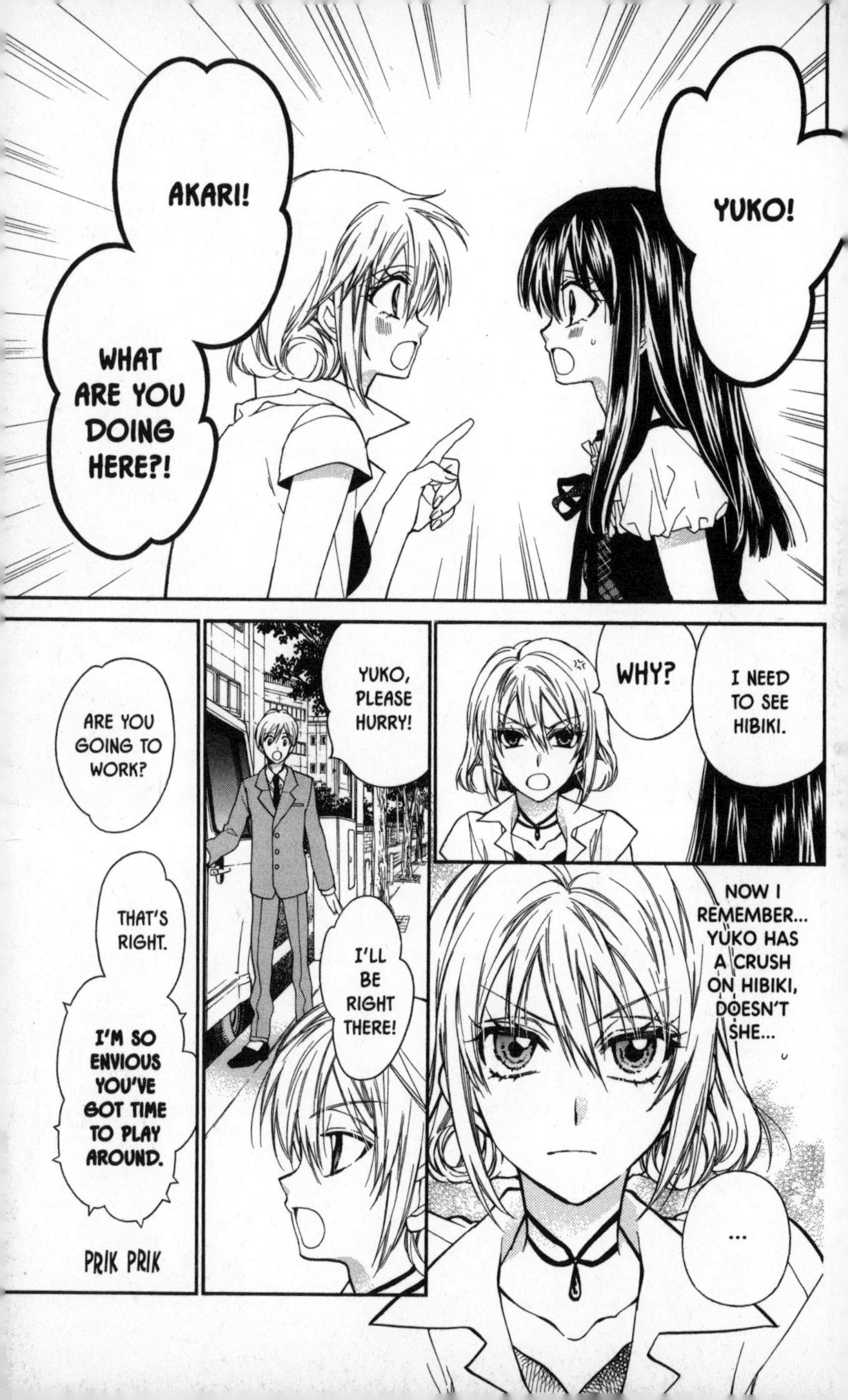
YUKO!
AKARI!
WHAT ARE YOU DOING HERE?!
I NEED TO SEE HIBIKI.
WHY?
NOW I REMEMBER... YUKO HAS A CRUSH ON HIBIKI, DOESN'T SHE...
...
YUKO, PLEASE HURRY!
I'LL BE RIGHT THERE!
ARE YOU GOING TO WORK?
THAT'S RIGHT.
I'M SO ENVIOUS YOU'VE GOT TIME TO PLAY AROUND.
PRIK PRIK

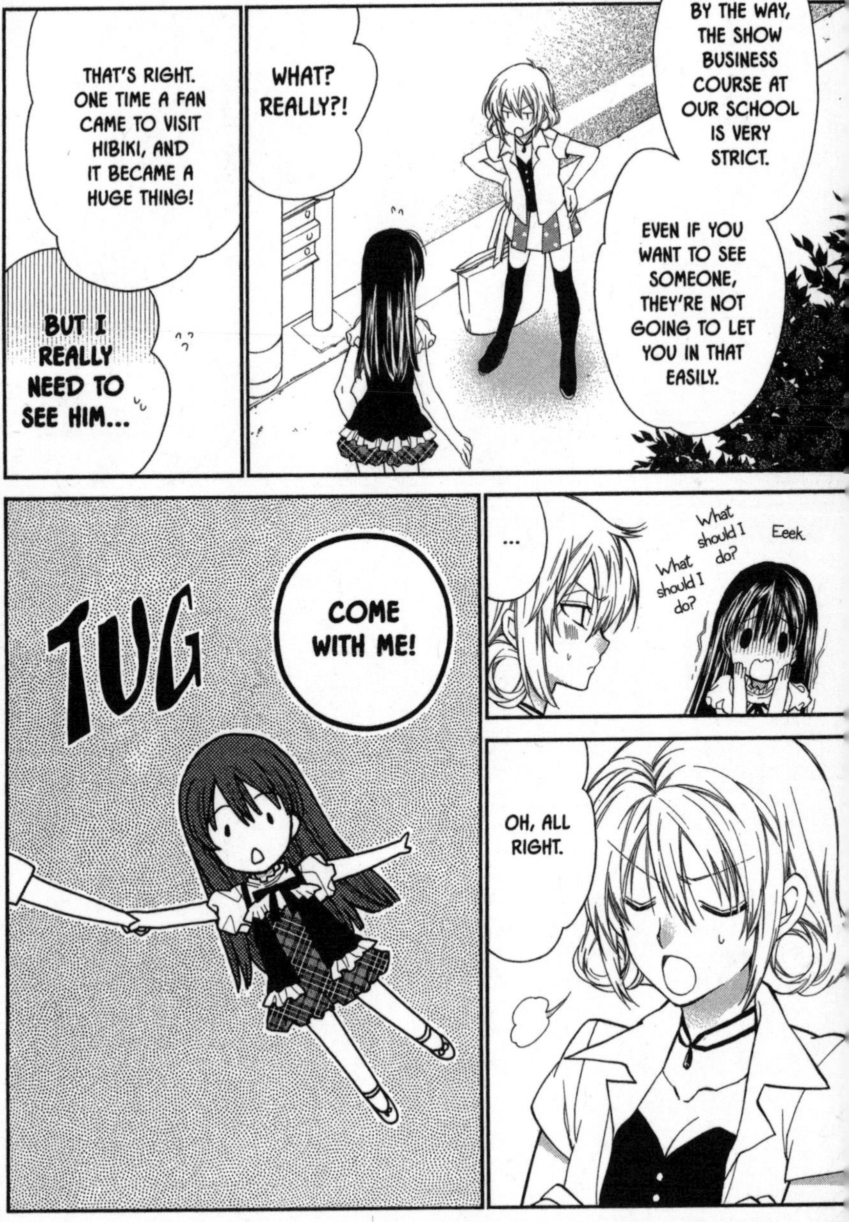
BY THE WAY, THE SHOW BUSINESS COURSE AT OUR SCHOOL IS VERY STRICT.
EVEN IF YOU WANT TO SEE SOMEONE, THEY'RE NOT GOING TO LET YOU IN THAT EASILY.
WHAT? REALLY?!
THAT'S RIGHT. ONE TIME A FAN CAME TO VISIT HIBIKI, AND IT BECAME A HUGE THING!
BUT I REALLY NEED TO SEE HIM...
...
Eeek.
What should I do?
What should I do?
OH, ALL RIGHT.
COME WITH ME!
TUG

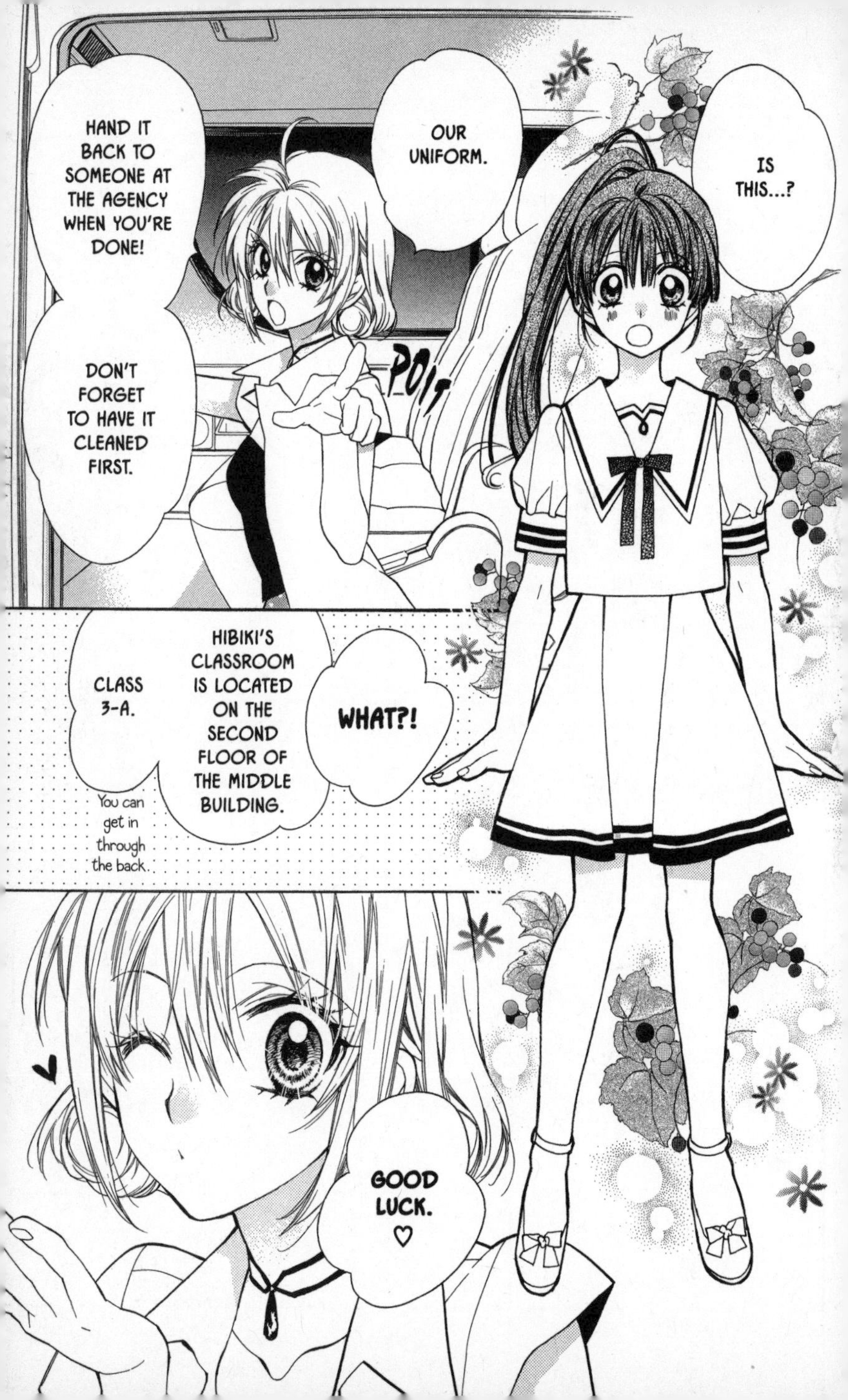
IS THIS...?
OUR UNIFORM.
POIT
HAND IT BACK TO SOMEONE AT THE AGENCY WHEN YOU'RE DONE!
DON'T FORGET TO HAVE IT CLEANED FIRST.
WHAT?!
HIBIKI'S CLASSROOM IS LOCATED ON THE SECOND FLOOR OF THE MIDDLE BUILDING.
CLASS 3-A.
You can get in through the back.
GOOD LUCK. ♡

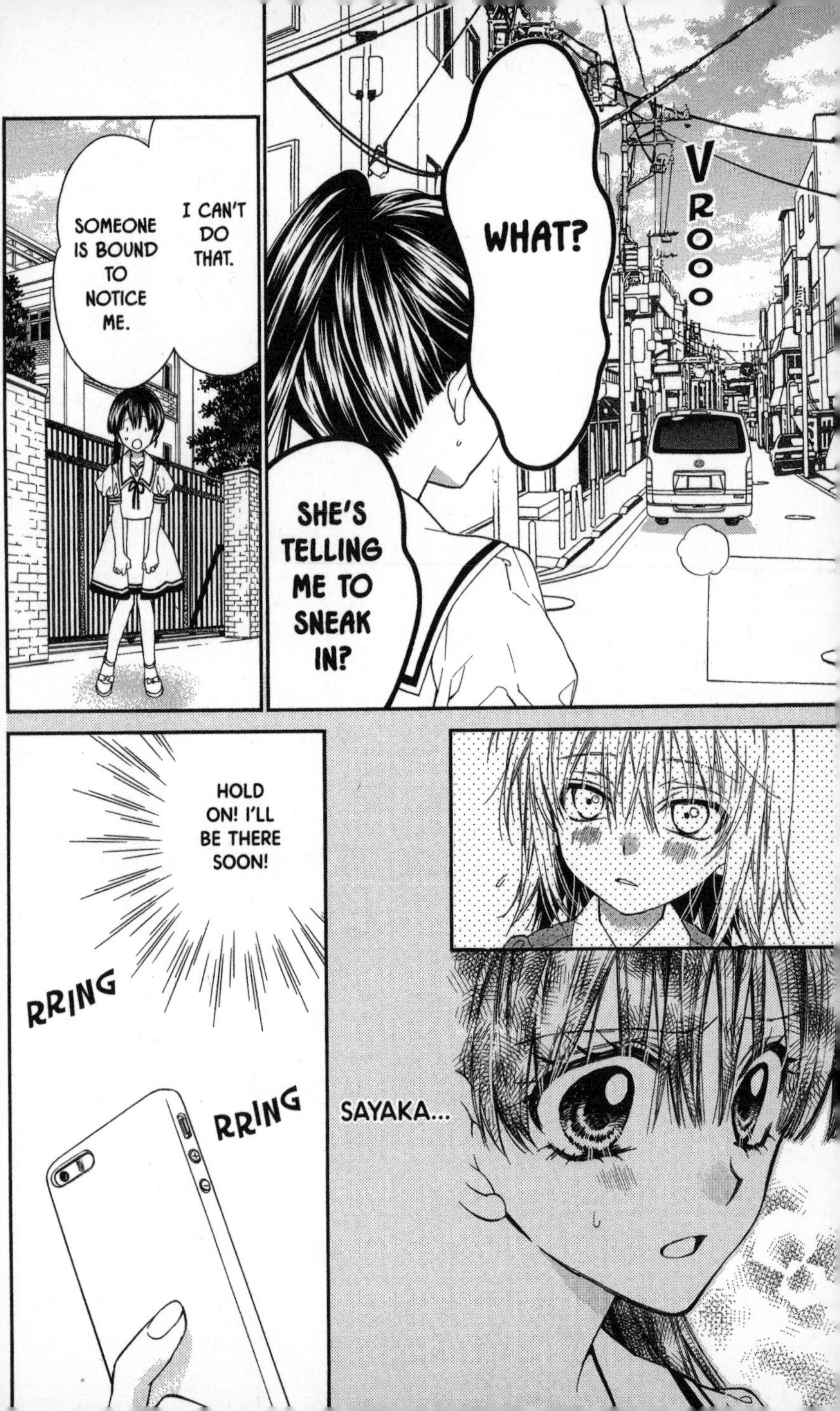
VROOO
WHAT?
SHE'S TELLING ME TO SNEAK IN?
I CAN'T DO THAT.
SOMEONE IS BOUND TO NOTICE ME.
SAYAKA...
HOLD ON! I'LL BE THERE SOON!
RRING
RRING

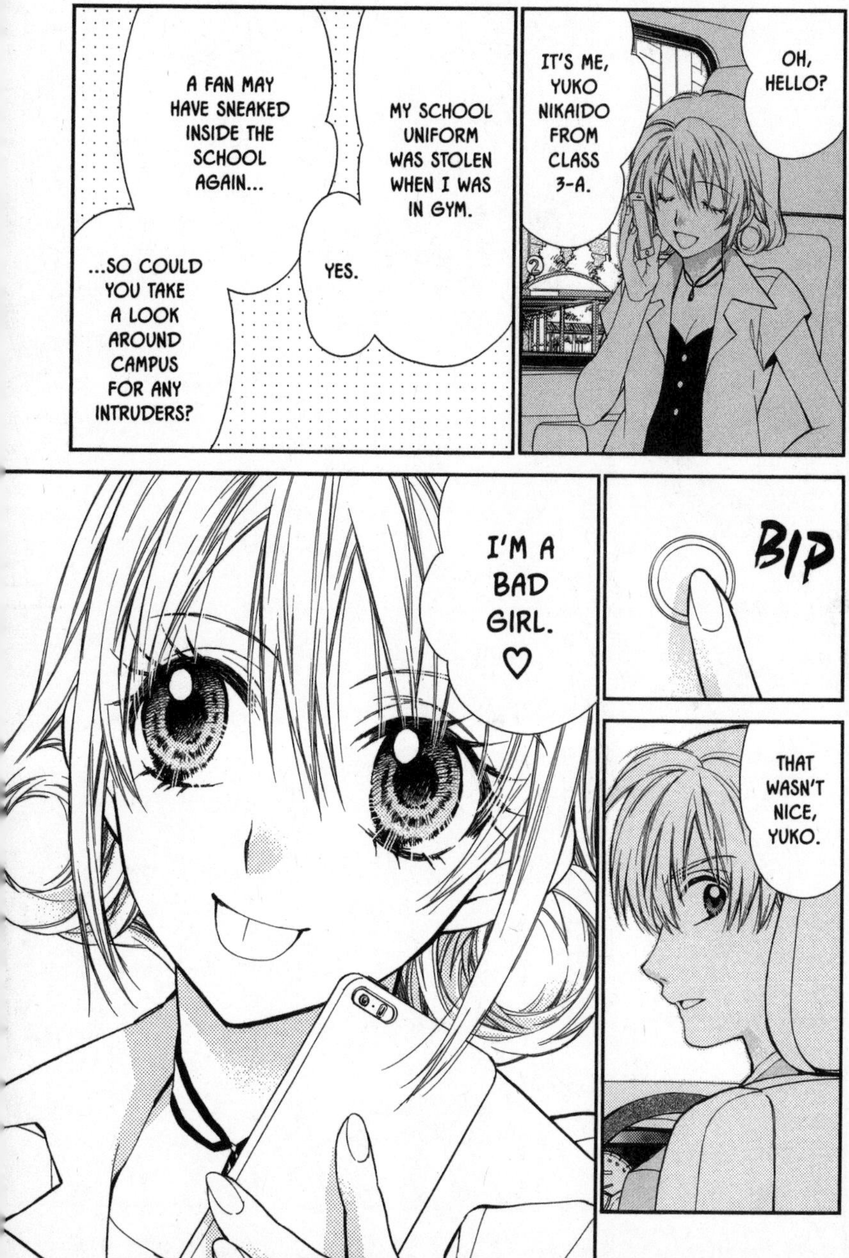
OH, HELLO?
IT'S ME, YUKO NIKAIDO FROM CLASS 3-A.
MY SCHOOL UNIFORM WAS STOLEN WHEN I WAS IN GYM.
A FAN MAY HAVE SNEAKED INSIDE THE SCHOOL AGAIN...
YES.
...SO COULD YOU TAKE A LOOK AROUND CAMPUS FOR ANY INTRUDERS?
BIP
THAT WASN'T NICE, YUKO.
I'M A BAD GIRL. ♡

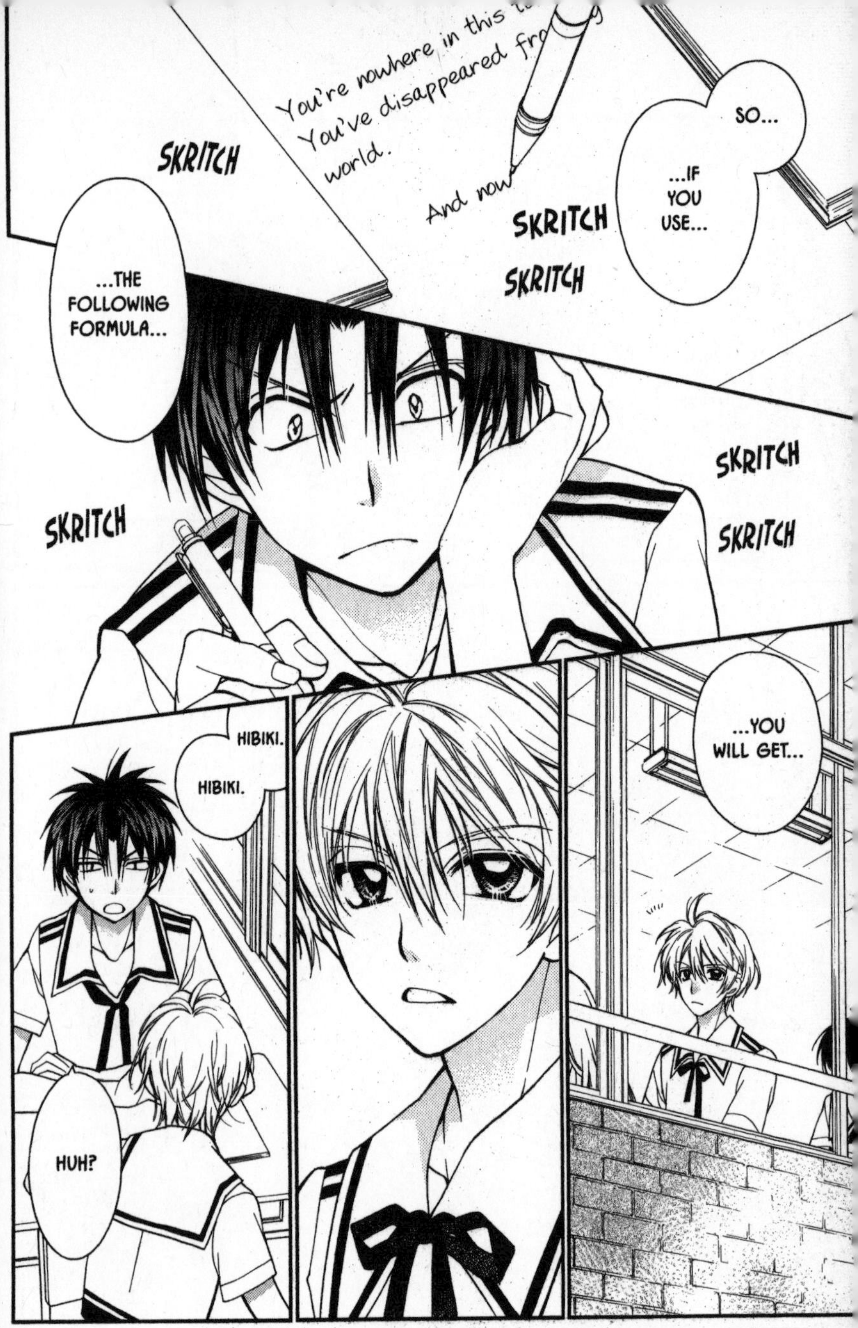
SO...
...IF YOU USE...
You're nowhere in this
You've disappeared
world.
And now
SKRITCH
SKRITCH
SKRITCH
...THE FOLLOWING FORMULA...
SKRITCH
SKRITCH
SKRITCH
...YOU WILL GET...
HIBIKI.
HIBIKI.
HUH?

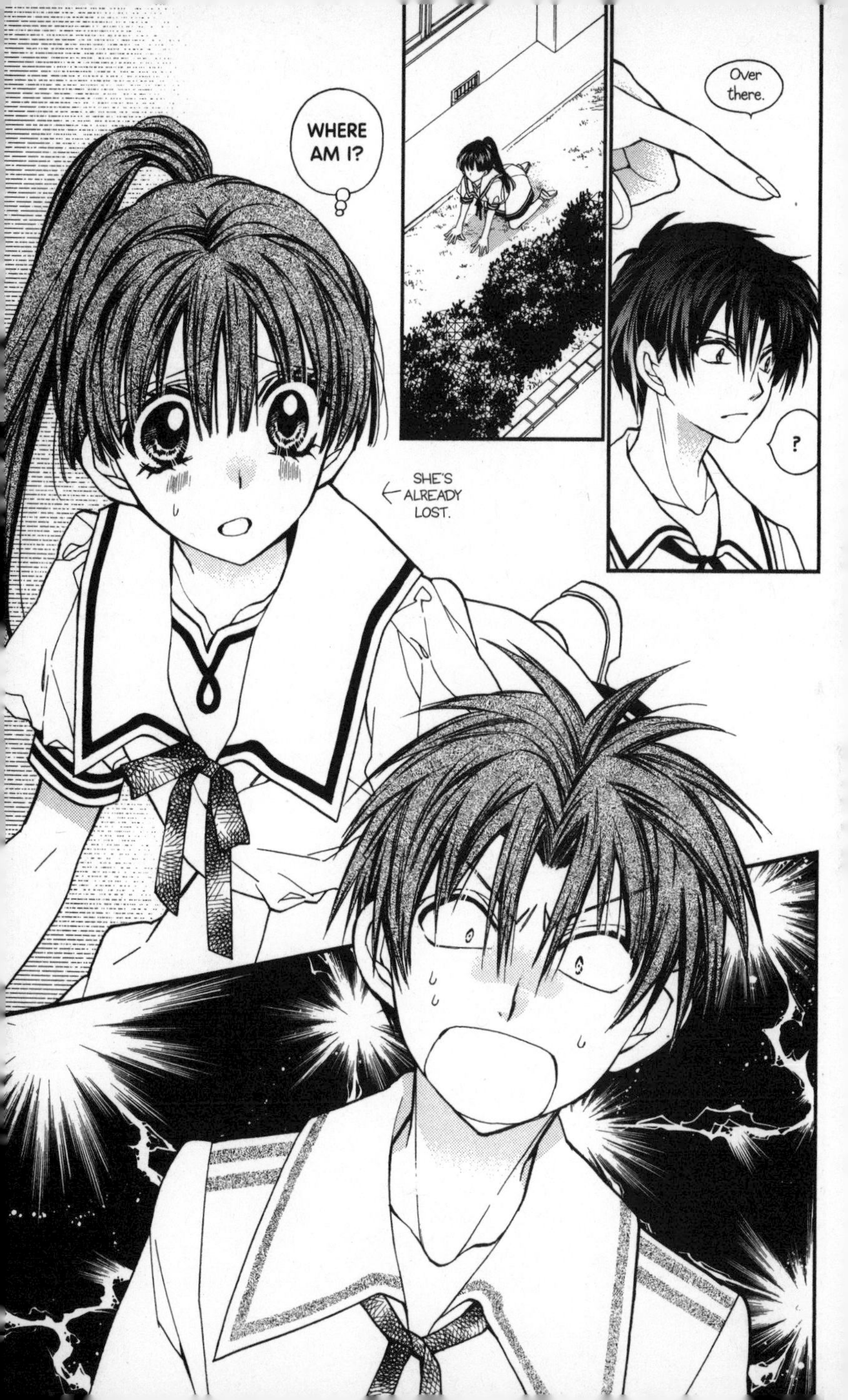
Over there.
?
WHERE AM I?
SHE'S ALREADY LOST.

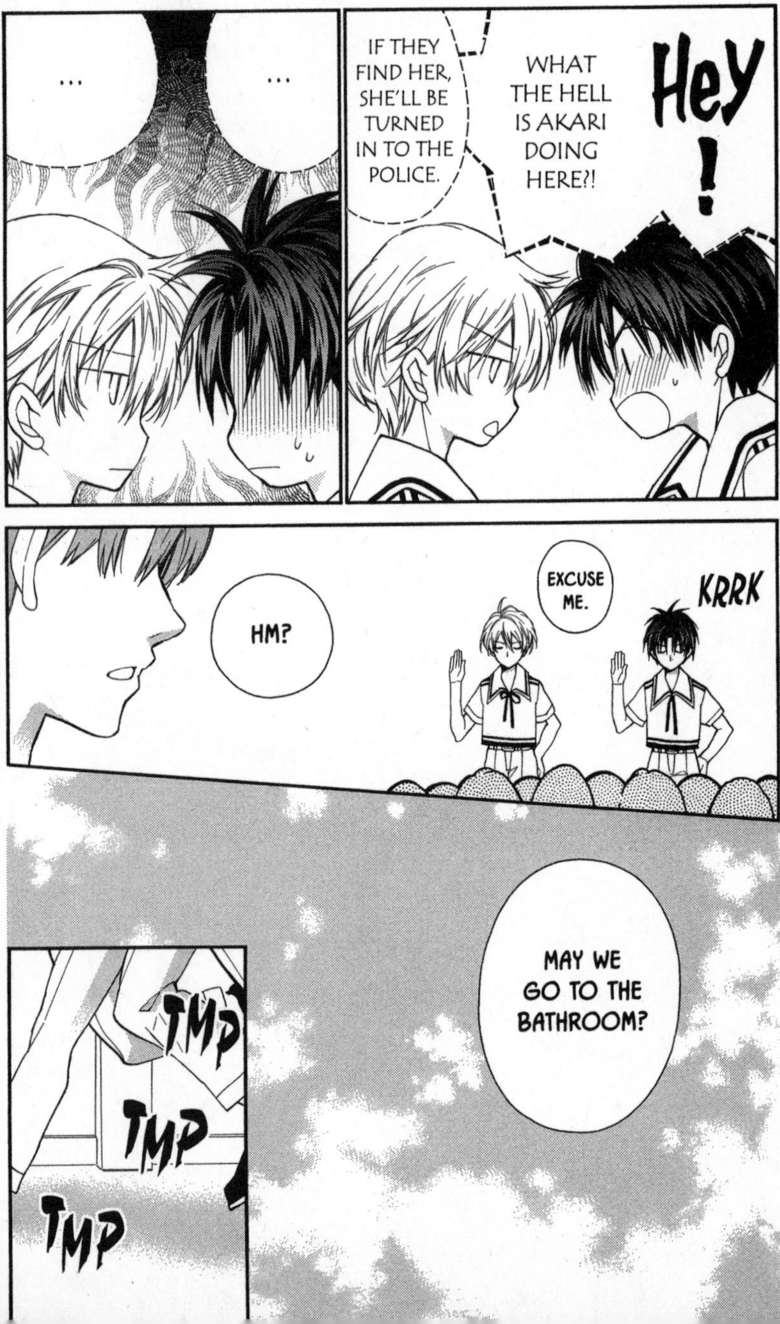
Hey!
WHAT THE HELL IS AKARI DOING HERE?!
IF THEY FIND HER, SHE'LL BE TURNED IN TO THE POLICE.
...
...
KRRK
EXCUSE ME.
HM?
MAY WE GO TO THE BATHROOM?
TMP
TMP
TMP

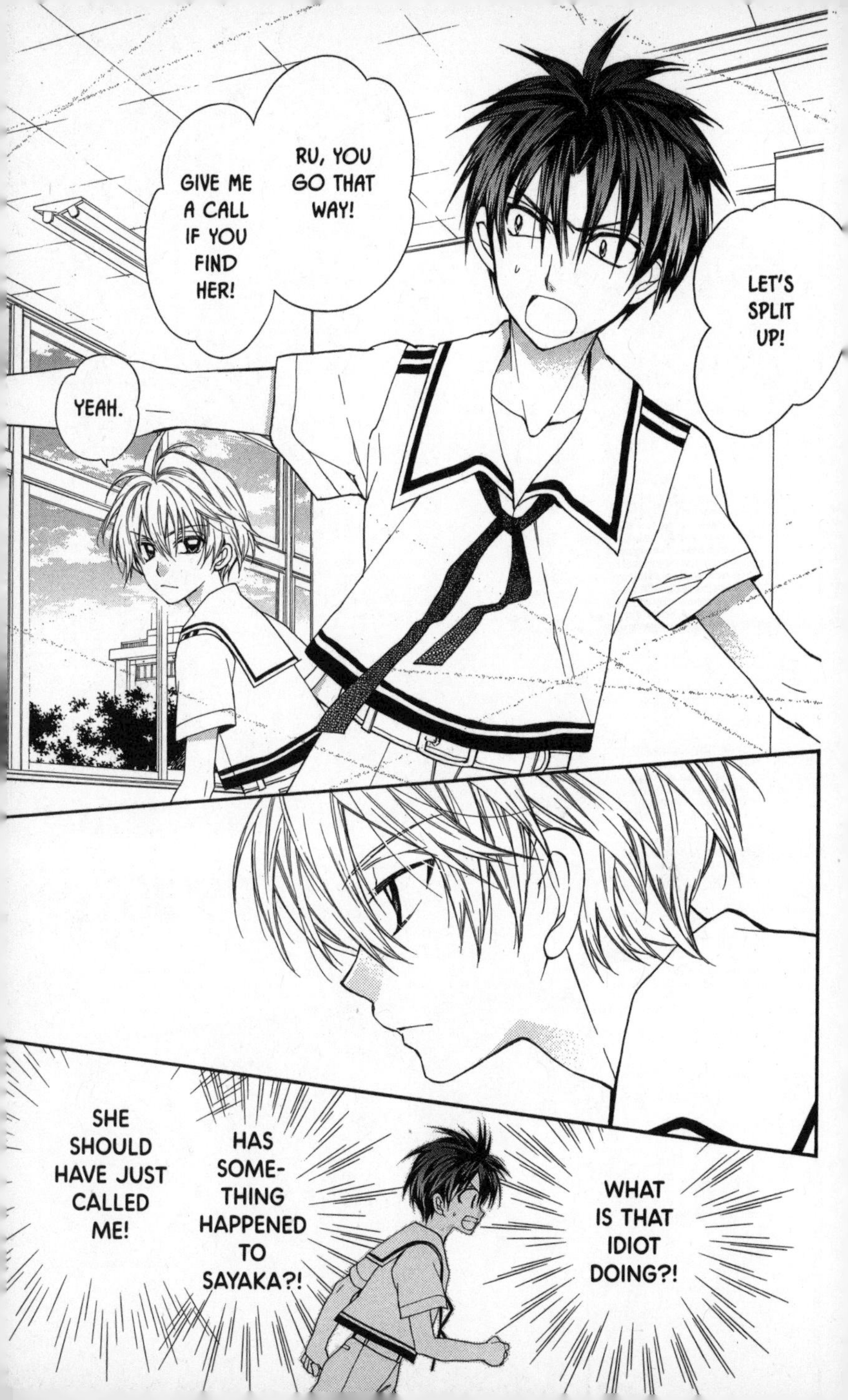
LET'S SPLIT UP!
RU, YOU GO THAT WAY!
GIVE ME A CALL IF YOU FIND HER!
YEAH.
WHAT IS THAT IDIOT DOING?!
HAS SOME-THING HAPPENED TO SAYAKA?!
SHE SHOULD HAVE JUST CALLED ME!

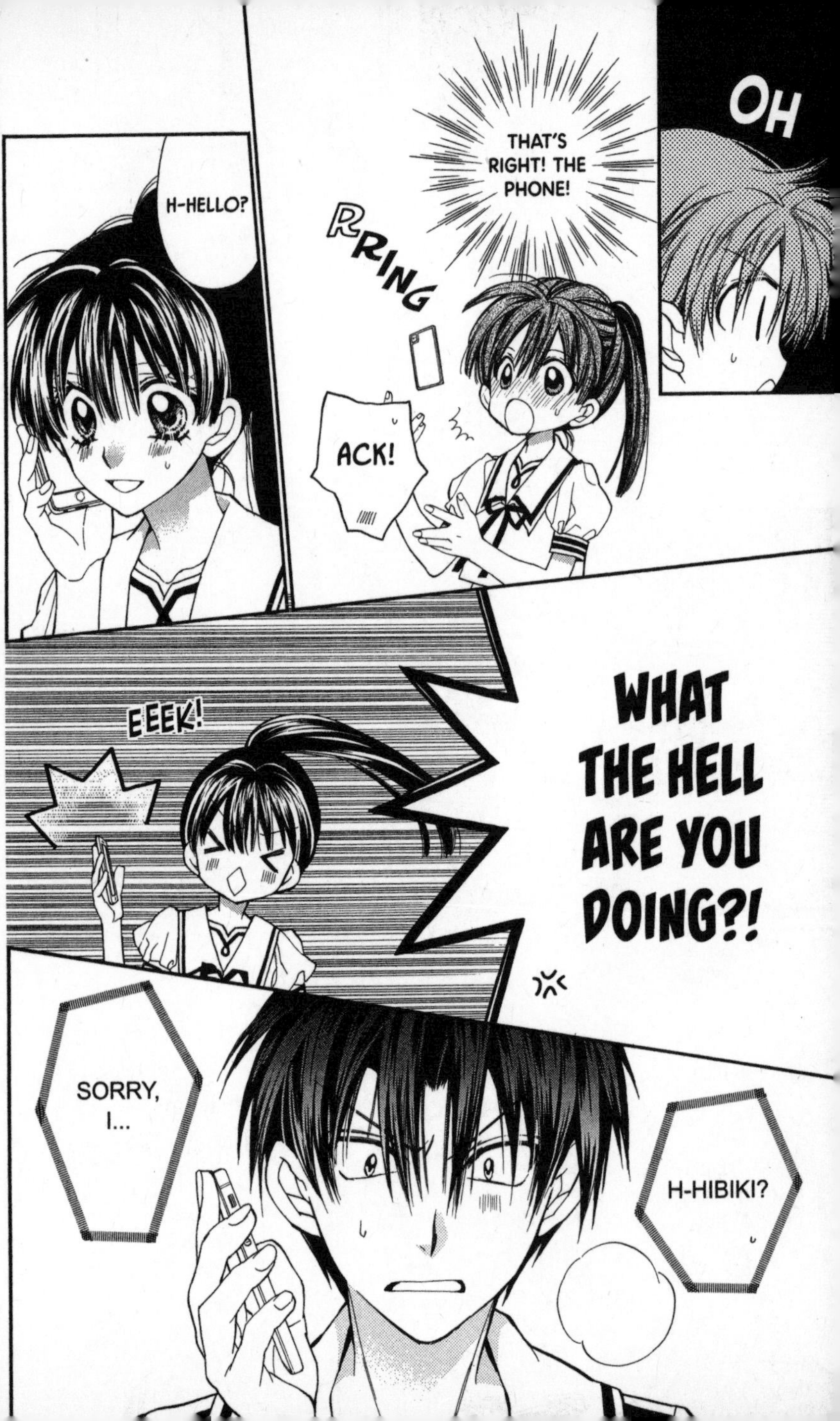
OH
THAT'S RIGHT! THE PHONE!
RRING
ACK!
H-HELLO?
WHAT THE HELL ARE YOU DOING?!
EEEK!
H-HIBIKI?
SORRY, I...

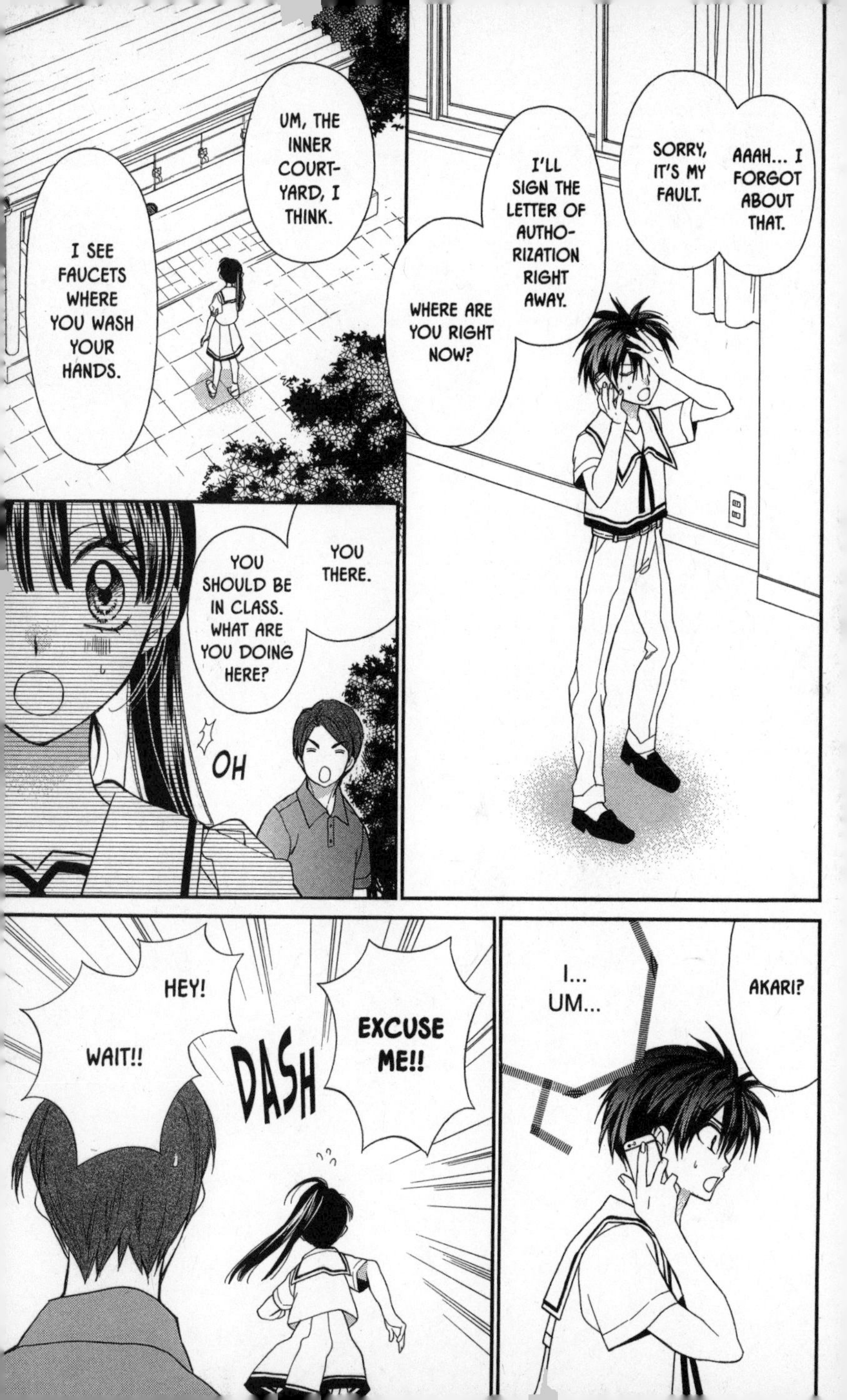
AAAH... I FORGOT ABOUT THAT.
SORRY, IT'S MY FAULT.
I'LL SIGN THE LETTER OF AUTHORIZATION RIGHT AWAY.
WHERE ARE YOU RIGHT NOW?
UM, THE INNER COURT-YARD, I THINK.
I SEE FAUCETS WHERE YOU WASH YOUR HANDS.
YOU THERE.
YOU SHOULD BE IN CLASS. WHAT ARE YOU DOING HERE?
OH
AKARI?
I... UM...
EXCUSE ME!!
DASH
HEY!
WAIT!!

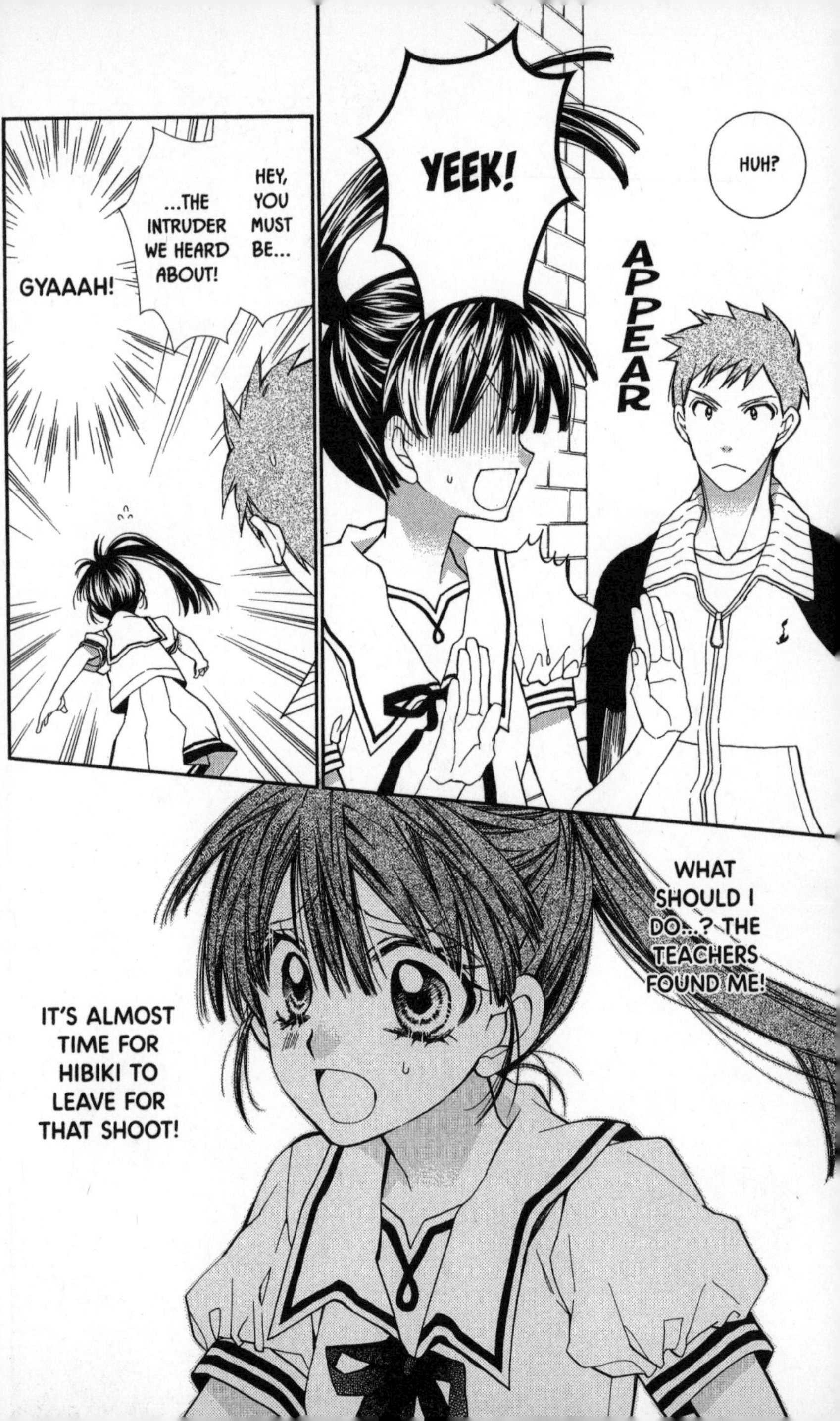
HUH?
APPEAR
YEEK!
HEY, YOU MUST BE...
...THE INTRUDER WE HEARD ABOUT!
GYAAAH!
WHAT SHOULD I DO...? THE TEACHERS FOUND ME!
IT'S ALMOST TIME FOR HIBIKI TO LEAVE FOR THAT SHOOT!

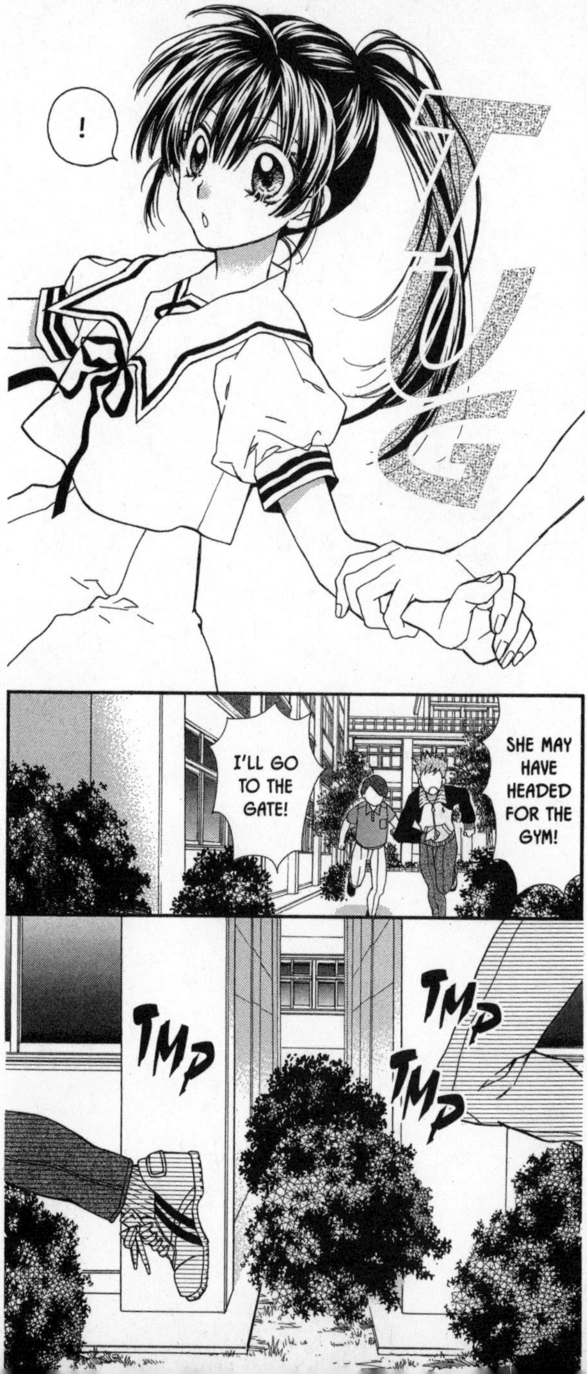
!
TUG
SHE MAY HAVE HEADED FOR THE GYM!
I'LL GO TO THE GATE!
TMP
TMP
TMP

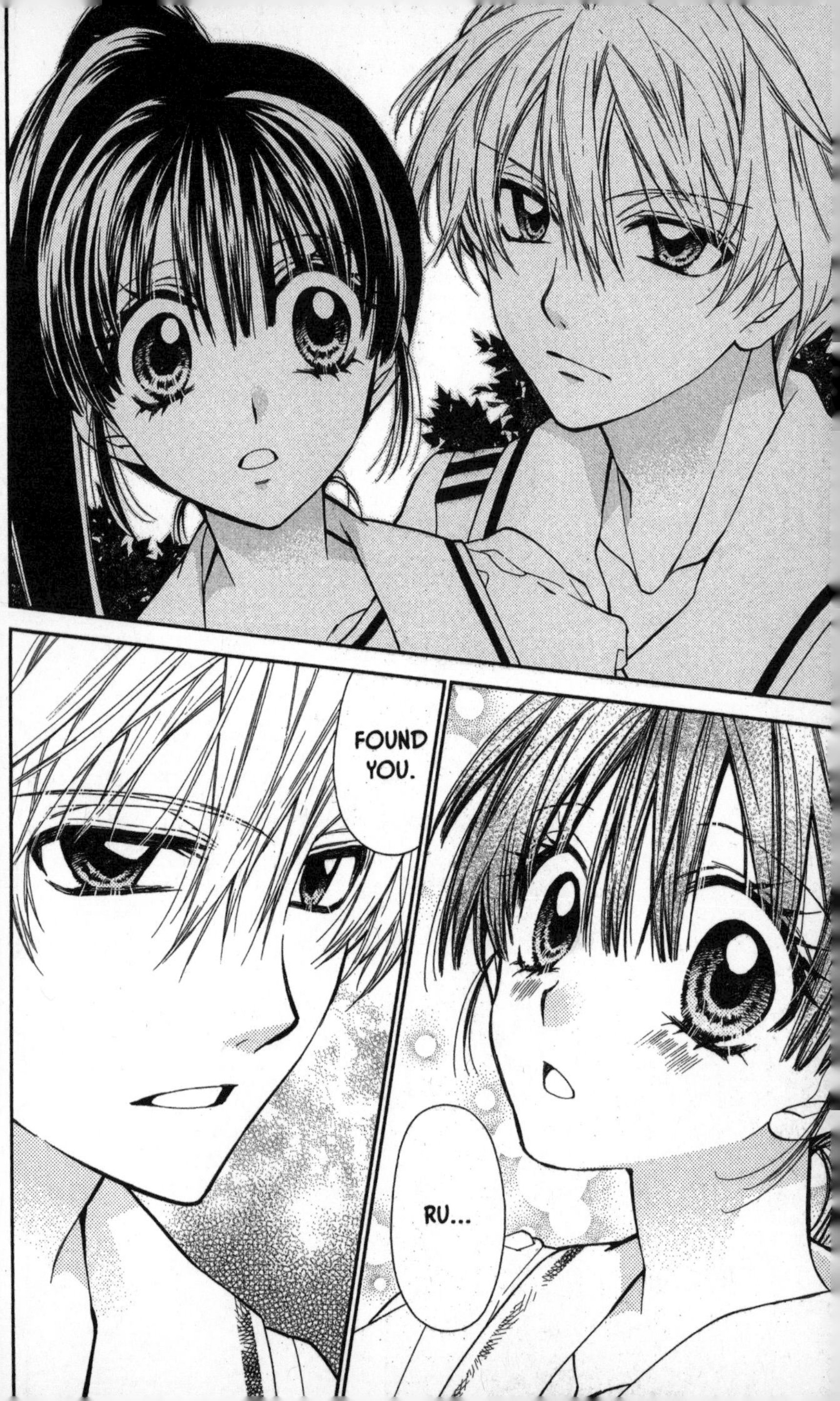
FOUND YOU.
RU...

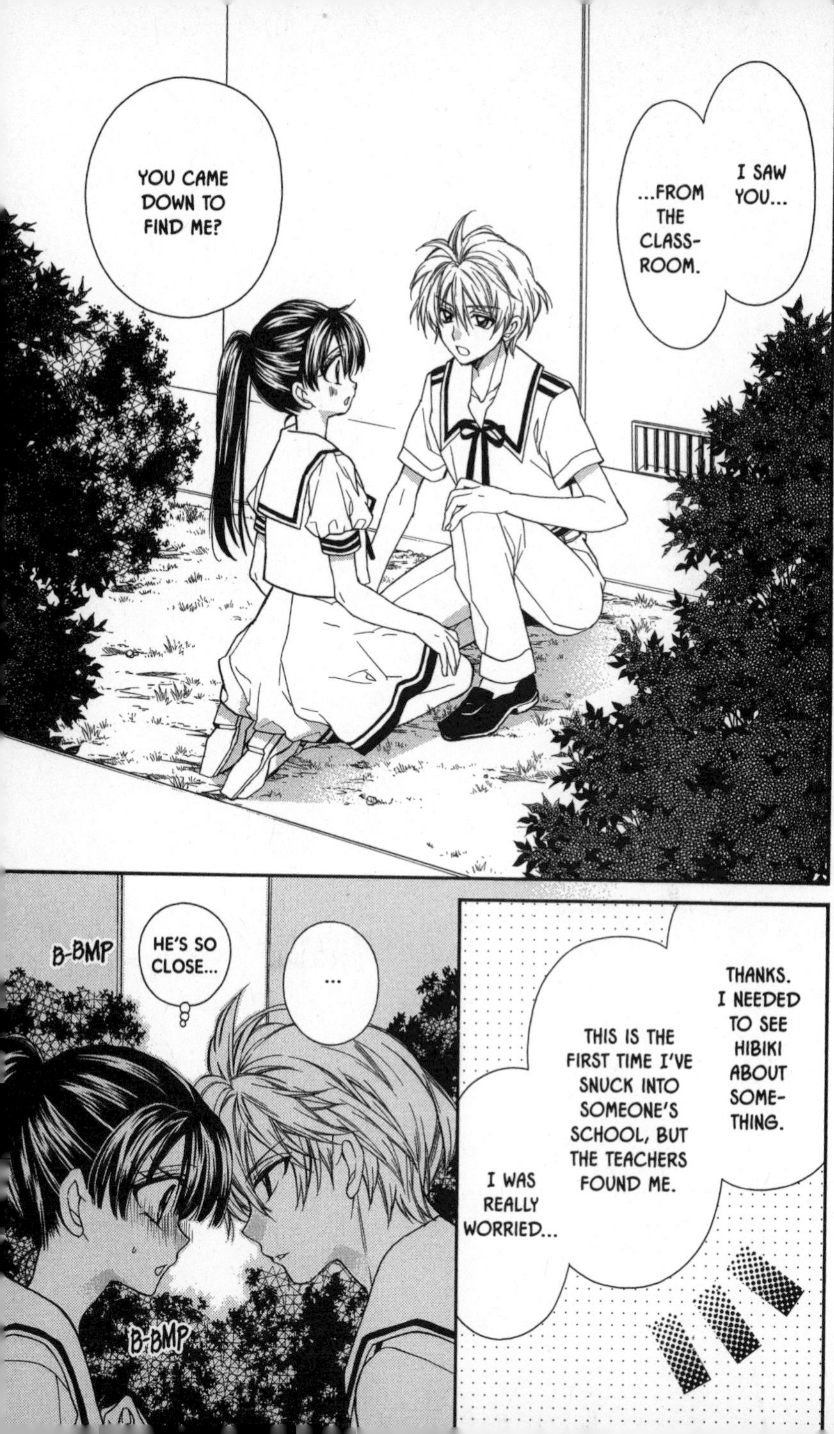

I SAW YOU...
...FROM THE CLASS-ROOM.
YOU CAME DOWN TO FIND ME?
THANKS. I NEEDED TO SEE HIBIKI ABOUT SOME-THING.
THIS IS THE FIRST TIME I'VE SNUCK INTO SOMEONE'S SCHOOL, BUT THE TEACHERS FOUND ME.
I WAS REALLY WORRIED...
...
HE'S SO CLOSE...
B-BMP
B-BMP

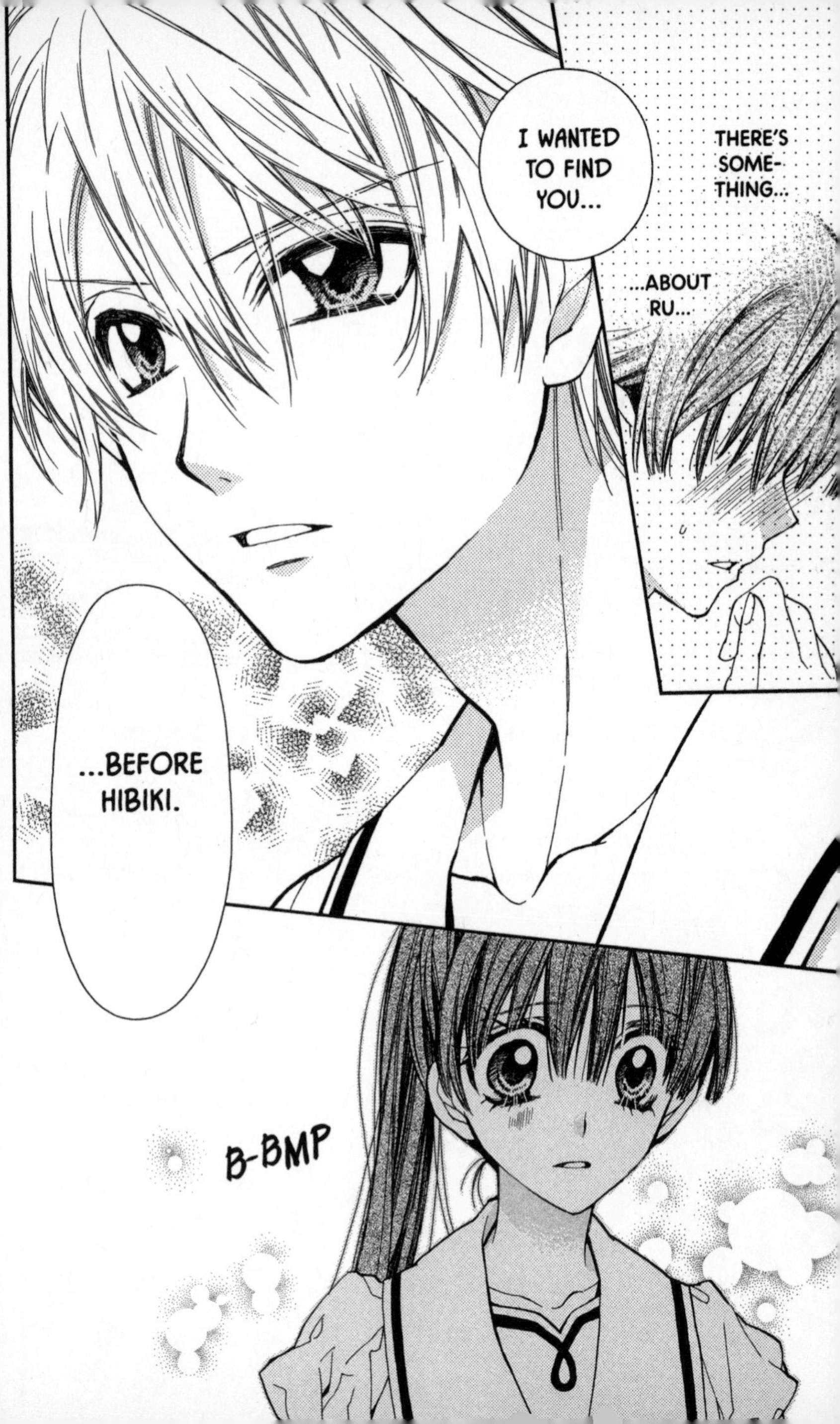
THERE'S SOME-THING...
...ABOUT RU...
I WANTED TO FIND YOU...
...BEFORE HIBIKI.
B-BMP

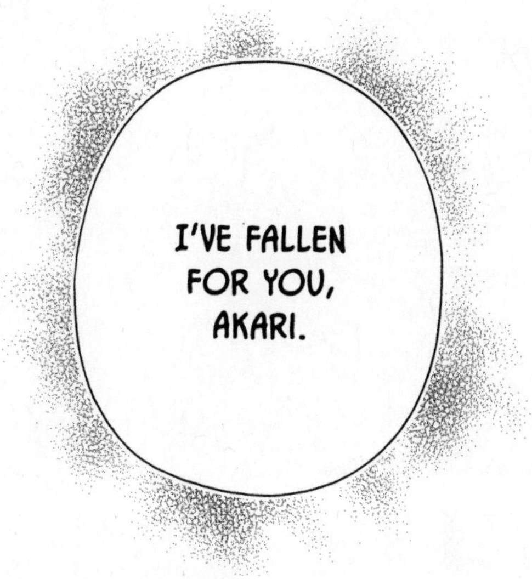
I'VE FALLEN FOR YOU, AKARI.

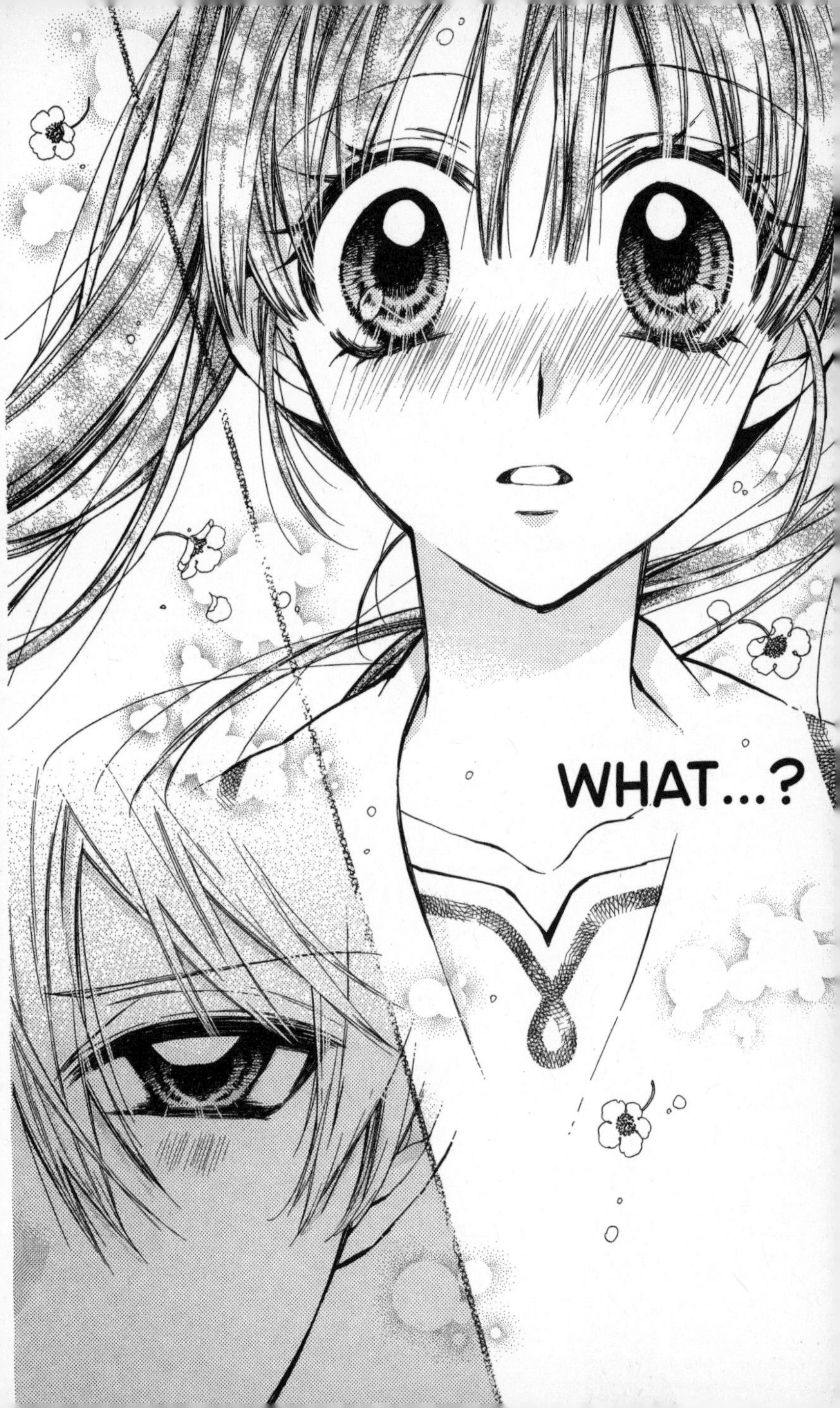
WHAT...?

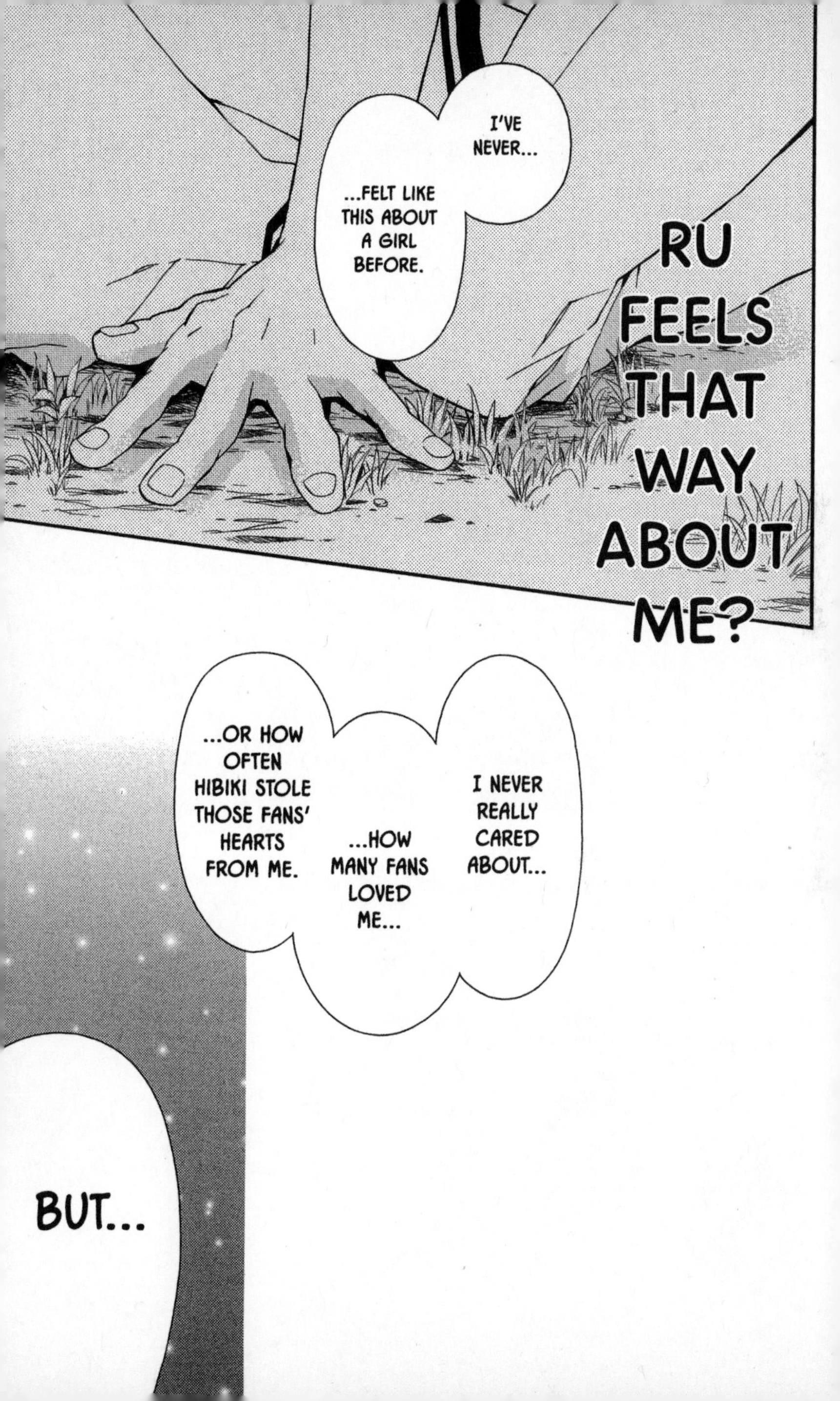
I'VE NEVER...
...FELT LIKE THIS ABOUT A GIRL BEFORE.
RU FEELS THAT WAY ABOUT ME?
I NEVER REALLY CARED ABOUT...
...HOW MANY FANS LOVED ME...
...OR HOW OFTEN HIBIKI STOLE THOSE FANS' HEARTS FROM ME.
BUT...

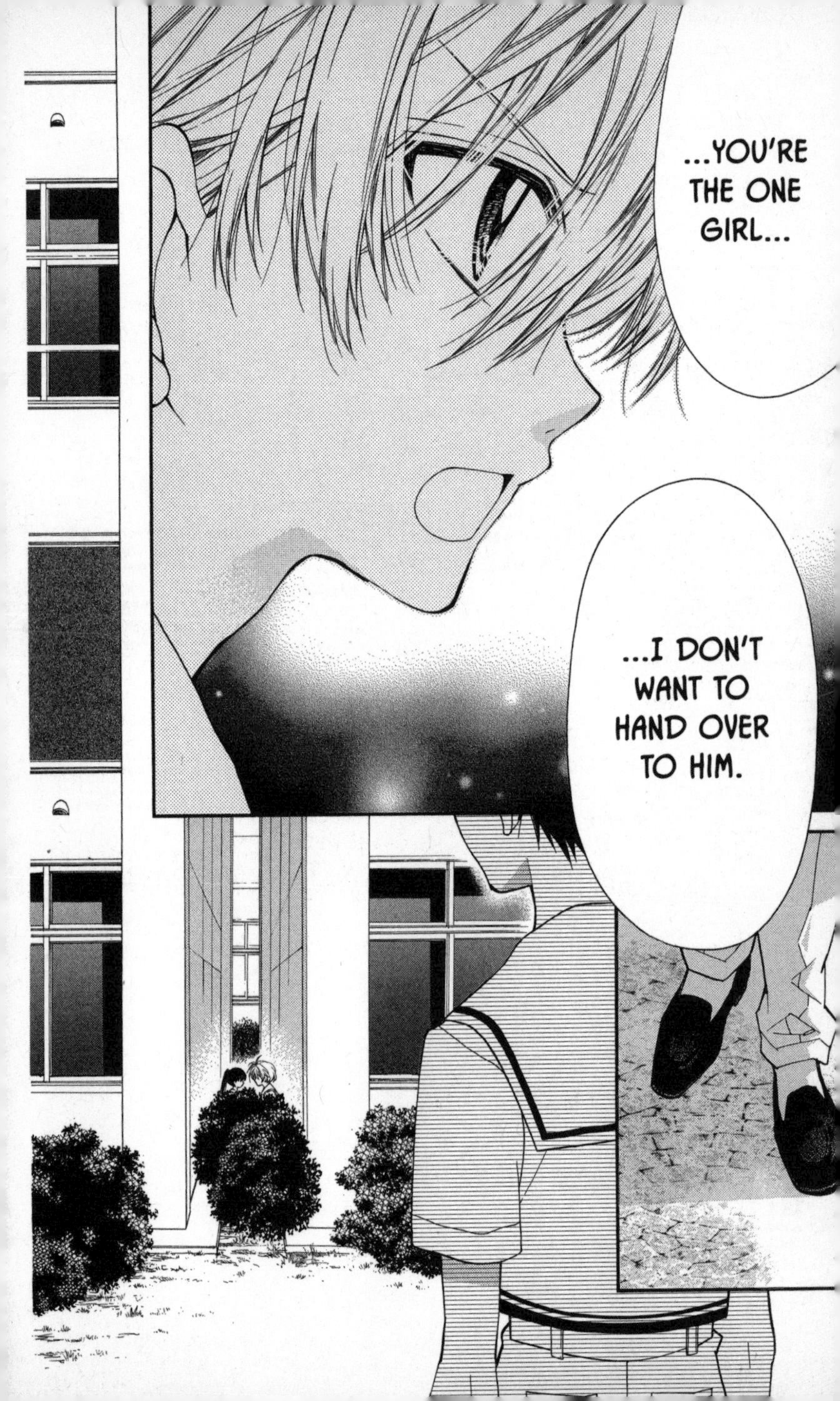
...YOU'RE THE ONE GIRL...
...I DON'T WANT TO HAND OVER TO HIM.

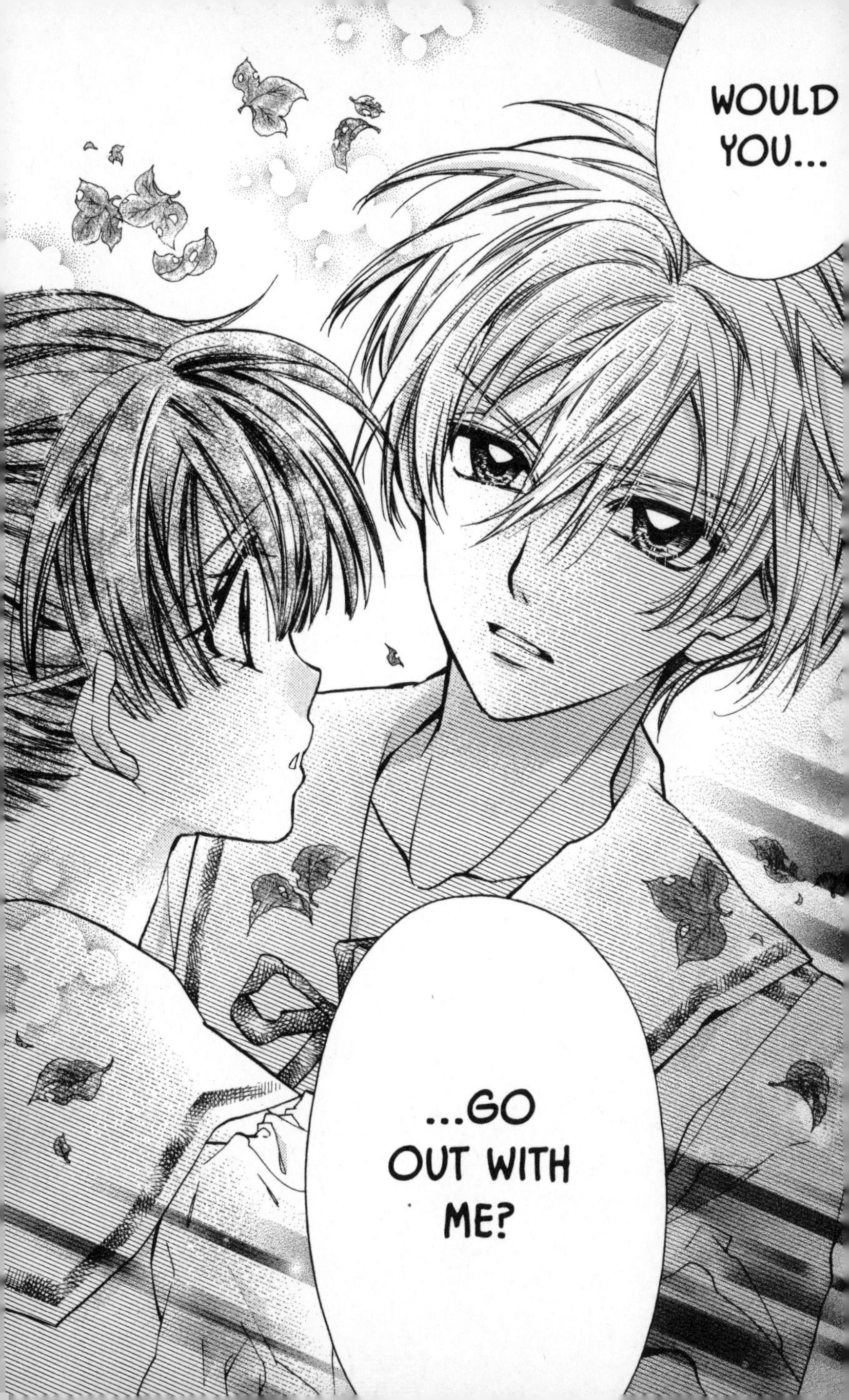
WOULD YOU...
...GO OUT WITH ME?

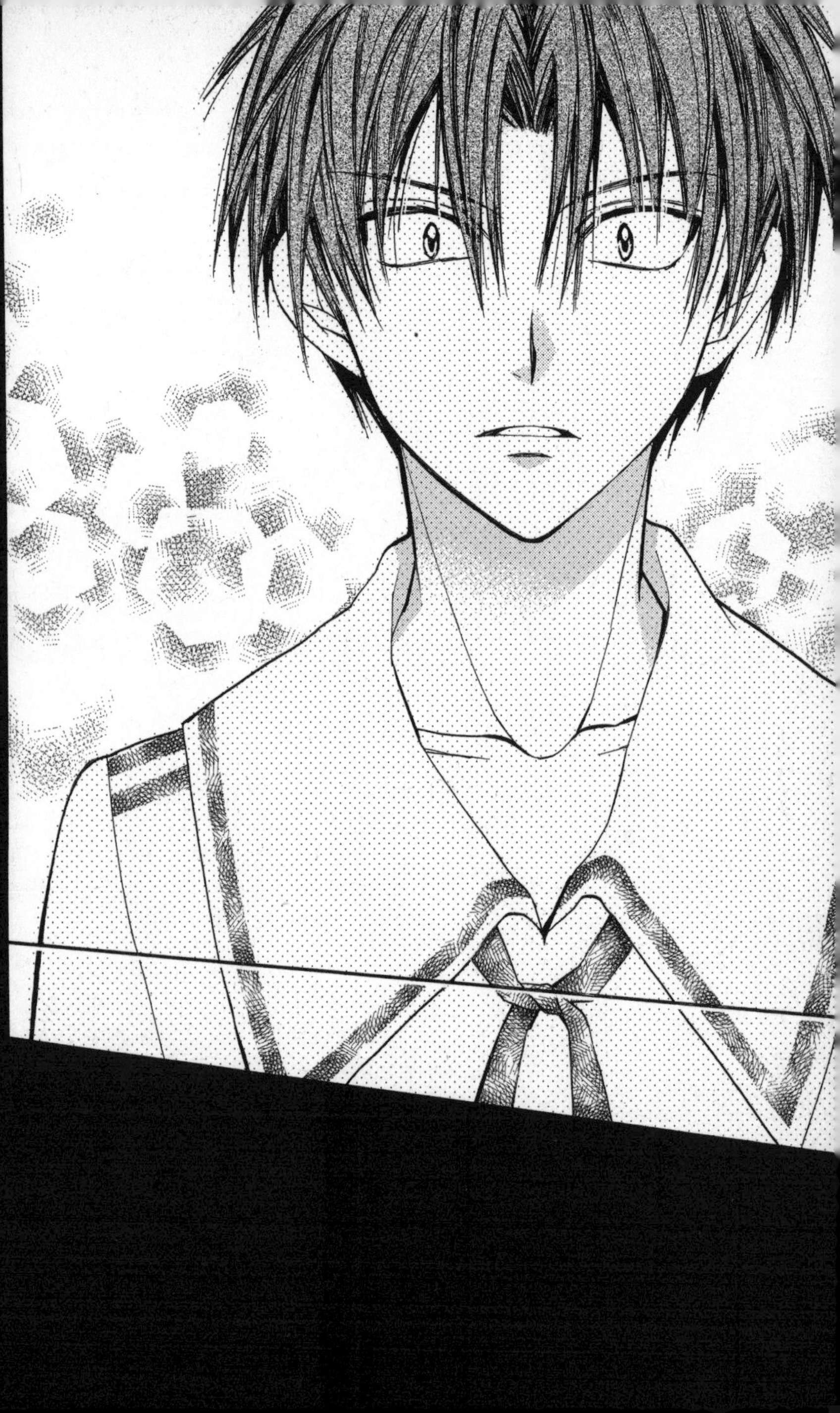

Chapter 15

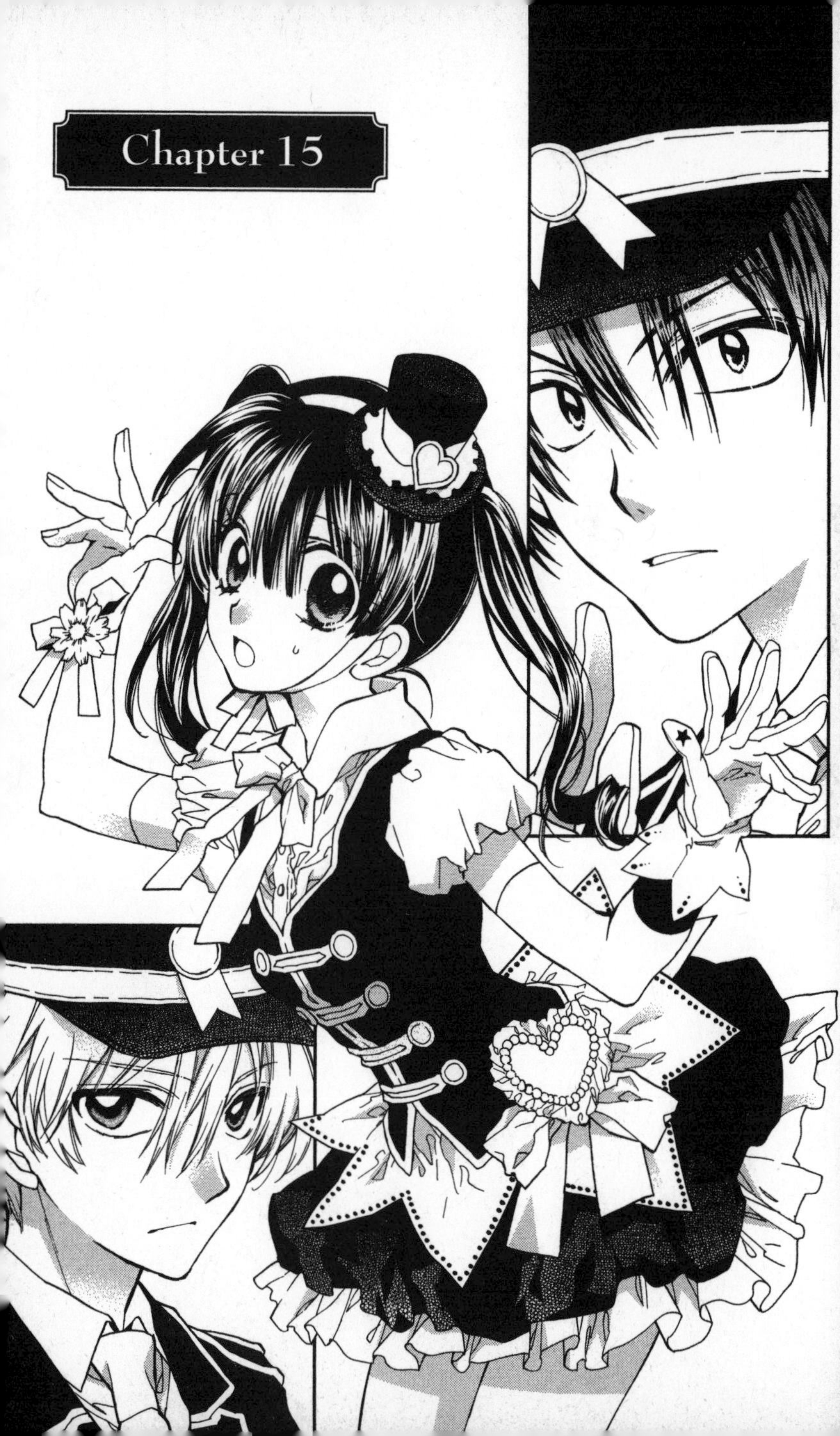

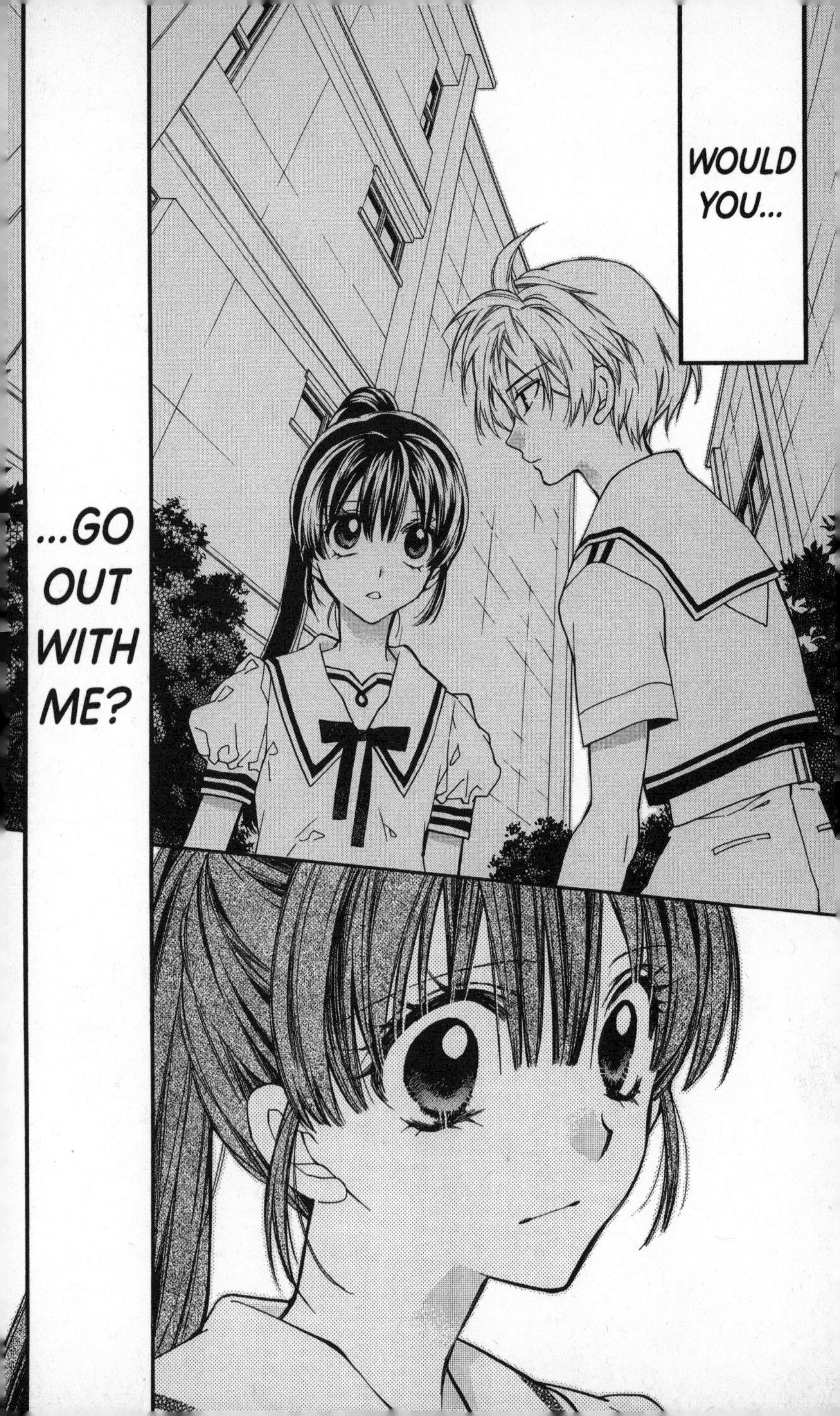
WOULD YOU...
...GO OUT WITH ME?

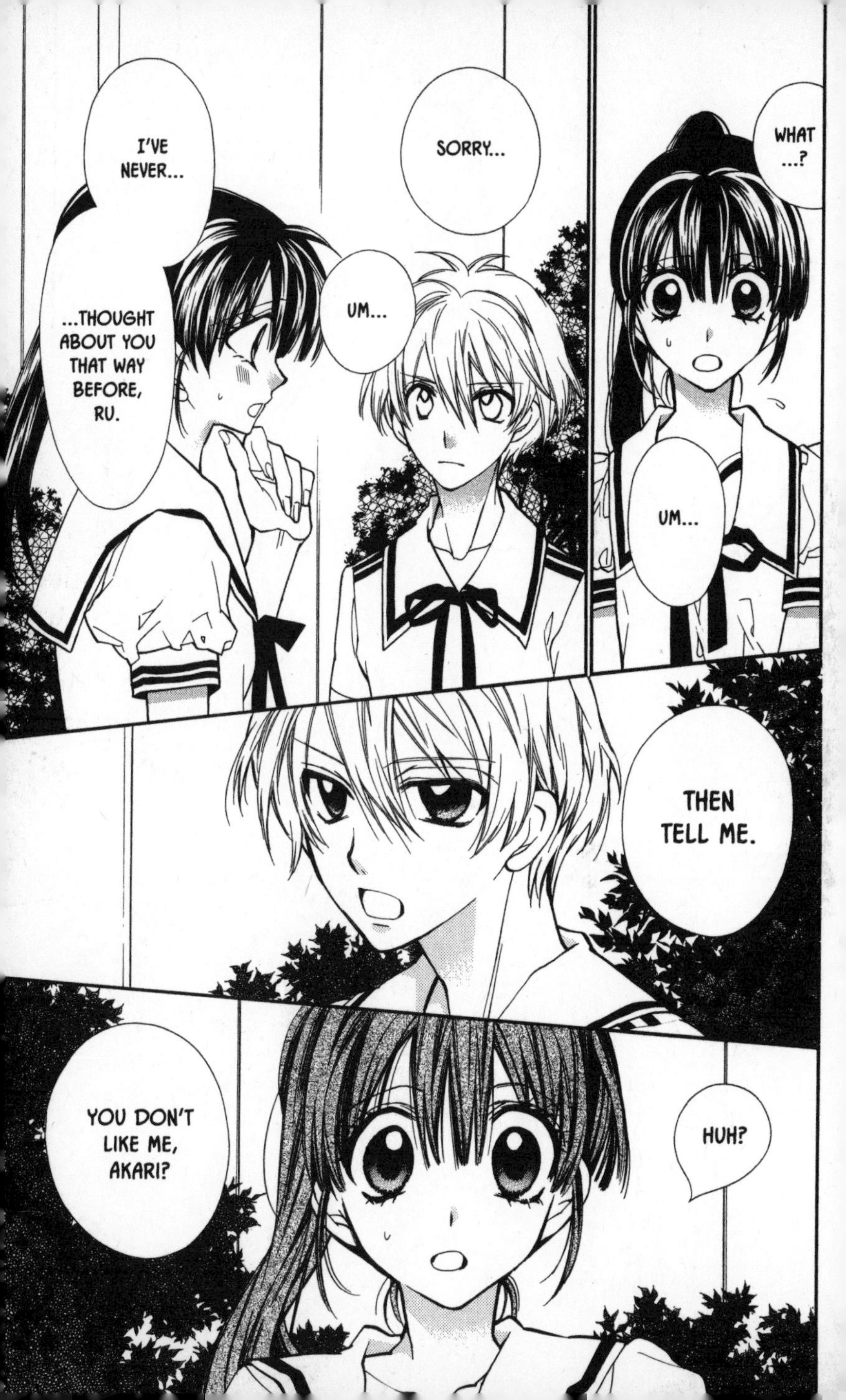
WHAT ...?
UM...
SORRY...
UM...
I'VE NEVER...
...THOUGHT ABOUT YOU THAT WAY BEFORE, RU.
THEN TELL ME.
YOU DON'T LIKE ME, AKARI?
HUH?

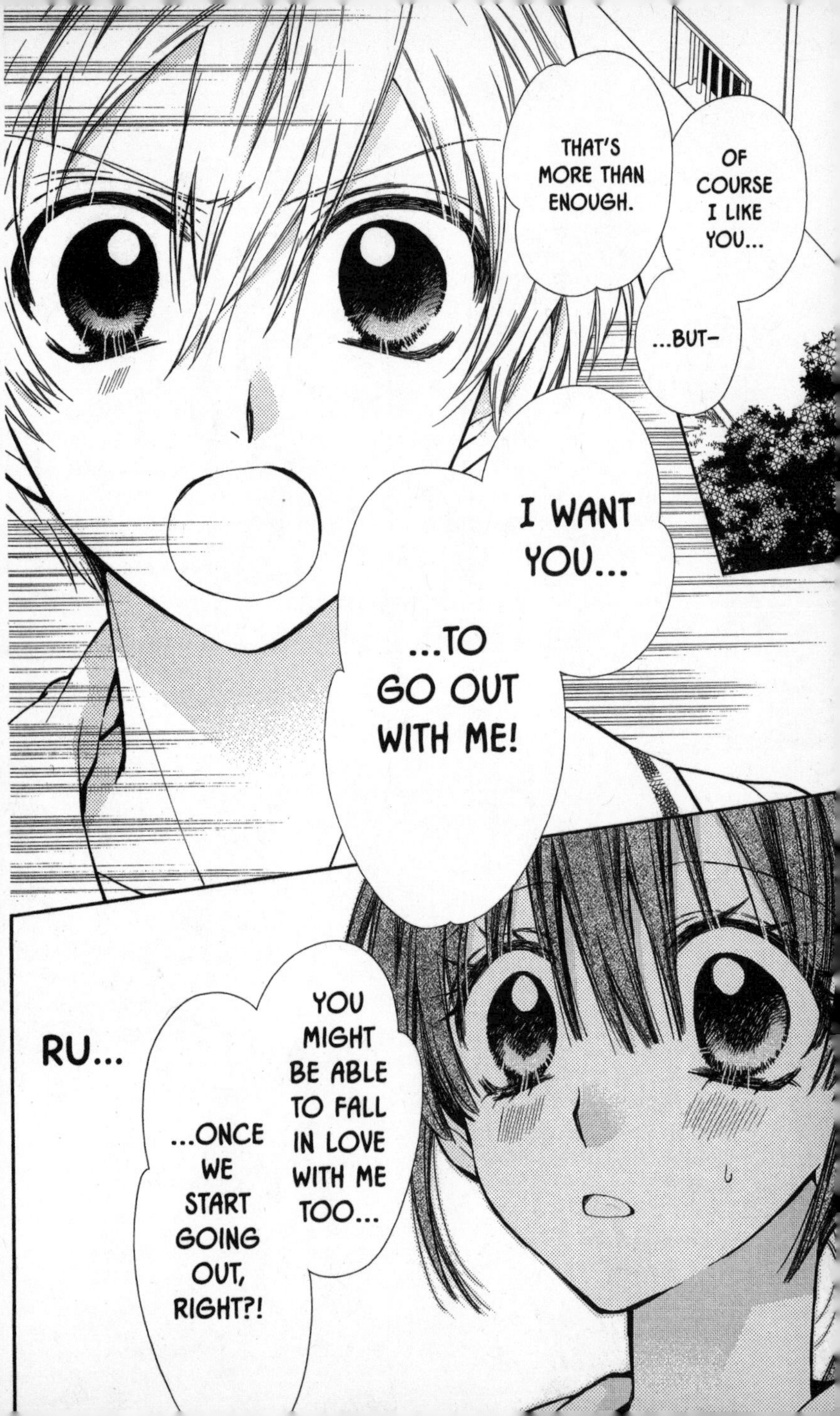
OF COURSE I LIKE YOU...
...BUT–
THAT'S MORE THAN ENOUGH.
I WANT YOU...
...TO GO OUT WITH ME!
YOU MIGHT BE ABLE TO FALL IN LOVE WITH ME TOO...
...ONCE WE START GOING OUT, RIGHT?!
RU...

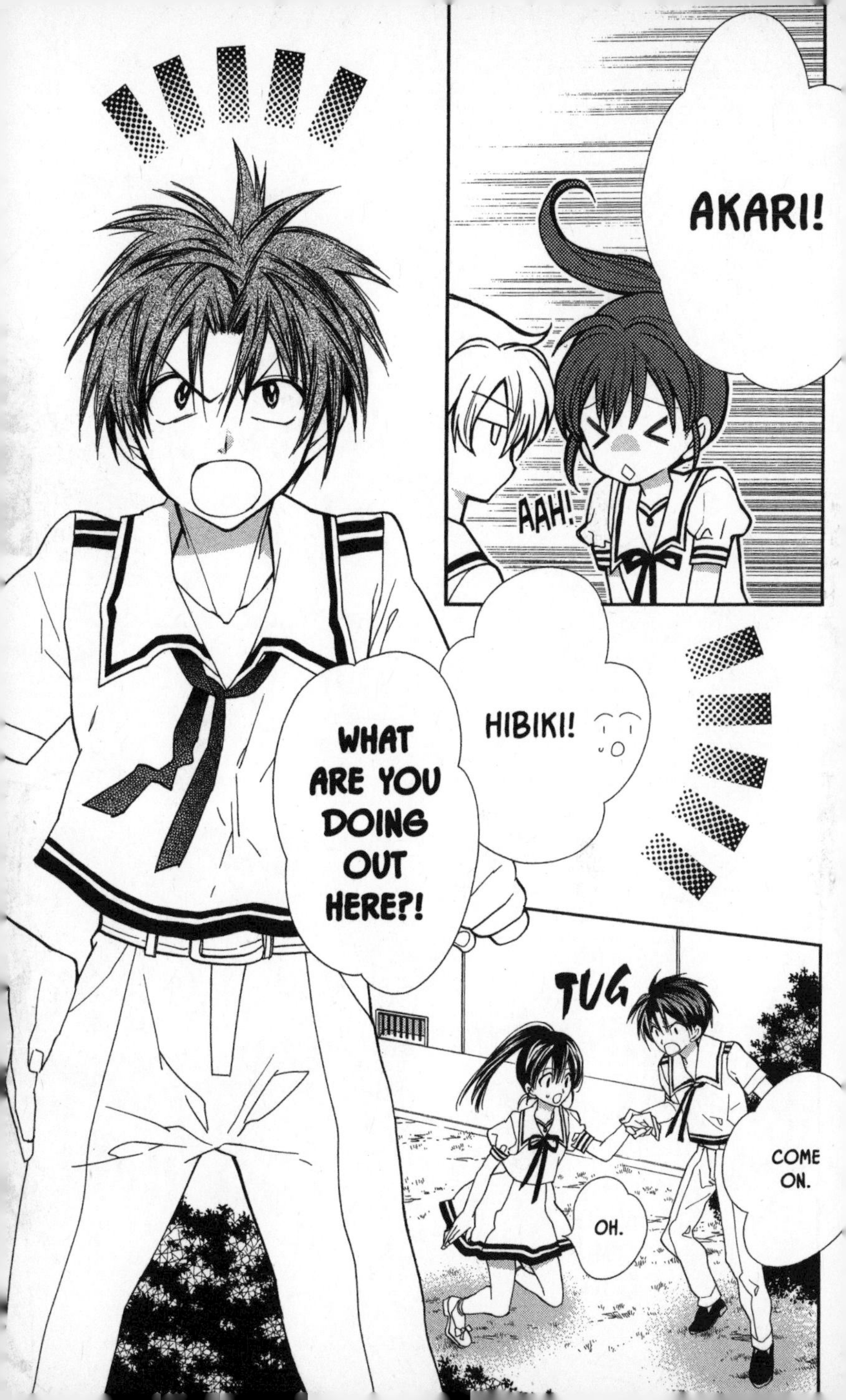
AKARI!
AAH!
HIBIKI!
WHAT ARE YOU DOING OUT HERE?!
TUG
COME ON.
OH.

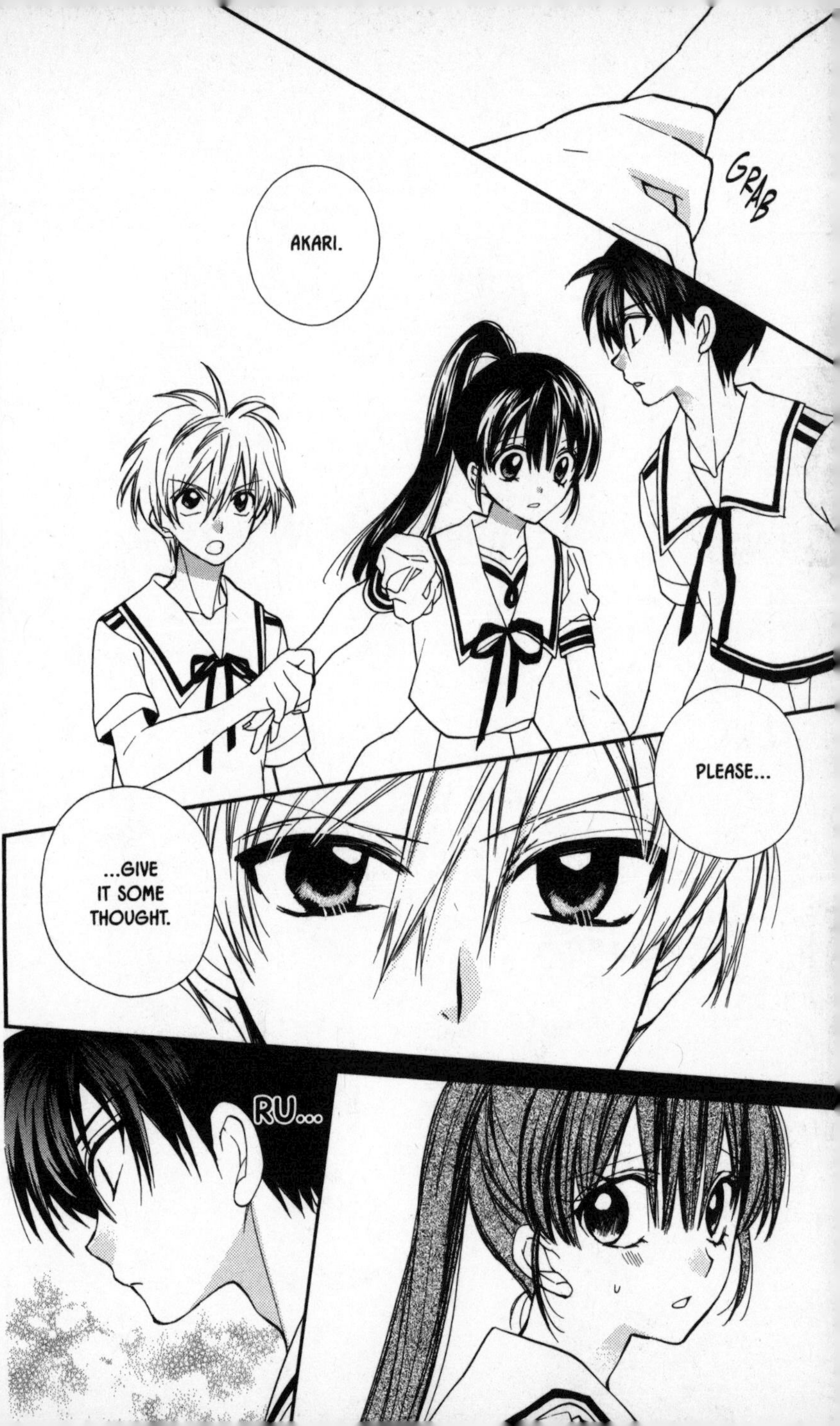
GRAB
AKARI.
PLEASE...
...GIVE IT SOME THOUGHT.
RU...

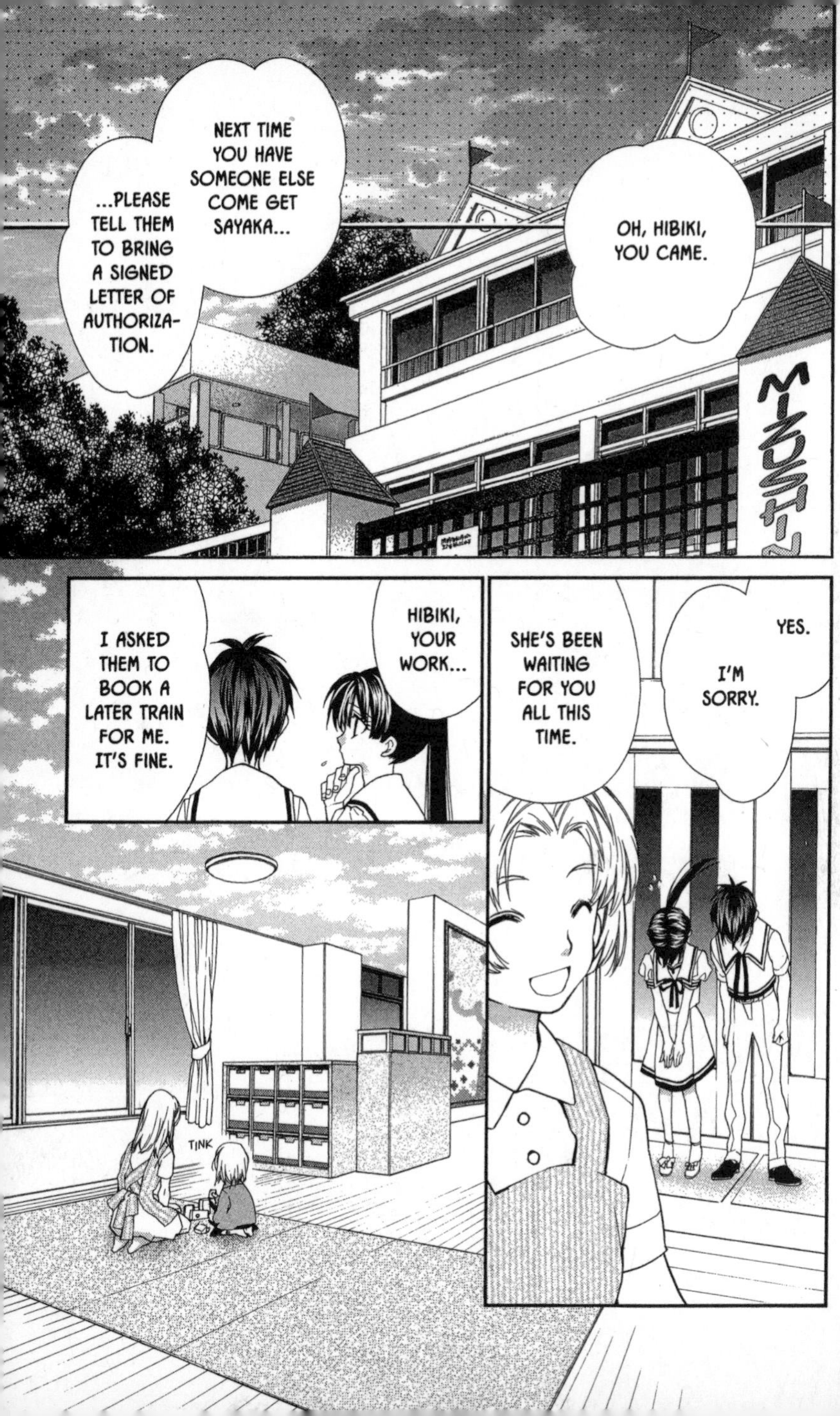
OH, HIBIKI, YOU CAME.
NEXT TIME YOU HAVE SOMEONE ELSE COME GET SAYAKA...
...PLEASE TELL THEM TO BRING A SIGNED LETTER OF AUTHORIZATION.
MIZUSHI
YES.
I'M SORRY.
SHE'S BEEN WAITING FOR YOU ALL THIS TIME.
HIBIKI, YOUR WORK...
I ASKED THEM TO BOOK A LATER TRAIN FOR ME. IT'S FINE.
TINK

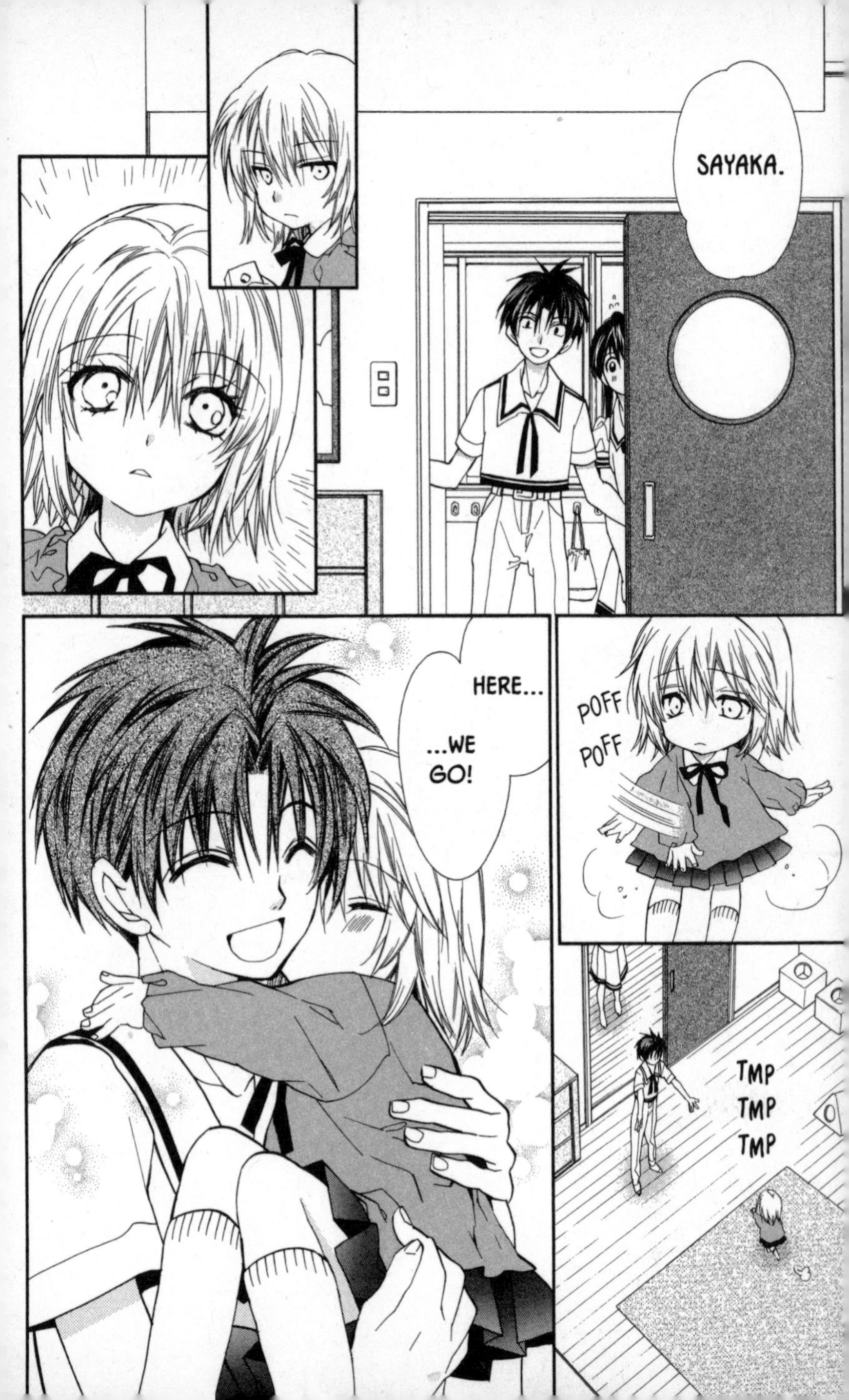
SAYAKA.
POFF POFF
TMP TMP TMP
HERE...
...WE GO!

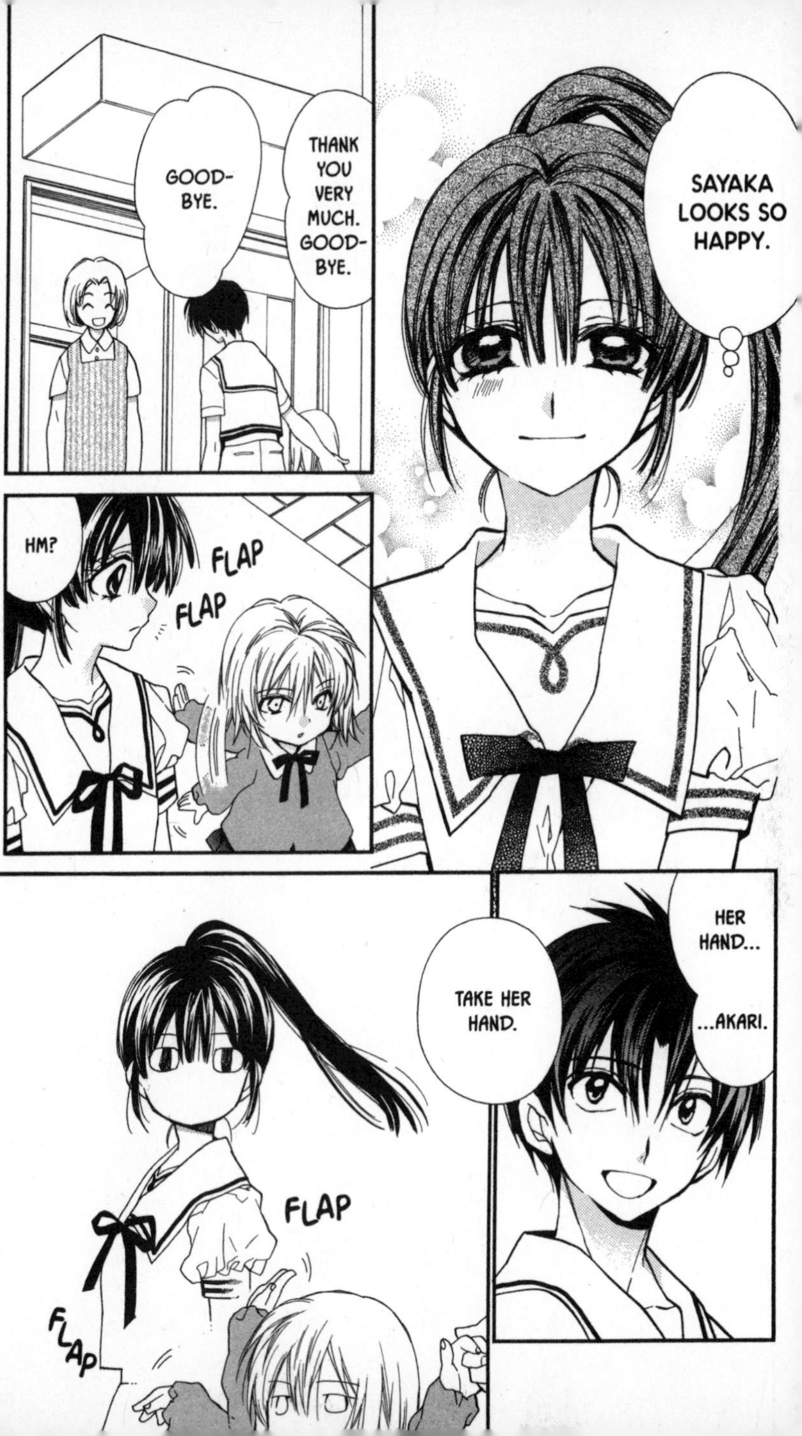
SAYAKA LOOKS SO HAPPY.
THANK YOU VERY MUCH. GOOD-BYE.
GOOD-BYE.
HM?
FLAP
FLAP
HER HAND...
...AKARI.
TAKE HER HAND.
FLAP
FLAP

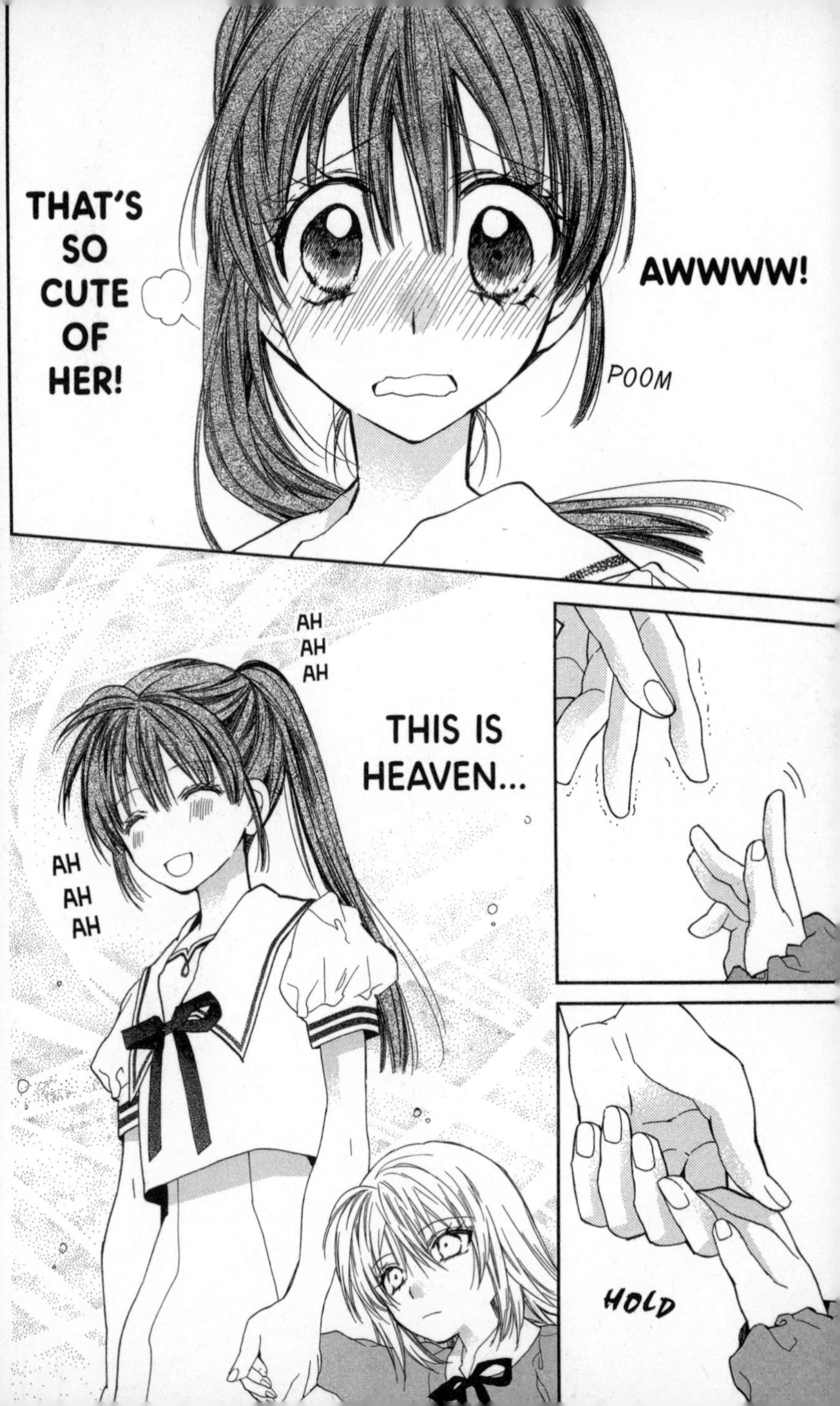
AWWWW!
POOM
THAT'S SO CUTE OF HER!
AH AH AH
THIS IS HEAVEN...
AH AH AH
HOLD

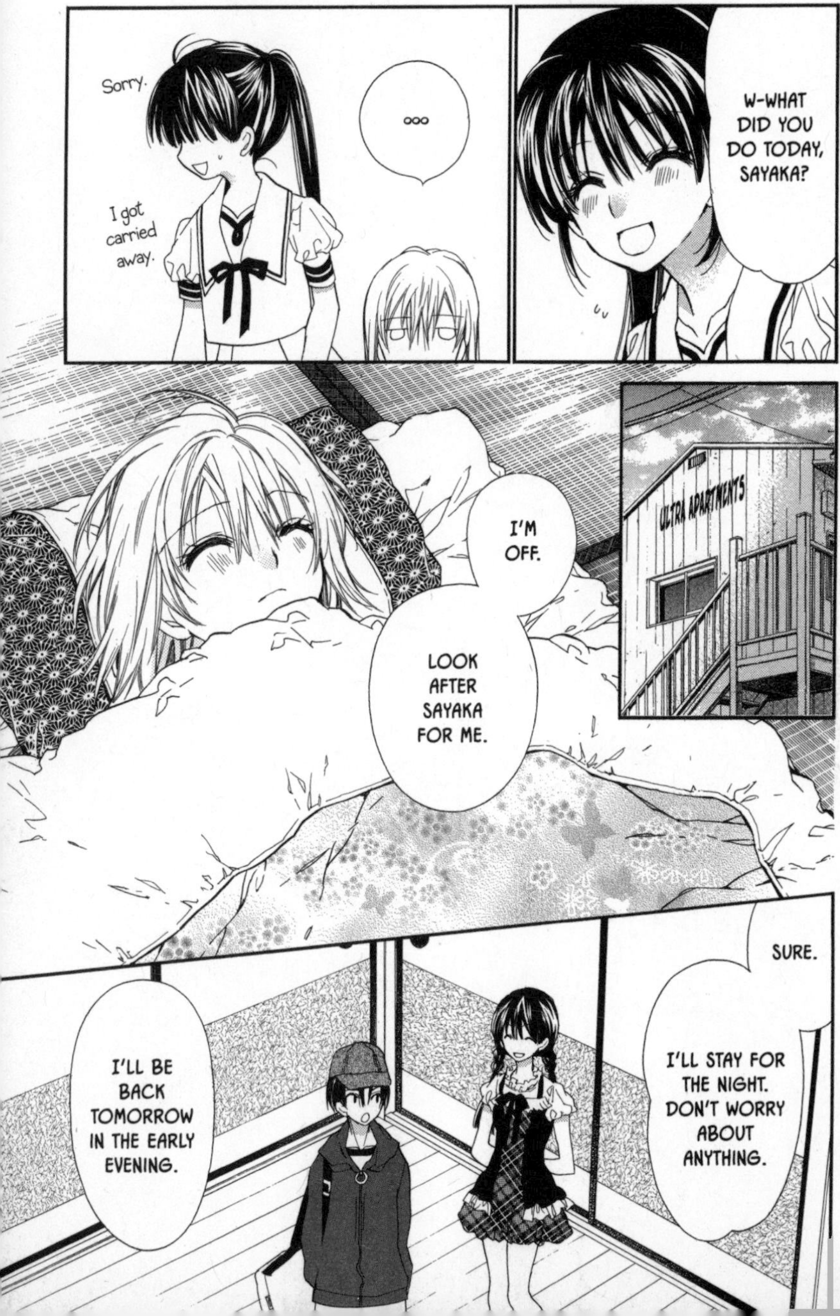
W-WHAT DID YOU DO TODAY, SAYAKA?
...
Sorry.
I got carried away.
ULTRA APARTMENTS
I'M OFF.
LOOK AFTER SAYAKA FOR ME.
SURE.
I'LL STAY FOR THE NIGHT. DON'T WORRY ABOUT ANYTHING.
I'LL BE BACK TOMORROW IN THE EARLY EVENING.

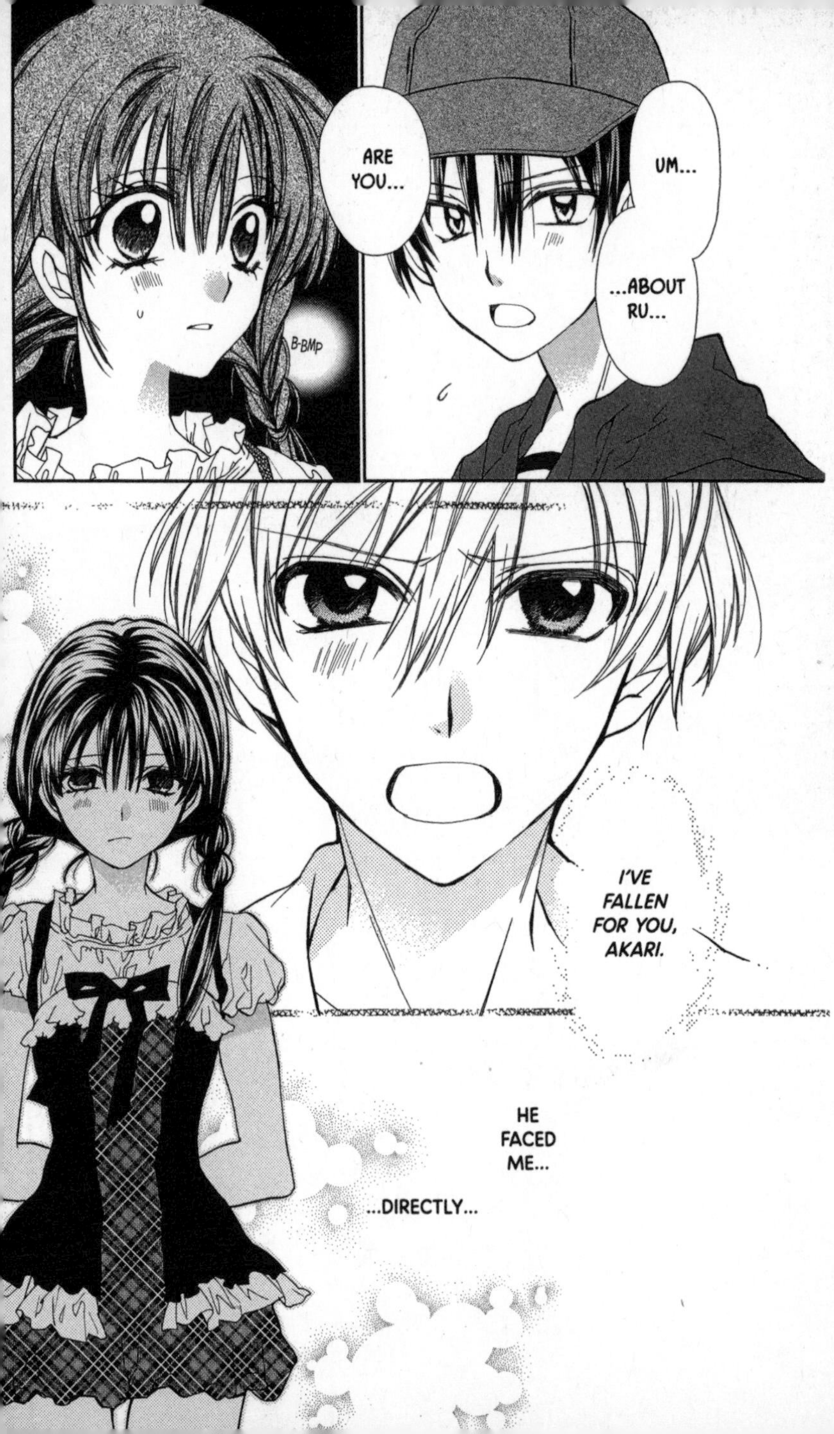
UM...
...ABOUT RU...
ARE YOU...
B-BMP
I'VE FALLEN FOR YOU, AKARI.
HE FACED ME...
...DIRECTLY...

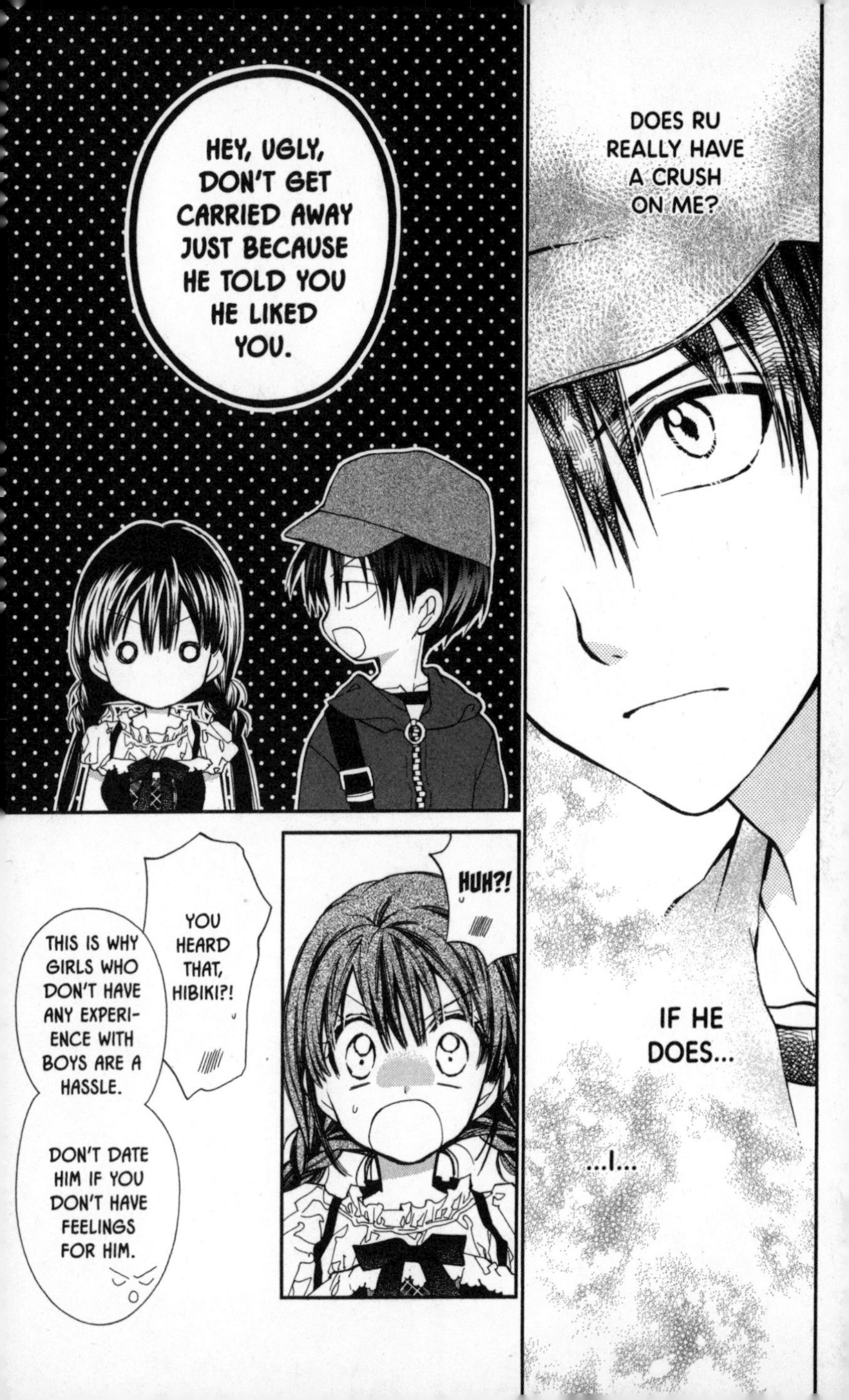
DOES RU REALLY HAVE A CRUSH ON ME?
IF HE DOES...
...I...
HEY, UGLY, DON'T GET CARRIED AWAY JUST BECAUSE HE TOLD YOU HE LIKED YOU.
HUH?!
YOU HEARD THAT, HIBIKI?!
THIS IS WHY GIRLS WHO DON'T HAVE ANY EXPERIENCE WITH BOYS ARE A HASSLE.
DON'T DATE HIM IF YOU DON'T HAVE FEELINGS FOR HIM.

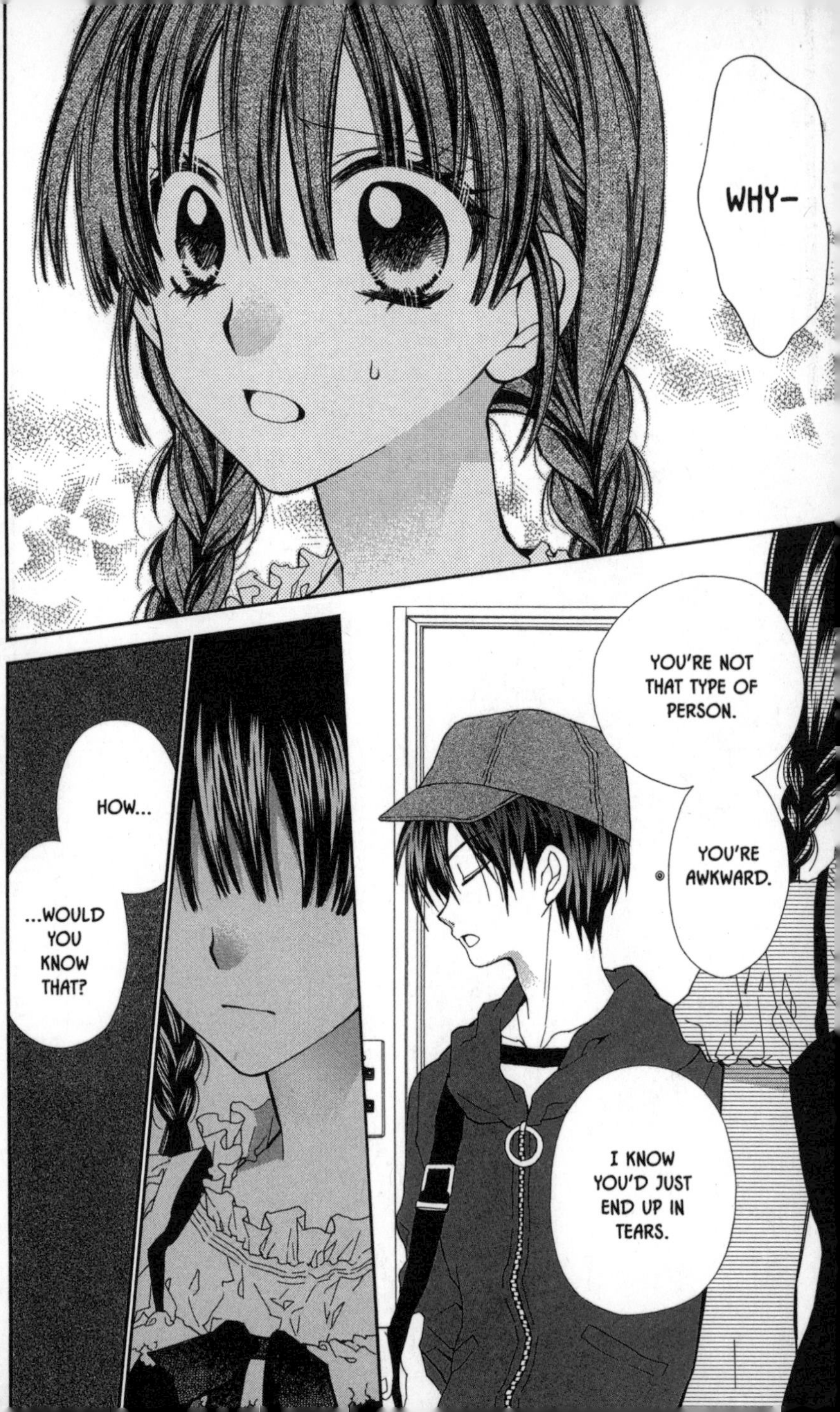
WHY–
YOU'RE NOT THAT TYPE OF PERSON.
YOU'RE AWKWARD.
I KNOW YOU'D JUST END UP IN TEARS.
HOW...
...WOULD YOU KNOW THAT?

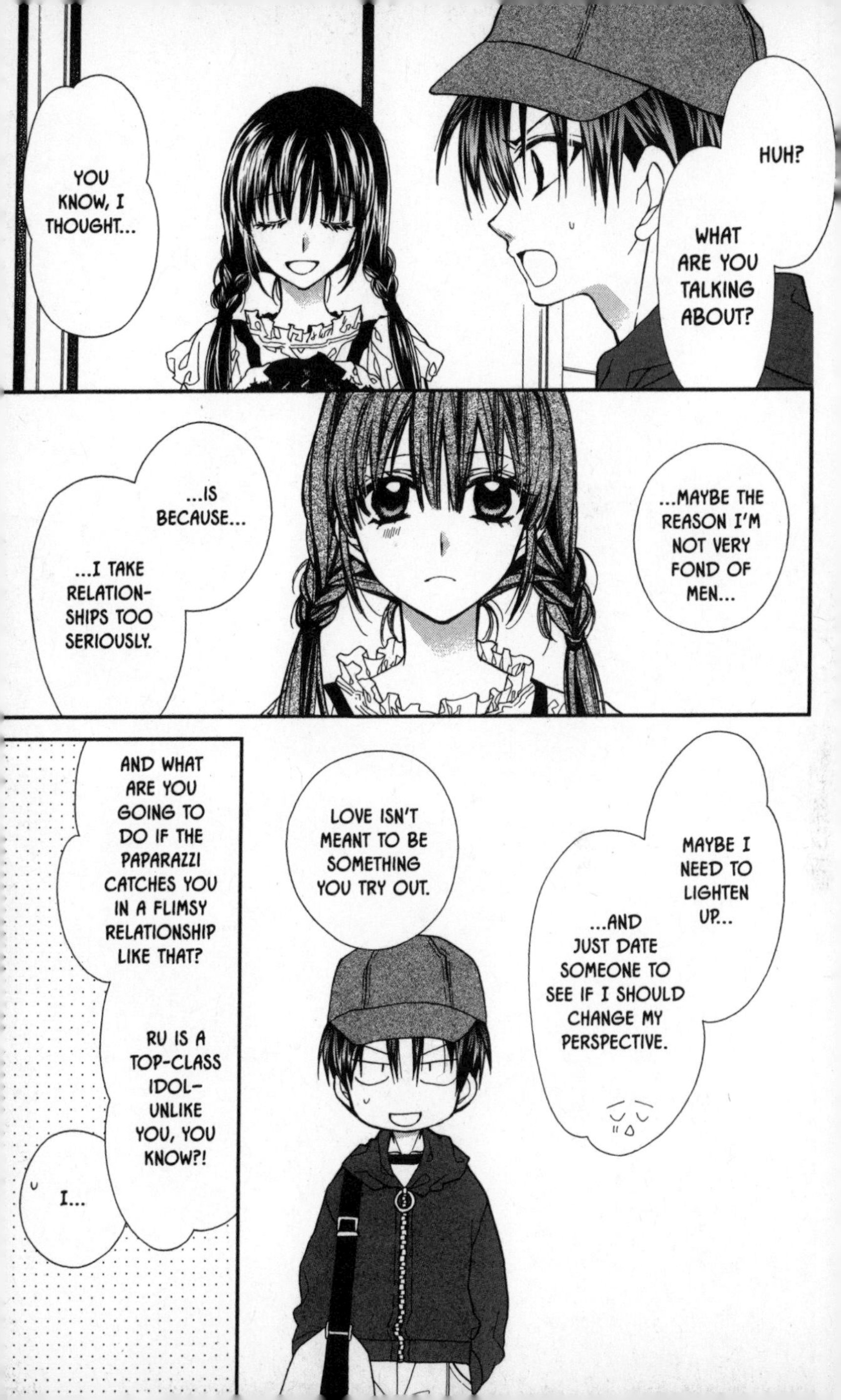
HUH?
WHAT ARE YOU TALKING ABOUT?
YOU KNOW, I THOUGHT...
...MAYBE THE REASON I'M NOT VERY FOND OF MEN...
...IS BECAUSE...
...I TAKE RELATION-SHIPS TOO SERIOUSLY.
MAYBE I NEED TO LIGHTEN UP...
...AND JUST DATE SOMEONE TO SEE IF I SHOULD CHANGE MY PERSPECTIVE.
LOVE ISN'T MEANT TO BE SOMETHING YOU TRY OUT.
AND WHAT ARE YOU GOING TO DO IF THE PAPARAZZI CATCHES YOU IN A FLIMSY RELATIONSHIP LIKE THAT?
RU IS A TOP-CLASS IDOL—UNLIKE YOU, YOU KNOW?!
I...

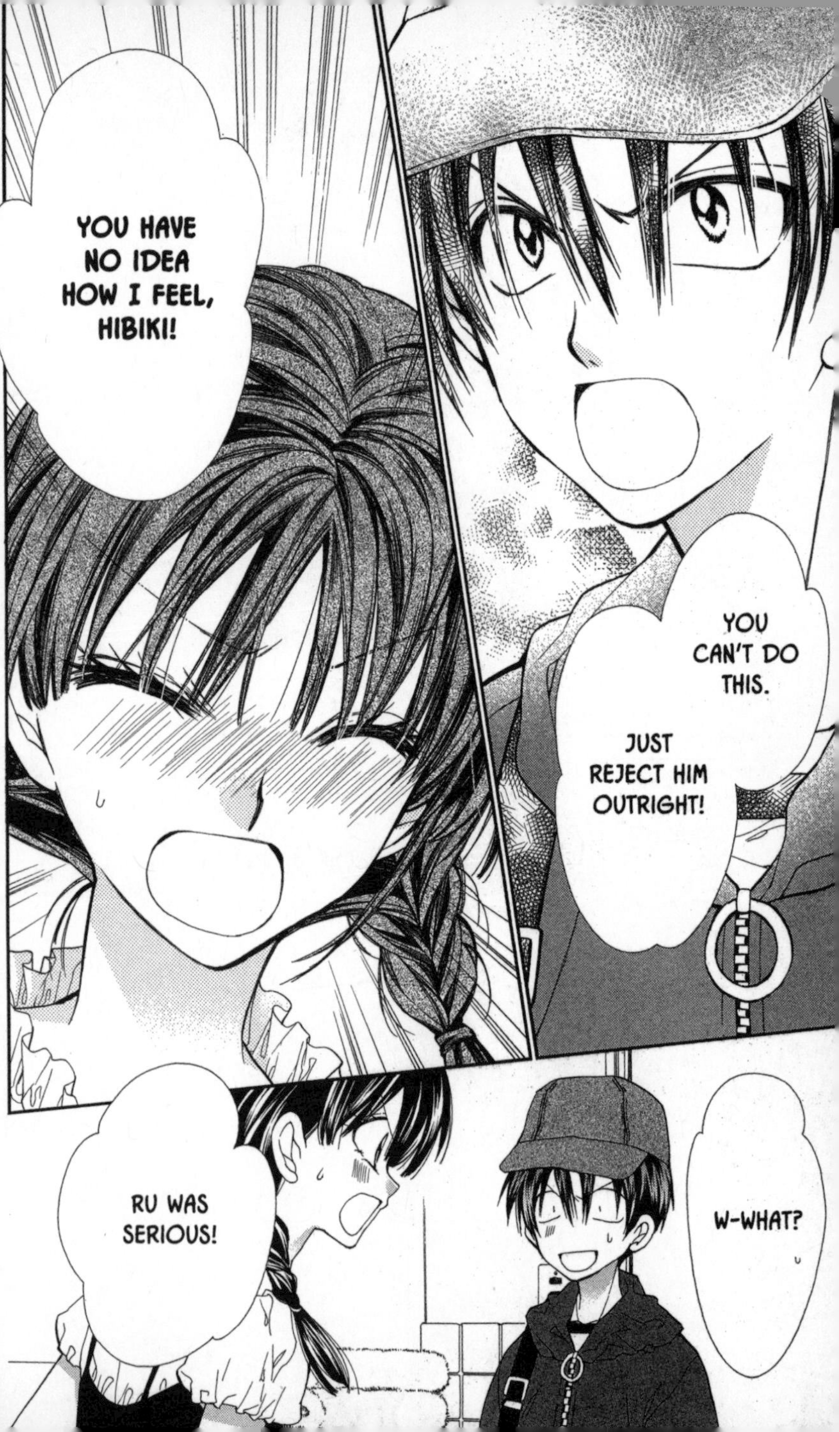
YOU CAN'T DO THIS.
JUST REJECT HIM OUTRIGHT!
YOU HAVE NO IDEA HOW I FEEL, HIBIKI!
W-WHAT?
RU WAS SERIOUS!

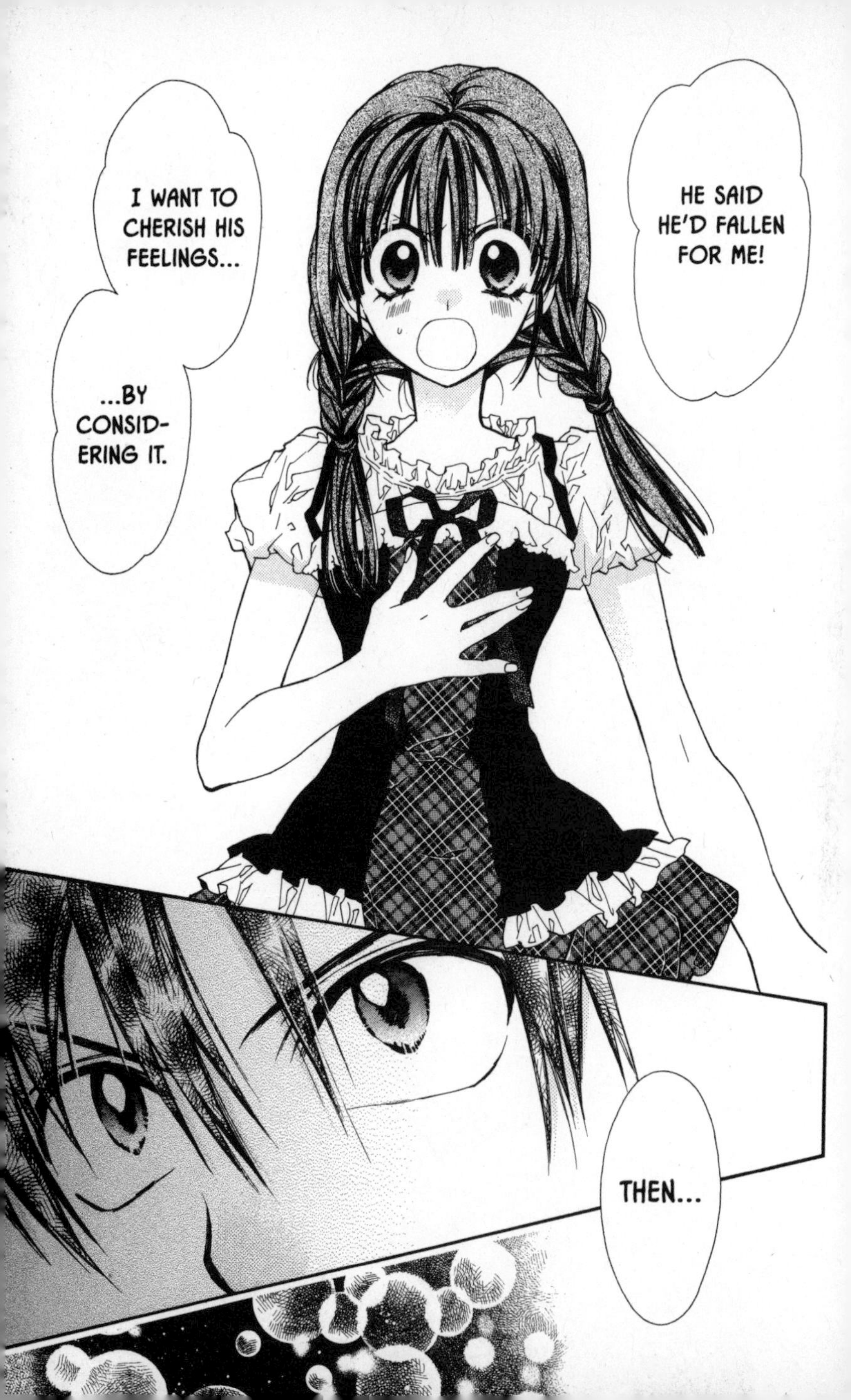
HE SAID HE'D FALLEN FOR ME!
I WANT TO CHERISH HIS FEELINGS...
...BY CONSID-ERING IT.
THEN...

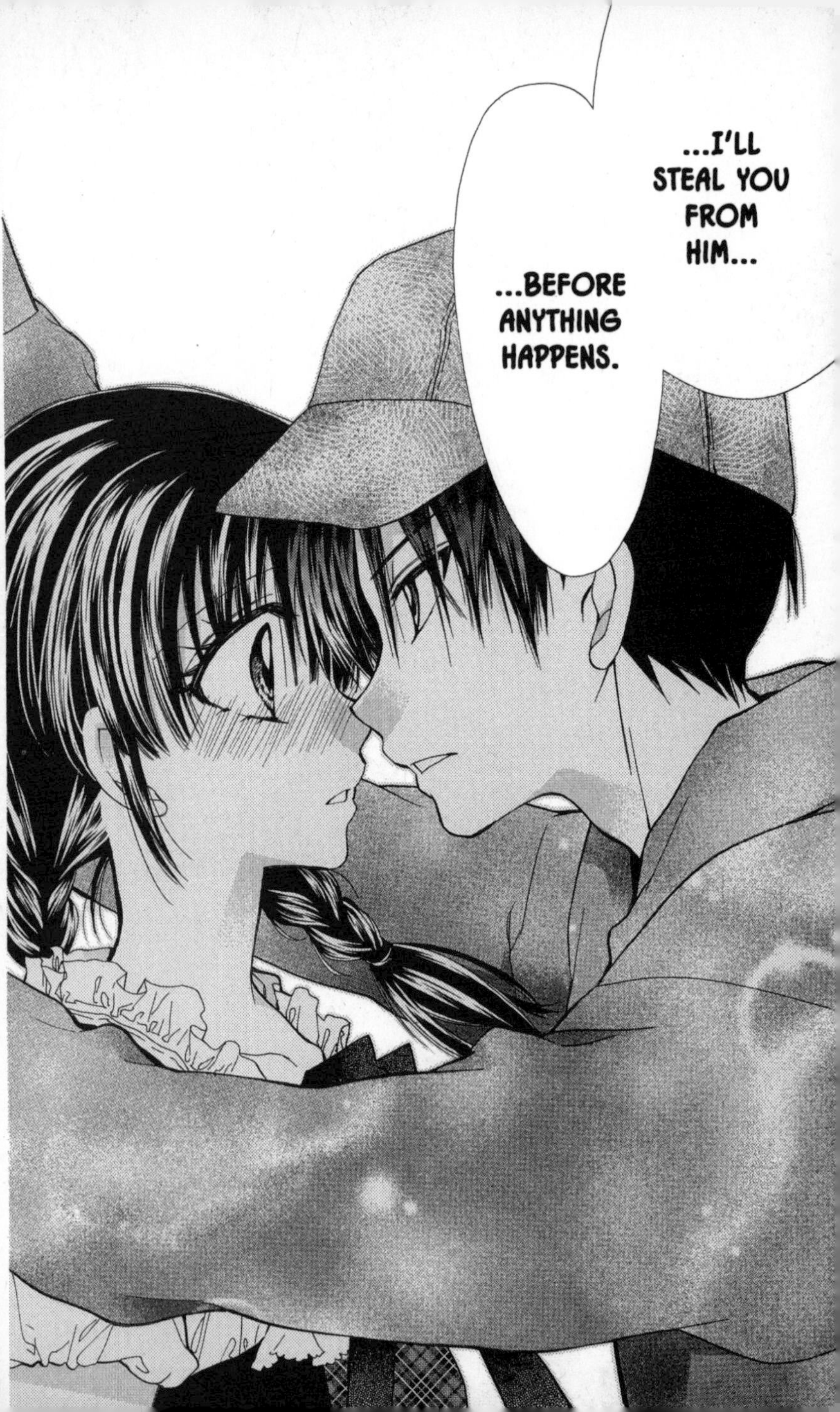
...I'LL STEAL YOU FROM HIM...
...BEFORE ANYTHING HAPPENS.

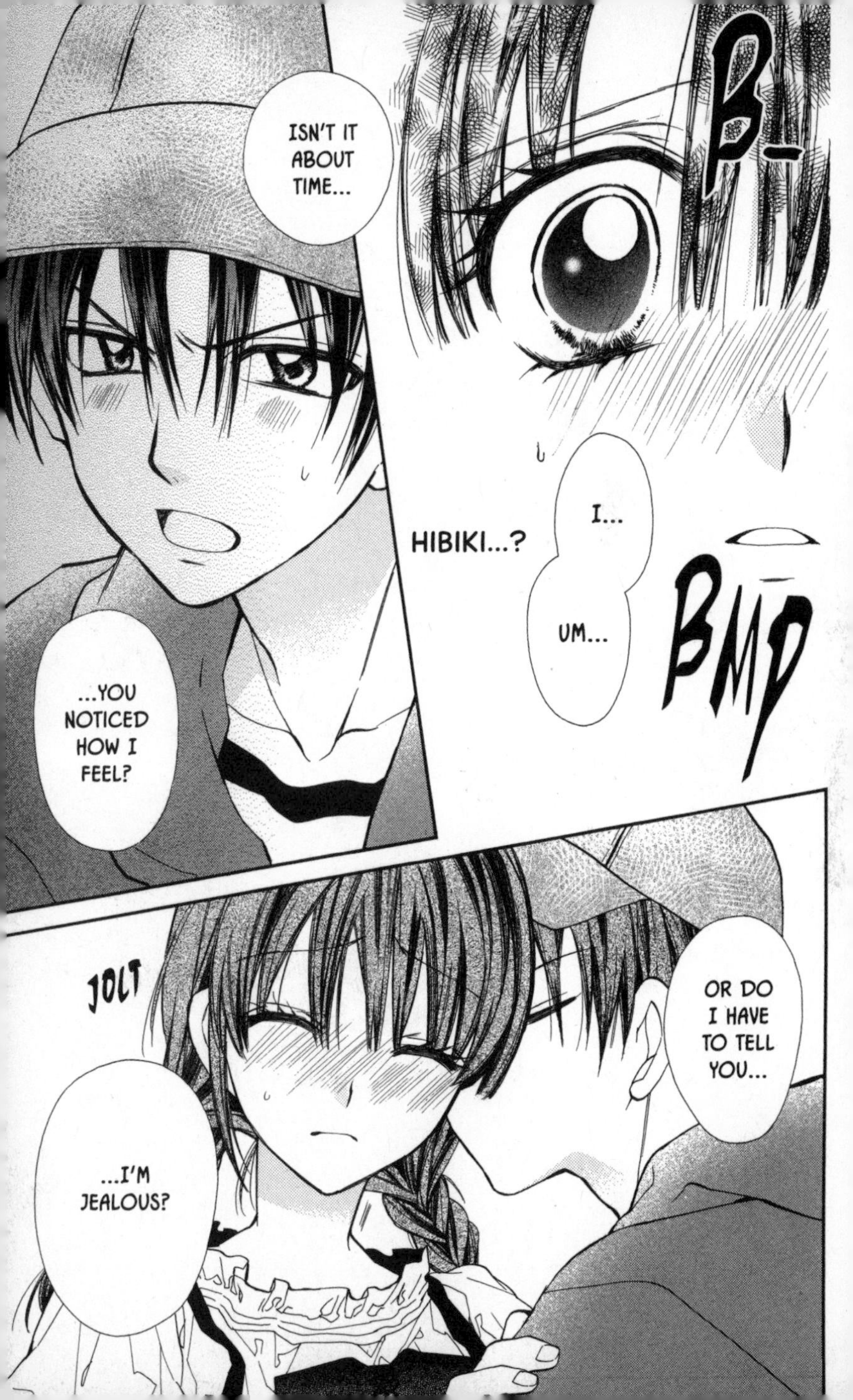
B-
I...
UM...
HIBIKI...?
BMP
ISN'T IT ABOUT TIME...
...YOU NOTICED HOW I FEEL?
OR DO I HAVE TO TELL YOU...
JOLT
...I'M JEALOUS?

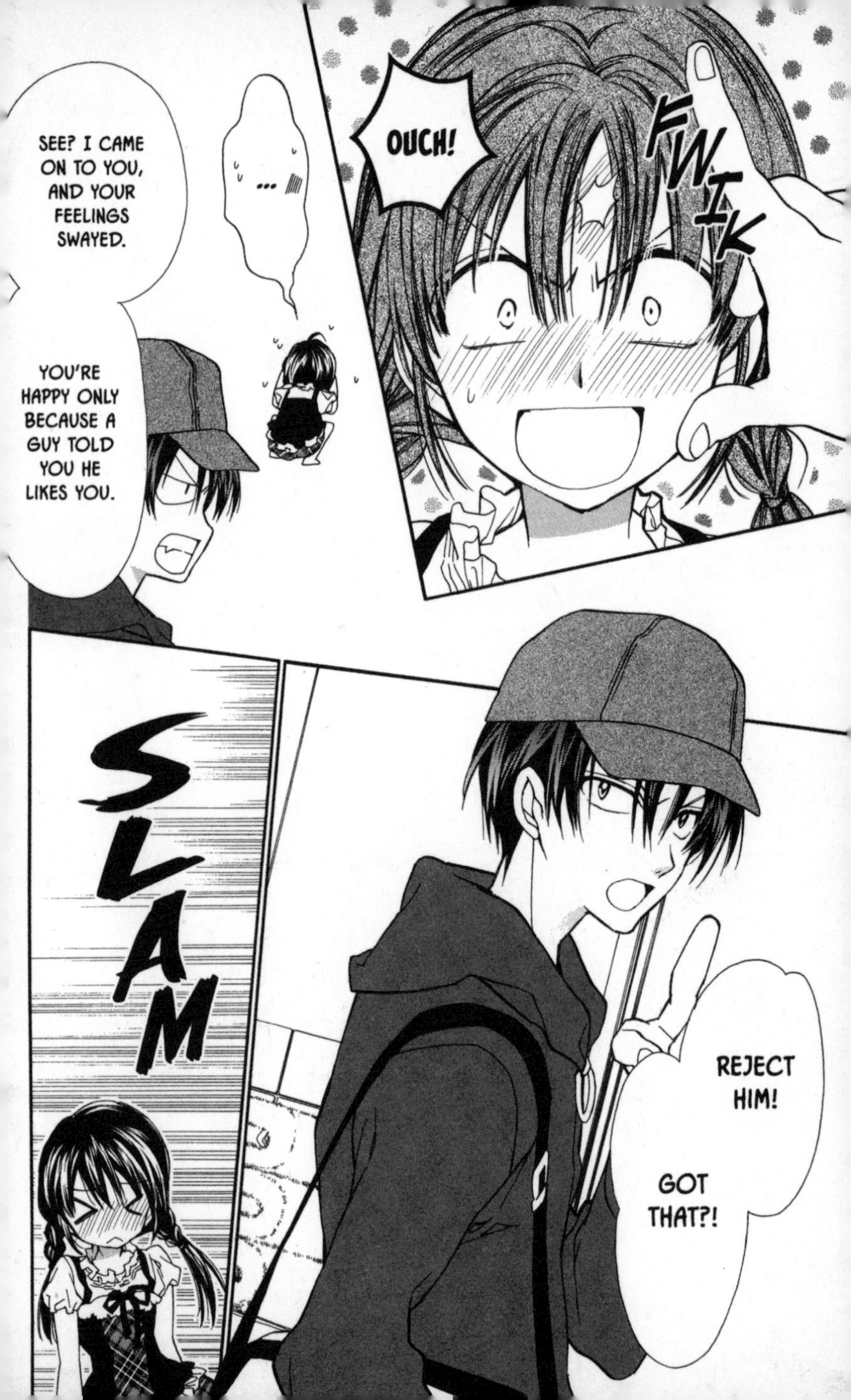

OUCH!
FWIK
...
SEE? I CAME ON TO YOU, AND YOUR FEELINGS SWAYED.
YOU'RE HAPPY ONLY BECAUSE A GUY TOLD YOU HE LIKES YOU.
REJECT HIM!
GOT THAT?!
SLAM

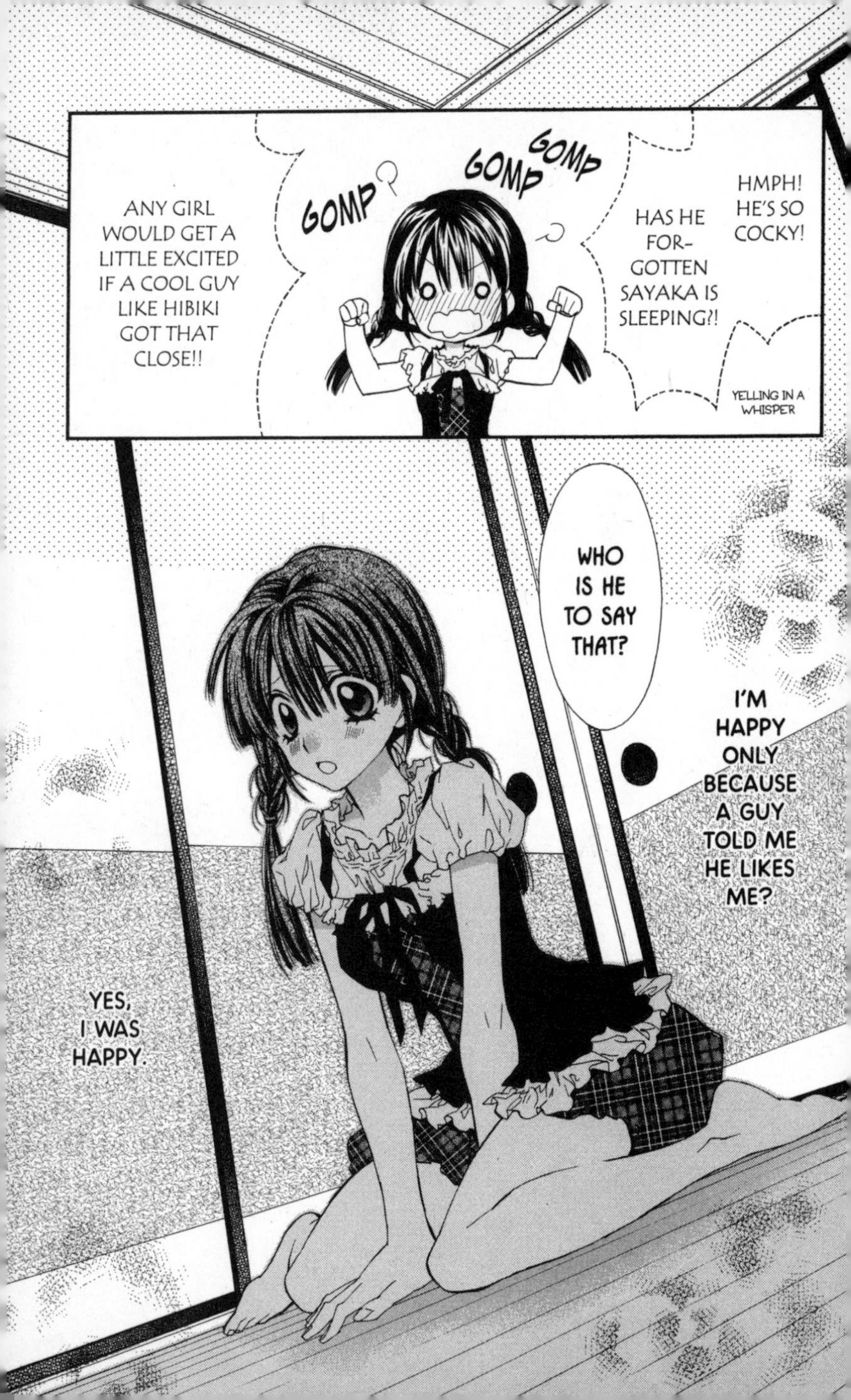
HMPH! HE'S SO COCKY!
HAS HE FOR-GOTTEN SAYAKA IS SLEEPING?!
YELLING IN A WHISPER
GOMP GOMP GOMP
ANY GIRL WOULD GET A LITTLE EXCITED IF A COOL GUY LIKE HIBIKI GOT THAT CLOSE!!
WHO IS HE TO SAY THAT?
I'M HAPPY ONLY BECAUSE A GUY TOLD ME HE LIKES ME?
YES, I WAS HAPPY.

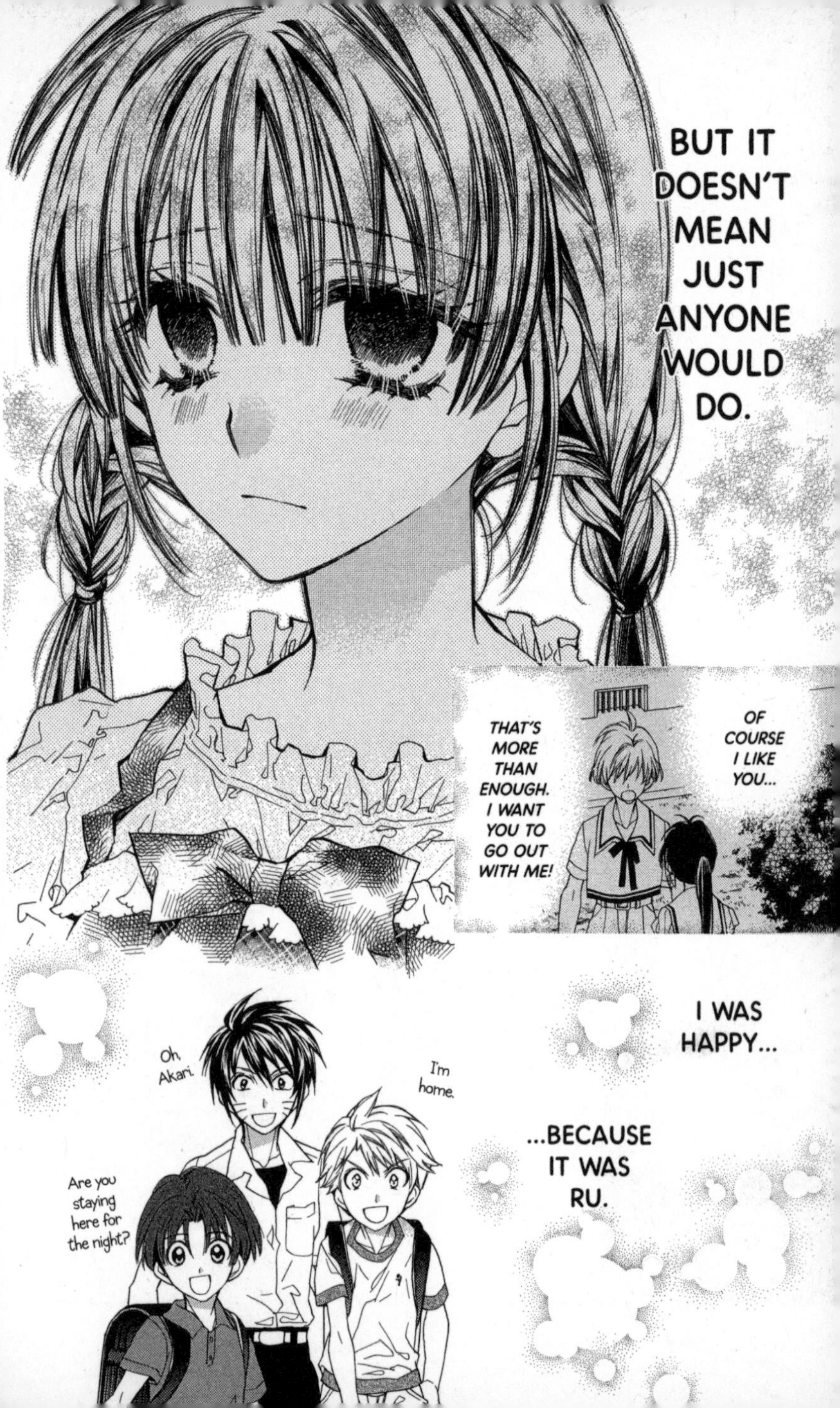
BUT IT DOESN'T MEAN JUST ANYONE WOULD DO.
OF COURSE I LIKE YOU...
THAT'S MORE THAN ENOUGH. I WANT YOU TO GO OUT WITH ME!
I WAS HAPPY...
...BECAUSE IT WAS RU.
I'm home.
Oh, Akari.
Are you staying here for the night?

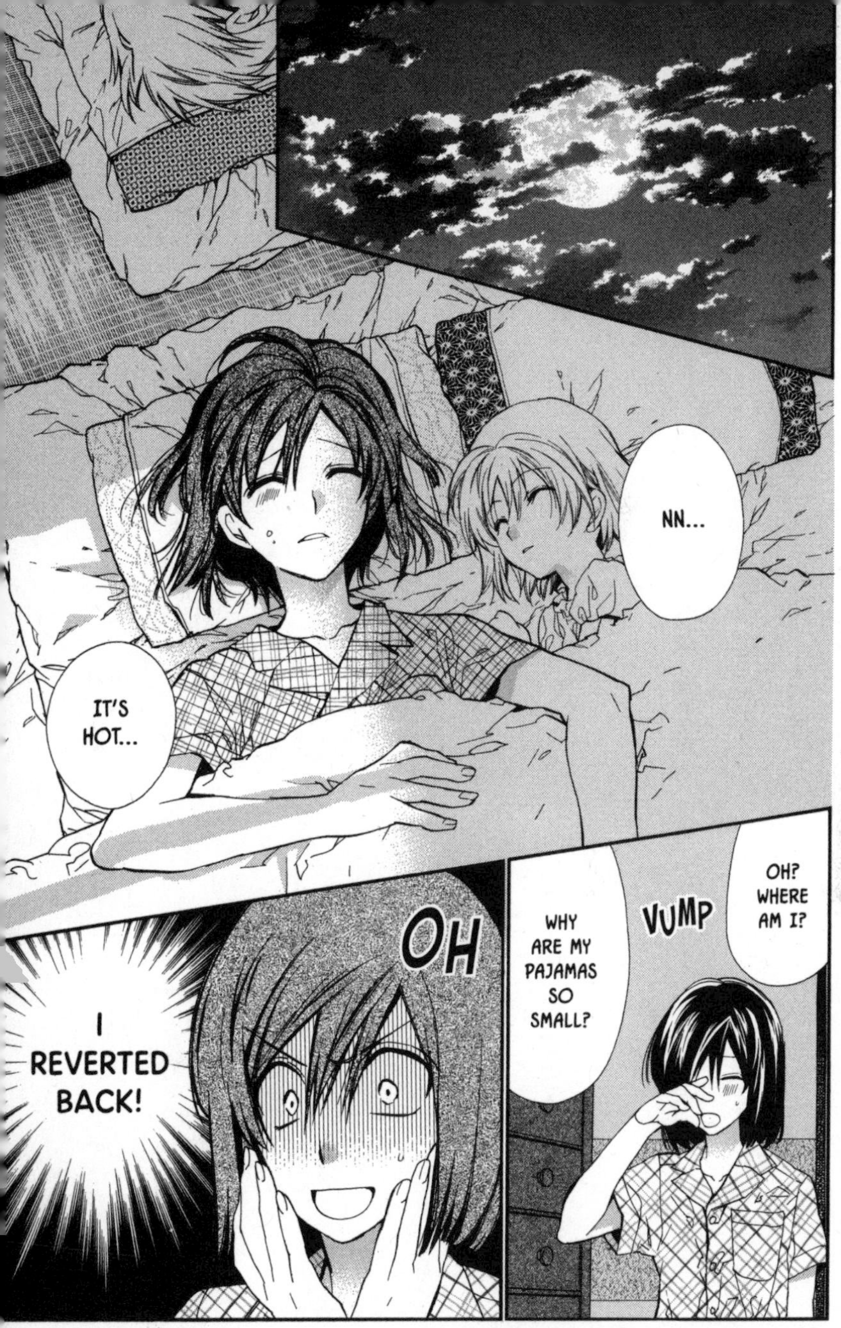
NN...
IT'S HOT...
OH? WHERE AM I?
VUMP
WHY ARE MY PAJAMAS SO SMALL?
OH
I REVERTED BACK!

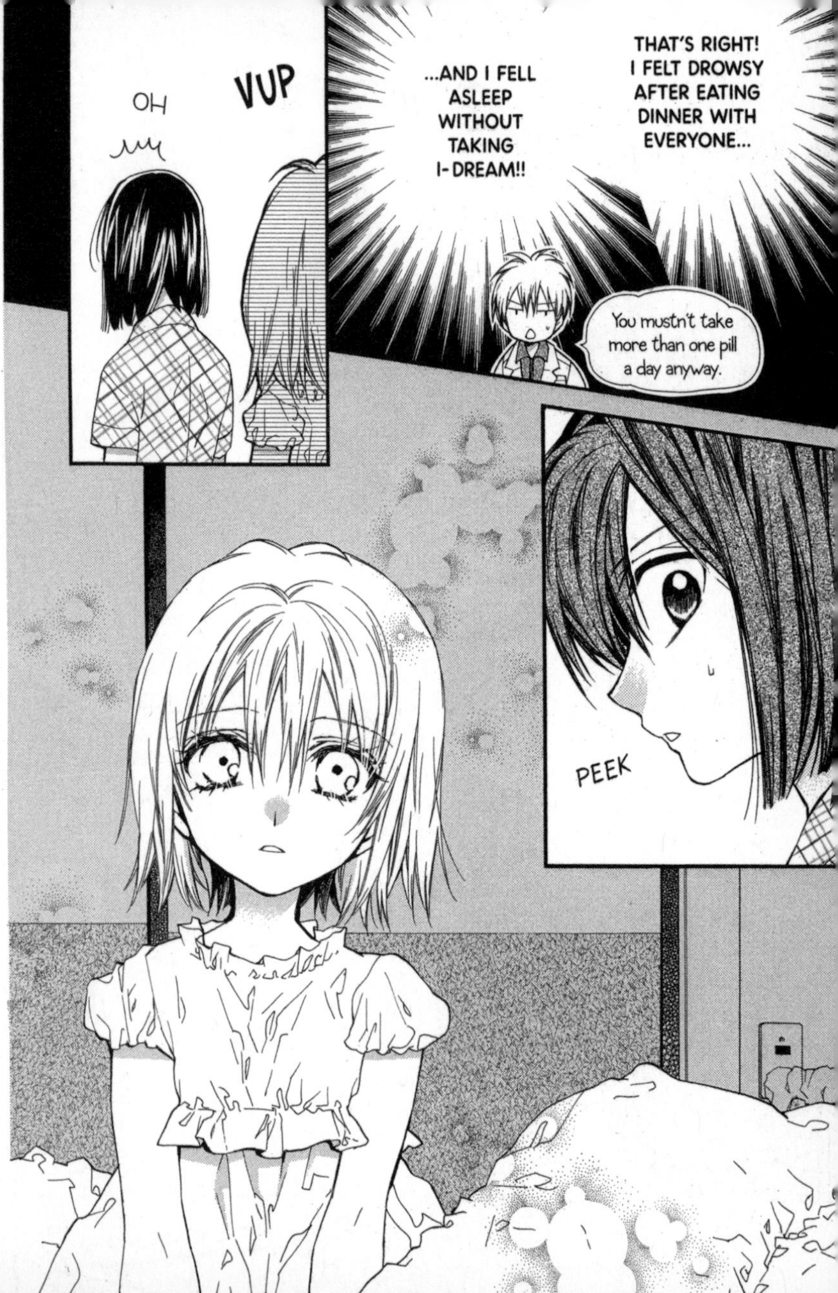
THAT'S RIGHT! I FELT DROWSY AFTER EATING DINNER WITH EVERYONE...
...AND I FELL ASLEEP WITHOUT TAKING I-DREAM!!
You mustn't take more than one pill a day anyway.
VUP
OH
PEEK

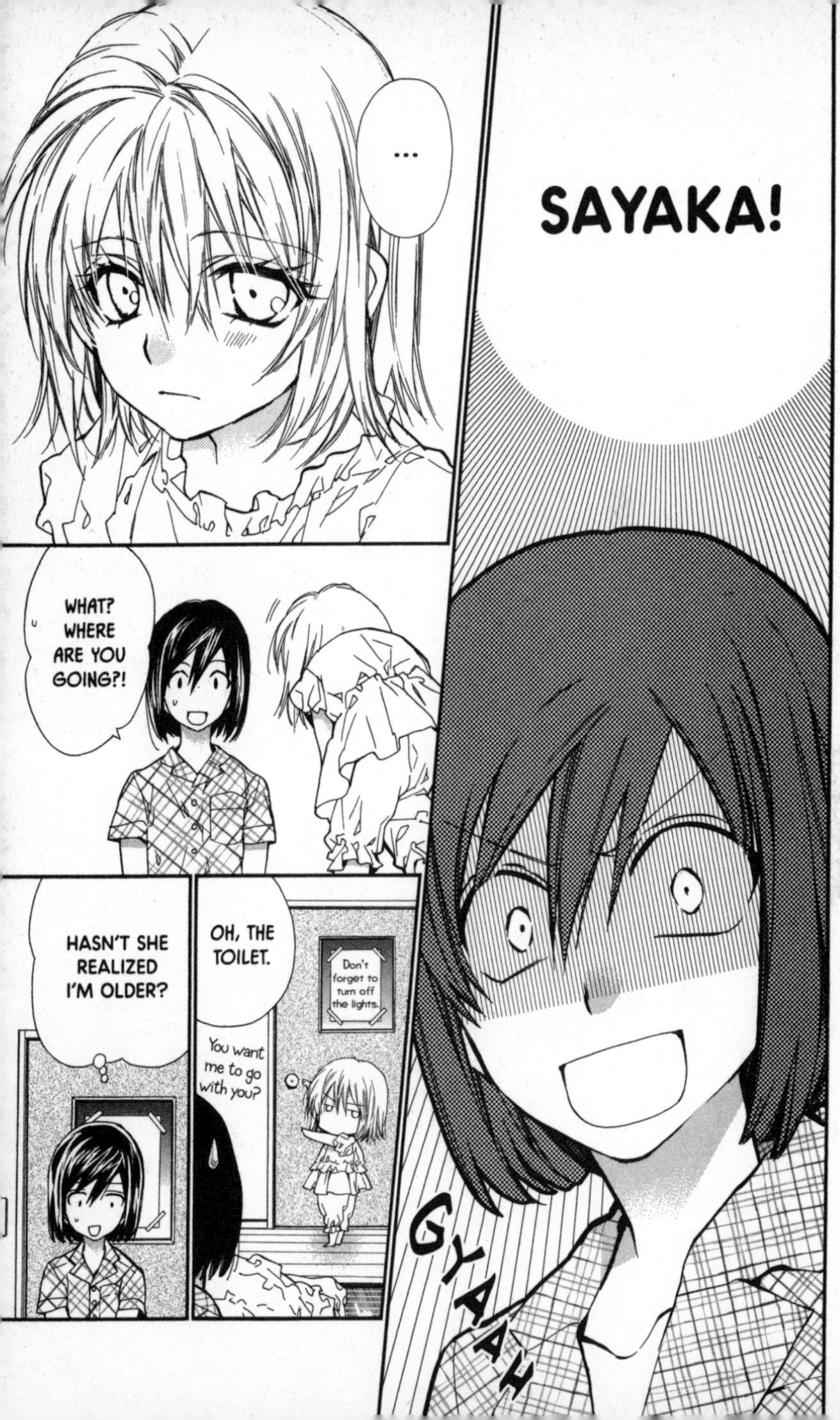
SAYAKA!
GYAAH
...
WHAT? WHERE ARE YOU GOING?!
OH, THE TOILET.
Don't forget to turn off the lights.
You want me to go with you?
HASN'T SHE REALIZED I'M OLDER?

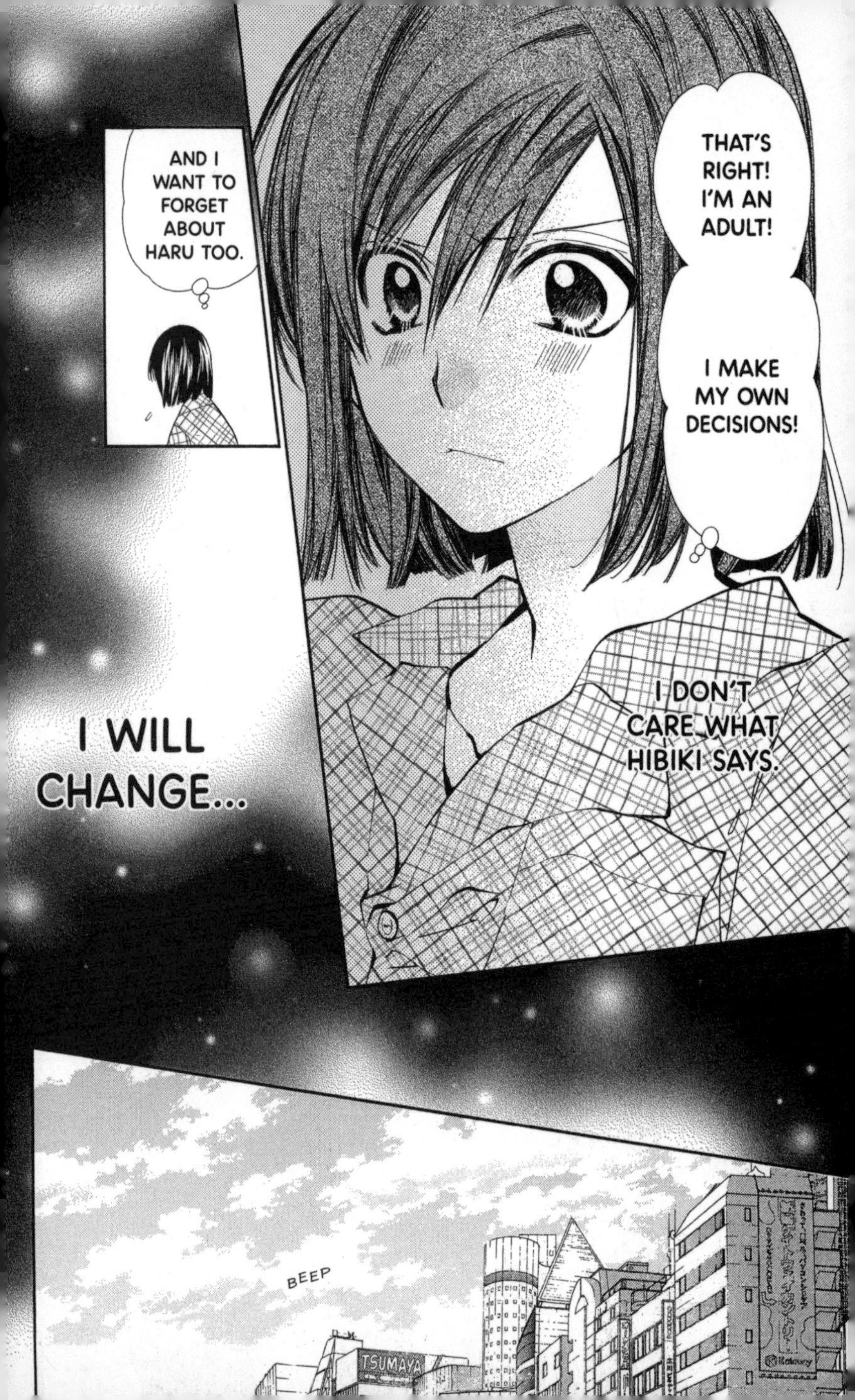
THAT'S RIGHT! I'M AN ADULT!
I MAKE MY OWN DECISIONS!
I DON'T CARE WHAT HIBIKI SAYS.
AND I WANT TO FORGET ABOUT HARU TOO.
I WILL CHANGE...
BEEP
TSUMAYA

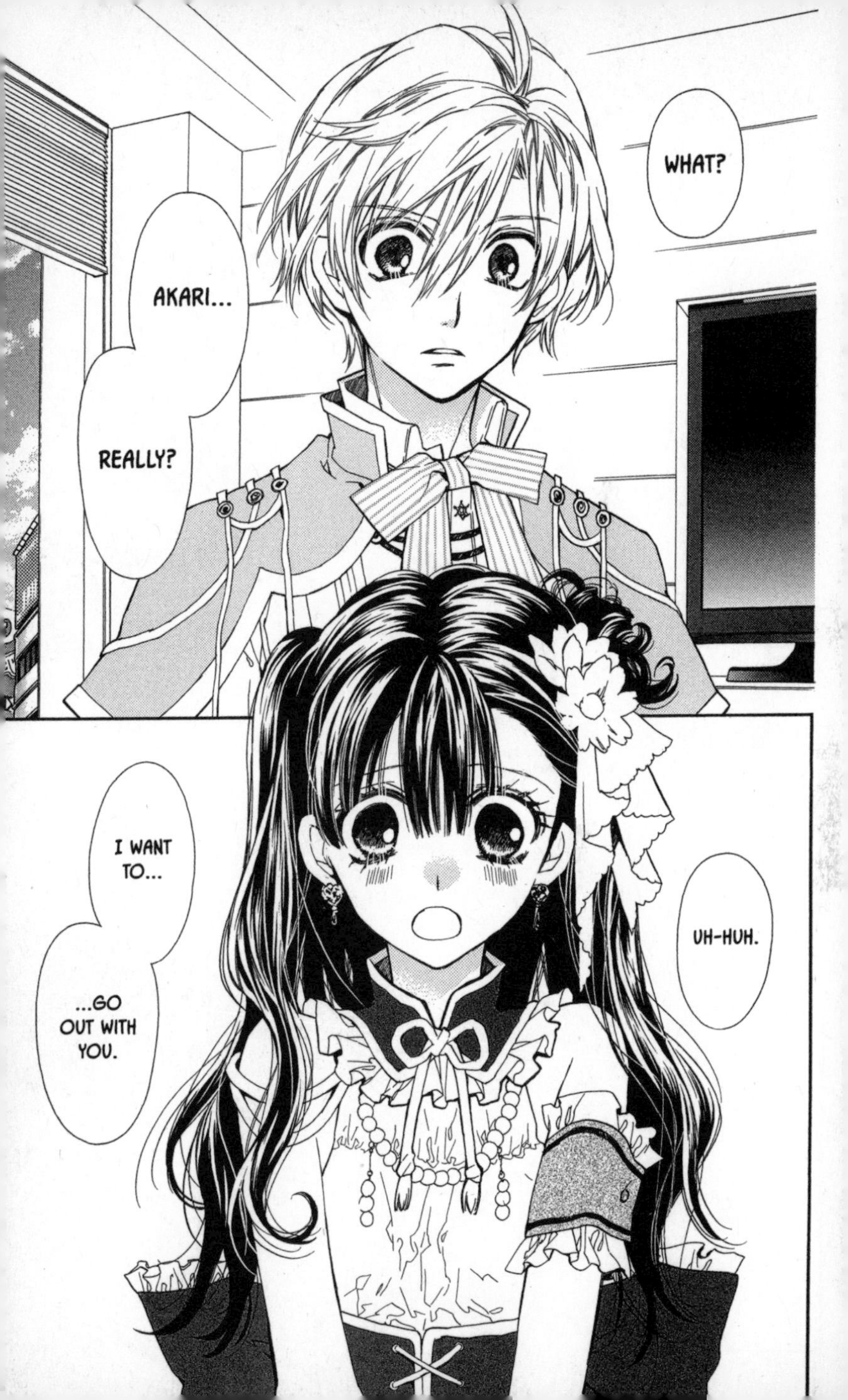
WHAT?
AKARI...
REALLY?
UH-HUH.
I WANT TO...
...GO OUT WITH YOU.

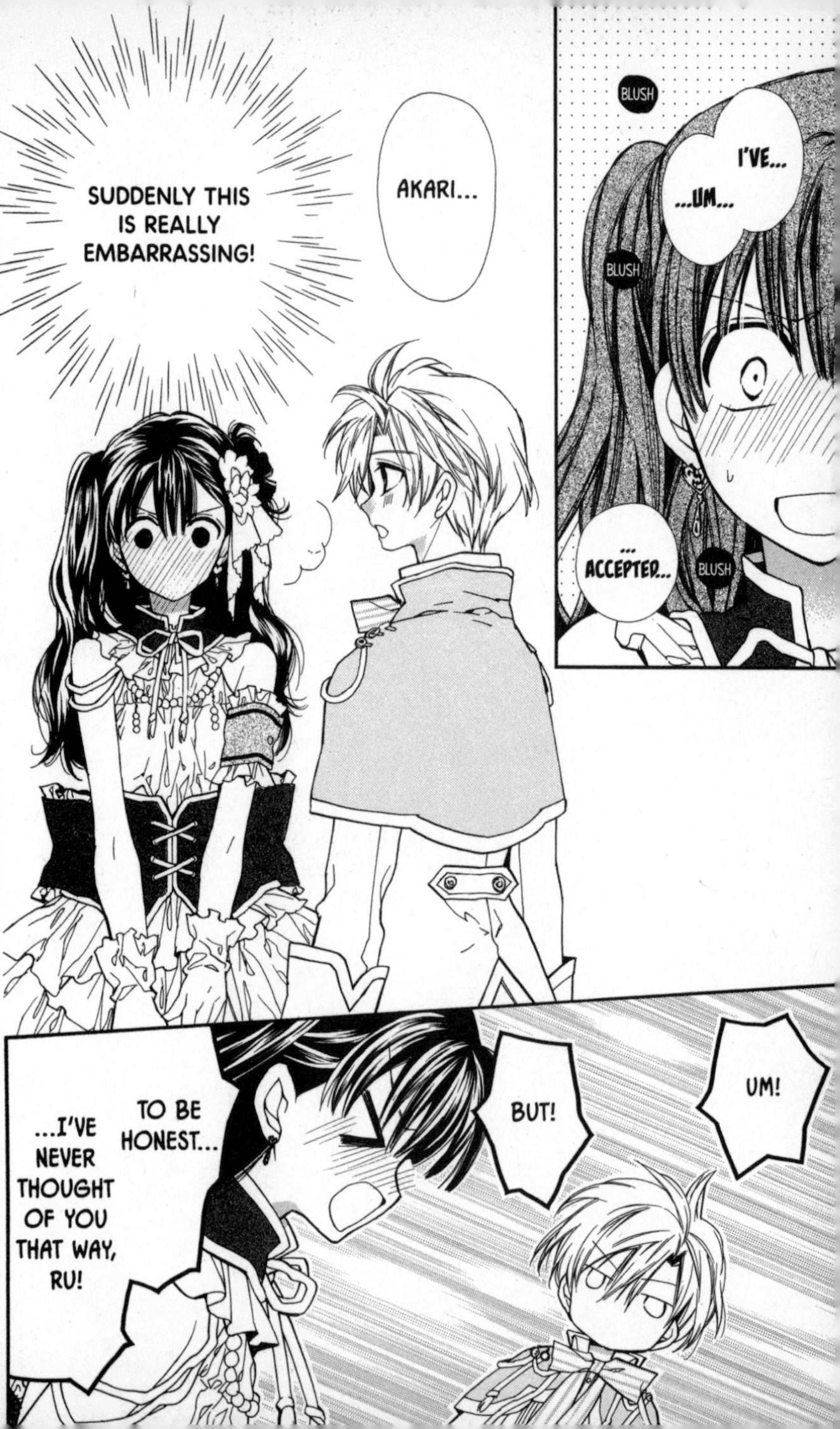
BLUSH
I'VE...
...UM...
BLUSH
...ACCEPTED...
BLUSH
AKARI...
SUDDENLY THIS IS REALLY EMBARRASSING!
UM!
BUT!
TO BE HONEST...
...I'VE NEVER THOUGHT OF YOU THAT WAY, RU!

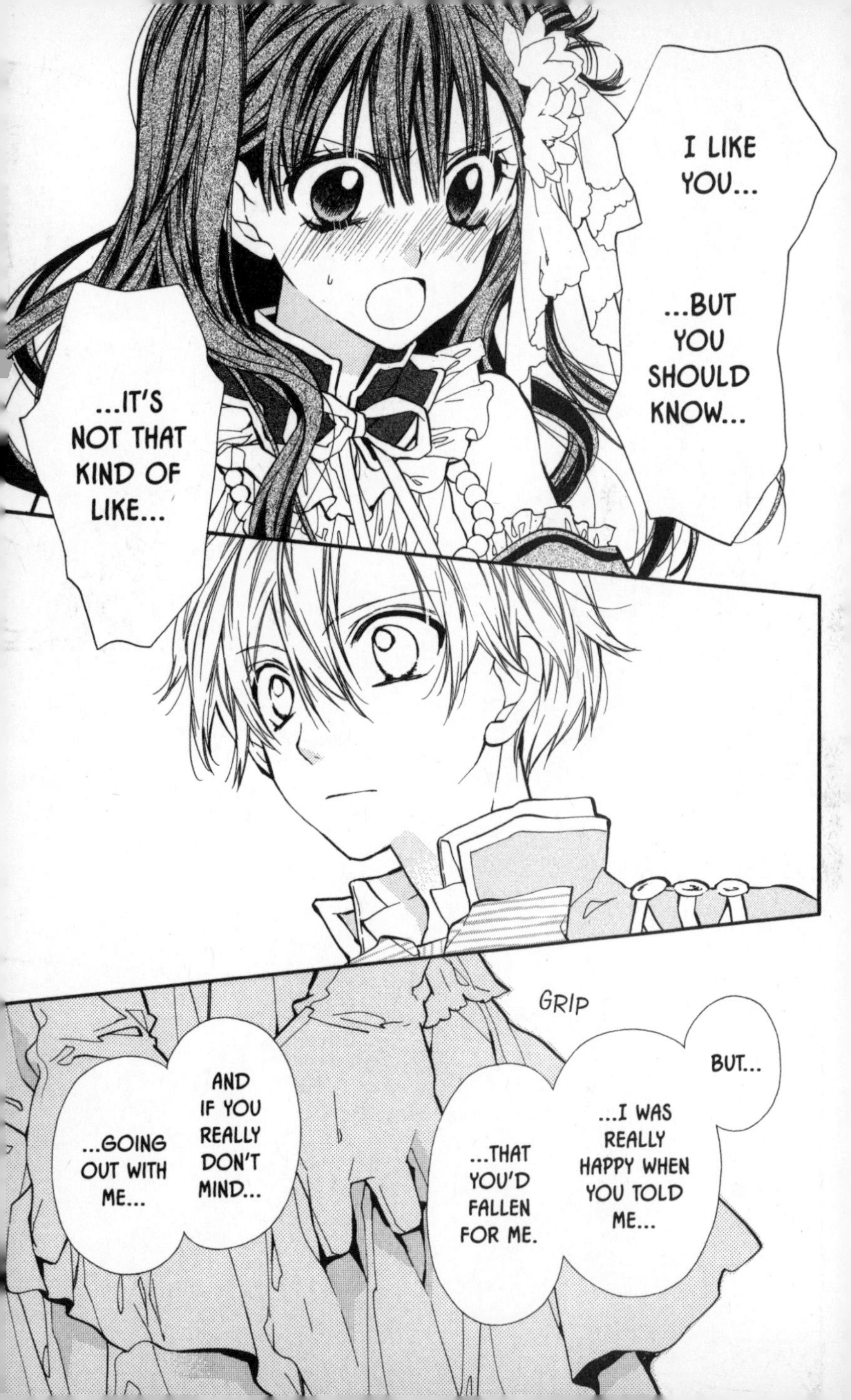
I LIKE YOU...
...BUT YOU SHOULD KNOW...
...IT'S NOT THAT KIND OF LIKE...
GRIP
BUT...
...I WAS REALLY HAPPY WHEN YOU TOLD ME...
...THAT YOU'D FALLEN FOR ME.
AND IF YOU REALLY DON'T MIND...
...GOING OUT WITH ME...

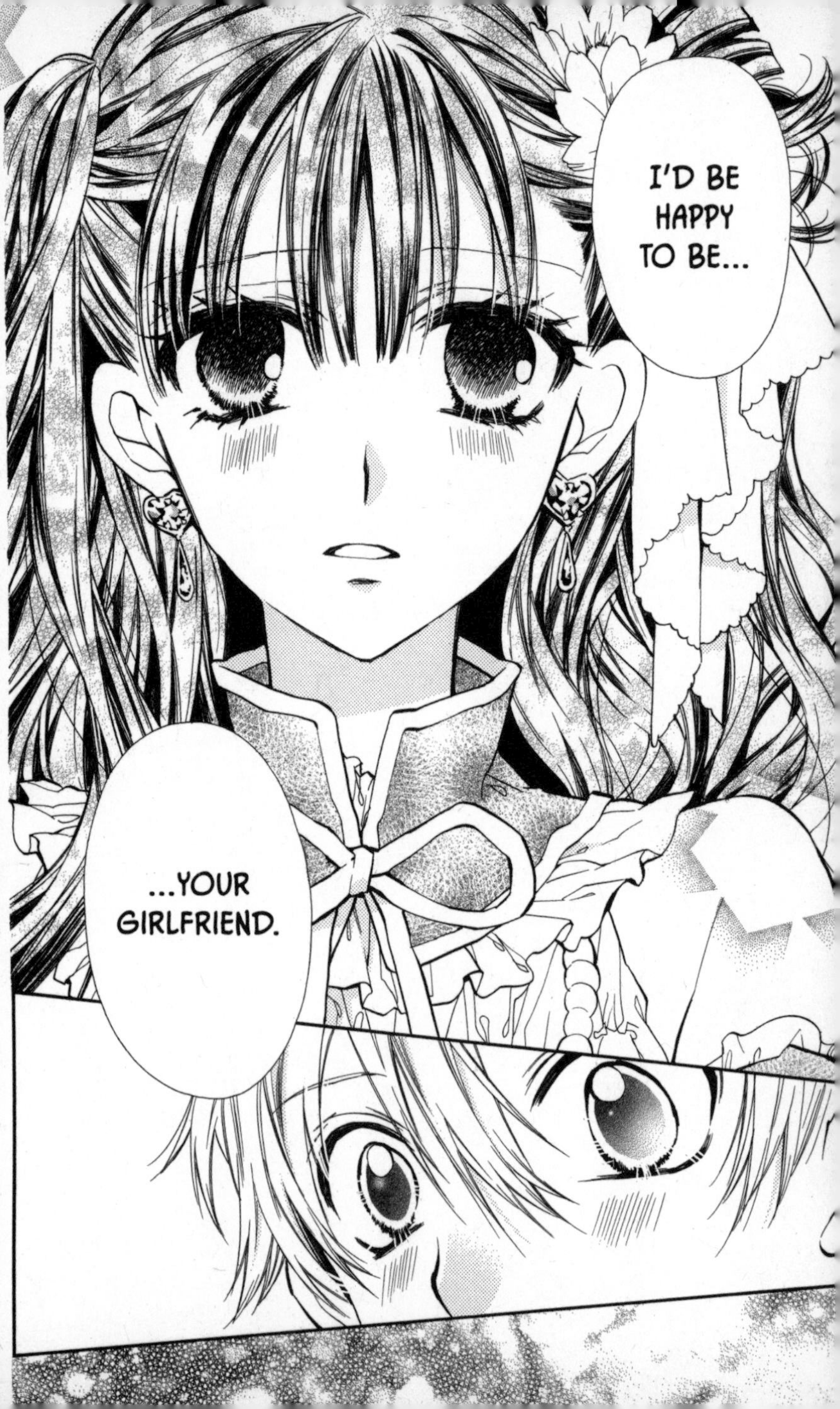
I'D BE HAPPY TO BE...
...YOUR GIRLFRIEND.

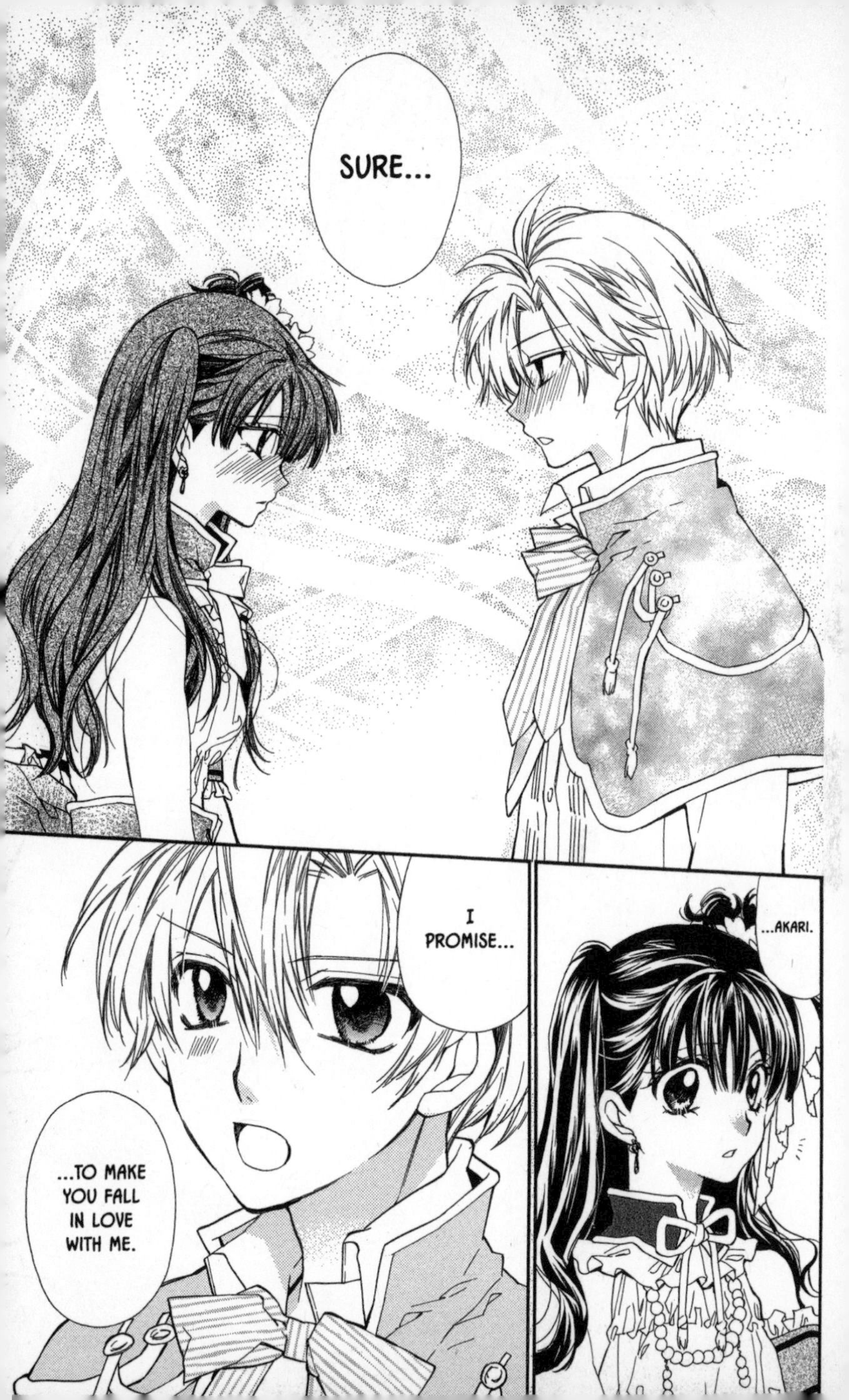
SURE...
...AKARI.
I PROMISE...
...TO MAKE YOU FALL IN LOVE WITH ME.

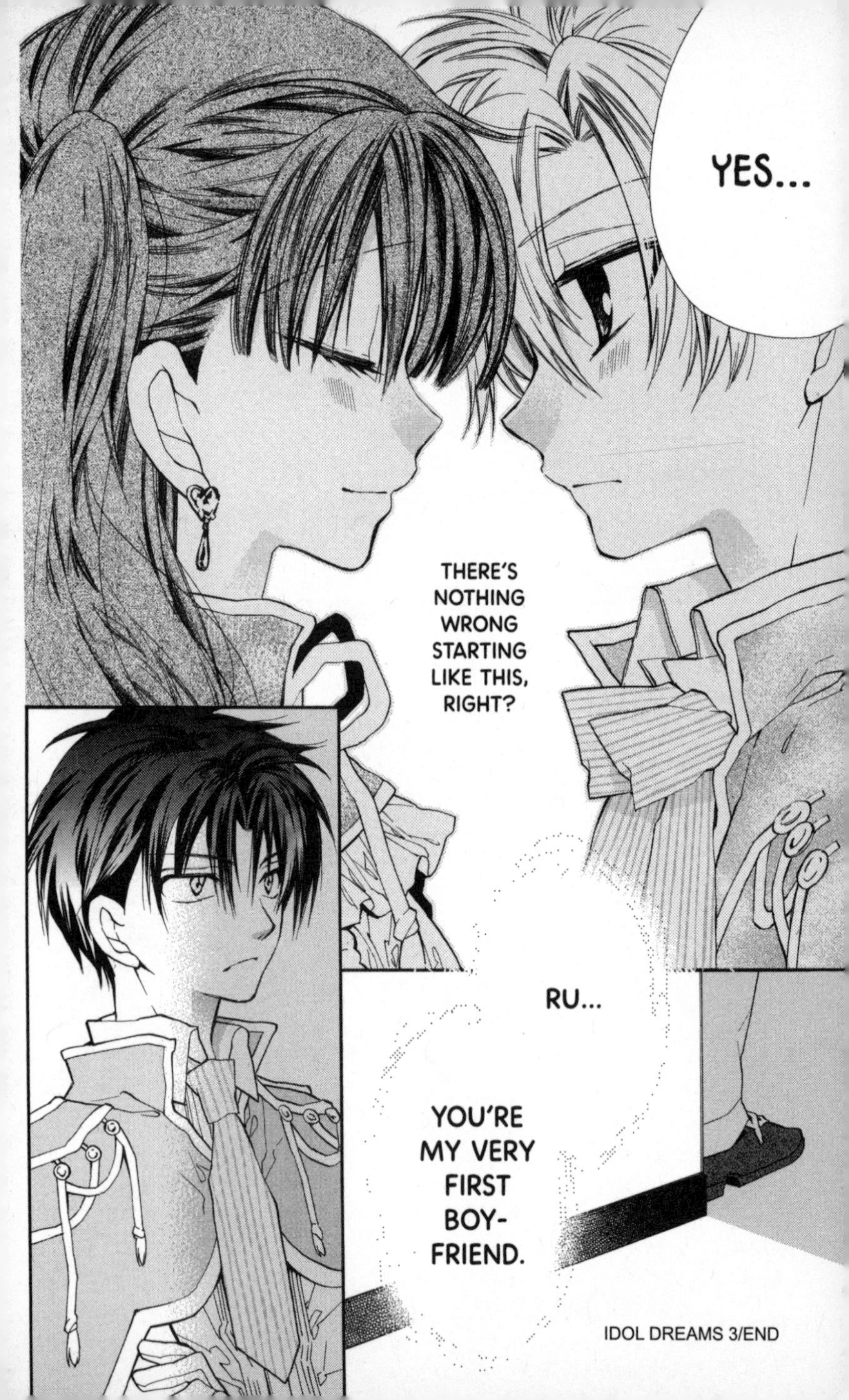
YES...
THERE'S NOTHING WRONG STARTING LIKE THIS, RIGHT?
RU...
YOU'RE MY VERY FIRST BOY-FRIEND.
IDOL DREAMS 3/END

The people around Chikage have slowly begun to
make moves in volume 3. This is a bimonthly series,
but I apologize for the slow pace of the story—I want
to express the emotions of the characters in detail.
And if the story moves too fast, Chikage will probably
get dizzy, so please understand. Volume 3 was
mainly about Chikage, but volume 4 will have more
chapters on Akari. Please look forward to it!

ARINA TANEMURA

Arina Tanemura began her manga career in 1996 when her short
stories debuted in *Ribon Original* magazine. She gained fame with the
1997 publication of *I•O•N*, and ever since her debut Tanemura has
been a major force in shojo manga with popular series *Phantom Thief
Jeanne*, *Time Stranger Kyoko*, *Full Moon*, *The Gentlemen's Alliance †* and
Sakura Hime: The Legend of Princess Sakura. Both *Phantom Thief Jeanne*
and *Full Moon* have been adapted into animated TV series.

SHOJO BEAT EDITION

STORY & ART BY **ARINA TANEMURA**

TRANSLATION **Tetsuichiro Miyaki**
TOUCH-UP ART & LETTERING **Inori Fukuda Trant**
DESIGN **Shawn Carrico**
EDITOR **Nancy Thistlethwaite**

Thirty One Idream by Arina Tanemura
© Arina Tanemura 2015
All rights reserved.
First published in Japan in 2015 by HAKUSENSHA, Inc., Tokyo.
English language translation rights arranged with HAKUSENSHA, Inc., Tokyo.

Printed in the U.S.A.

Published by VIZ Media, LLC
P.O. Box 77010
San Francisco, CA 94107

10 9 8 7 6 5 4 3 2 1
First printing, September 2016

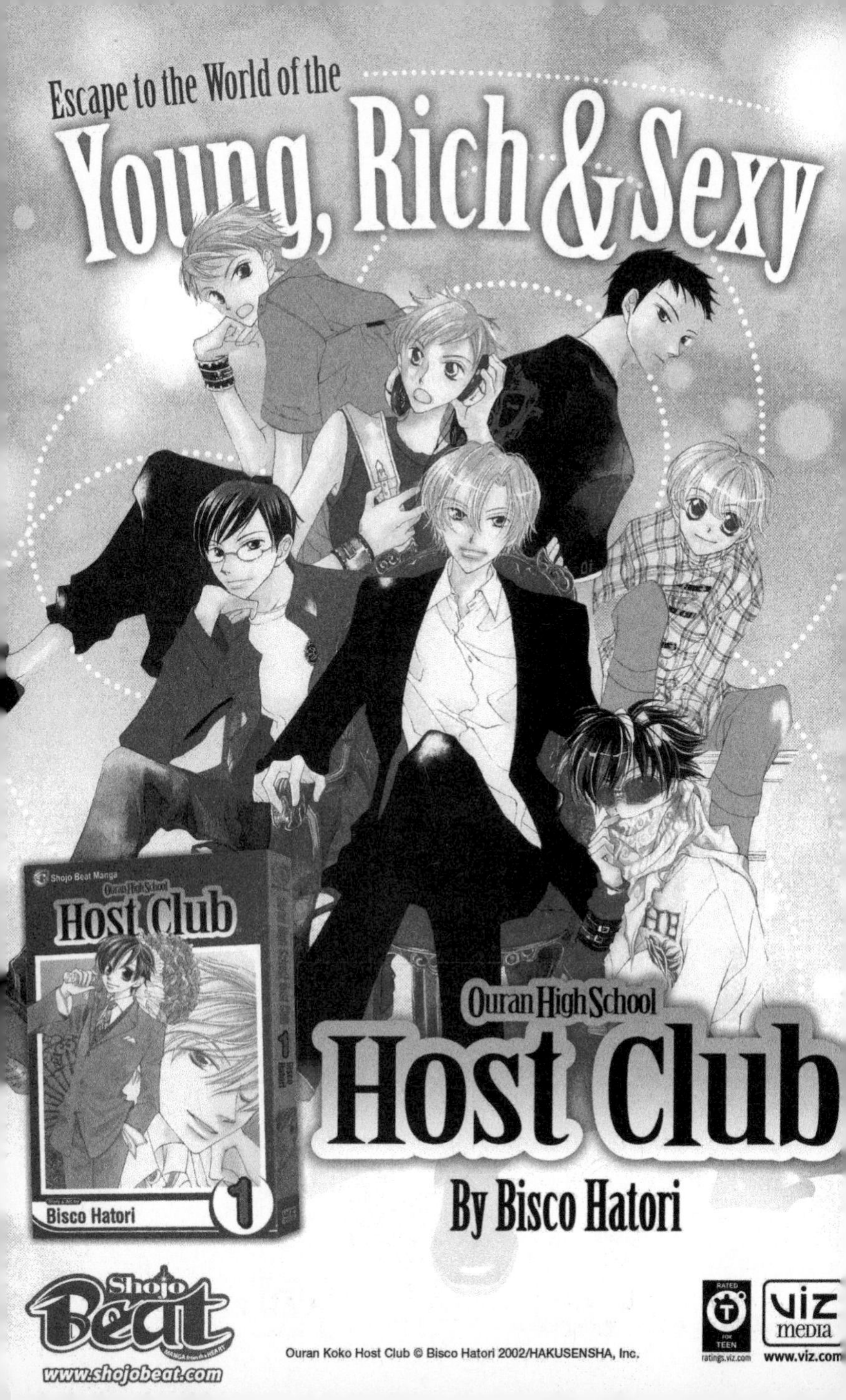
Escape to the World of the
Young, Rich & Sexy
Shojo Beat Manga
Ouran High School
Host Club
1
Bisco Hatori
Ouran High School
Host Club
By Bisco Hatori
Shojo Beat
www.shojobeat.com
Ouran Koko Host Club © Bisco Hatori 2002/HAKUSENSHA, Inc.
RATED T FOR TEEN
ratings.viz.com
VIZ media
www.viz.com

Shuriken ⭐ and Pleats

When the master she has sworn to protect is killed, Mikage Kirio, a skilled ninja, travels to Japan to start a new, peaceful life for herself. But as soon as she arrives, she finds herself fighting to protect the life of Mahito Wakashimatsu, a man who is under attack by a band of ninja. From that time on, Mikage is drawn deeper into the machinations of his powerful family.

Natsume's BOOK of FRIENDS

STORY and ART by
Yuki Midorikawa

Make Some Unusual New Friends

The power to see hidden spirits has always felt like a curse to troubled high schooler Takashi Natsume. But he's about to discover he inherited a lot more than just the Sight from his mysterious grandmother!

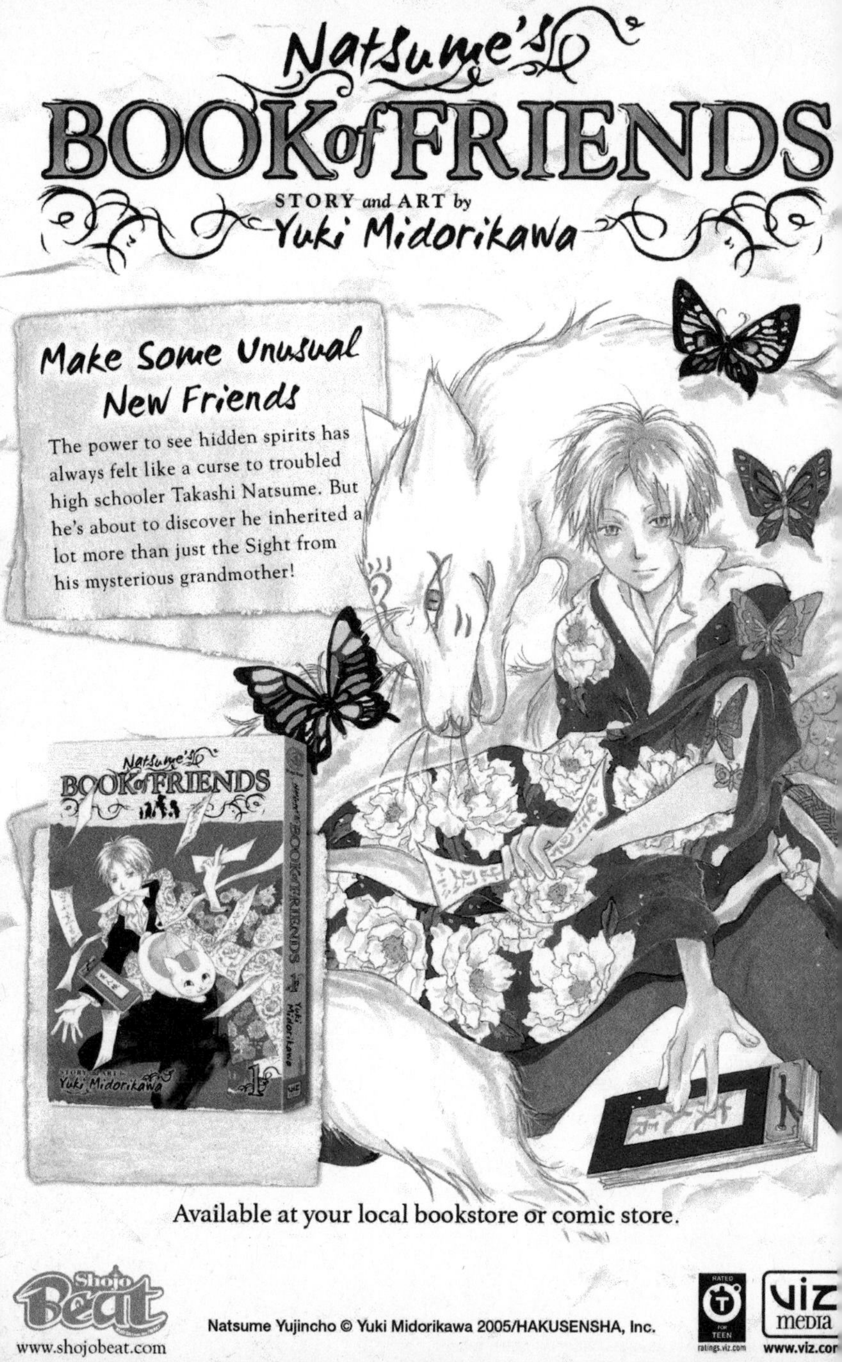

Natsume's BOOK of FRIENDS
STORY and ART by
Yuki Midorikawa
1

Available at your local bookstore or comic store.

Shojo Beat
www.shojobeat.com

RATED T FOR TEEN
ratings.viz.com

VIZ media
www.viz.com

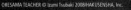

Don't Hide What's *Inside*

OTOMEN

by **AYA KANNO**

Despite his tough jock exterior, Asuka Masamune harbors a secret love for sewing, shojo manga, and all things girly. But when he finds himself drawn to his domestically inept classmate Ryo, his carefully crafted persona is put to the test. Can Asuka ever show his true self to anyone, much less to the girl he's falling for?

Find out in the *Otomen* manga—buy yours today!

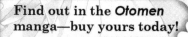

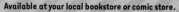

STOP!
YOU MAY BE READING THE WRONG WAY!

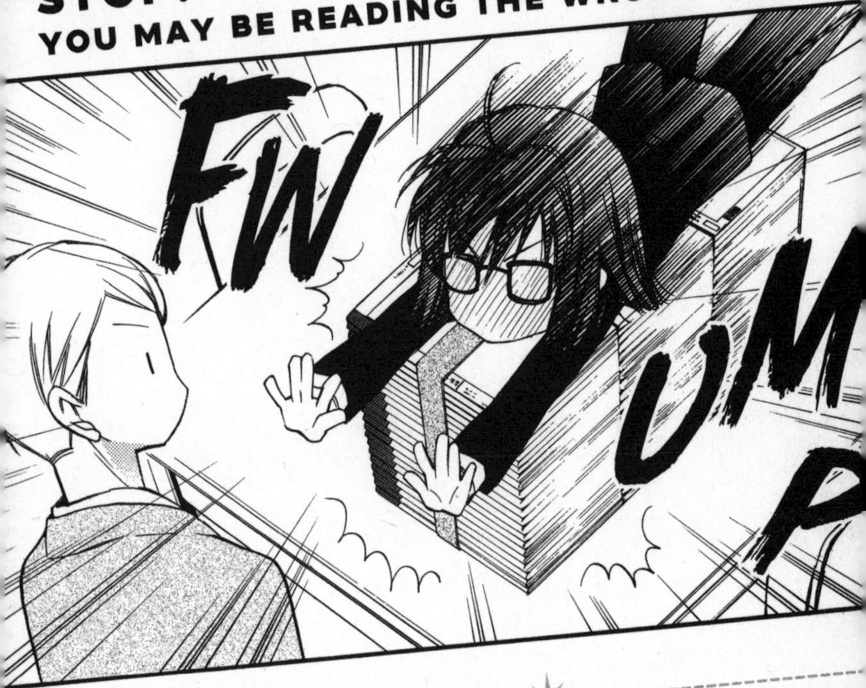
FWUMP

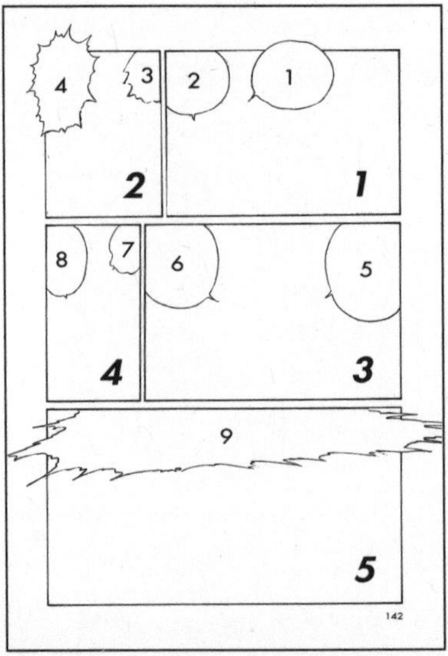
1
2
1
3
4
2
5
6
3
7
8
4
9
5
142

In keeping with the original Japanese comic format, this book reads from right to left—so action, sound effects and word balloons are completely reversed to preserve the orientation of the original artwork.

Check out the diagram shown here to get the hang of things, and then turn to the other side of the book to get started!